GRANBLUE FANTASY

グランブルーファンタジー

volume.

05

Original story: Cygames   Art: cocho   Layouts: Makoto Fugetsu

CONTENTS
GRANBLUE FANTASY

volume.
05

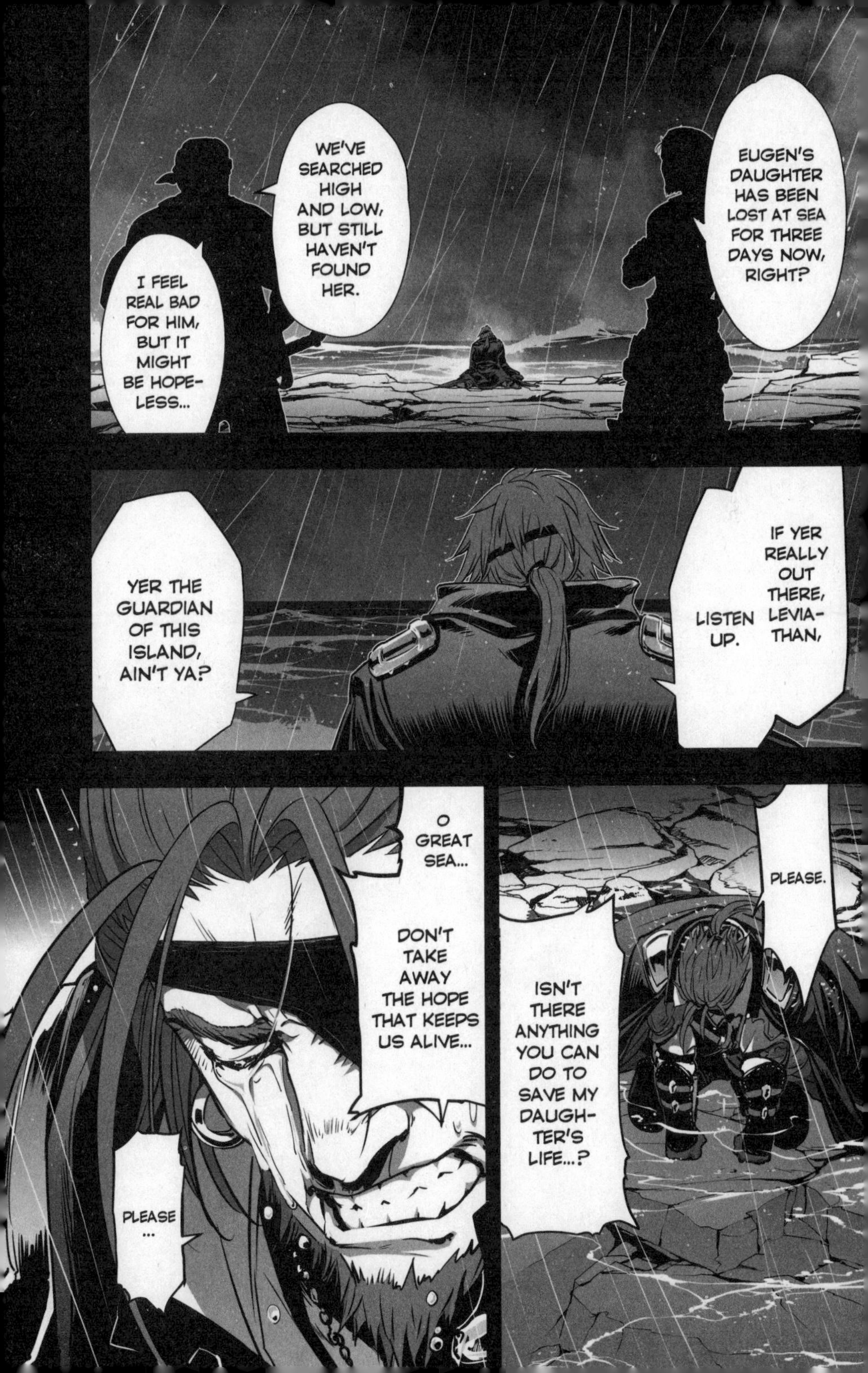
EUGEN'S DAUGHTER HAS BEEN LOST AT SEA FOR THREE DAYS NOW, RIGHT?
WE'VE SEARCHED HIGH AND LOW, BUT STILL HAVEN'T FOUND HER.
I FEEL REAL BAD FOR HIM, BUT IT MIGHT BE HOPE-LESS...
IF YER REALLY OUT THERE, LEVIA-THAN,
LISTEN UP.
YER THE GUARDIAN OF THIS ISLAND, AIN'T YA?
PLEASE.
ISN'T THERE ANYTHING YOU CAN DO TO SAVE MY DAUGH-TER'S LIFE...?
O GREAT SEA...
DON'T TAKE AWAY THE HOPE THAT KEEPS US ALIVE...
PLEASE ...

CHAPTER 25: Leviathan

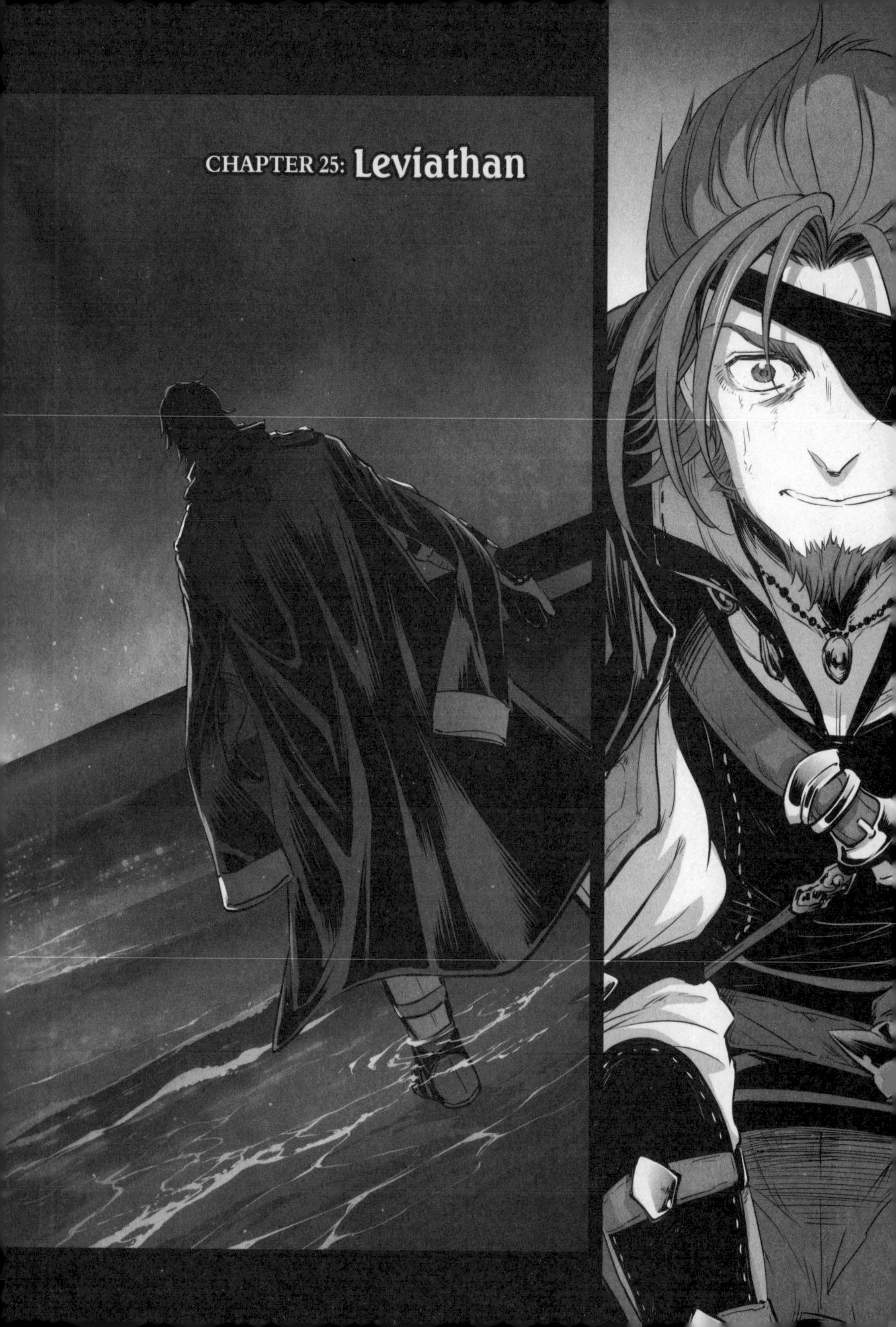

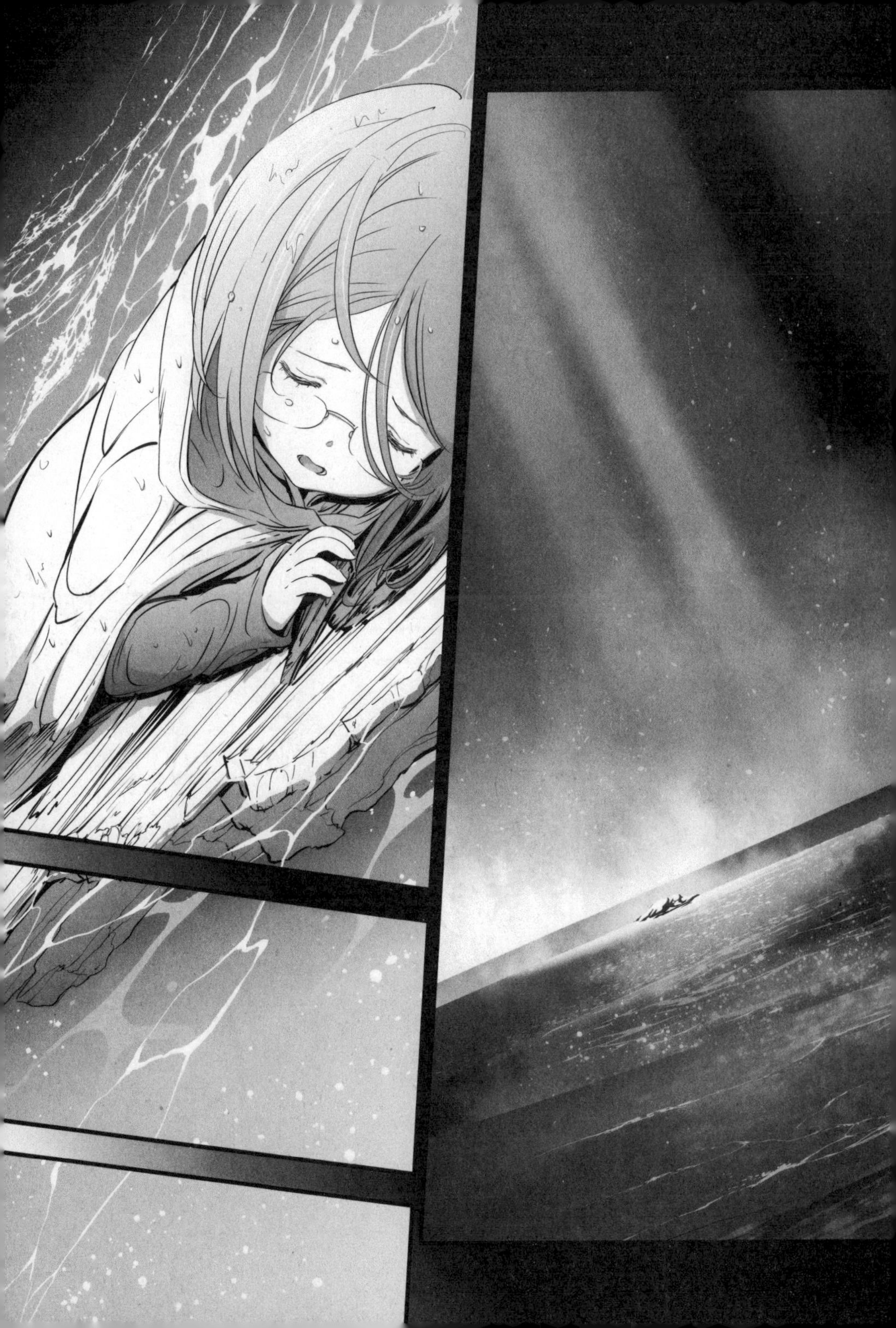

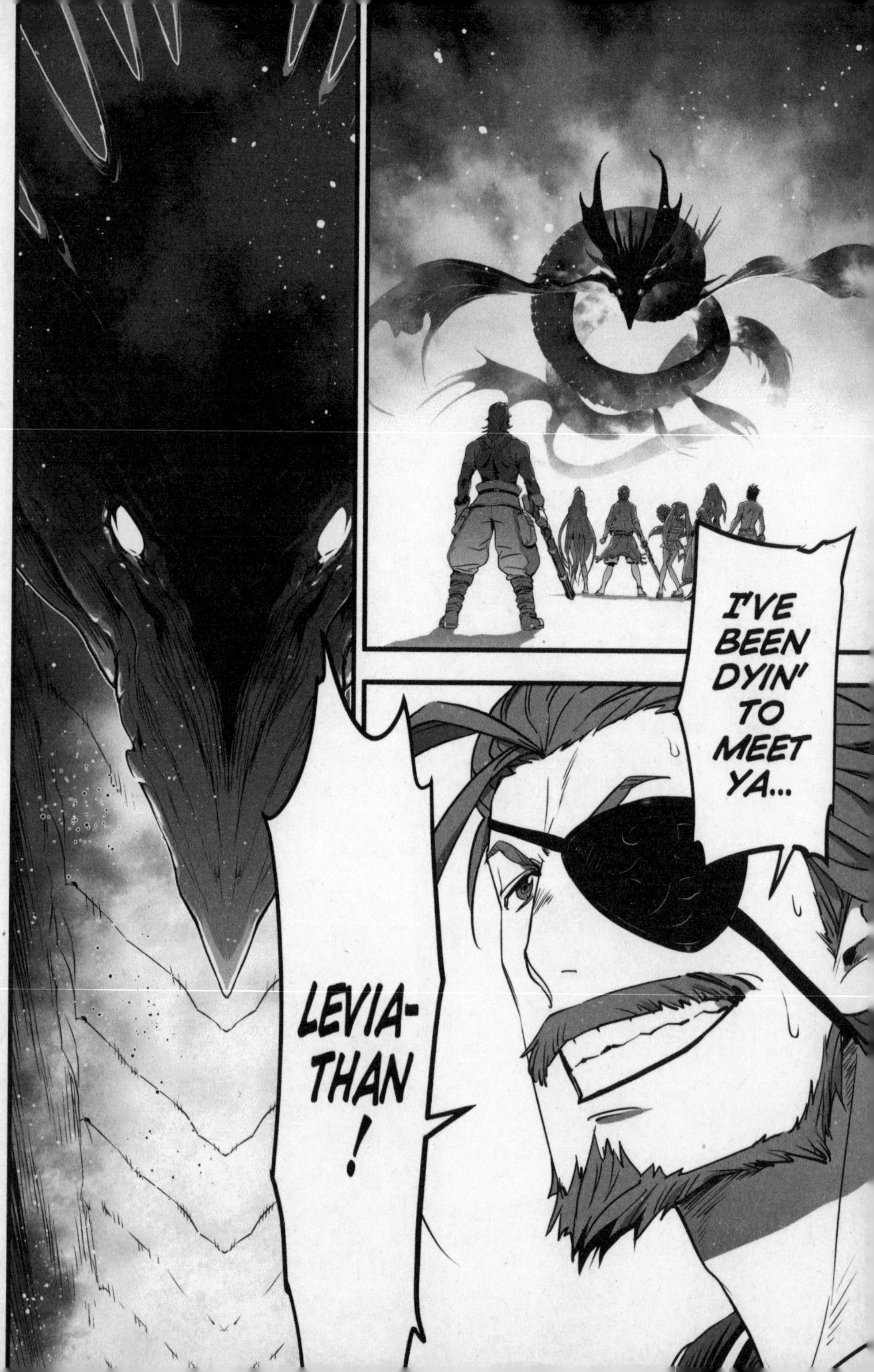
I'VE BEEN DYIN' TO MEET YA...
LEVIA-THAN!

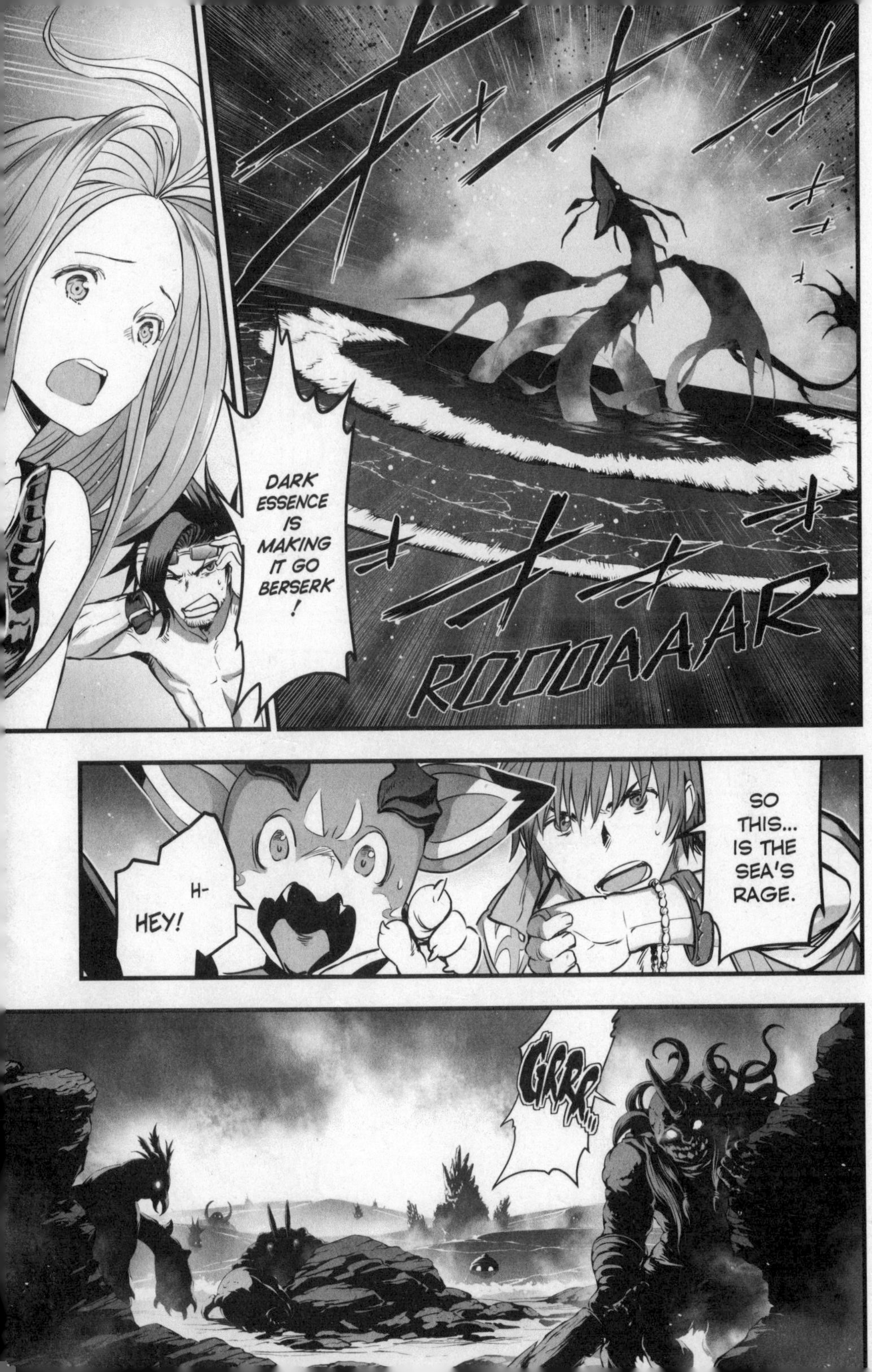
DARK ESSENCE IS MAKING IT GO BERSERK!
ROOOAAAR
SO THIS... IS THE SEA'S RAGE.
H- HEY!
GRRR...

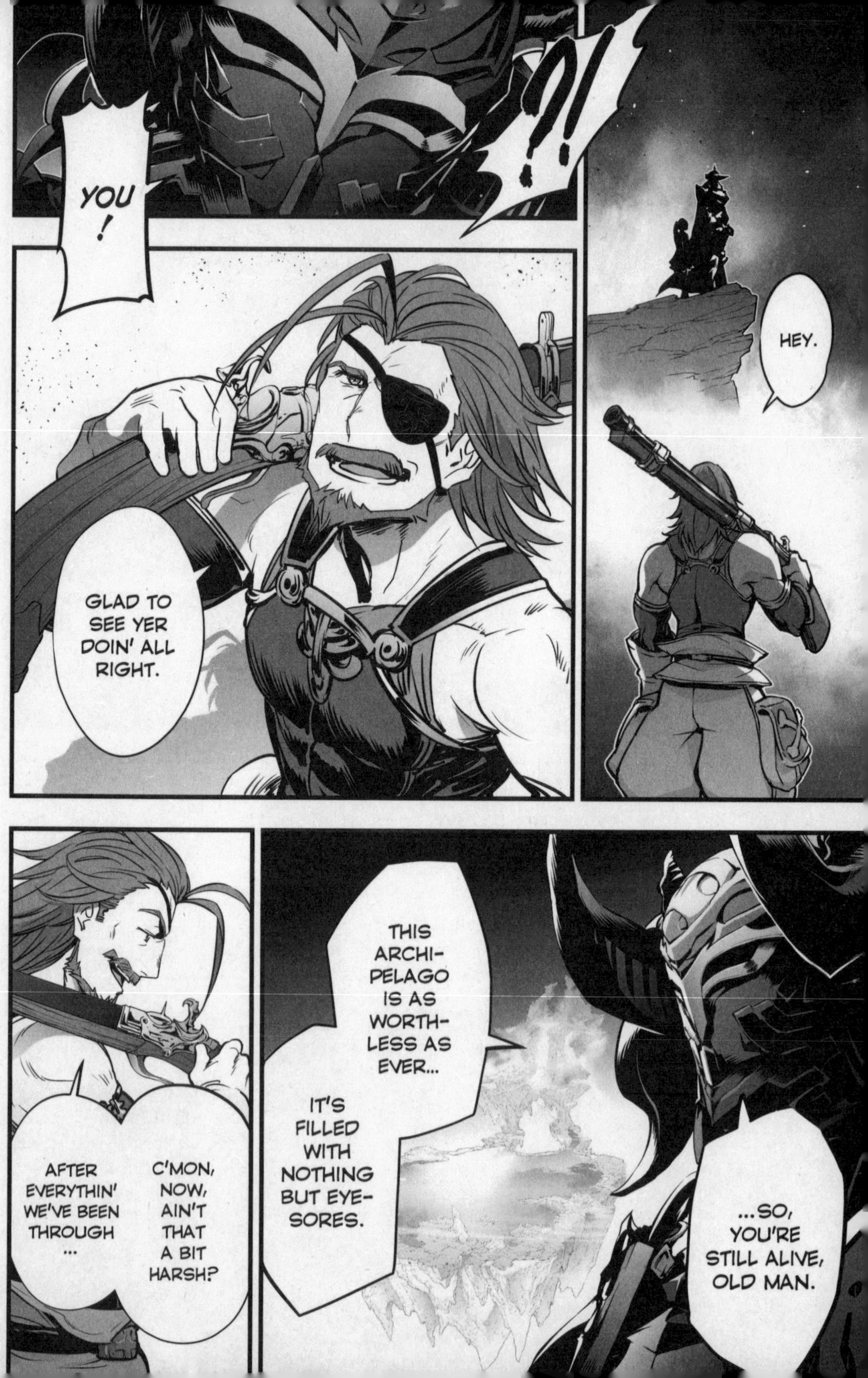
HEY.
?!!
YOU!
GLAD TO SEE YER DOIN' ALL RIGHT.
...SO, YOU'RE STILL ALIVE, OLD MAN.
THIS ARCHI-PELAGO IS AS WORTH-LESS AS EVER...
IT'S FILLED WITH NOTHING BUT EYE-SORES.
C'MON, NOW, AIN'T THAT A BIT HARSH?
AFTER EVERYTHIN' WE'VE BEEN THROUGH...

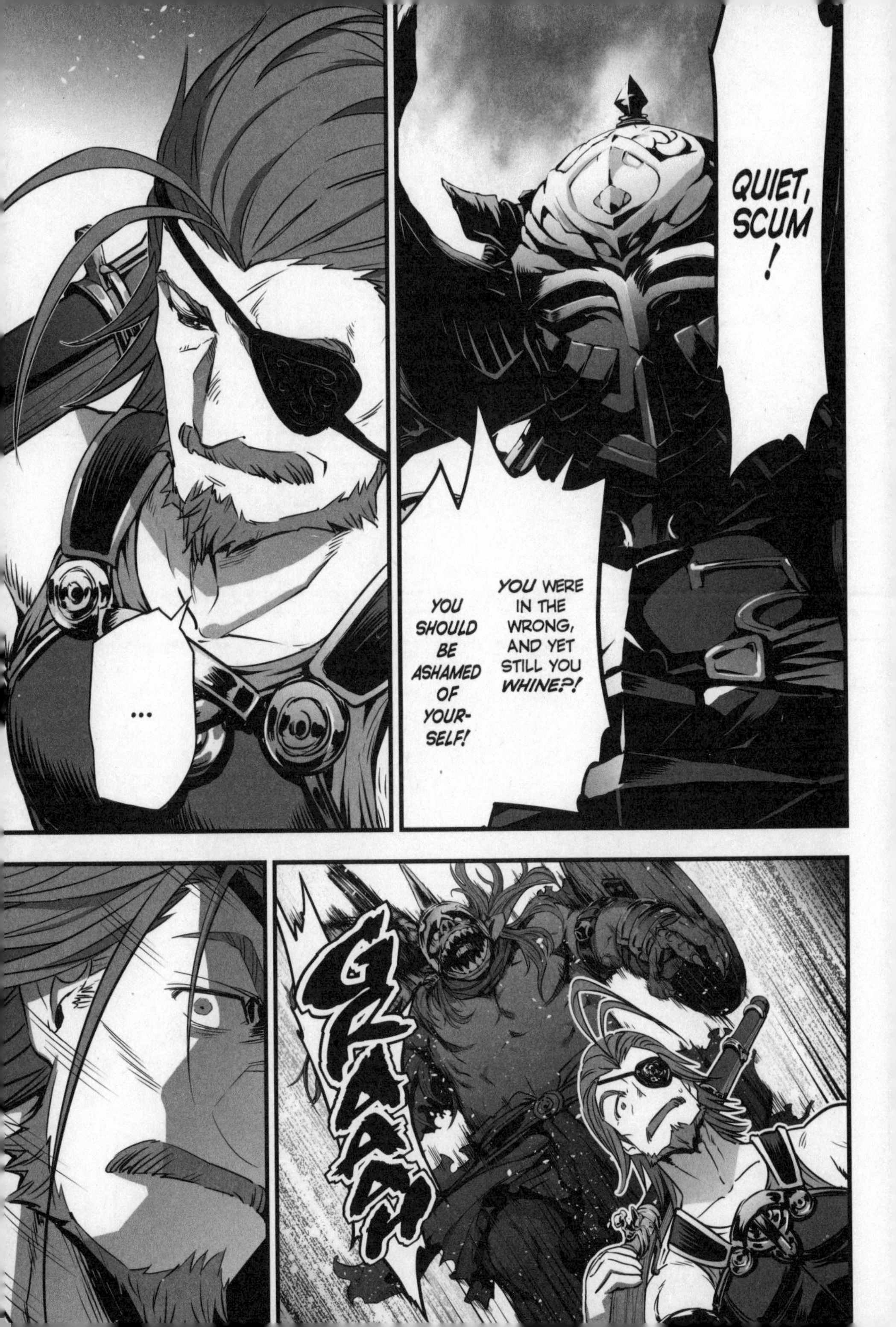
QUIET, SCUM!
YOU WERE IN THE WRONG, AND YET STILL YOU WHINE?!
YOU SHOULD BE ASHAMED OF YOURSELF!
...

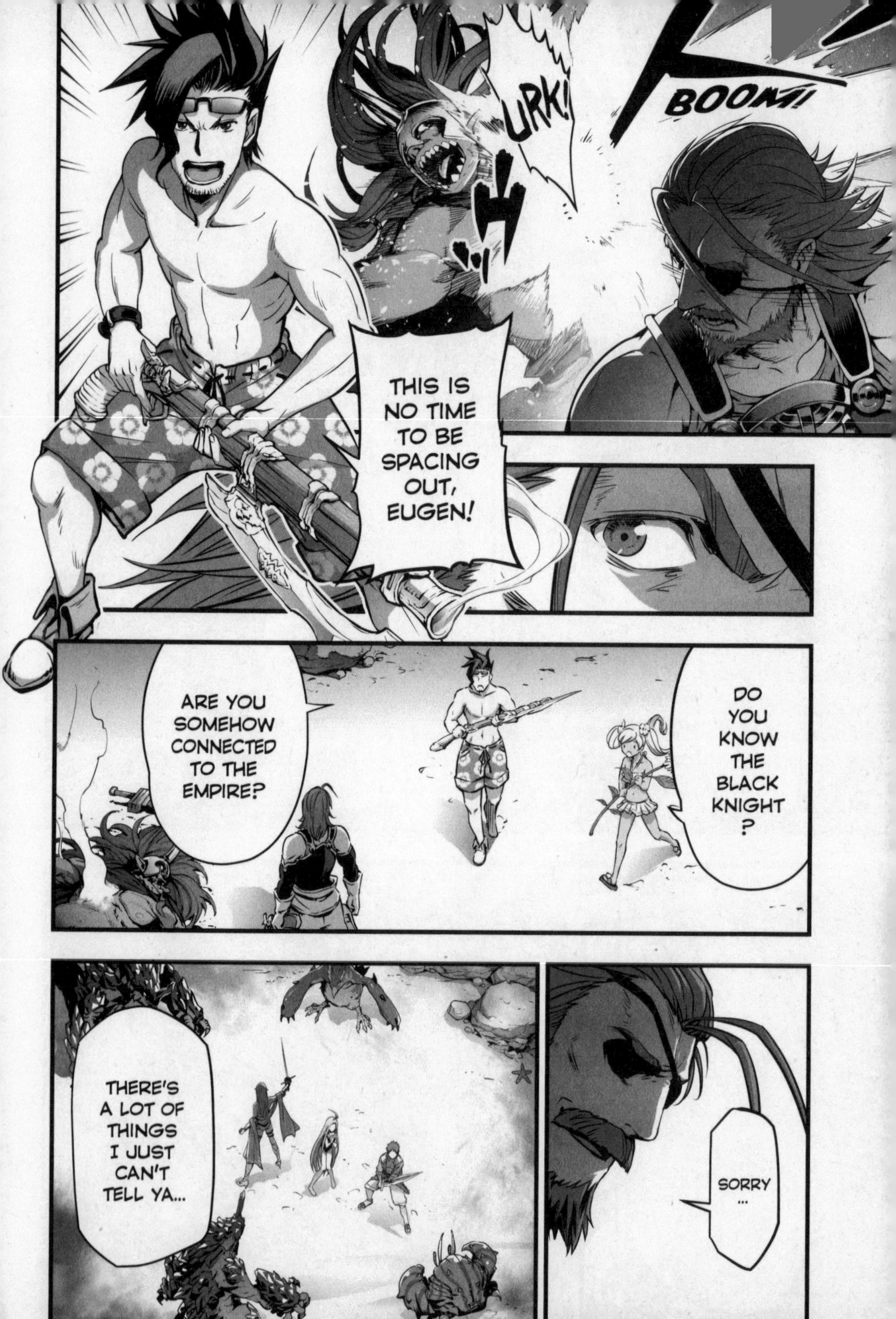
BOOM!
URK!
THIS IS NO TIME TO BE SPACING OUT, EUGEN!
DO YOU KNOW THE BLACK KNIGHT?
ARE YOU SOMEHOW CONNECTED TO THE EMPIRE?
SORRY...
THERE'S A LOT OF THINGS I JUST CAN'T TELL YA...

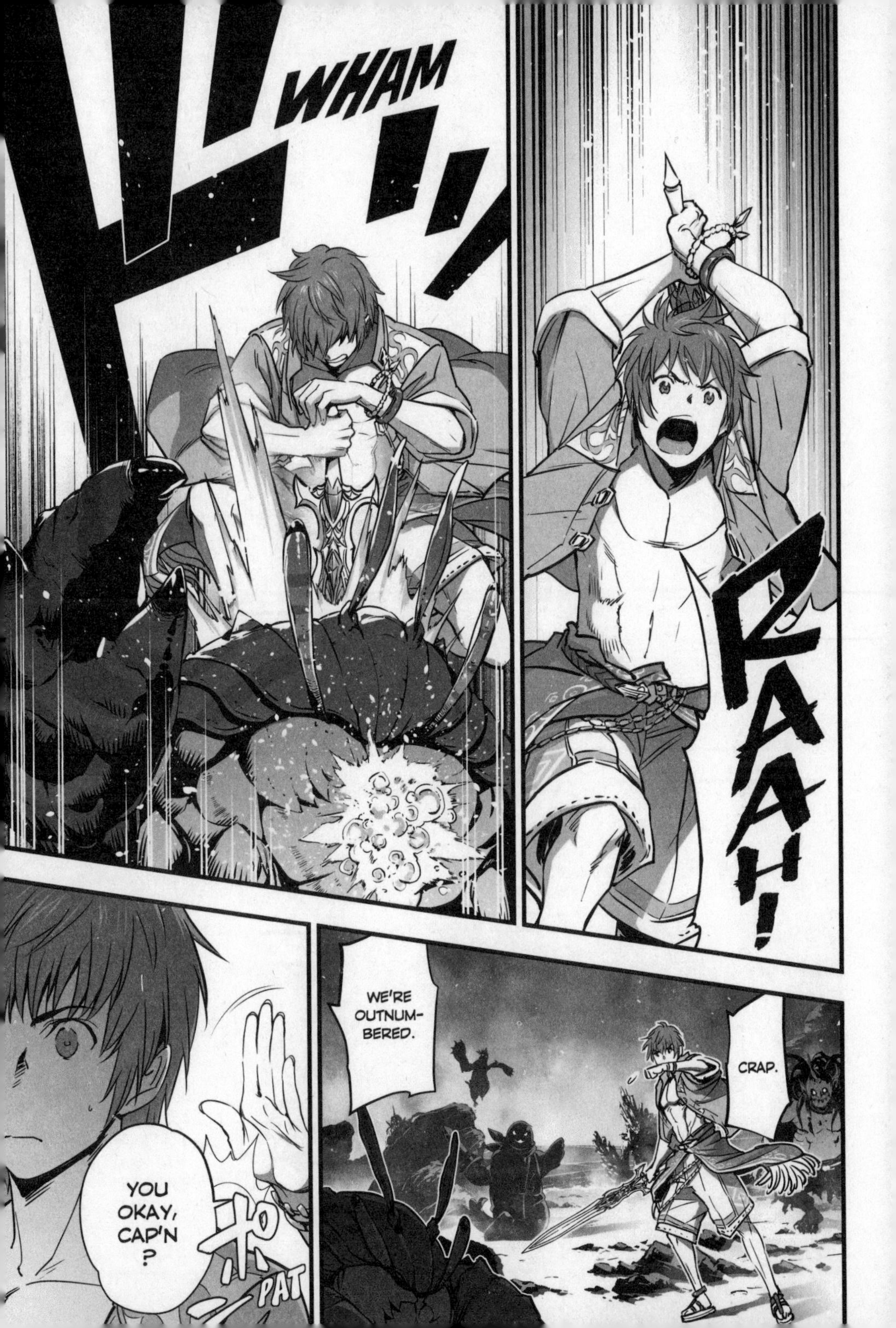
RAAAH!
WHAM
CRAP.
WE'RE OUTNUM-BERED.
YOU OKAY, CAP'N?
PAT

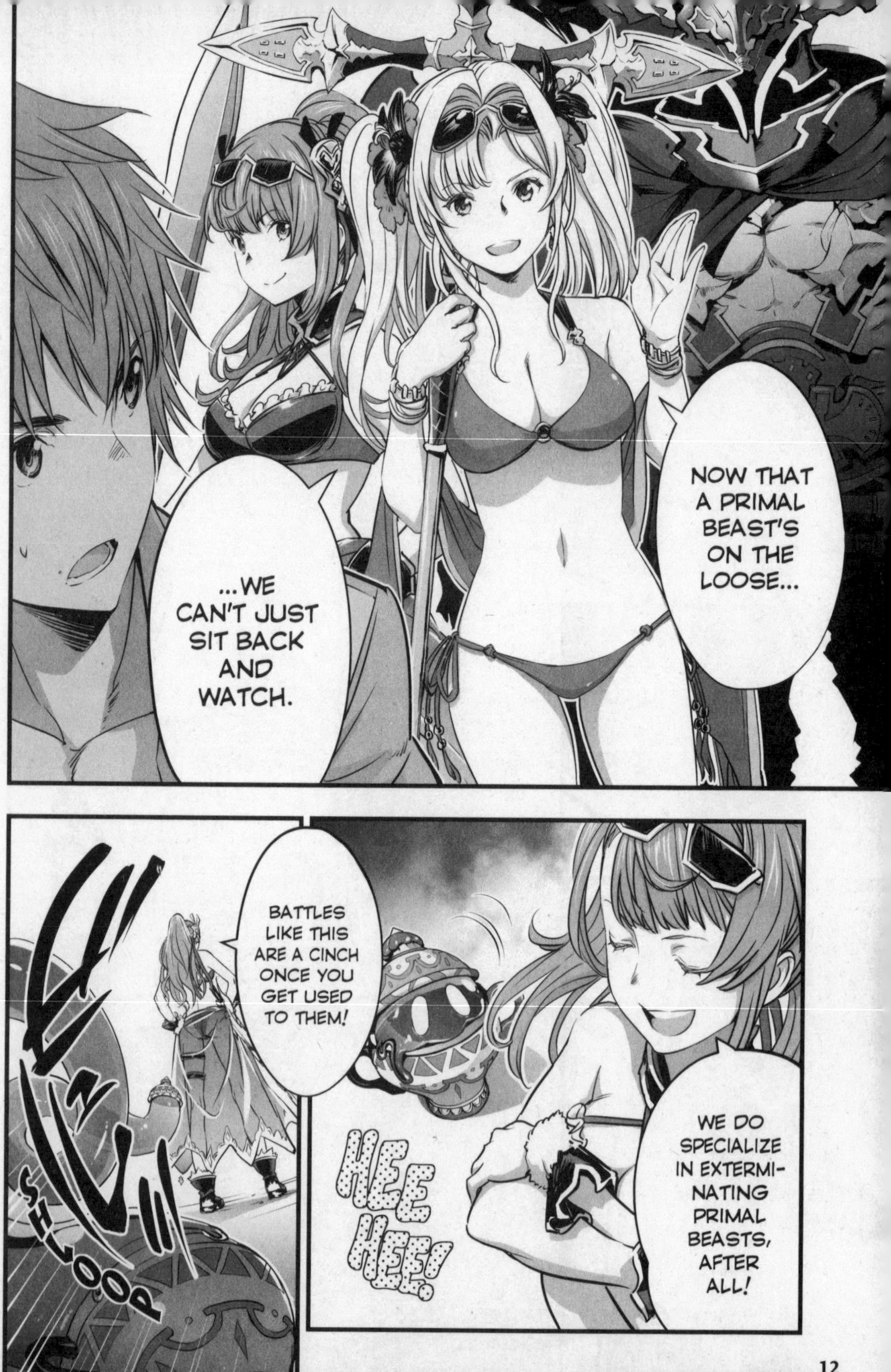
NOW THAT A PRIMAL BEAST'S ON THE LOOSE...
...WE CAN'T JUST SIT BACK AND WATCH.
BATTLES LIKE THIS ARE A CINCH ONCE YOU GET USED TO THEM!
HEE HEE!
WE DO SPECIALIZE IN EXTERMINATING PRIMAL BEASTS, AFTER ALL!
SHLOOP

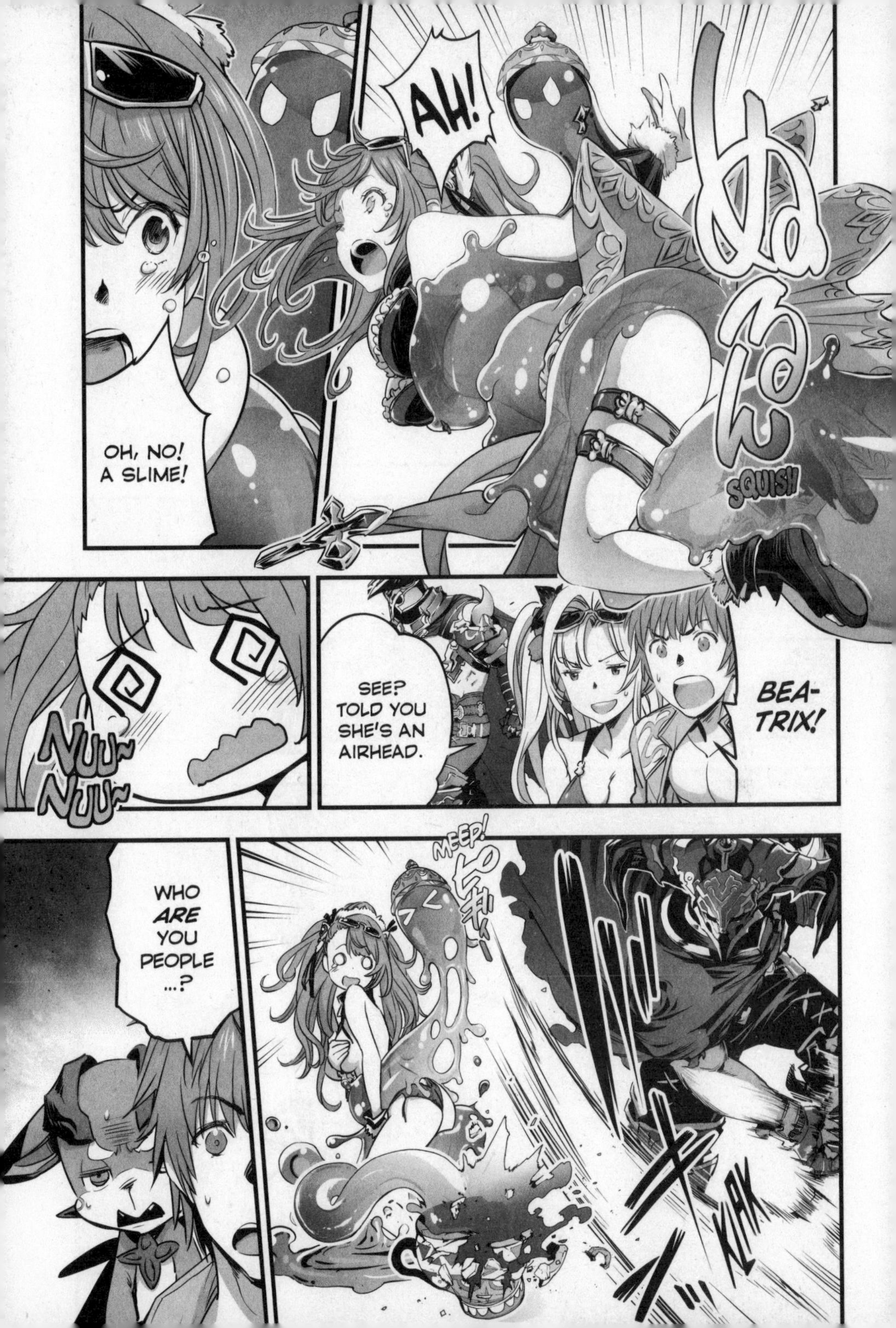
AH!
ぬるん
SQUISH!
OH, NO! A SLIME!
BEA-TRIX!
SEE? TOLD YOU SHE'S AN AIRHEAD.
NUU~ NUU~
MEEP!
KRAK
WHO *ARE* YOU PEOPLE ...?

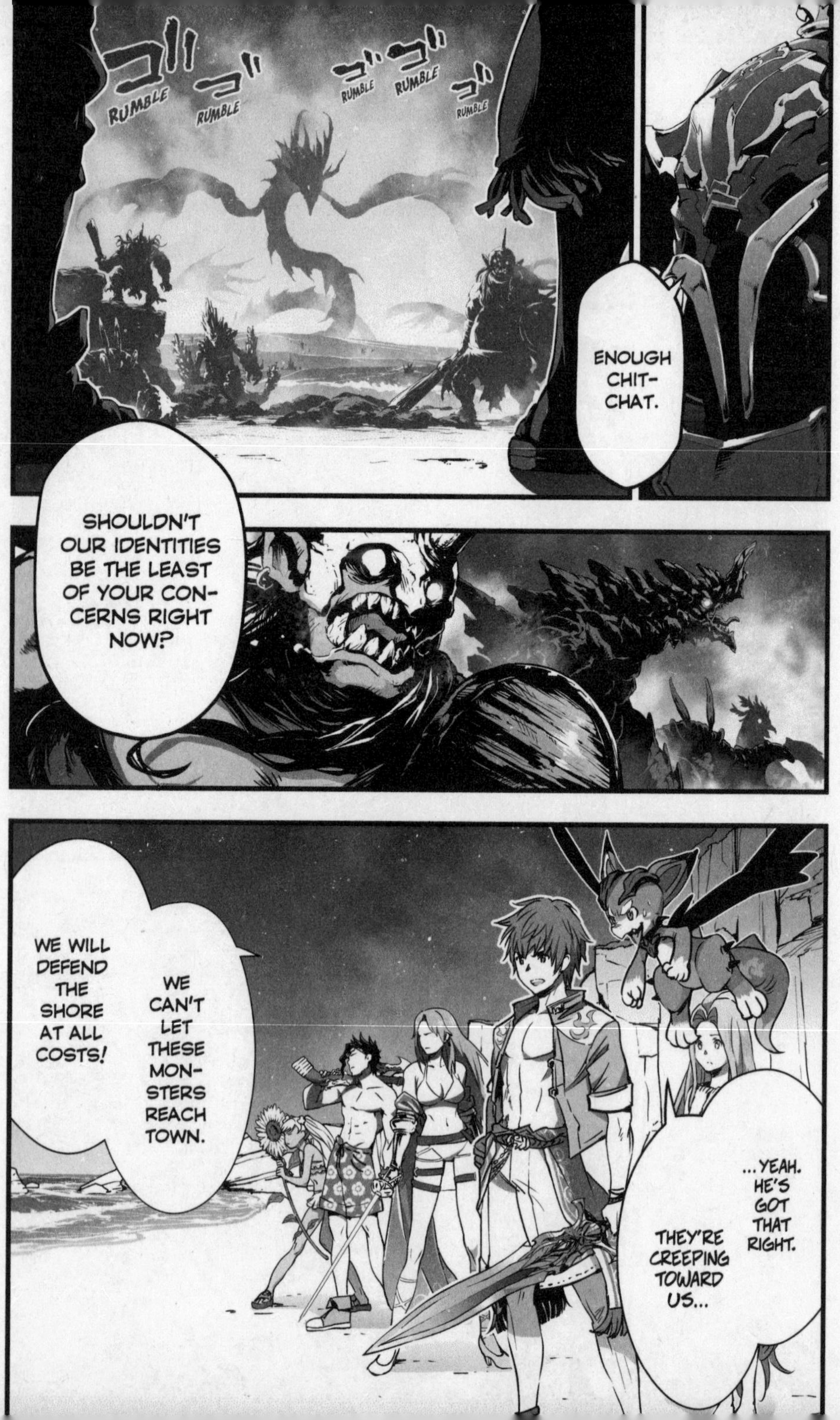
ENOUGH CHIT-CHAT.
RUMBLE
RUMBLE
RUMBLE
RUMBLE
RUMBLE
SHOULDN'T OUR IDENTITIES BE THE LEAST OF YOUR CONCERNS RIGHT NOW?
...YEAH. HE'S GOT THAT RIGHT.
THEY'RE CREEPING TOWARD US...
WE CAN'T LET THESE MONSTERS REACH TOWN.
WE WILL DEFEND THE SHORE AT ALL COSTS!

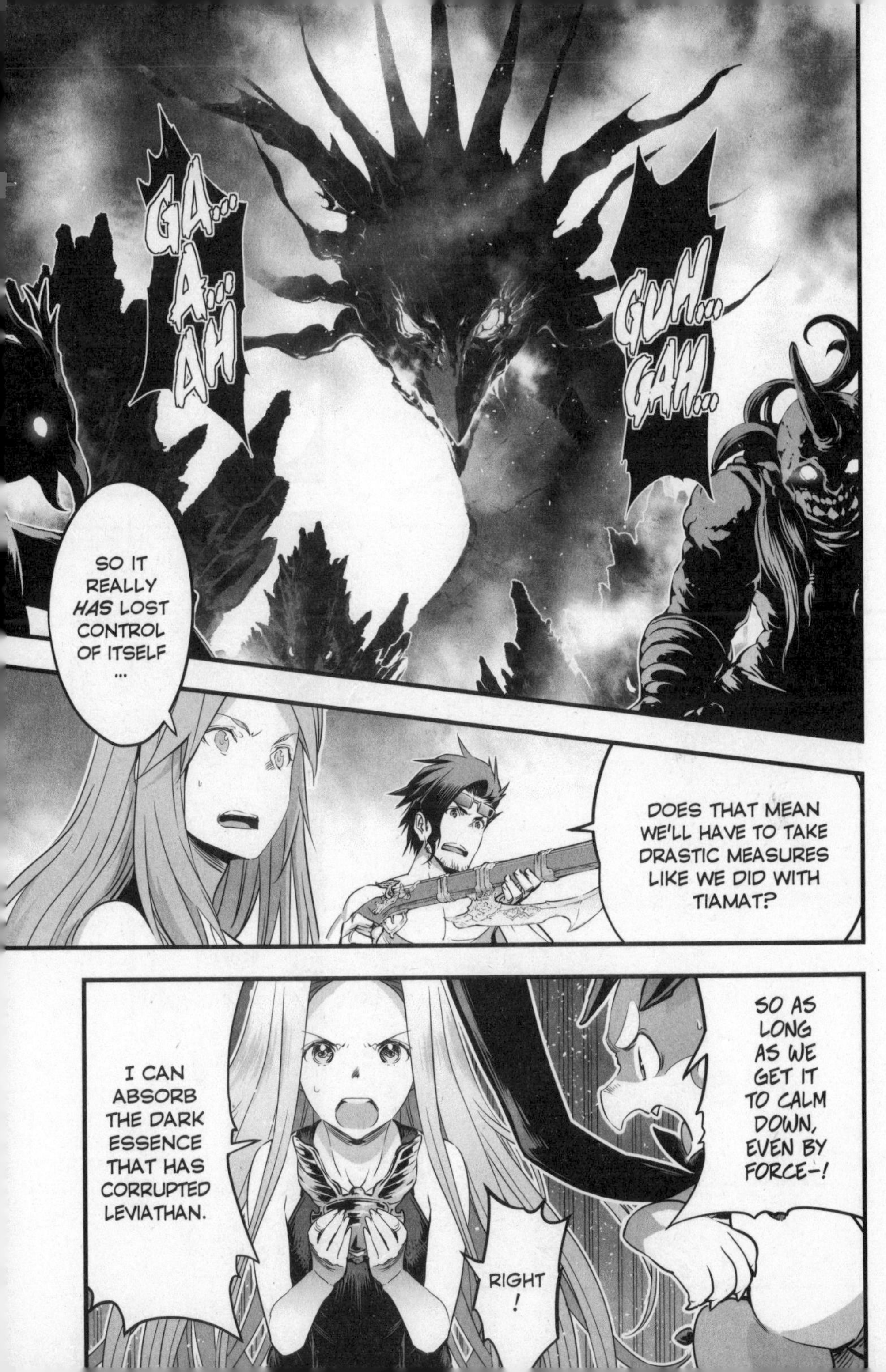
GUH... GAH...
GA... A... AH
SO IT REALLY HAS LOST CONTROL OF ITSELF ...
DOES THAT MEAN WE'LL HAVE TO TAKE DRASTIC MEASURES LIKE WE DID WITH TIAMAT?
SO AS LONG AS WE GET IT TO CALM DOWN, EVEN BY FORCE–!
I CAN ABSORB THE DARK ESSENCE THAT HAS CORRUPTED LEVIATHAN.
RIGHT!

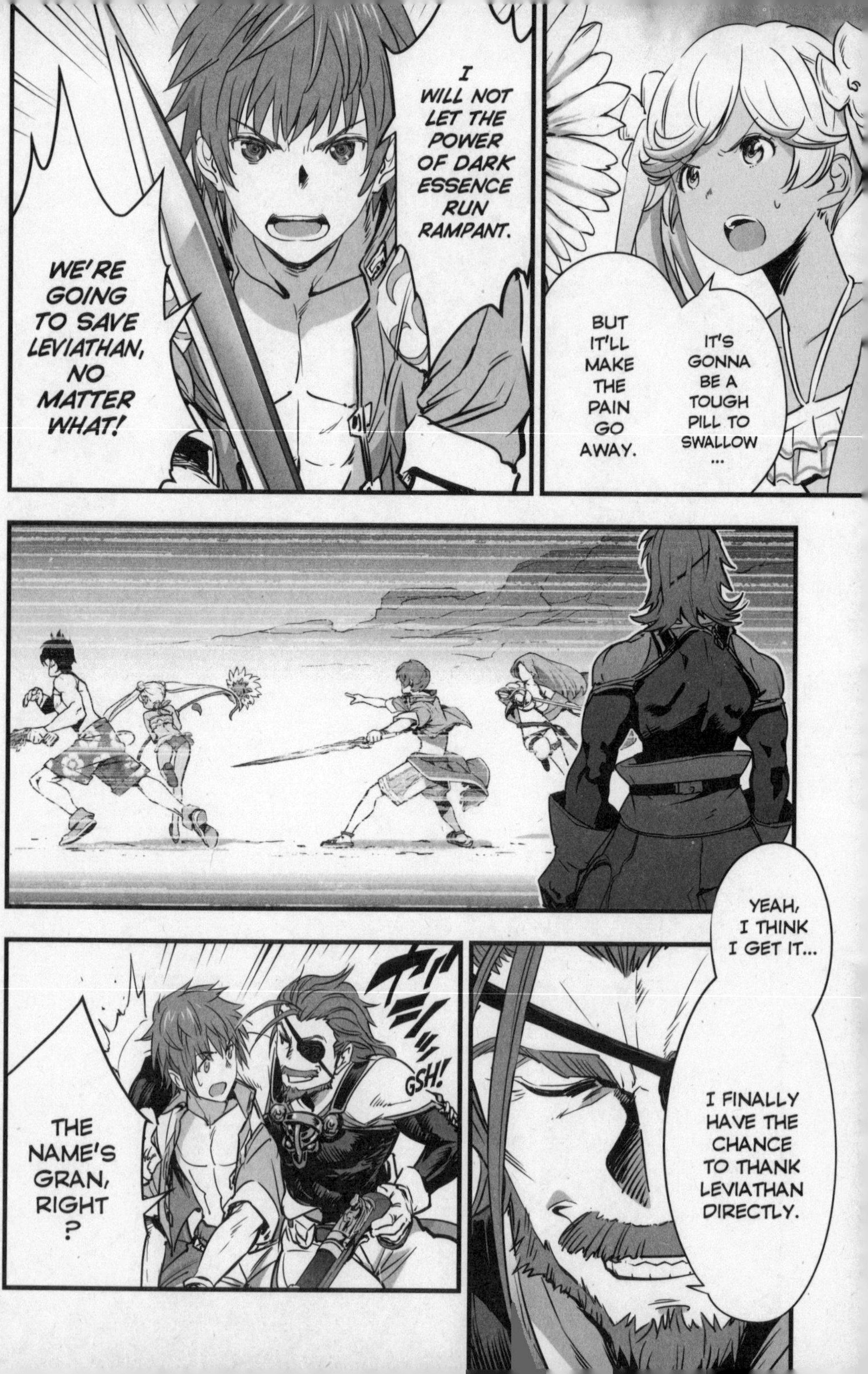
IT'S GONNA BE A TOUGH PILL TO SWALLOW...
BUT IT'LL MAKE THE PAIN GO AWAY.
I WILL NOT LET THE POWER OF DARK ESSENCE RUN RAMPANT.
WE'RE GOING TO SAVE LEVIATHAN, NO MATTER WHAT!
YEAH, I THINK I GET IT...
I FINALLY HAVE THE CHANCE TO THANK LEVIATHAN DIRECTLY.
GSH!
THE NAME'S GRAN, RIGHT?

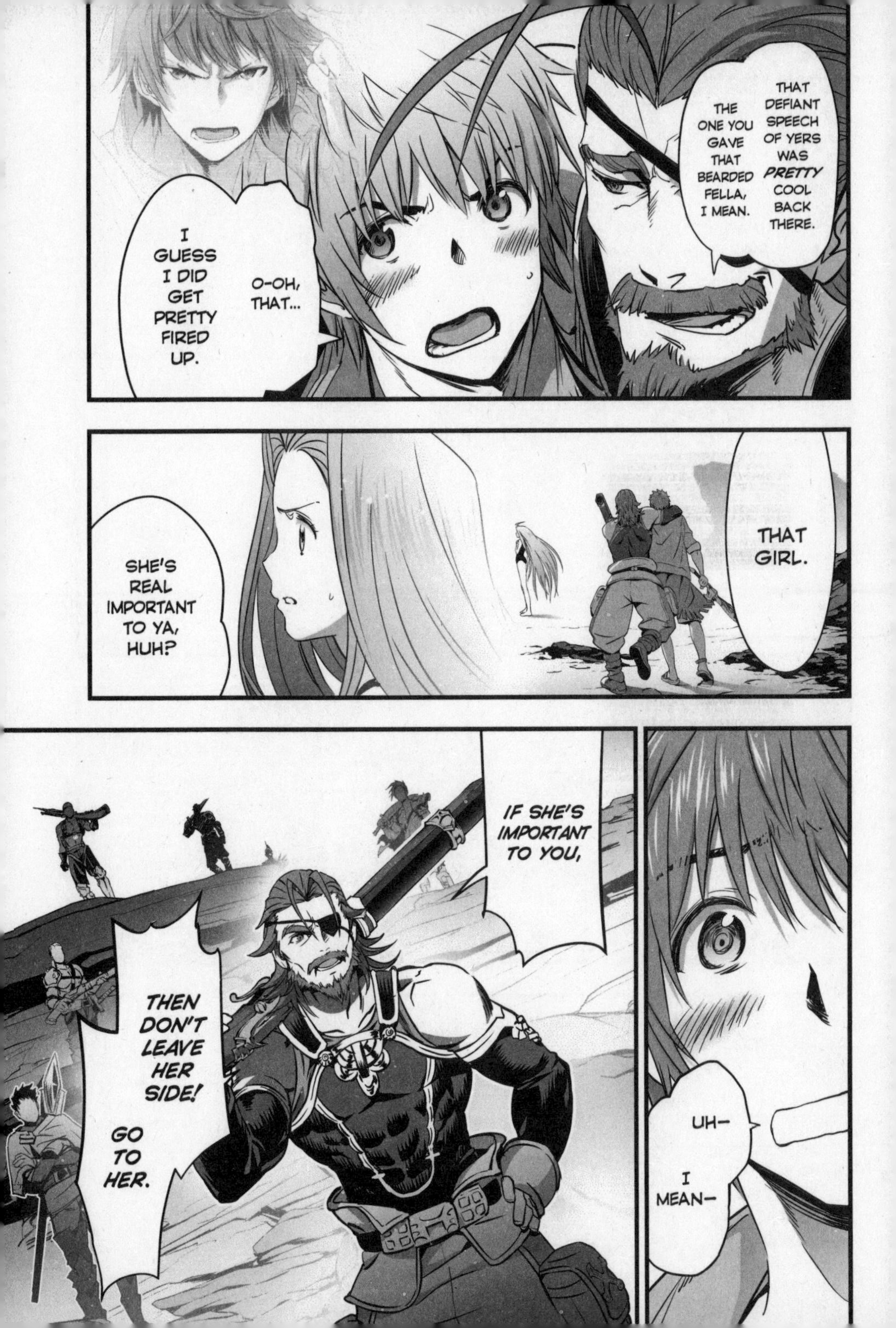
THAT DEFIANT SPEECH OF YERS WAS PRETTY COOL BACK THERE.
THE ONE YOU GAVE THAT BEARDED FELLA, I MEAN.
O-OH, THAT...
I GUESS I DID GET PRETTY FIRED UP.
THAT GIRL.
SHE'S REAL IMPORTANT TO YA, HUH?
UH-
I MEAN-
IF SHE'S IMPORTANT TO YOU,
THEN DON'T LEAVE HER SIDE!
GO TO HER.

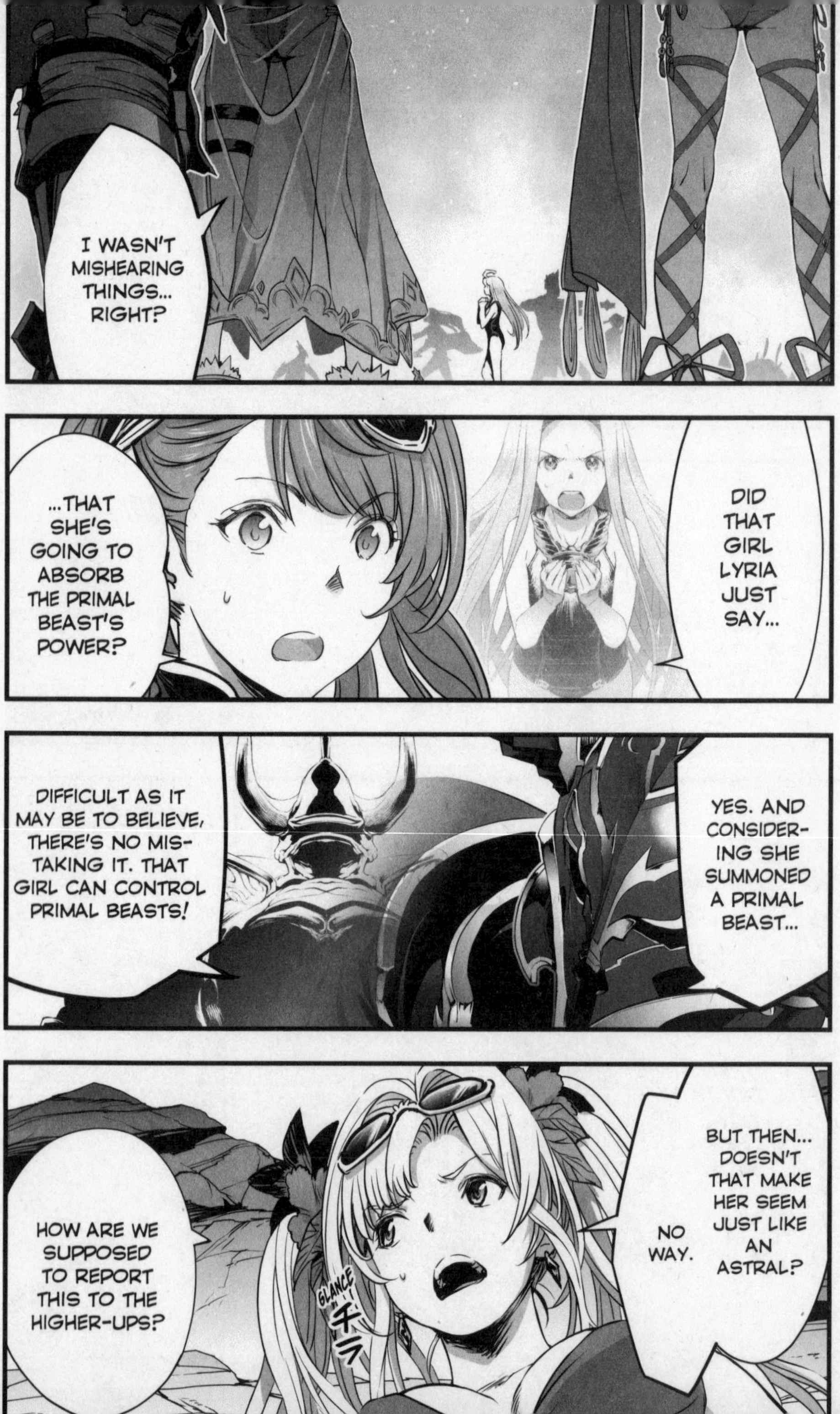
I WASN'T MISHEARING THINGS... RIGHT?
DID THAT GIRL LYRIA JUST SAY...
...THAT SHE'S GOING TO ABSORB THE PRIMAL BEAST'S POWER?
YES. AND CONSIDERING SHE SUMMONED A PRIMAL BEAST...
DIFFICULT AS IT MAY BE TO BELIEVE, THERE'S NO MIS-TAKING IT. THAT GIRL CAN CONTROL PRIMAL BEASTS!
BUT THEN... DOESN'T THAT MAKE HER SEEM JUST LIKE AN ASTRAL?
NO WAY.
GLANCE
チラ
HOW ARE WE SUPPOSED TO REPORT THIS TO THE HIGHER-UPS?

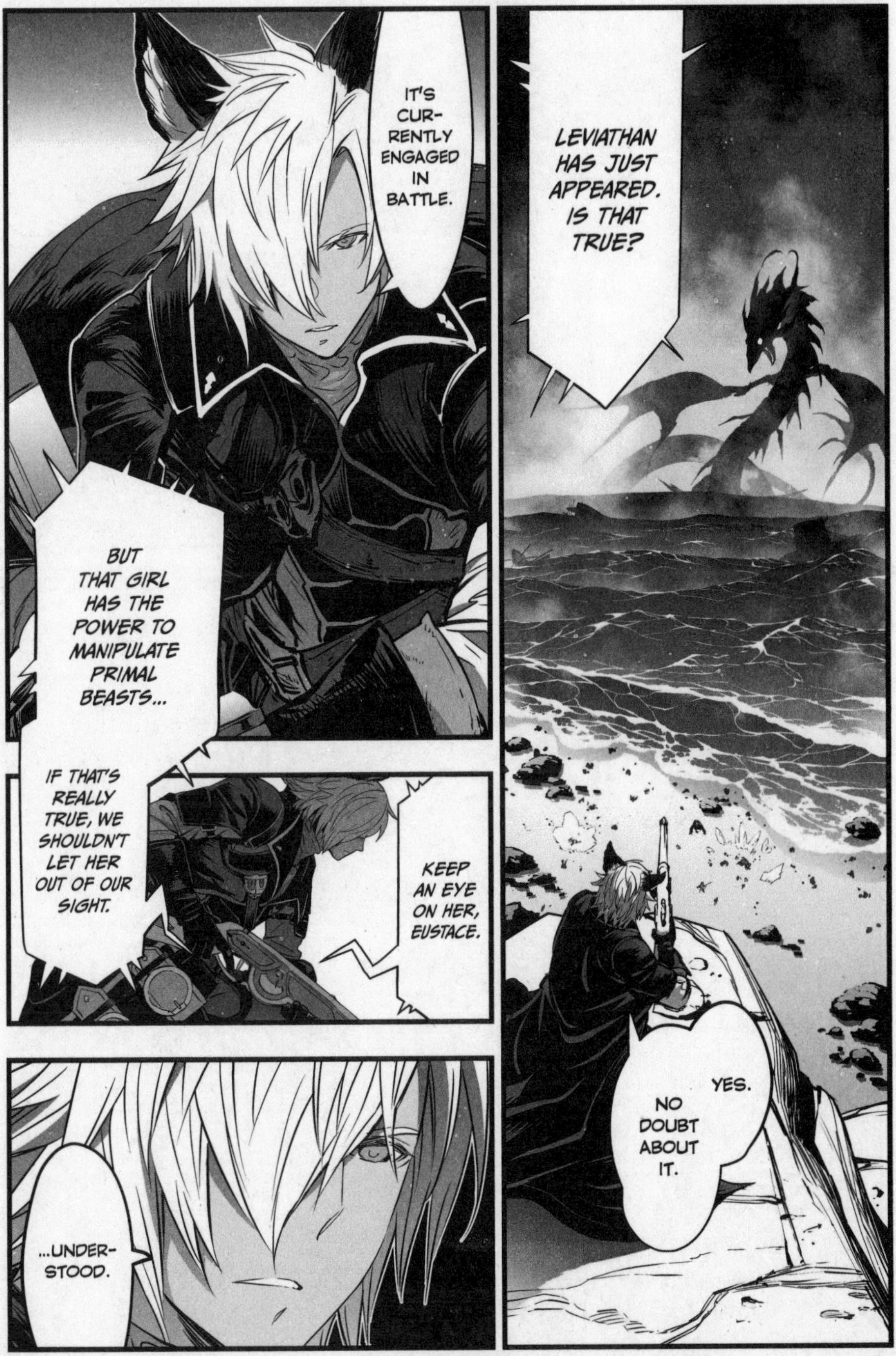
LEVIATHAN HAS JUST APPEARED. IS THAT TRUE?
YES.
NO DOUBT ABOUT IT.
IT'S CUR-RENTLY ENGAGED IN BATTLE.
BUT THAT GIRL HAS THE POWER TO MANIPULATE PRIMAL BEASTS...
IF THAT'S REALLY TRUE, WE SHOULDN'T LET HER OUT OF OUR SIGHT.
KEEP AN EYE ON HER, EUSTACE.
...UNDER-STOOD.

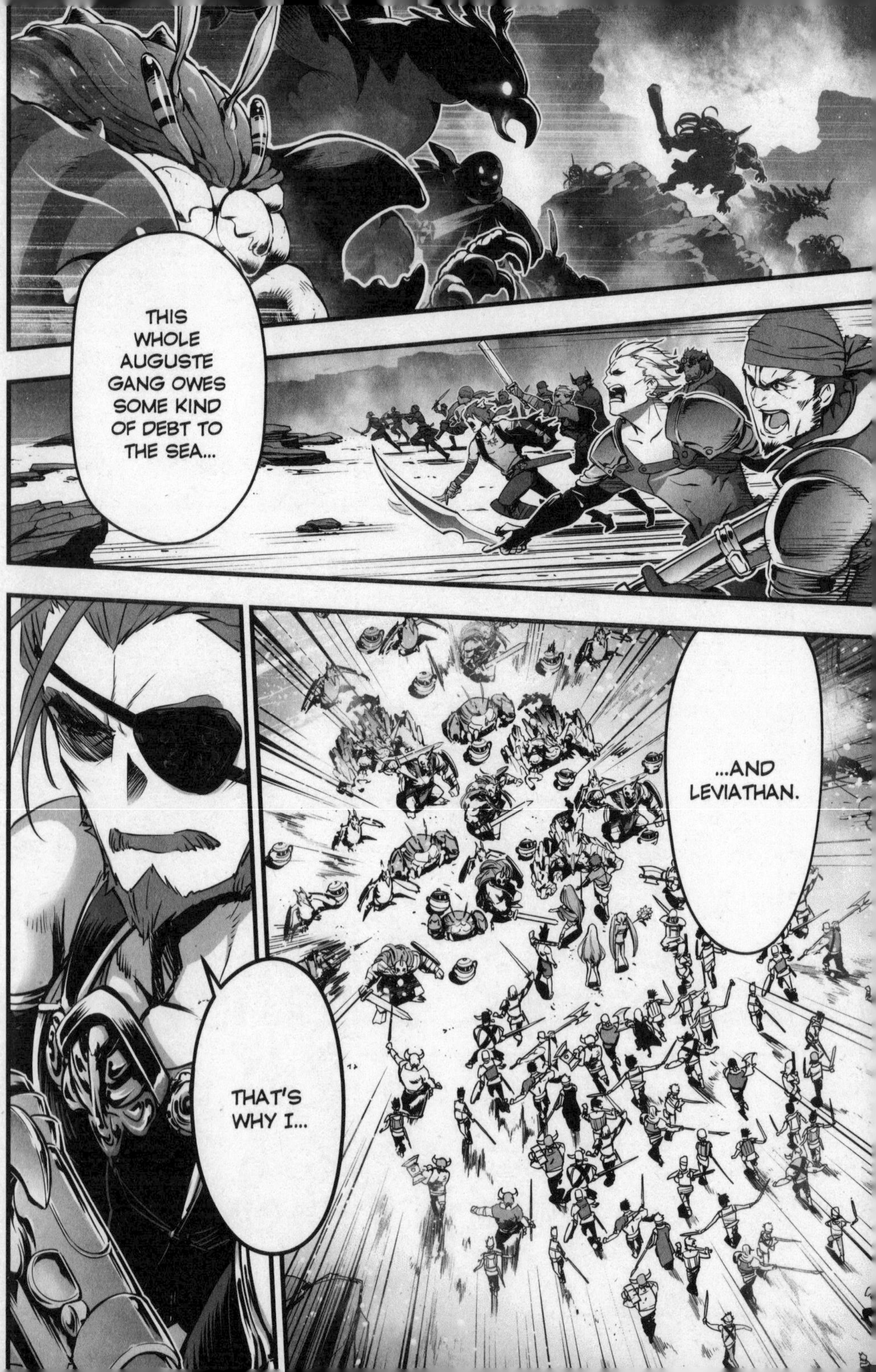
THIS WHOLE AUGUSTE GANG OWES SOME KIND OF DEBT TO THE SEA...
...AND LEVIATHAN.
THAT'S WHY I...

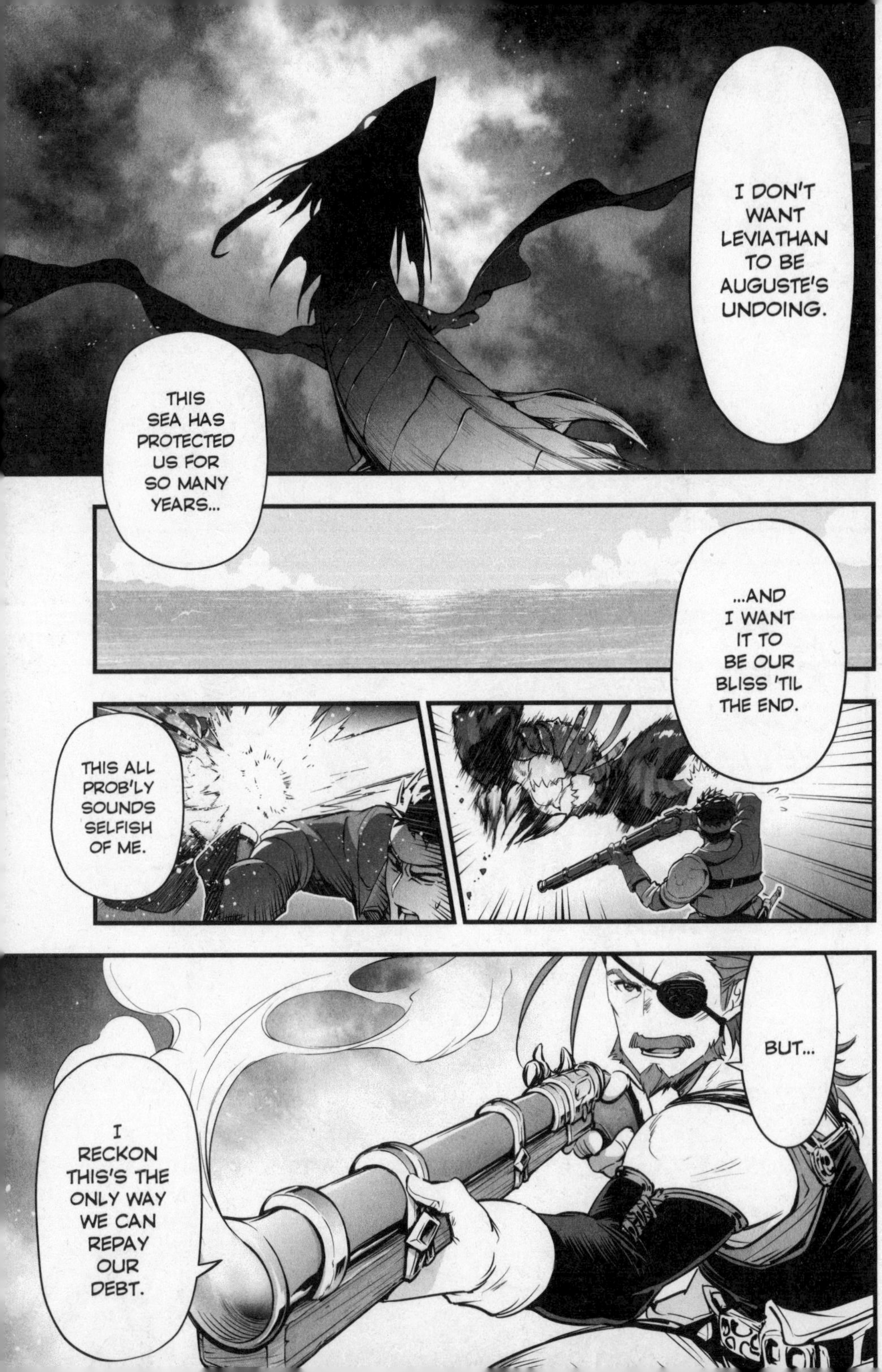
I DON'T WANT LEVIATHAN TO BE AUGUSTE'S UNDOING.
THIS SEA HAS PROTECTED US FOR SO MANY YEARS...
...AND I WANT IT TO BE OUR BLISS 'TIL THE END.
THIS ALL PROB'LY SOUNDS SELFISH OF ME.
BUT...
I RECKON THIS'S THE ONLY WAY WE CAN REPAY OUR DEBT.

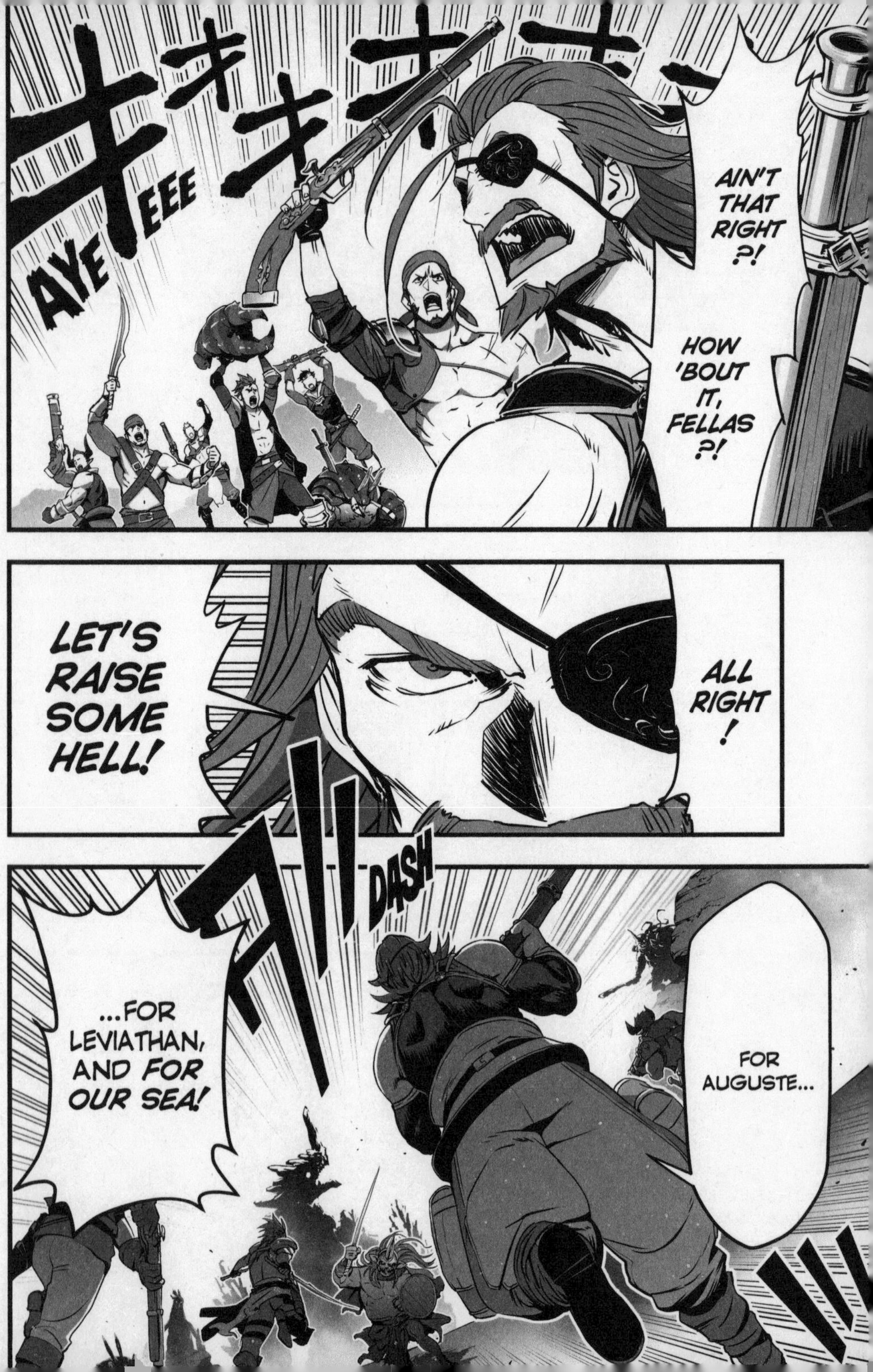
AIN'T THAT RIGHT?!
HOW 'BOUT IT, FELLAS?!
AYEEEE
ALL RIGHT!
LET'S RAISE SOME HELL!
DASH
FOR AUGUSTE...
...FOR LEVIATHAN, AND FOR OUR SEA!

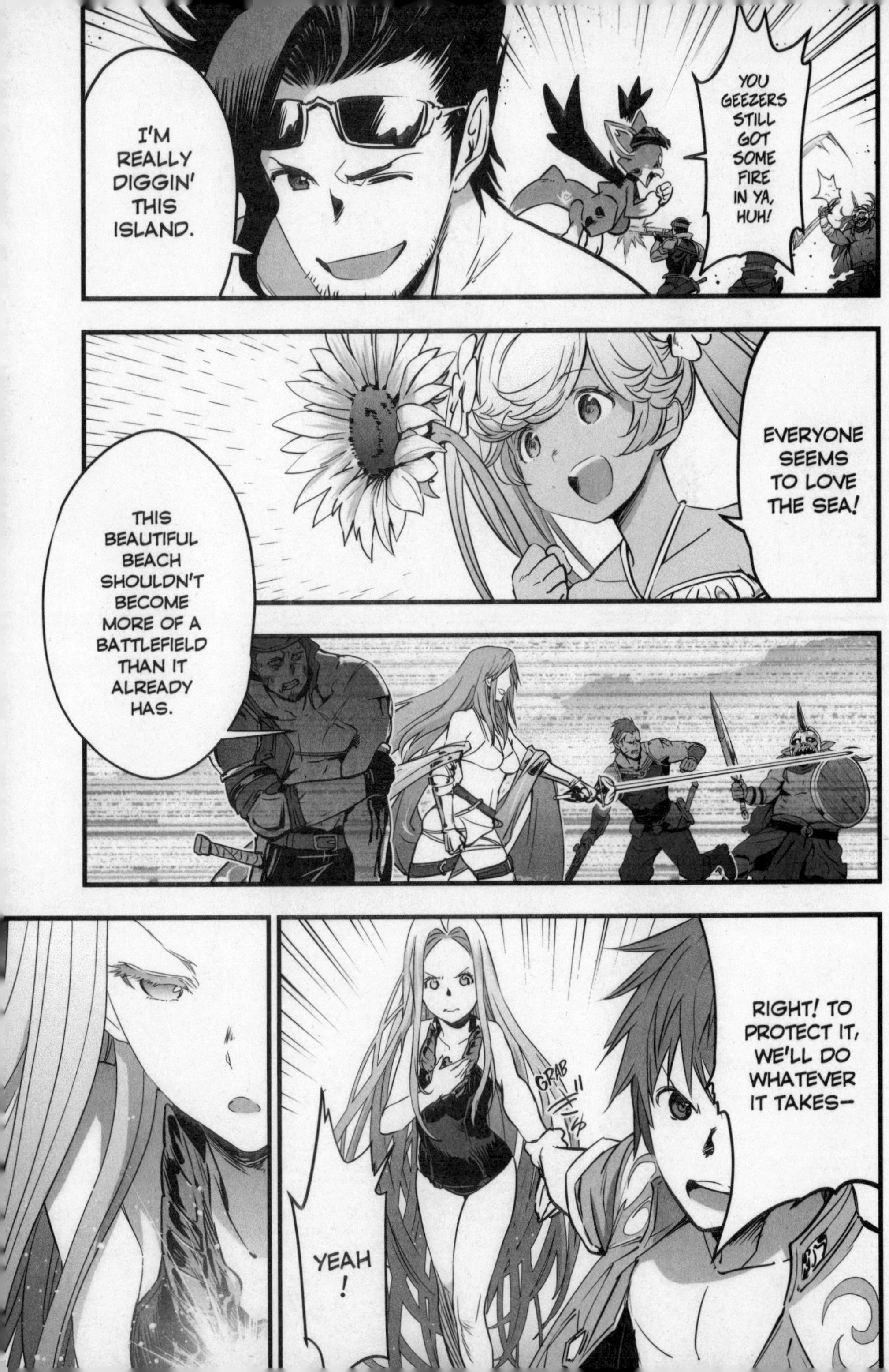
YOU GEEZERS STILL GOT SOME FIRE IN YA, HUH!
I'M REALLY DIGGIN' THIS ISLAND.
EVERYONE SEEMS TO LOVE THE SEA!
THIS BEAUTIFUL BEACH SHOULDN'T BECOME MORE OF A BATTLEFIELD THAN IT ALREADY HAS.
RIGHT! TO PROTECT IT, WE'LL DO WHATEVER IT TAKES—
GRAB
YEAH!

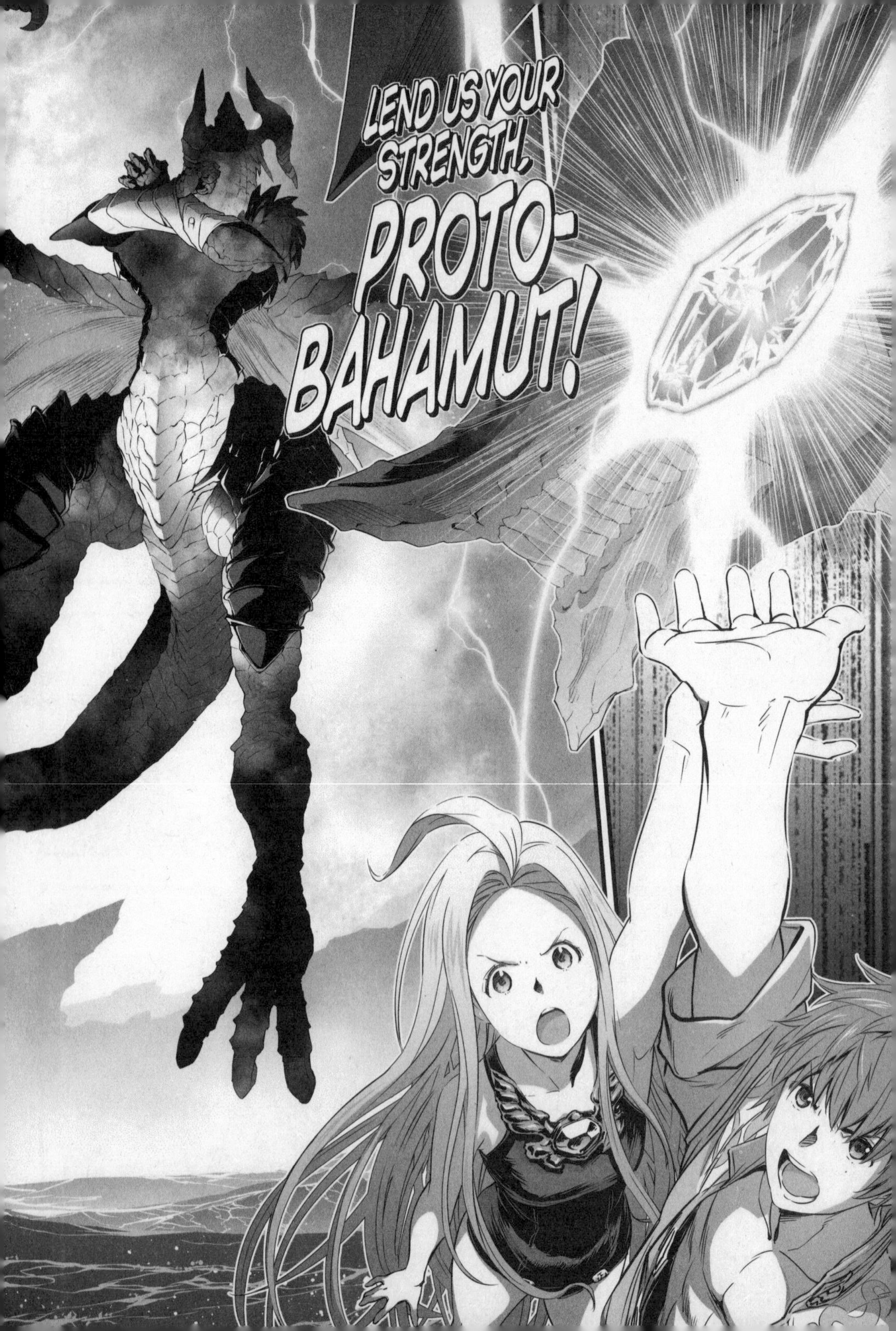
LEND US YOUR STRENGTH, PROTO-BAHAMUT!

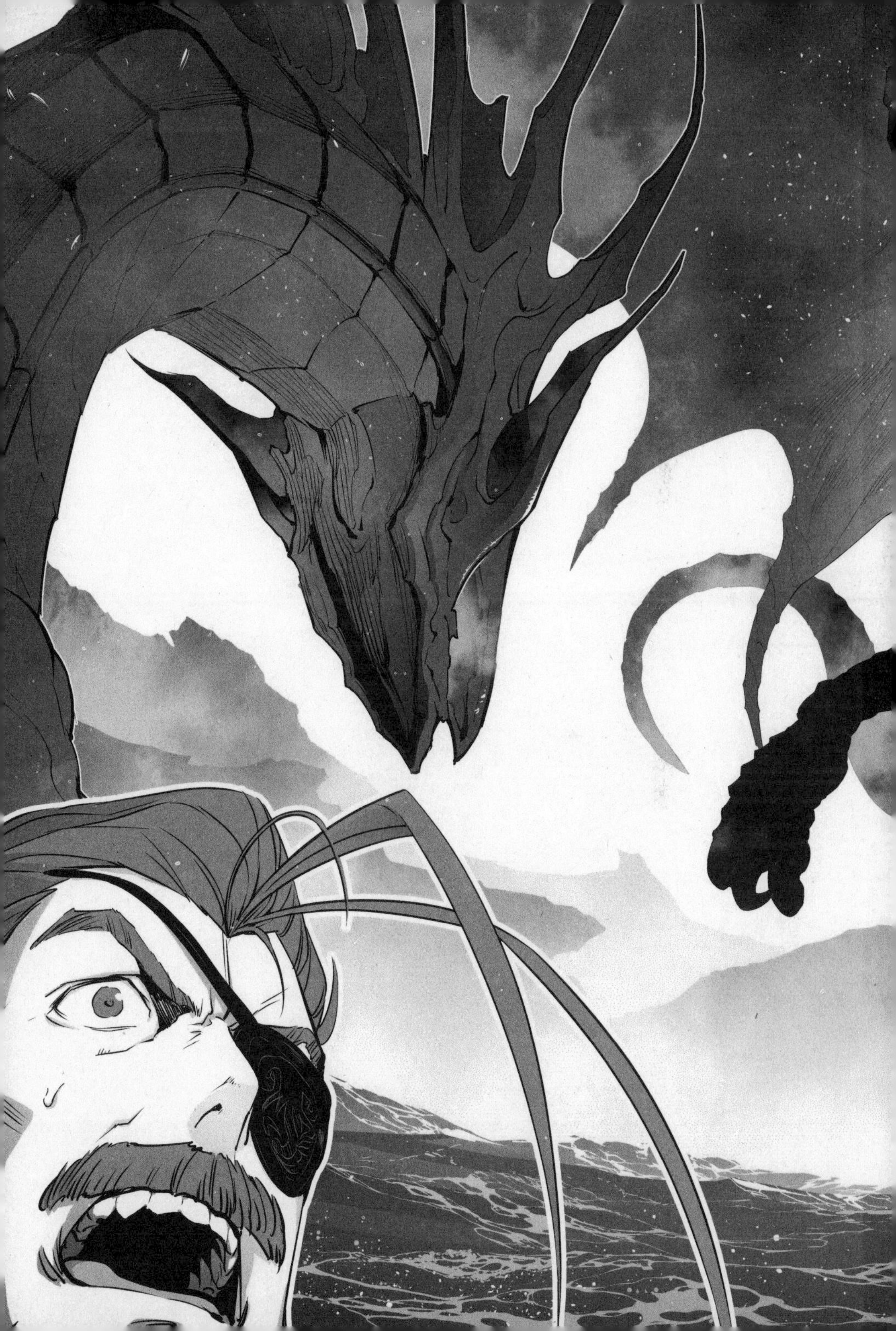

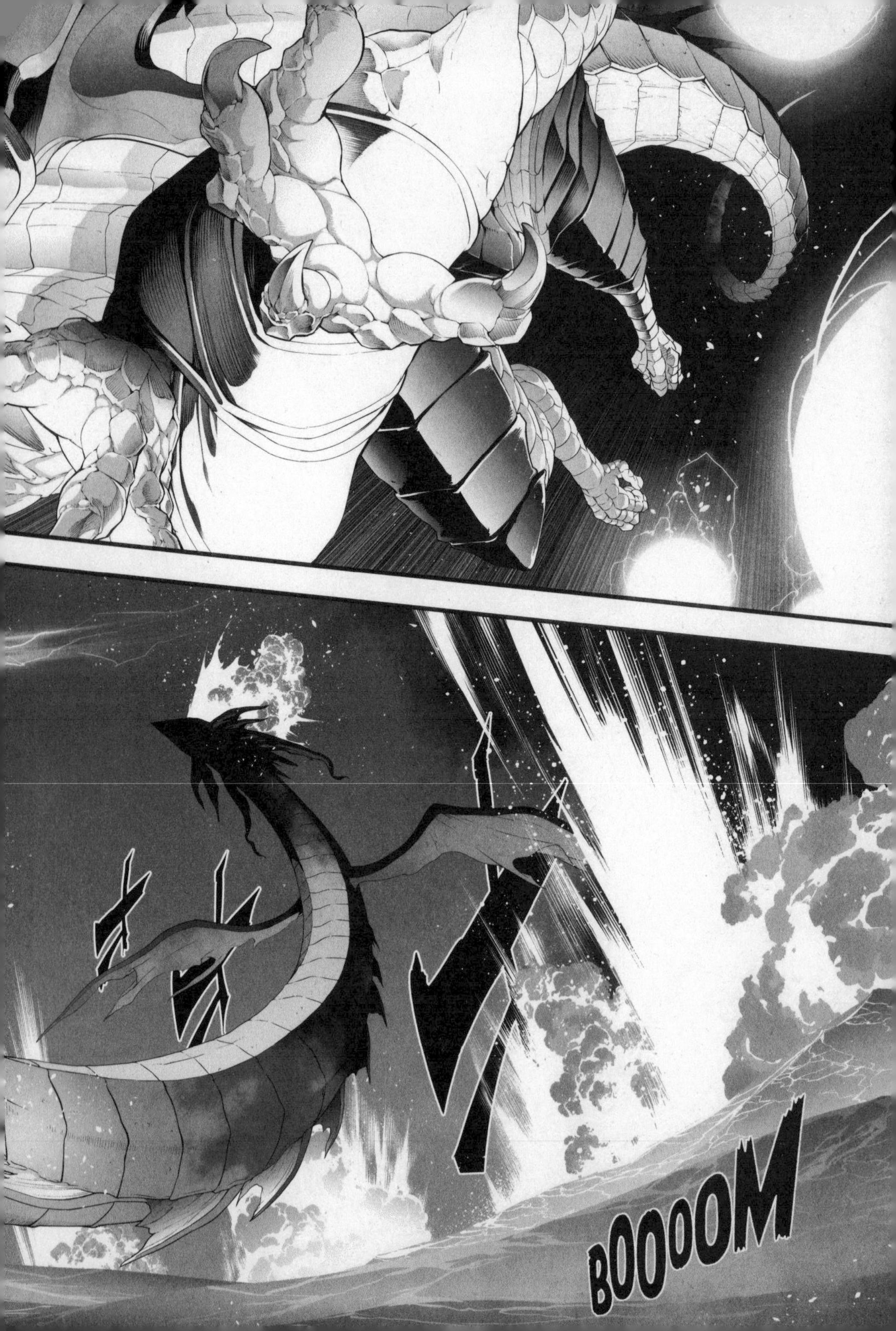
BOOOOM

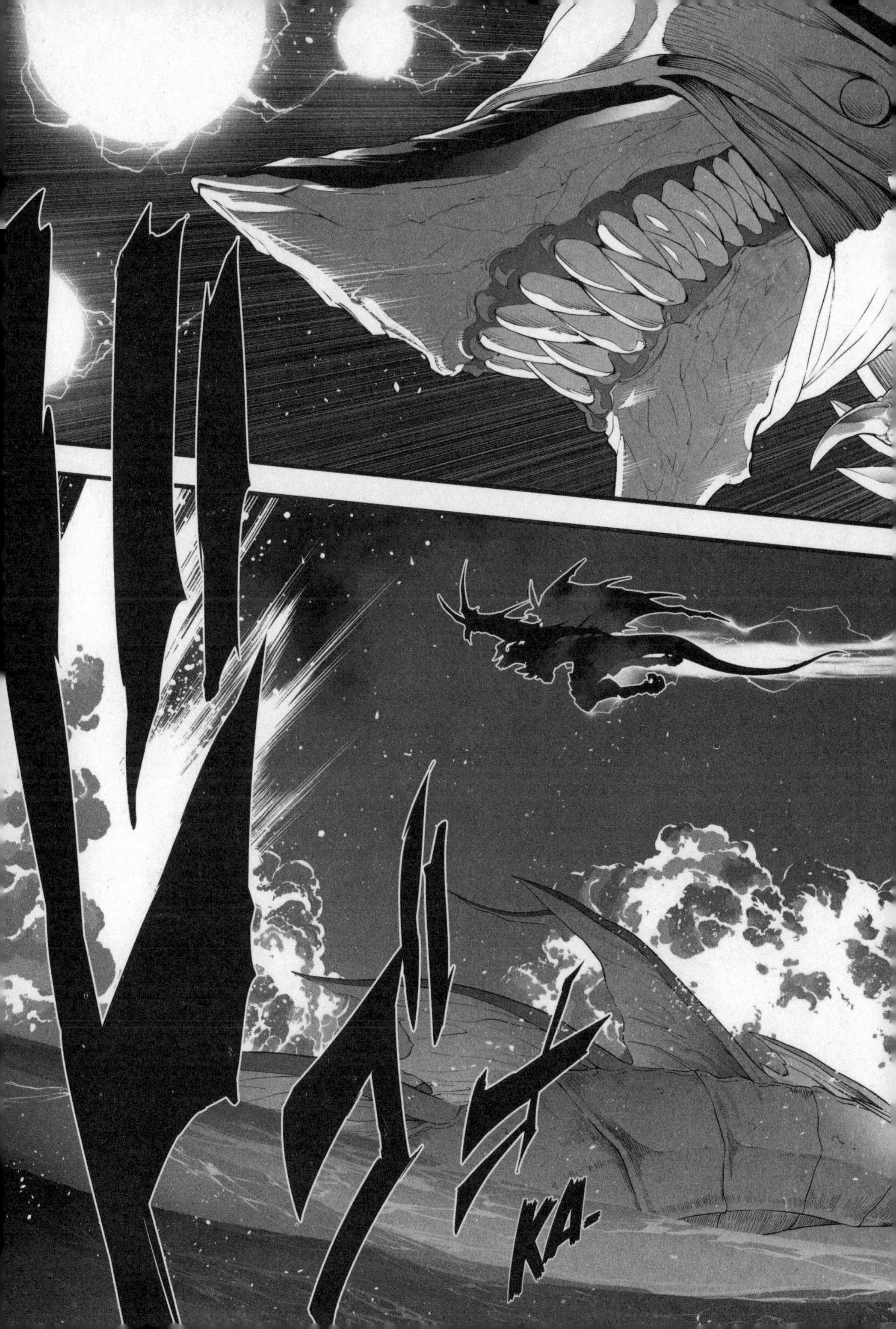
KA-

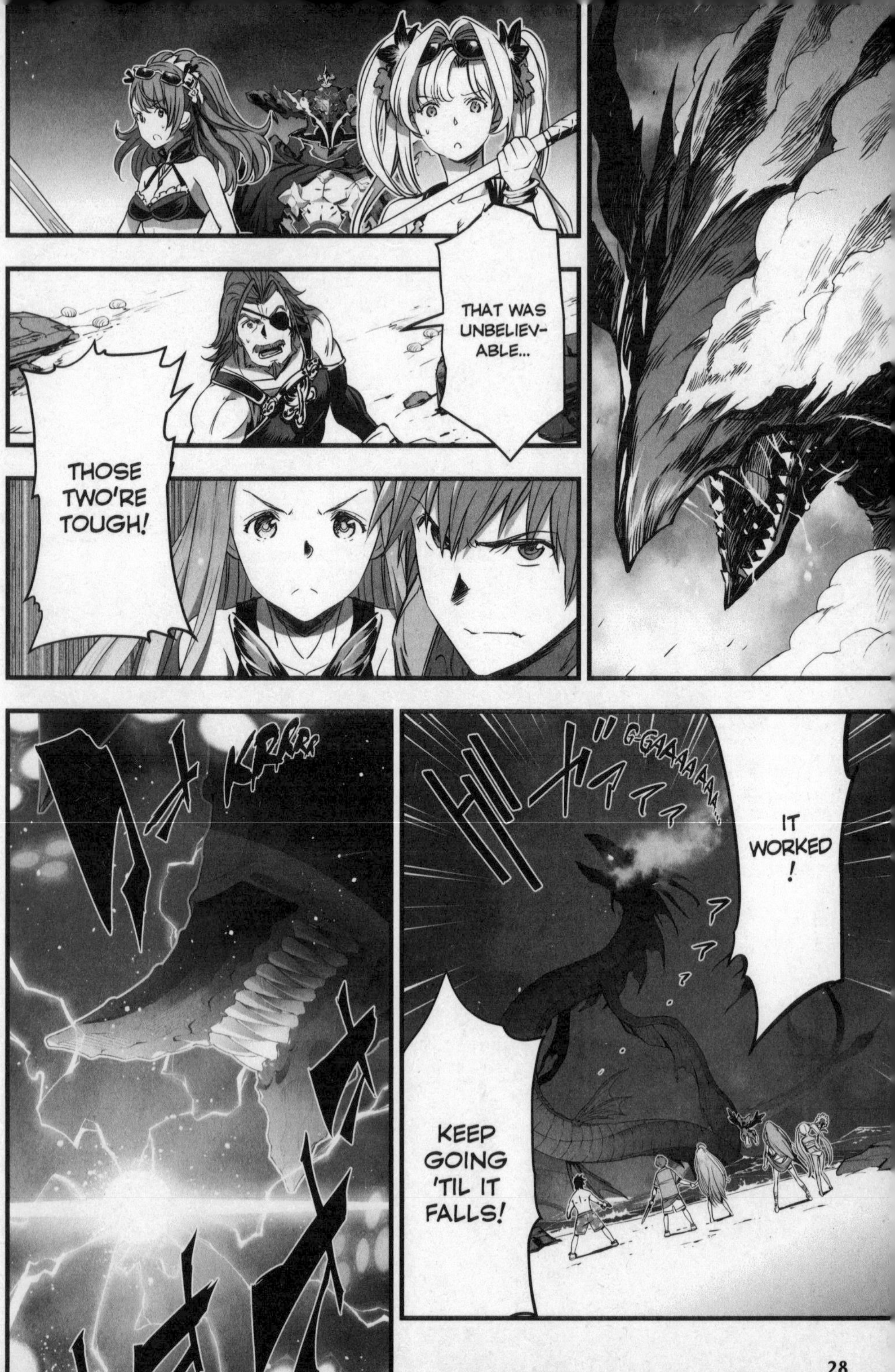
THAT WAS UNBELIEV-ABLE...
THOSE TWO'RE TOUGH!
G-GAAAAA AAA...
IT WORKED!
KEEP GOING 'TIL IT FALLS!
KRRRRR

REGINLEIV!!!

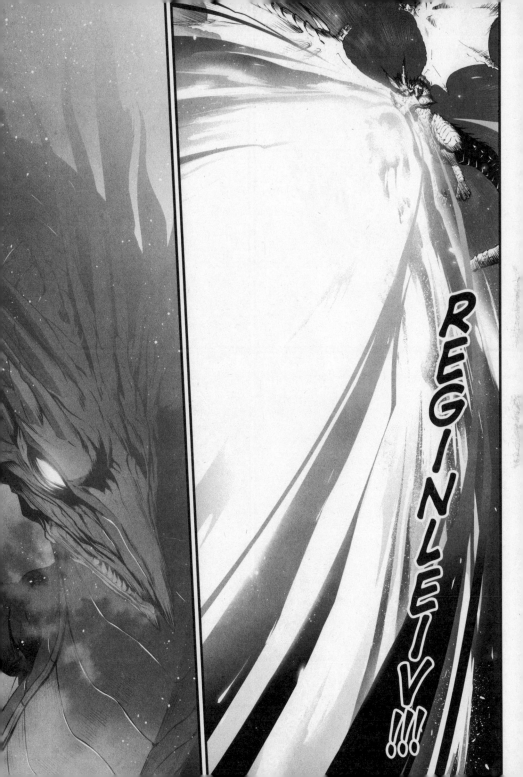

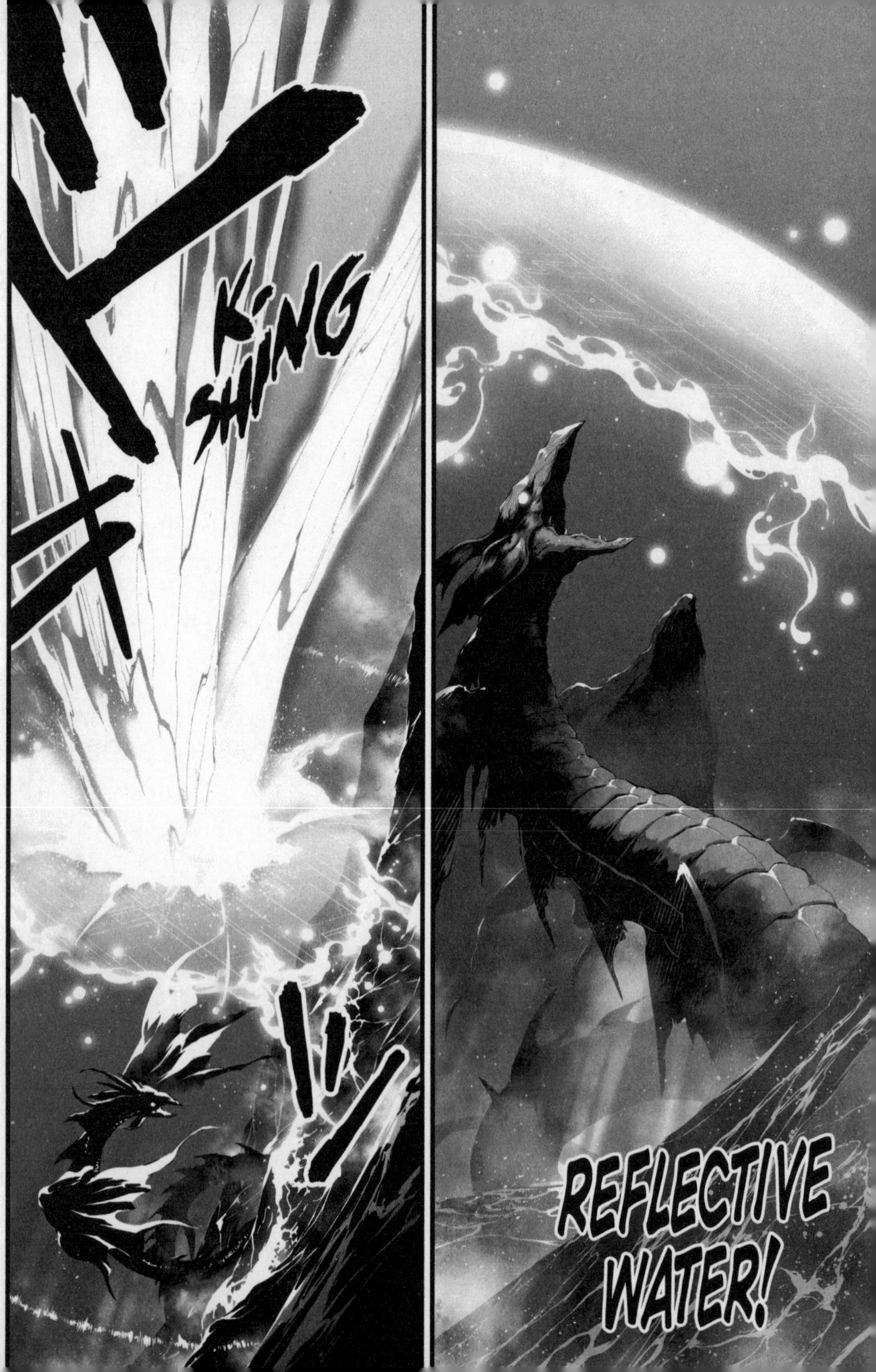
REFLECTIVE WATER!
KING SHING

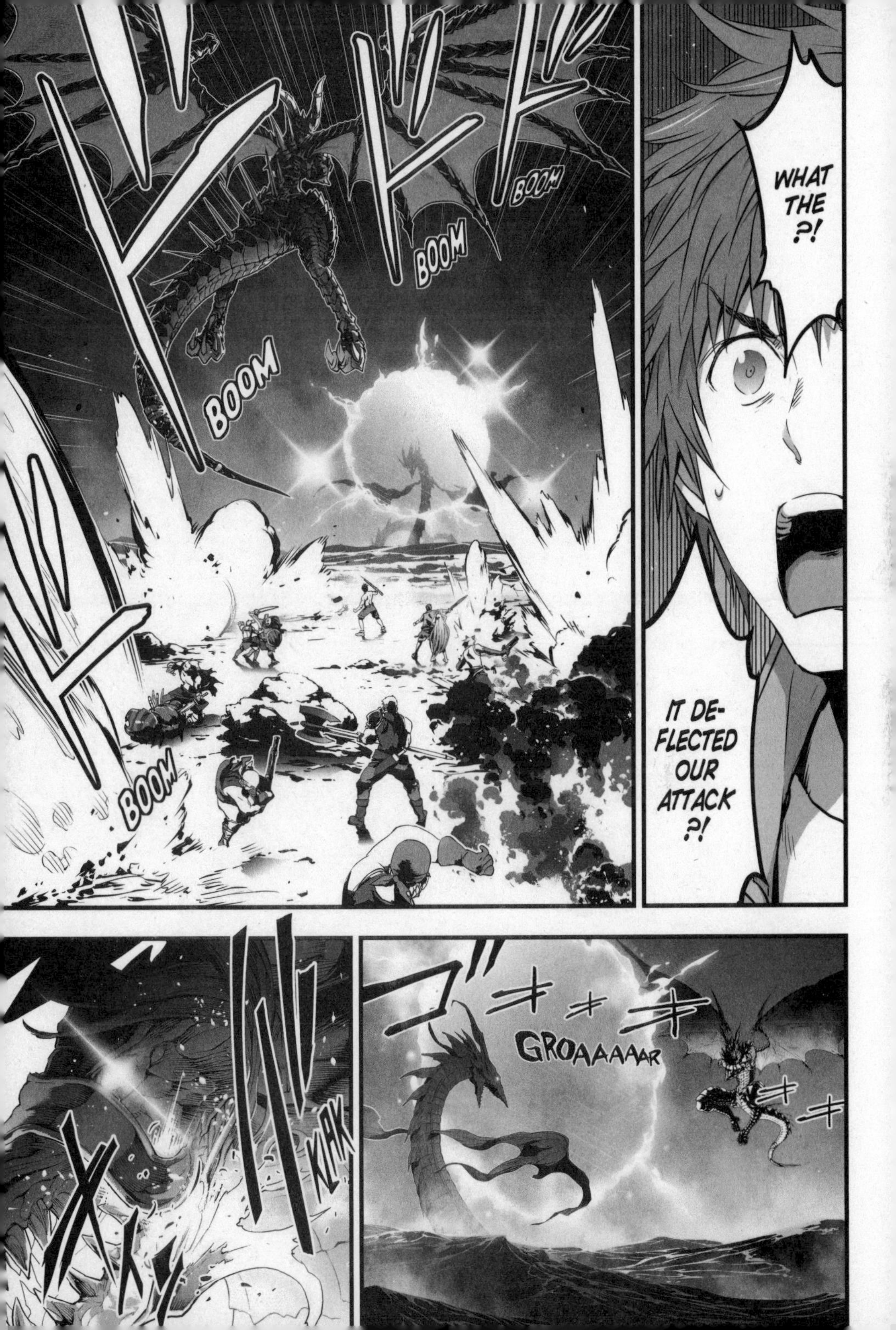
WHAT THE ?!
IT DE-FLECTED OUR ATTACK ?!
BOOM
BOOM
BOOM
BOOM
BOOM
GROAAAAAR
KRAK

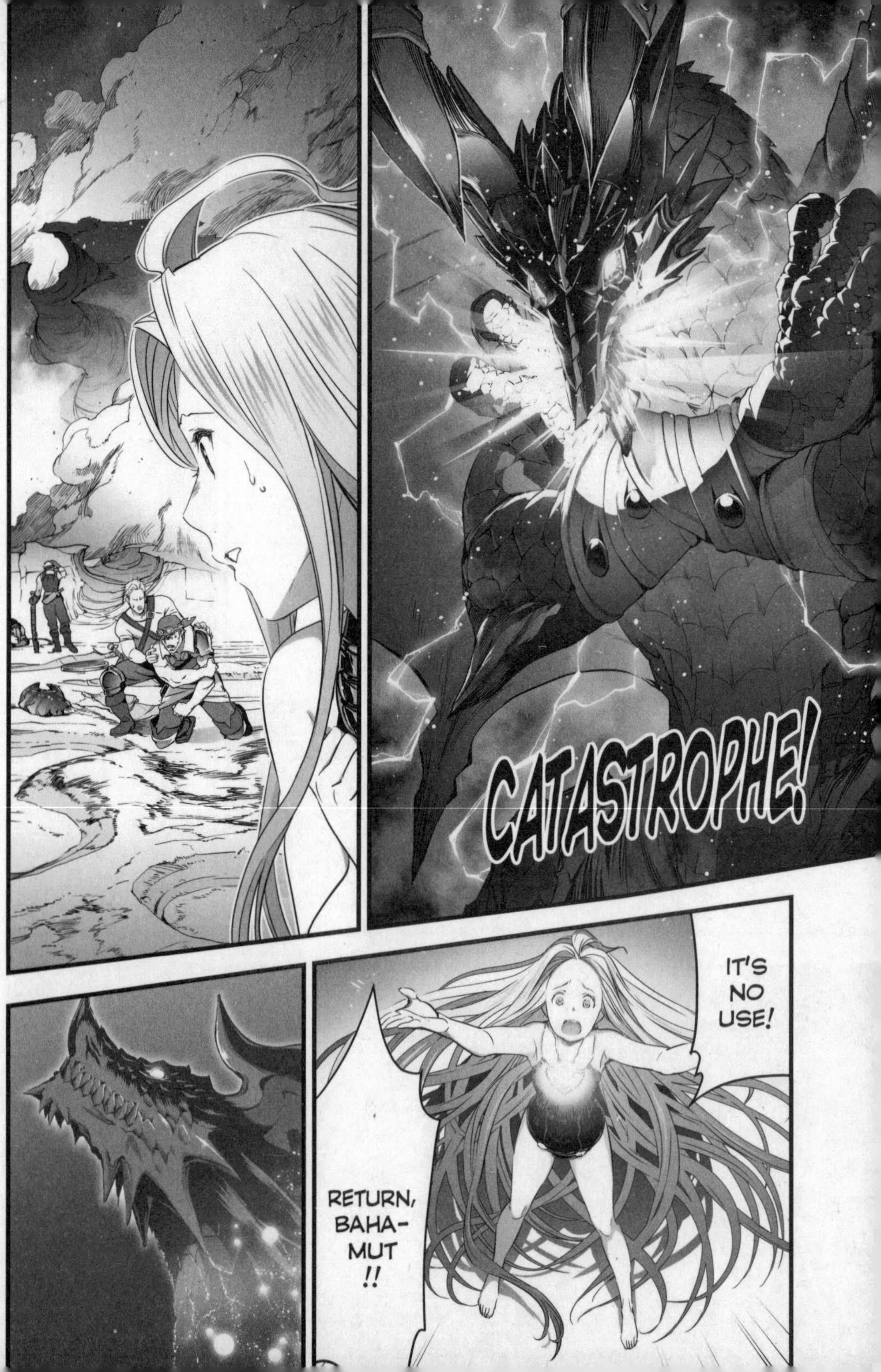
CATASTROPHE!
IT'S NO USE!
RETURN, BAHA-MUT!!

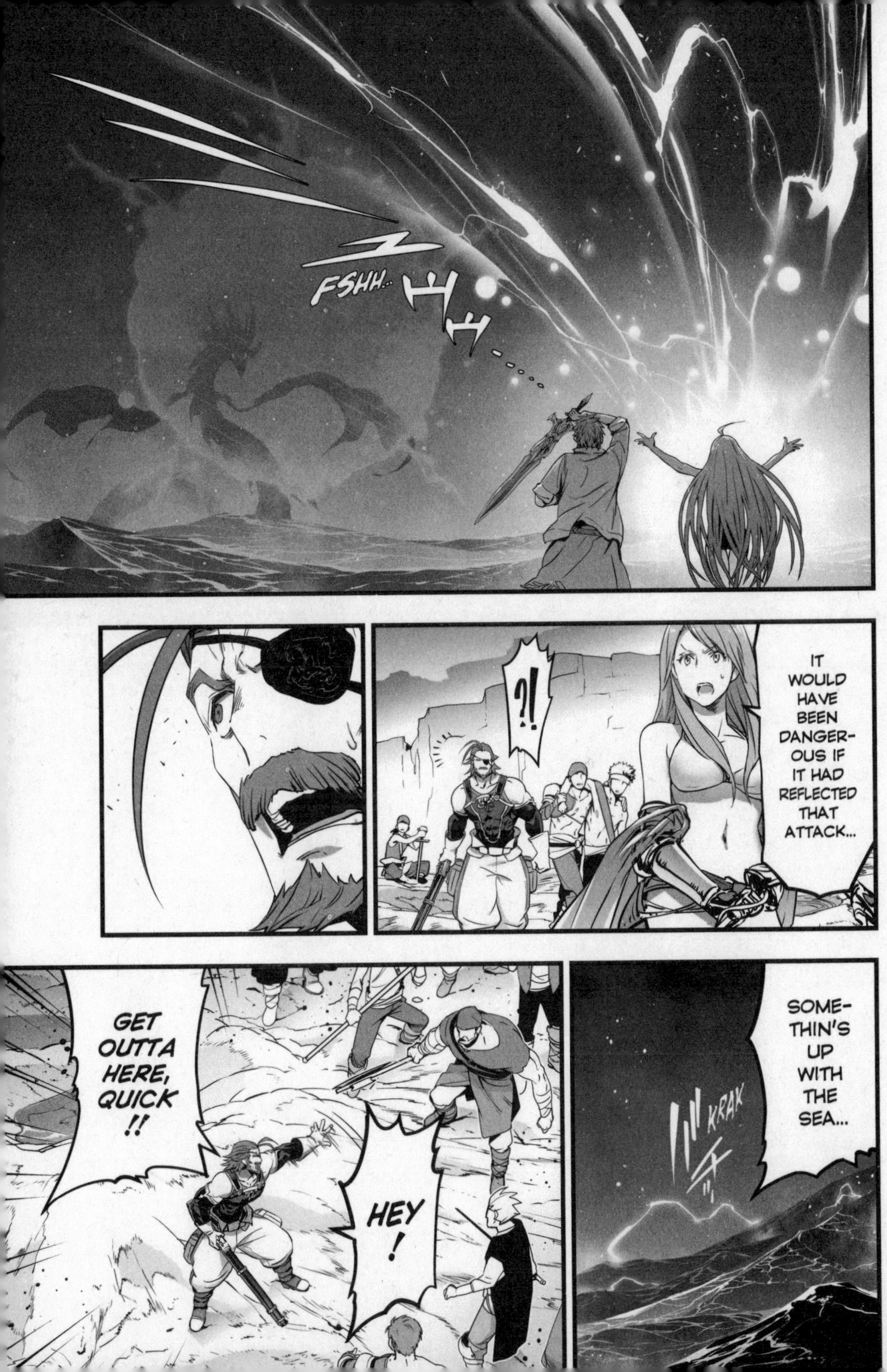
FSHH...
IT WOULD HAVE BEEN DANGER-OUS IF IT HAD REFLECTED THAT ATTACK...
?!
SOME-THIN'S UP WITH THE SEA...
KRAK
GET OUTTA HERE, QUICK!!
HEY!

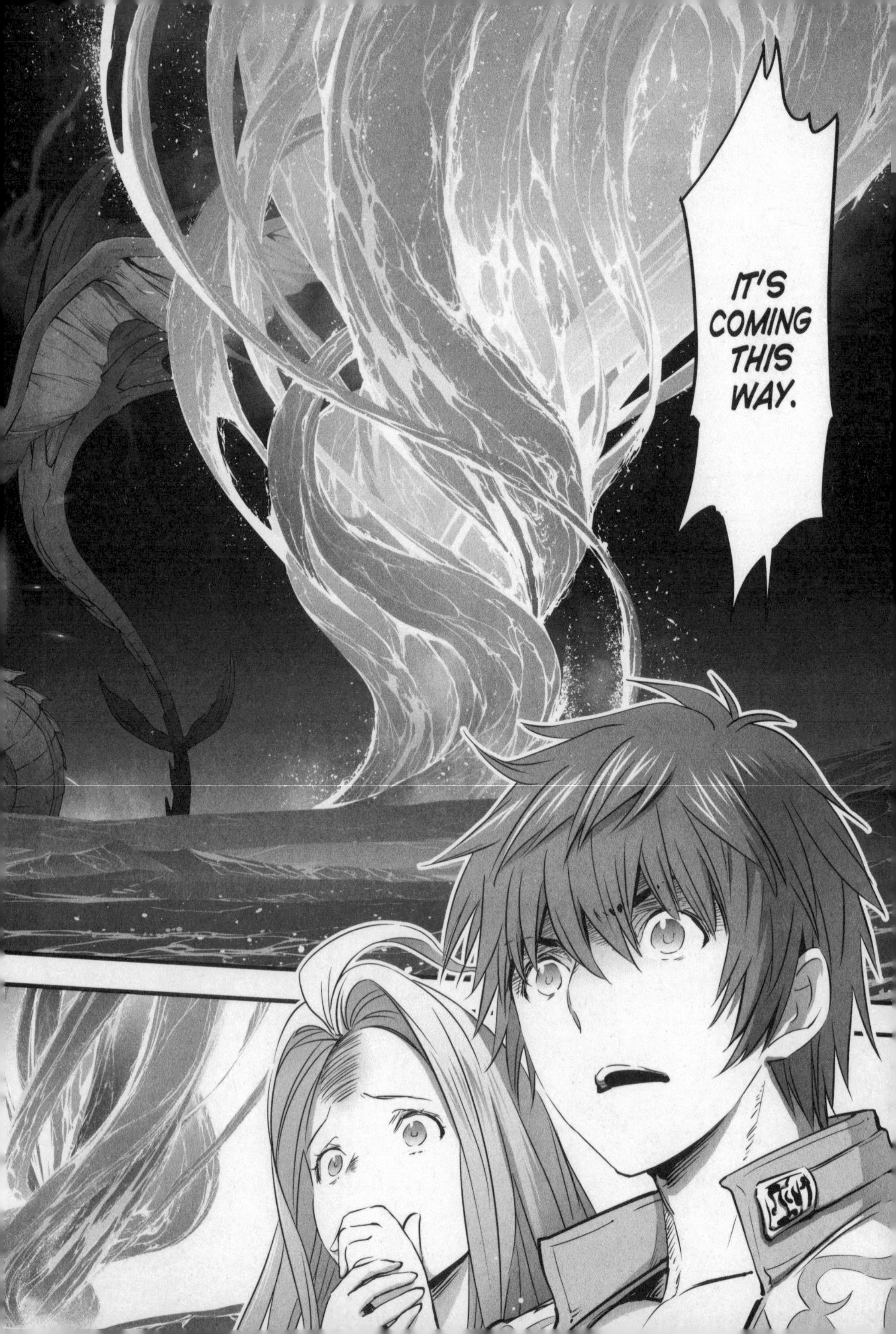
IT'S COMING THIS WAY.

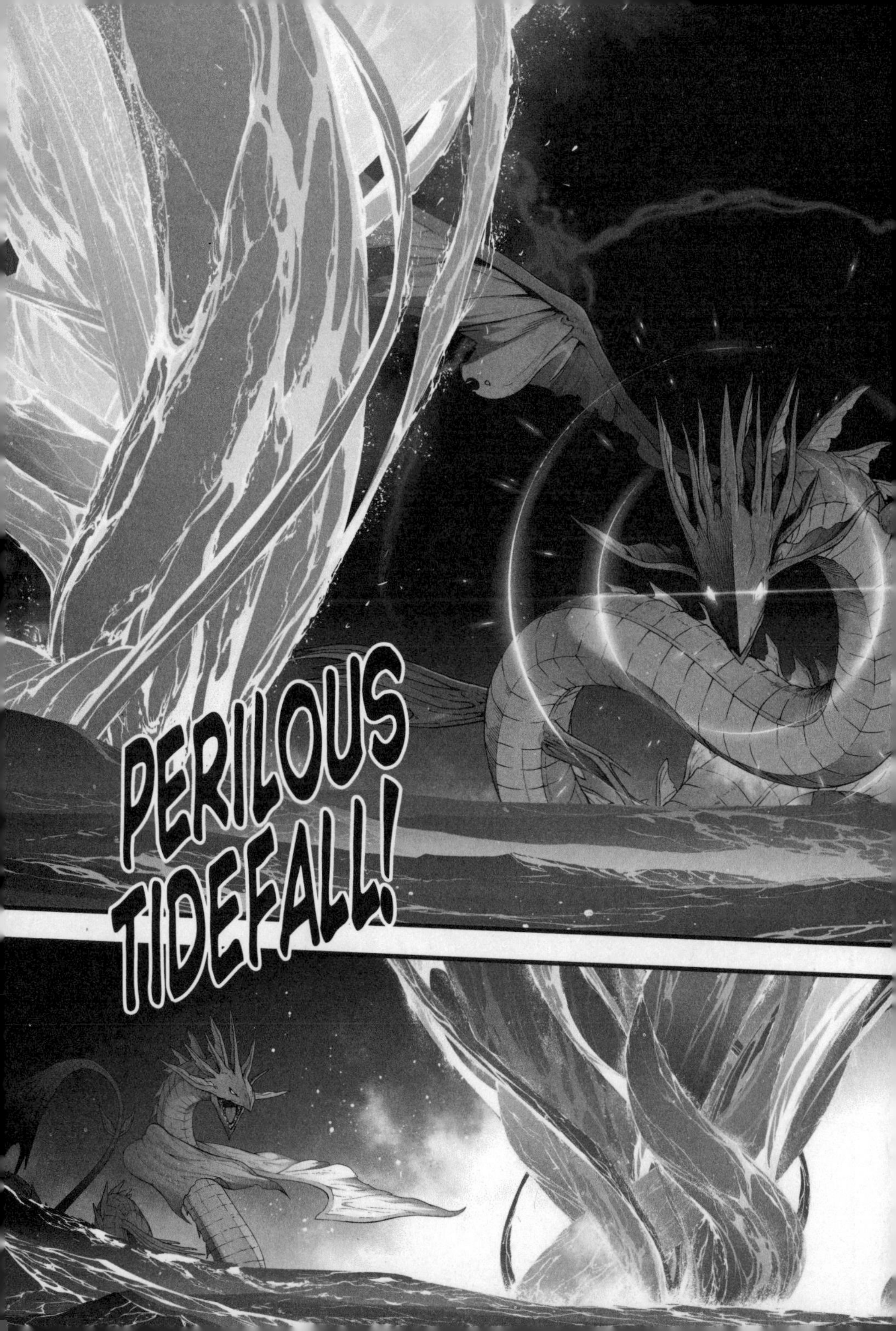
PERILOUS TIDEFALL!

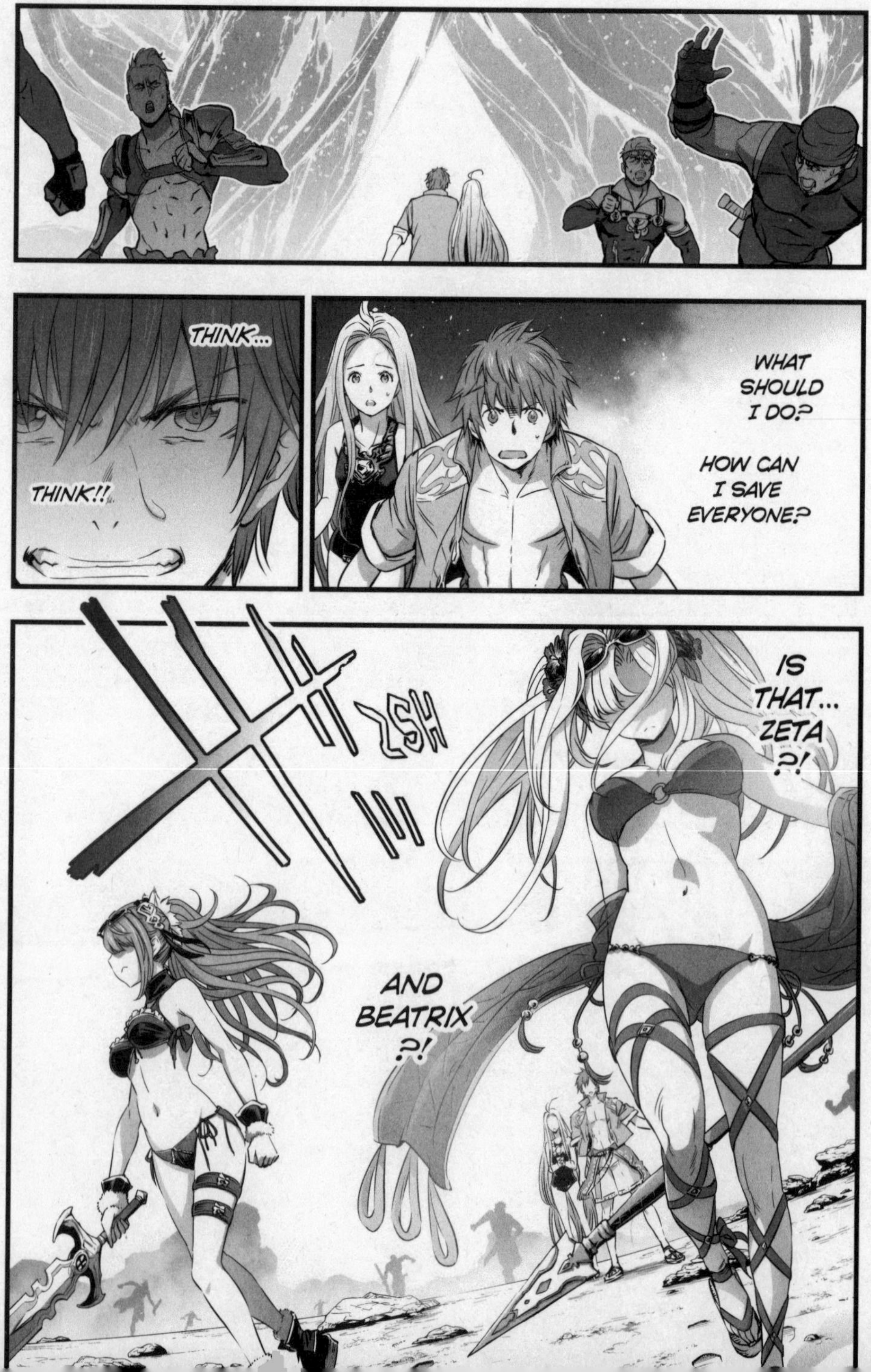
WHAT SHOULD I DO?
HOW CAN I SAVE EVERYONE?
THINK...
THINK!!
IS THAT... ZETA ?!
AND BEATRIX ?!

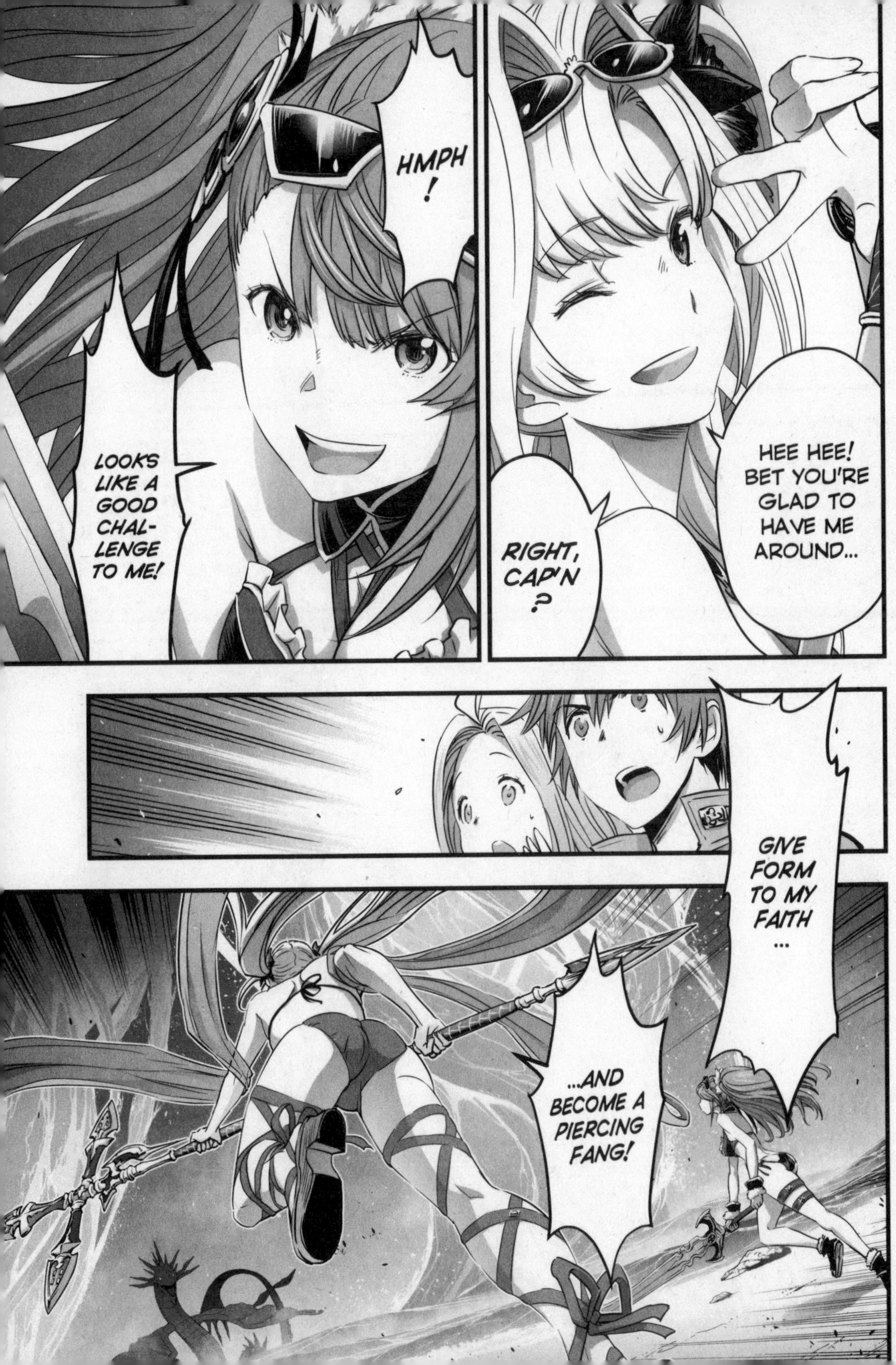
HEE HEE! BET YOU'RE GLAD TO HAVE ME AROUND...
RIGHT, CAP'N?
HMPH!
LOOKS LIKE A GOOD CHAL-LENGE TO ME!
GIVE FORM TO MY FAITH...
...AND BECOME A PIERCING FANG!

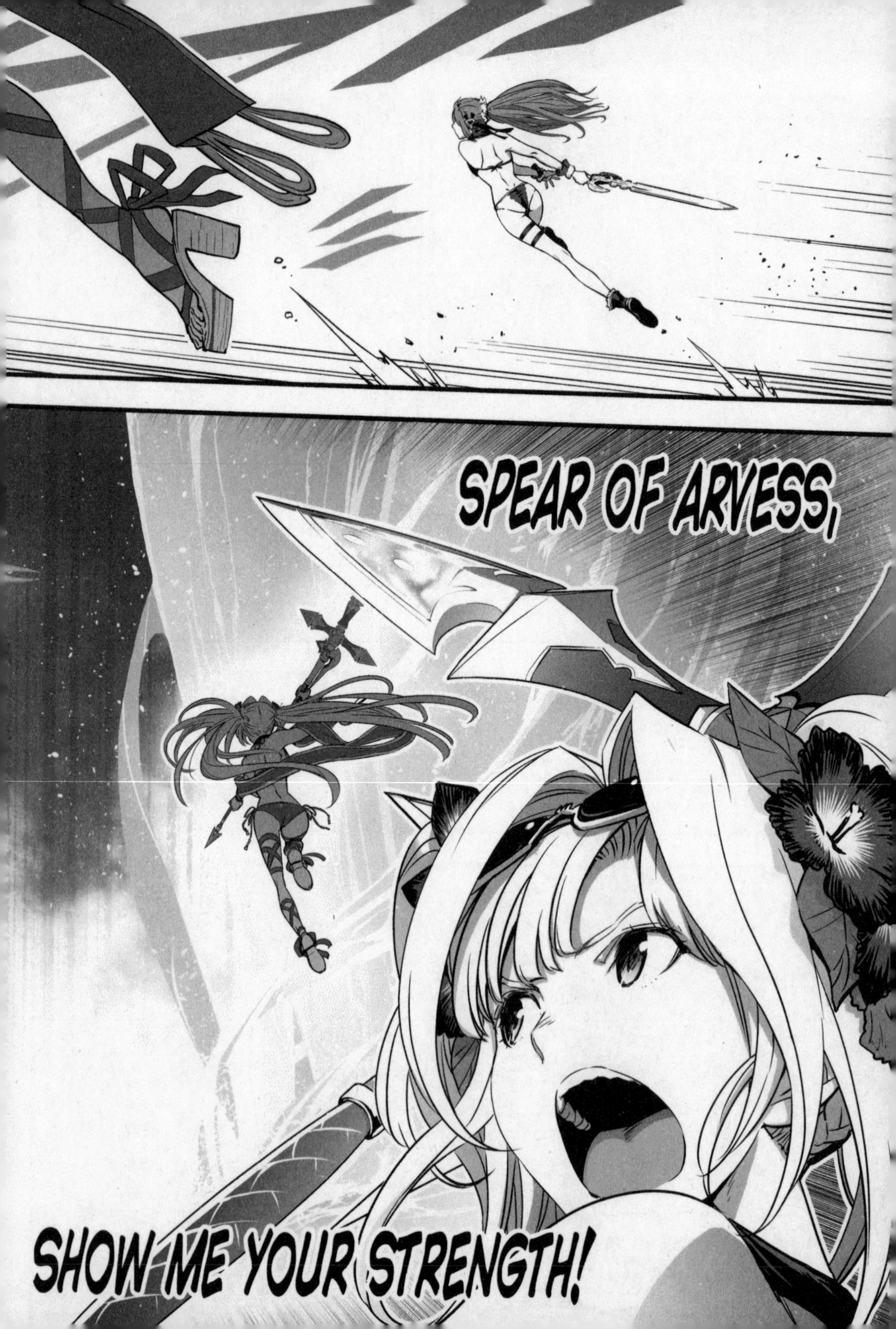
SPEAR OF ARVESS,
SHOW ME YOUR STRENGTH!

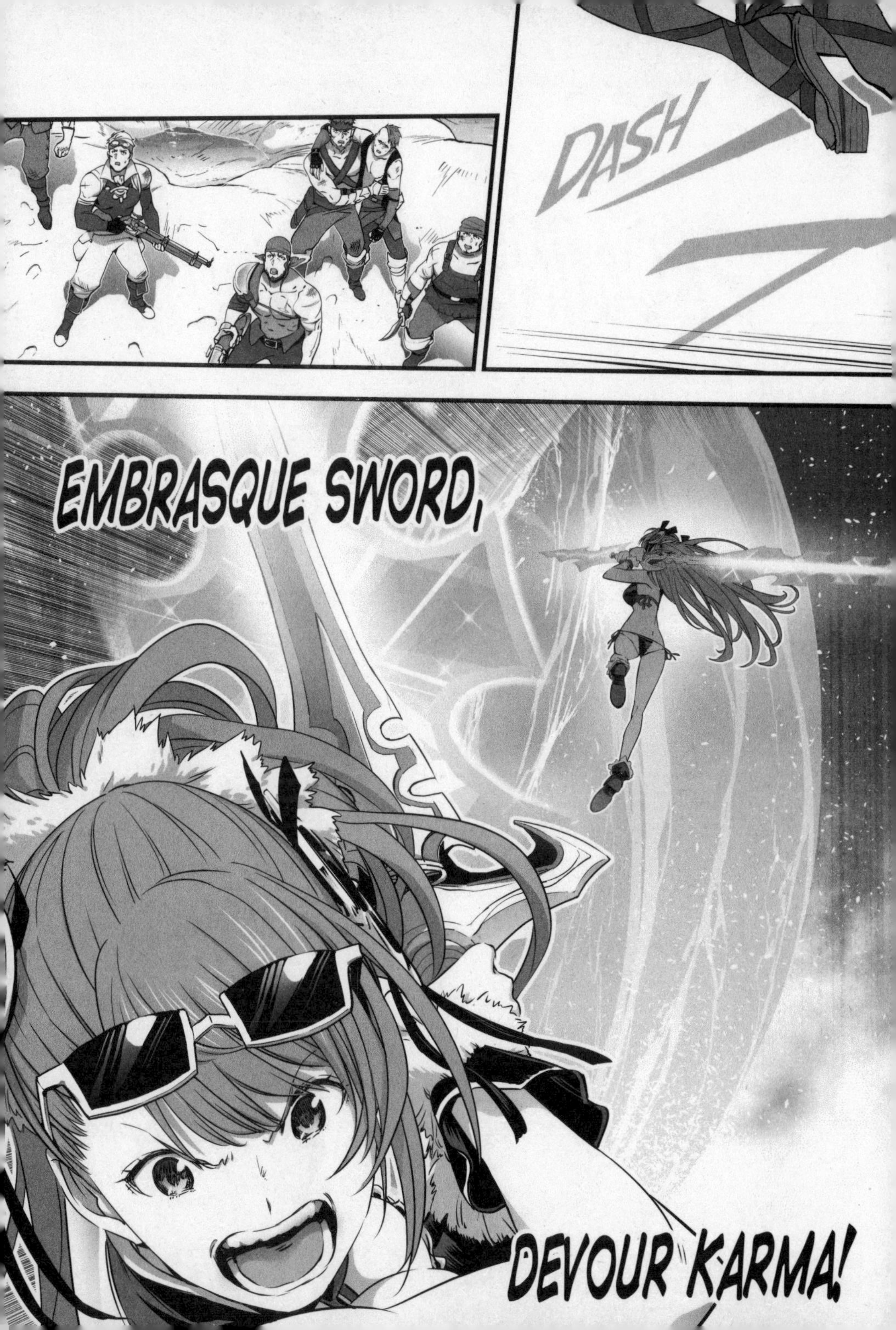
DASH
EMBRASQUE SWORD,
DEVOUR KARMA!

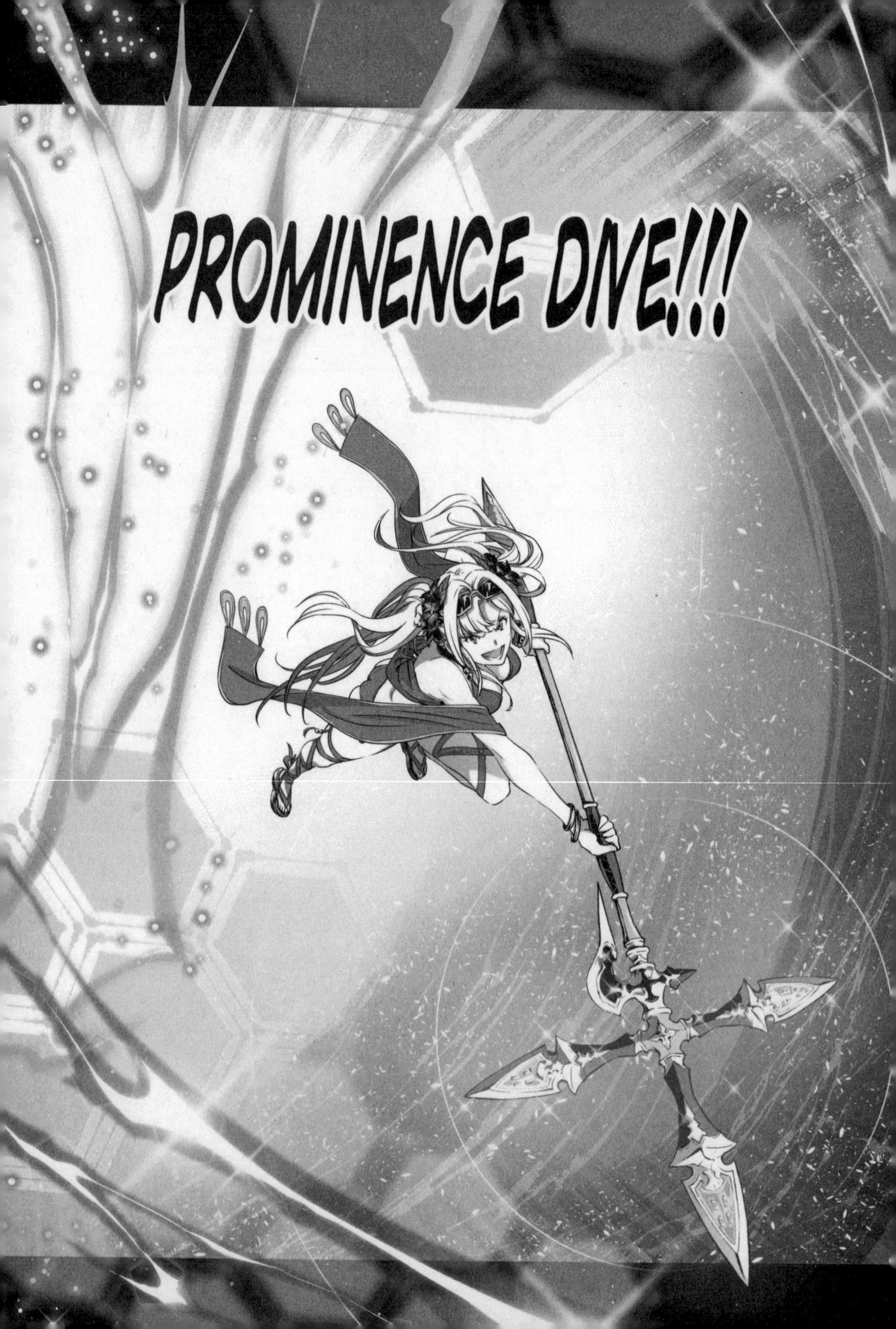
PROMINENCE DIVE!!!

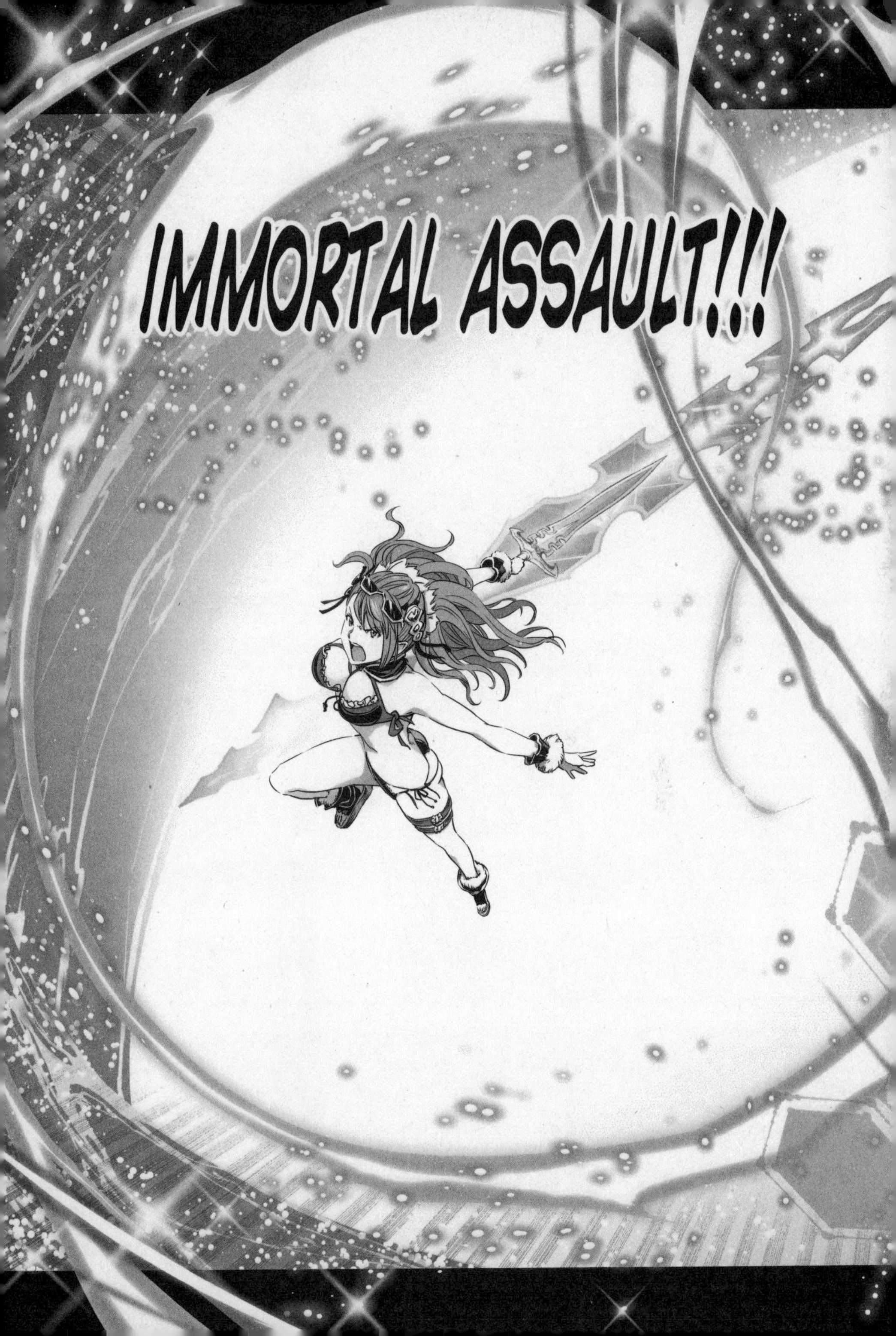
IMMORTAL ASSAULT!!!

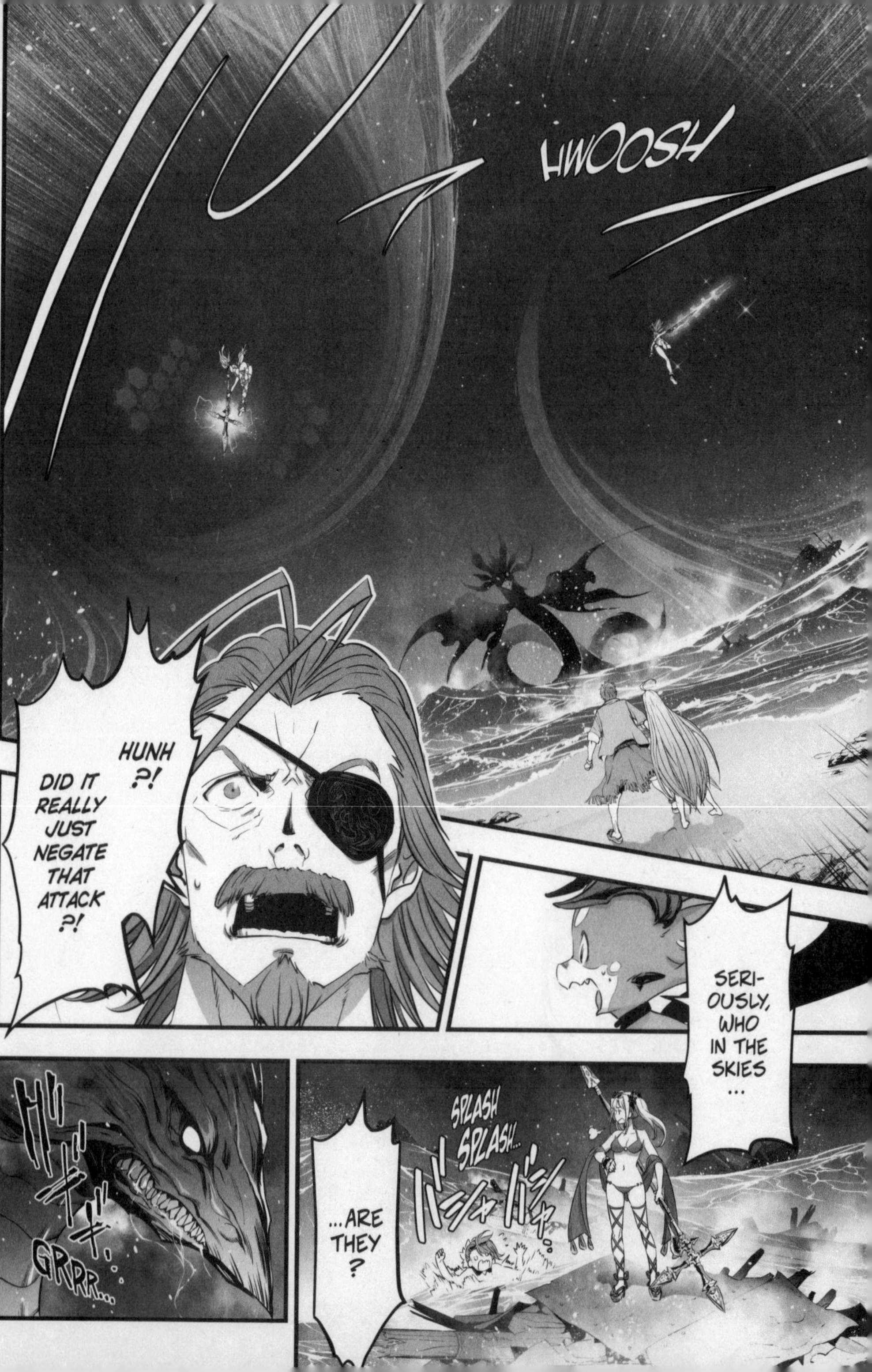
HWOOSH
HUNH ?!
DID IT REALLY JUST NEGATE THAT ATTACK ?!
SERI-OUSLY, WHO IN THE SKIES ...
SPLASH SPLASH...
...ARE THEY ?
GRRR...

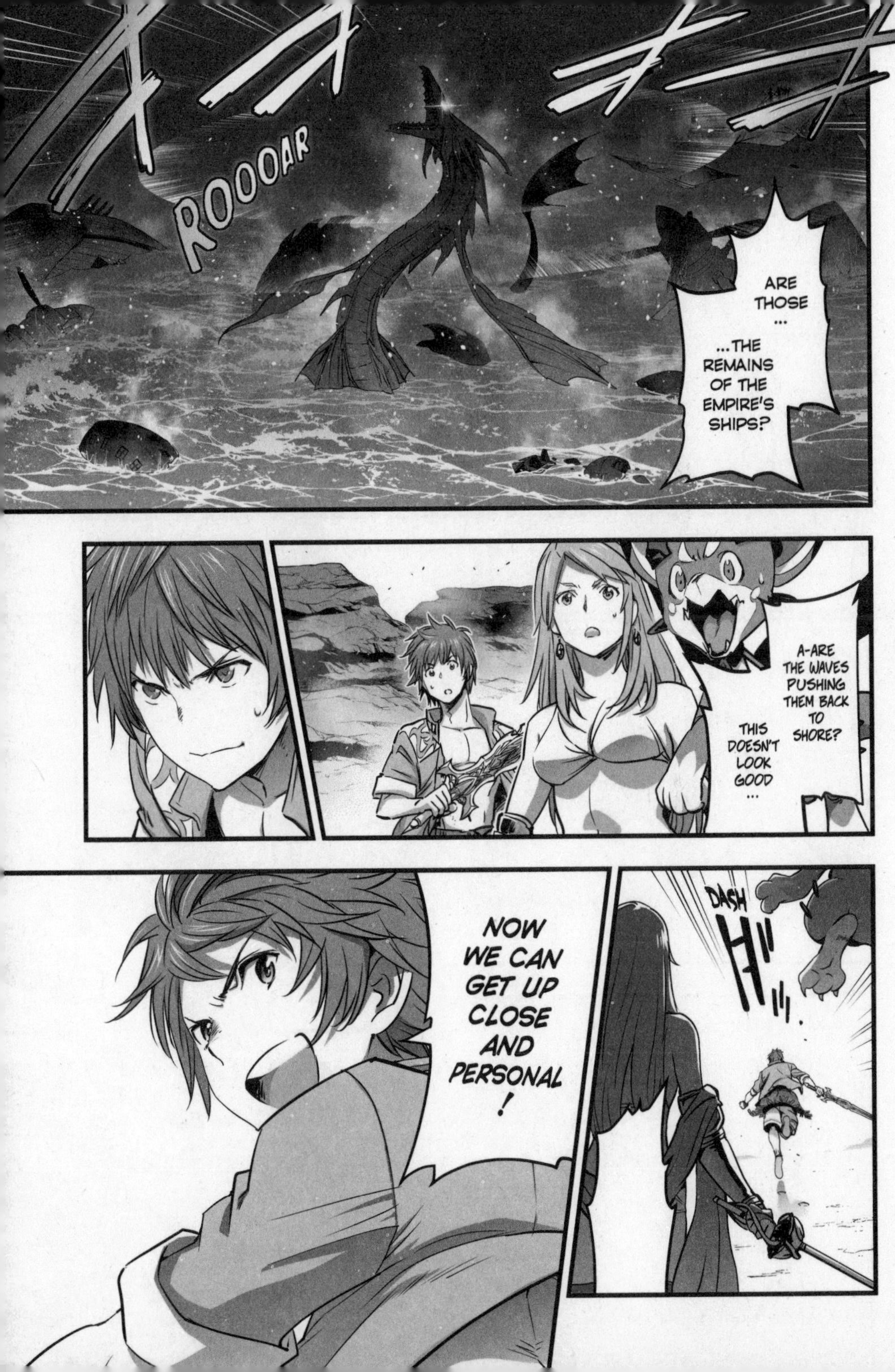
ROOOAR
ARE THOSE ...
...THE REMAINS OF THE EMPIRE'S SHIPS?
A-ARE THE WAVES PUSHING THEM BACK TO SHORE?
THIS DOESN'T LOOK GOOD ...
DASH
NOW WE CAN GET UP CLOSE AND PERSONAL!

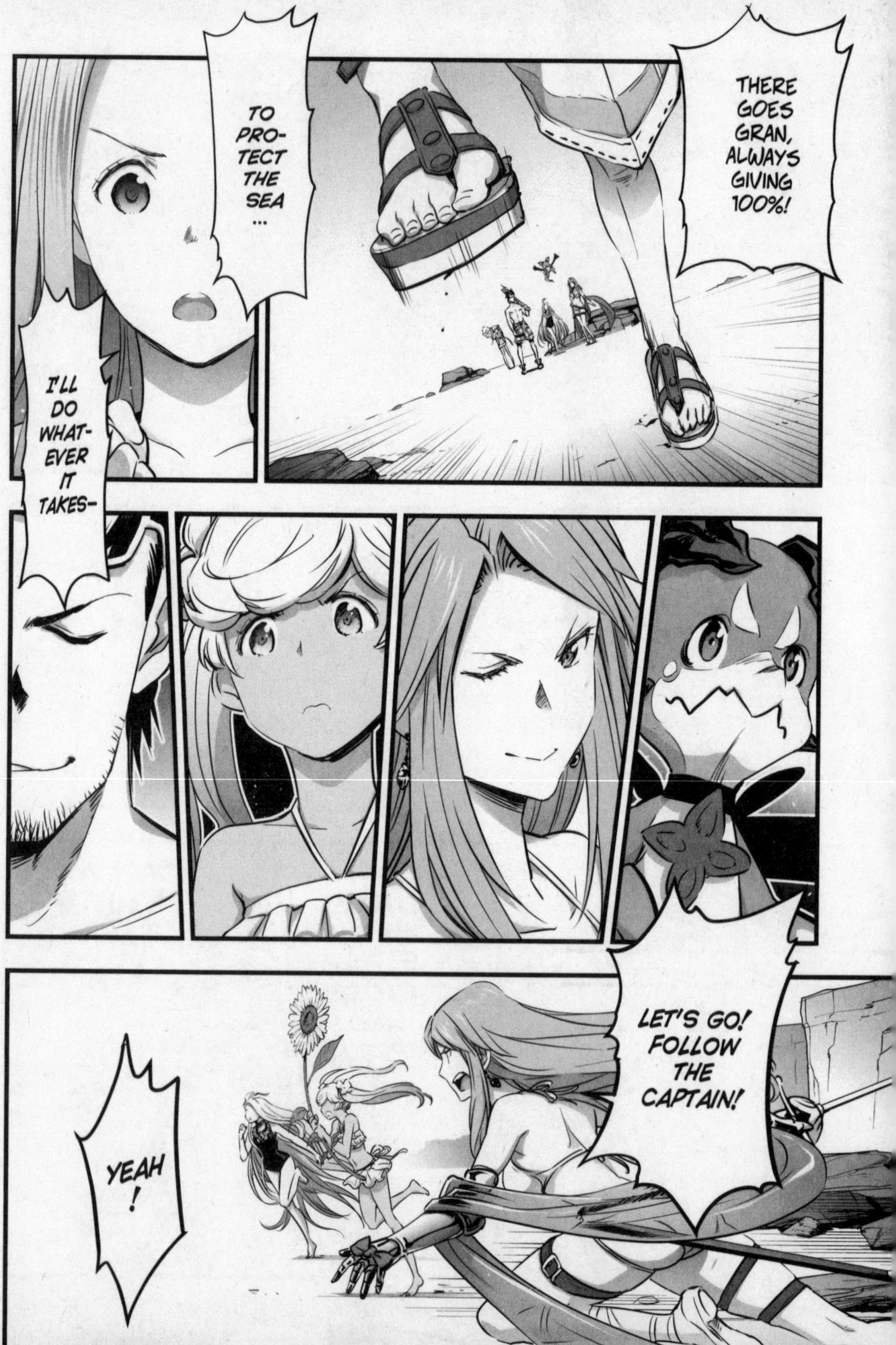
THERE GOES GRAN, ALWAYS GIVING 100%!
TO PROTECT THE SEA...
I'LL DO WHATEVER IT TAKES-
LET'S GO! FOLLOW THE CAPTAIN!
YEAH!

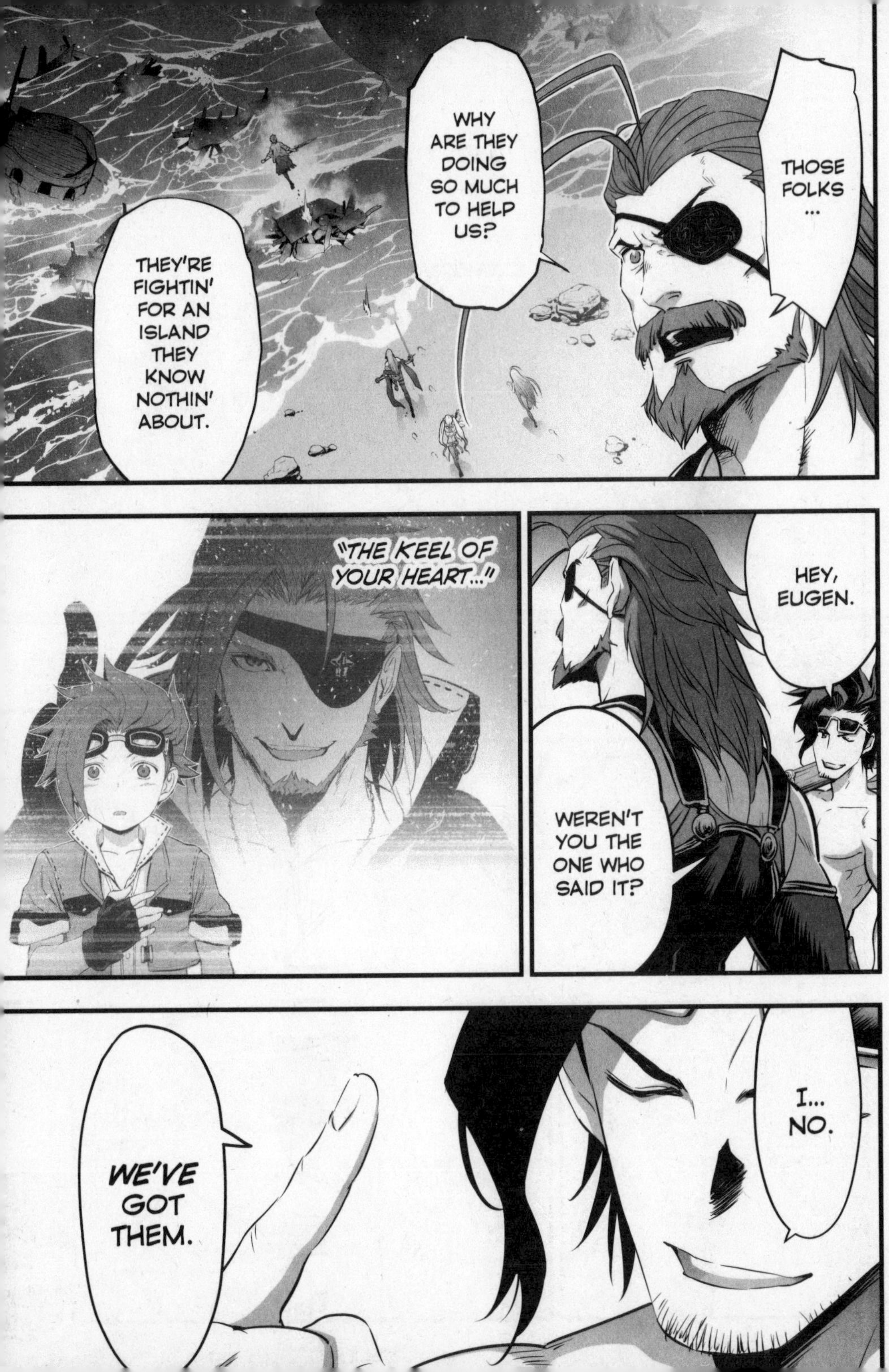
THOSE FOLKS ...
WHY ARE THEY DOING SO MUCH TO HELP US?
THEY'RE FIGHTIN' FOR AN ISLAND THEY KNOW NOTHIN' ABOUT.
HEY, EUGEN.
WEREN'T YOU THE ONE WHO SAID IT?
"THE KEEL OF YOUR HEART..."
I... NO.
WE'VE GOT THEM.

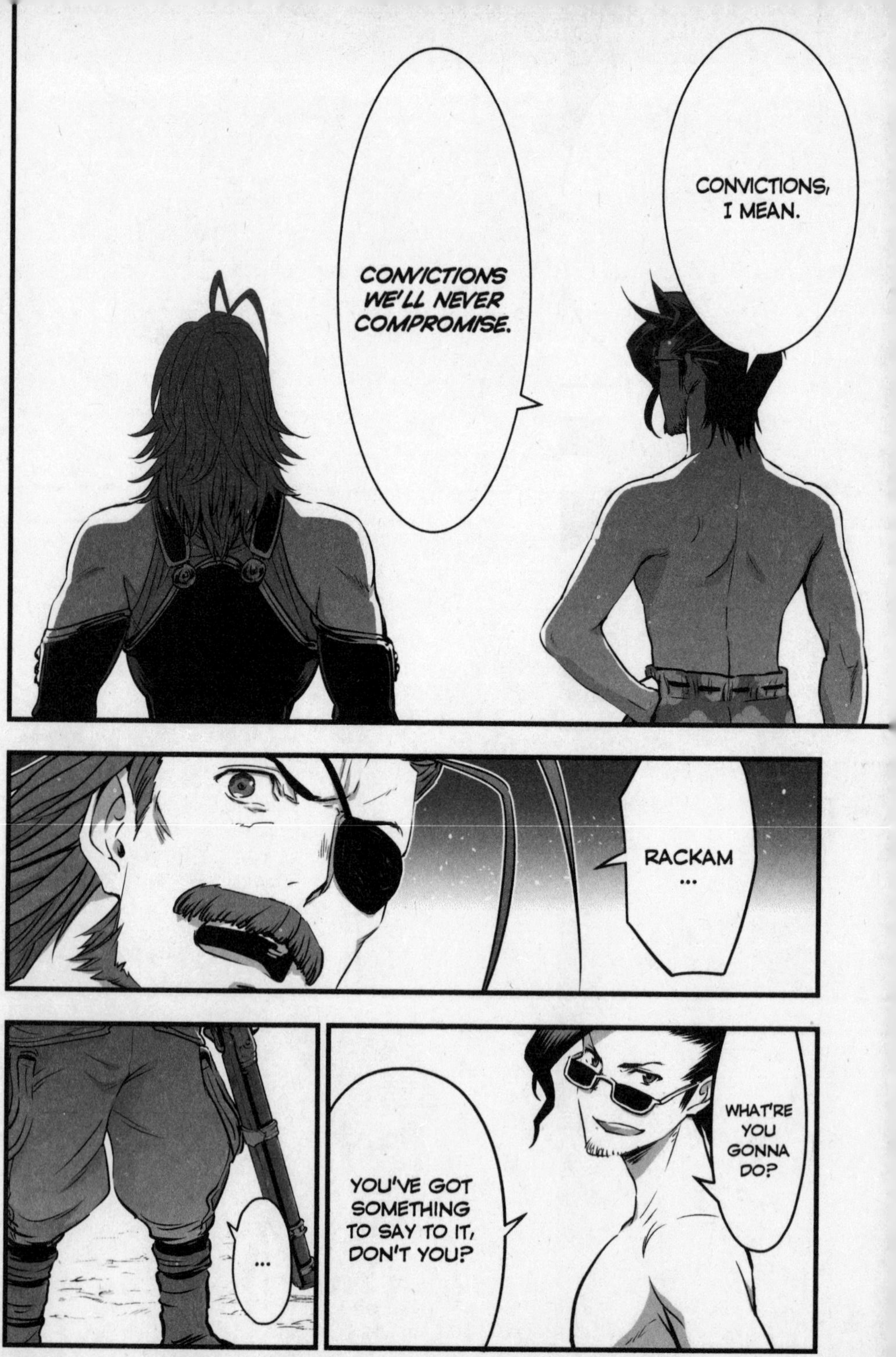
CONVICTIONS, I MEAN.
CONVICTIONS WE'LL NEVER COMPROMISE.
RACKAM ...
WHAT'RE YOU GONNA DO?
YOU'VE GOT SOMETHING TO SAY TO IT, DON'T YOU?
...

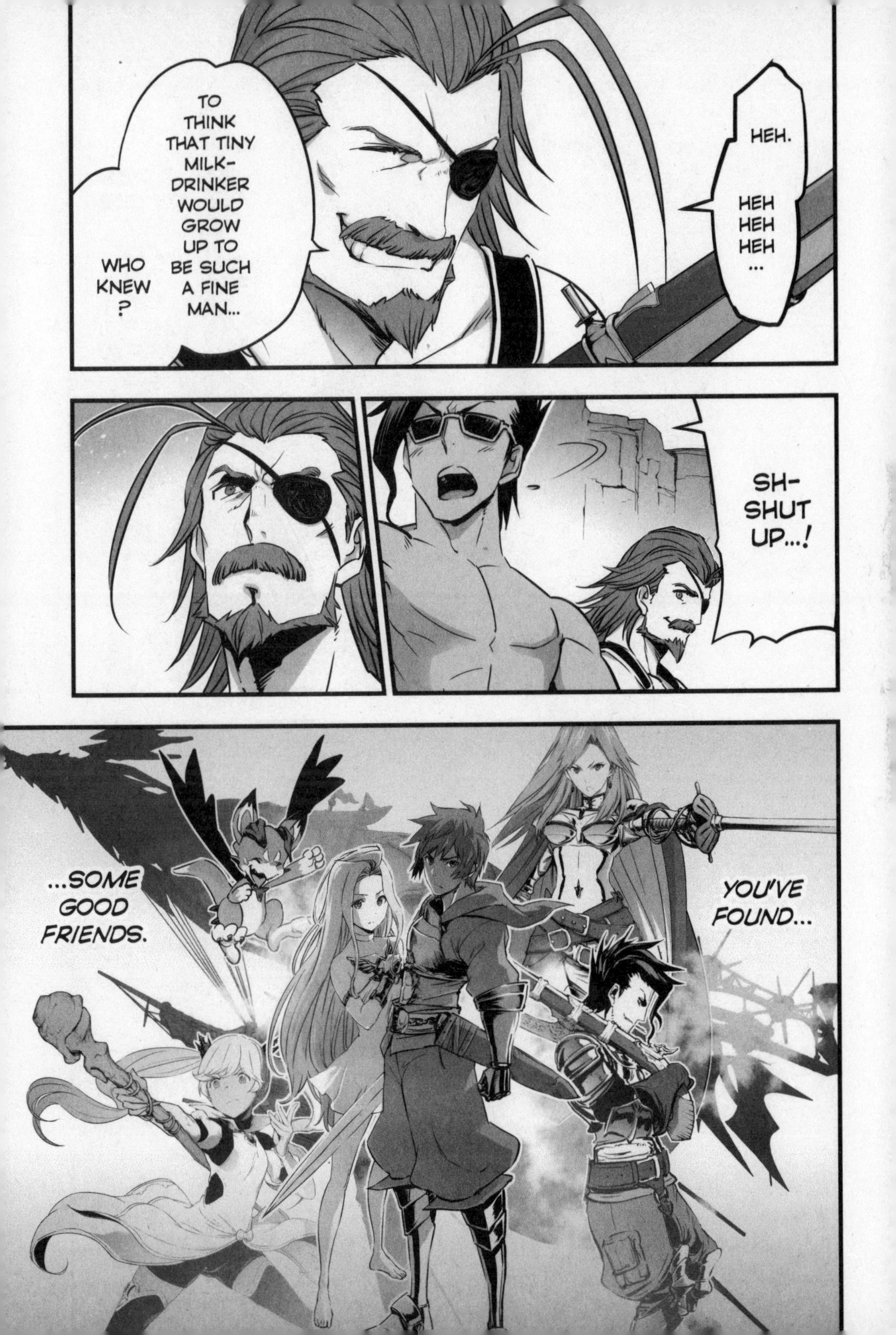
HEH.
HEH HEH HEH ...
TO THINK THAT TINY MILK-DRINKER WOULD GROW UP TO BE SUCH A FINE MAN...
WHO KNEW?
SH-SHUT UP...!
YOU'VE FOUND...
...SOME GOOD FRIENDS.

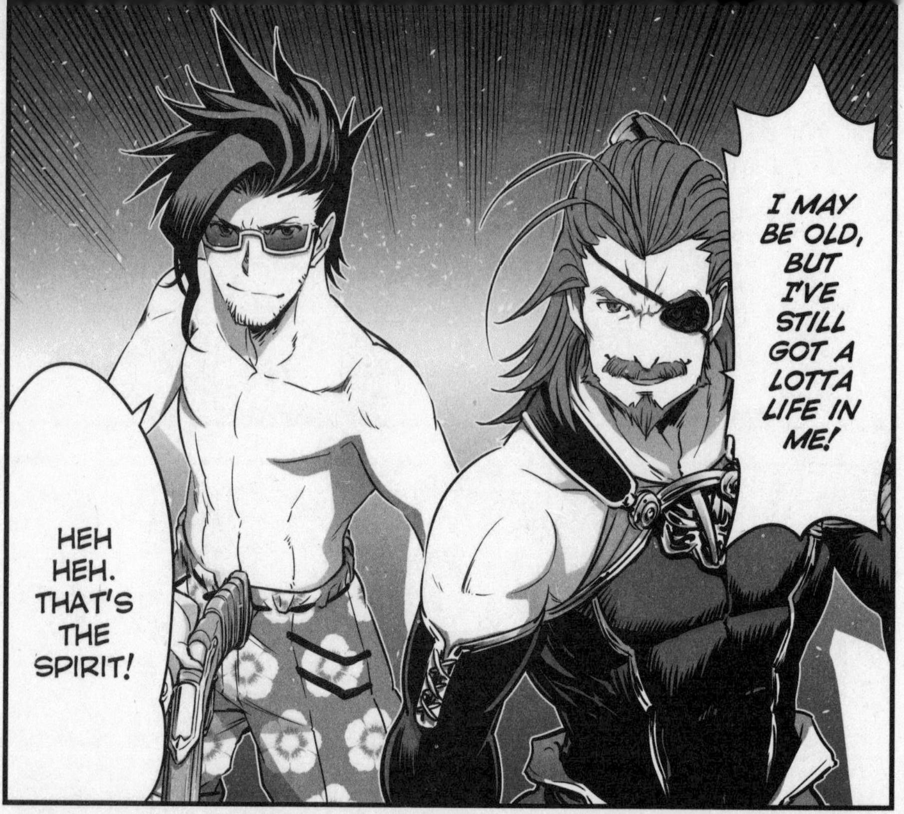
I MAY BE OLD, BUT I'VE STILL GOT A LOTTA LIFE IN ME!
HEH HEH. THAT'S THE SPIRIT!

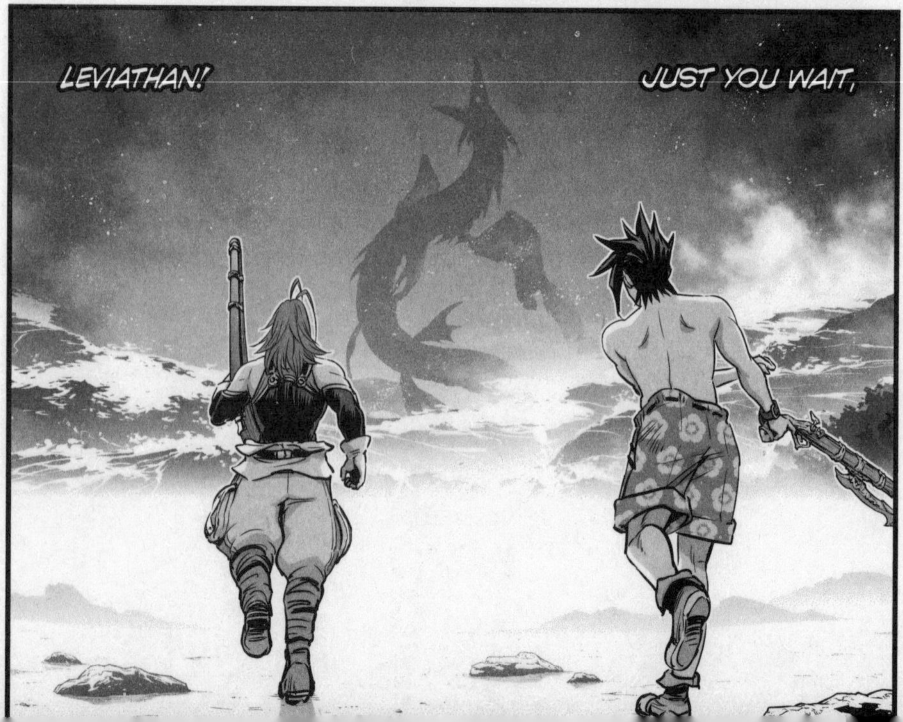
JUST YOU WAIT,
LEVIATHAN!

GRANBLUE FANTASY
グランブルーファンタジー

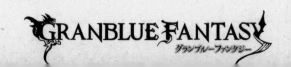

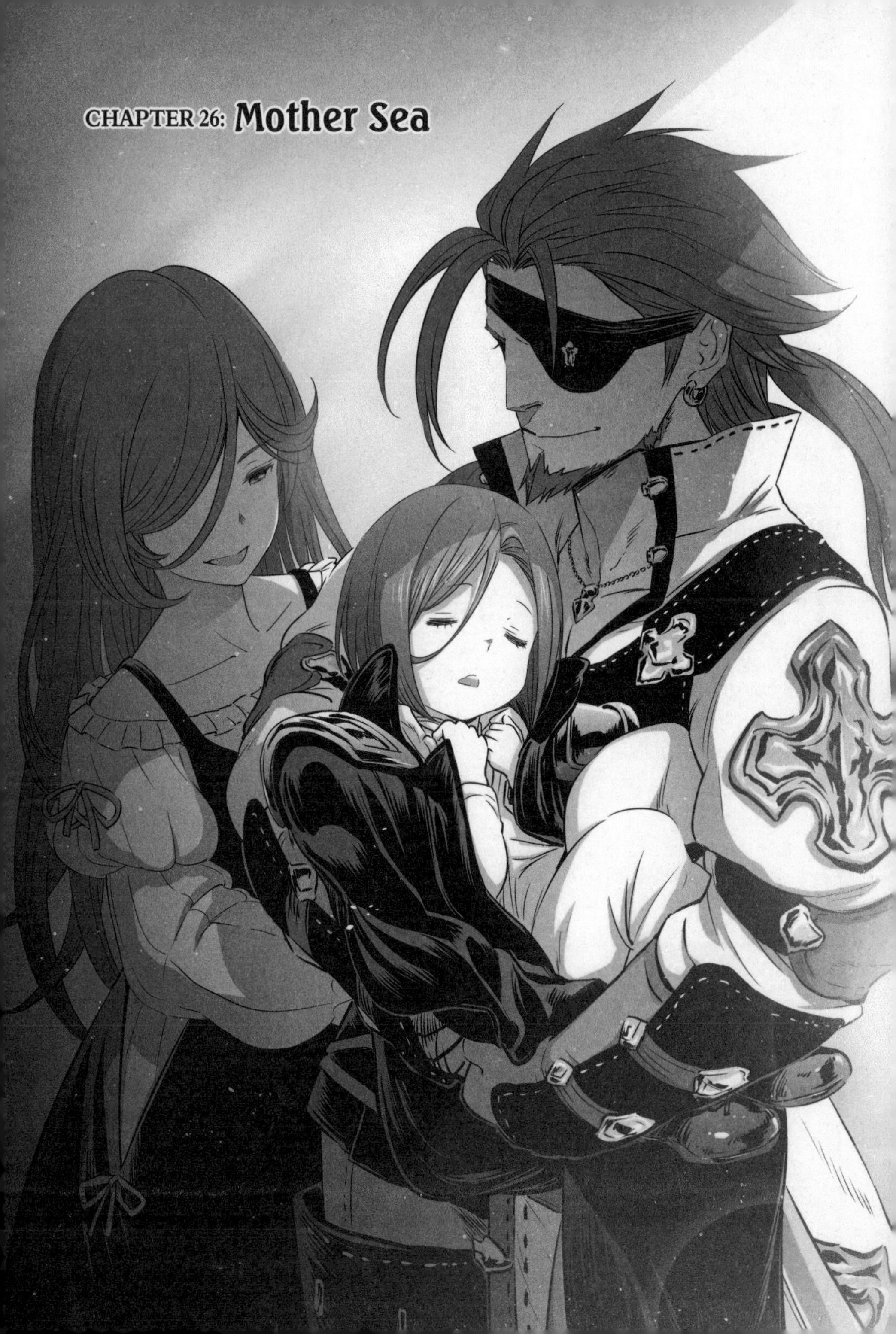
CHAPTER 26: Mother Sea

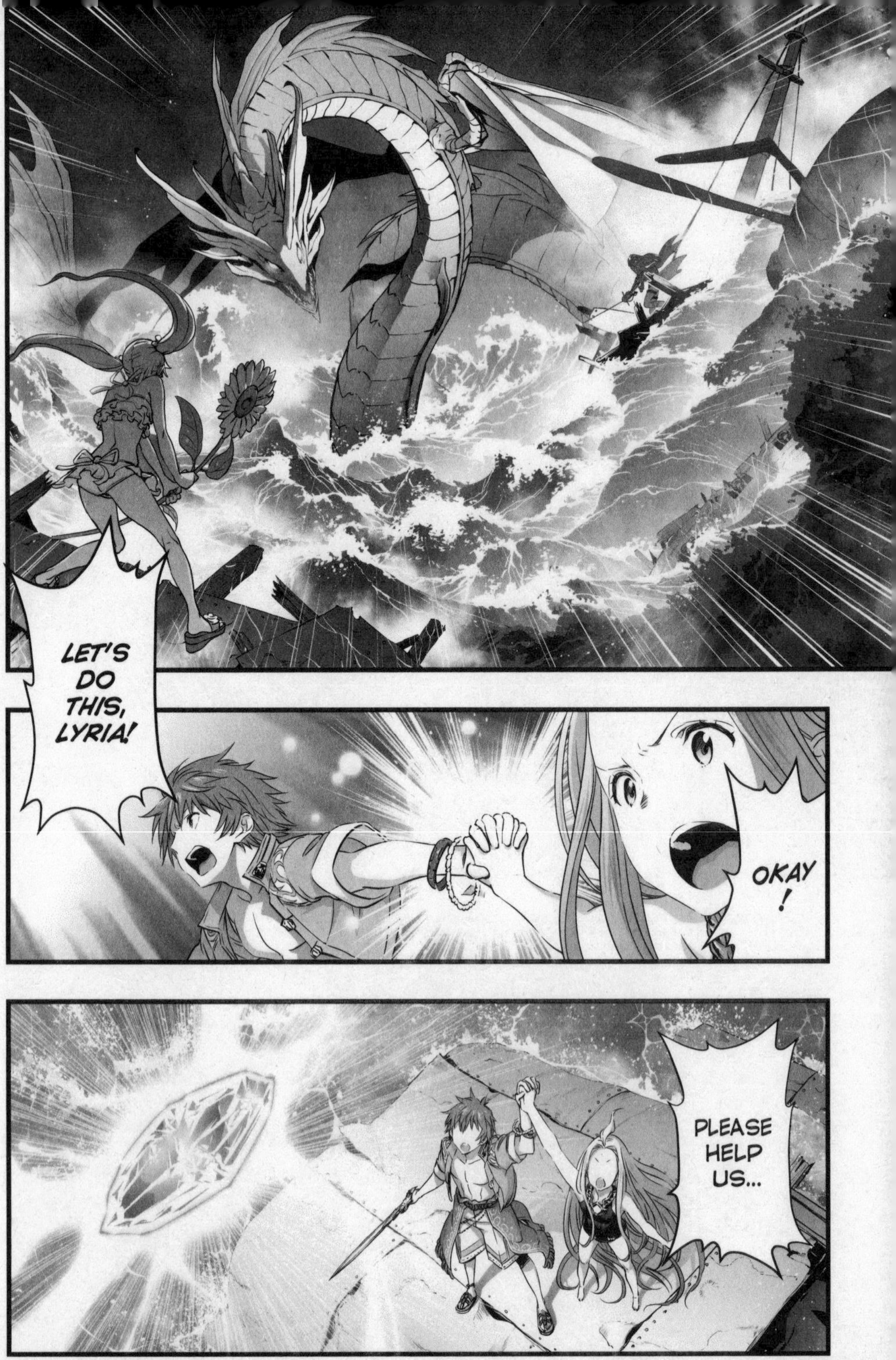
LET'S DO THIS, LYRIA!
OKAY!
PLEASE HELP US...

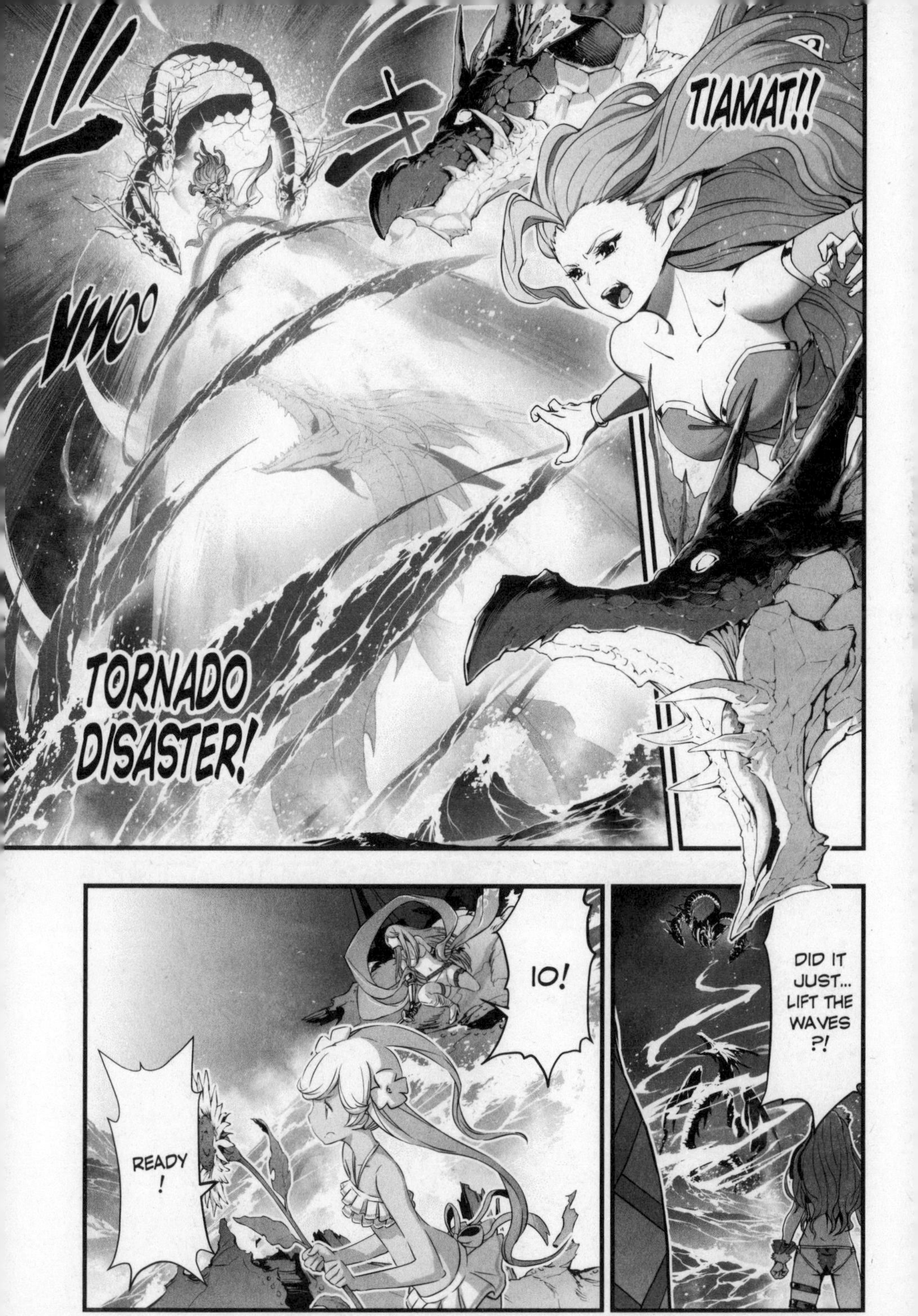
TIAMAT!!
VWOO
TORNADO DISASTER!
DID IT JUST... LIFT THE WAVES ?!
IO!
READY !

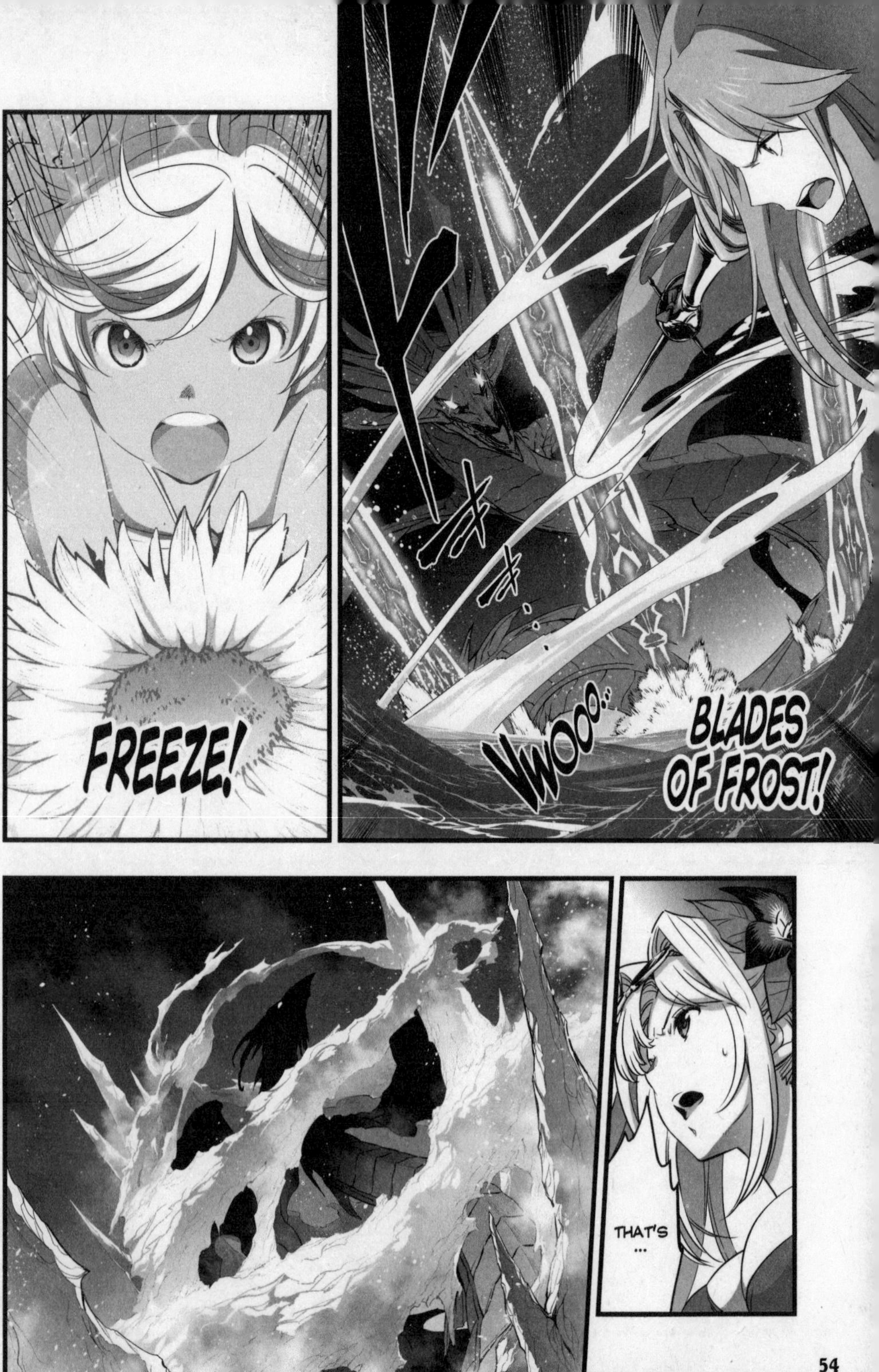
BLADES OF FROST!
VWOOO...
FREEZE!
THAT'S ...

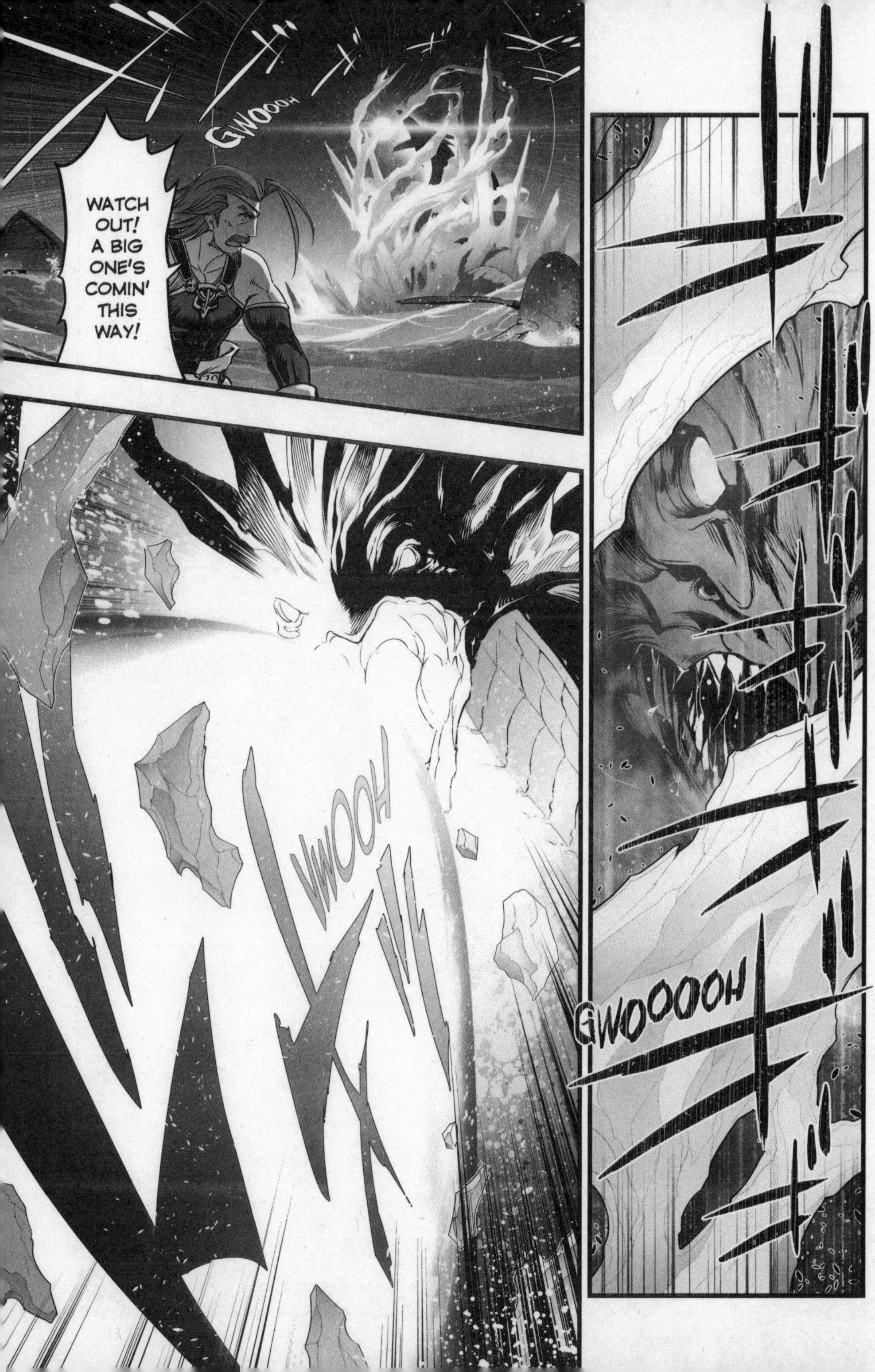
GWOOOOH
GWOOOH
WATCH OUT! A BIG ONE'S COMIN' THIS WAY!
VWOOH

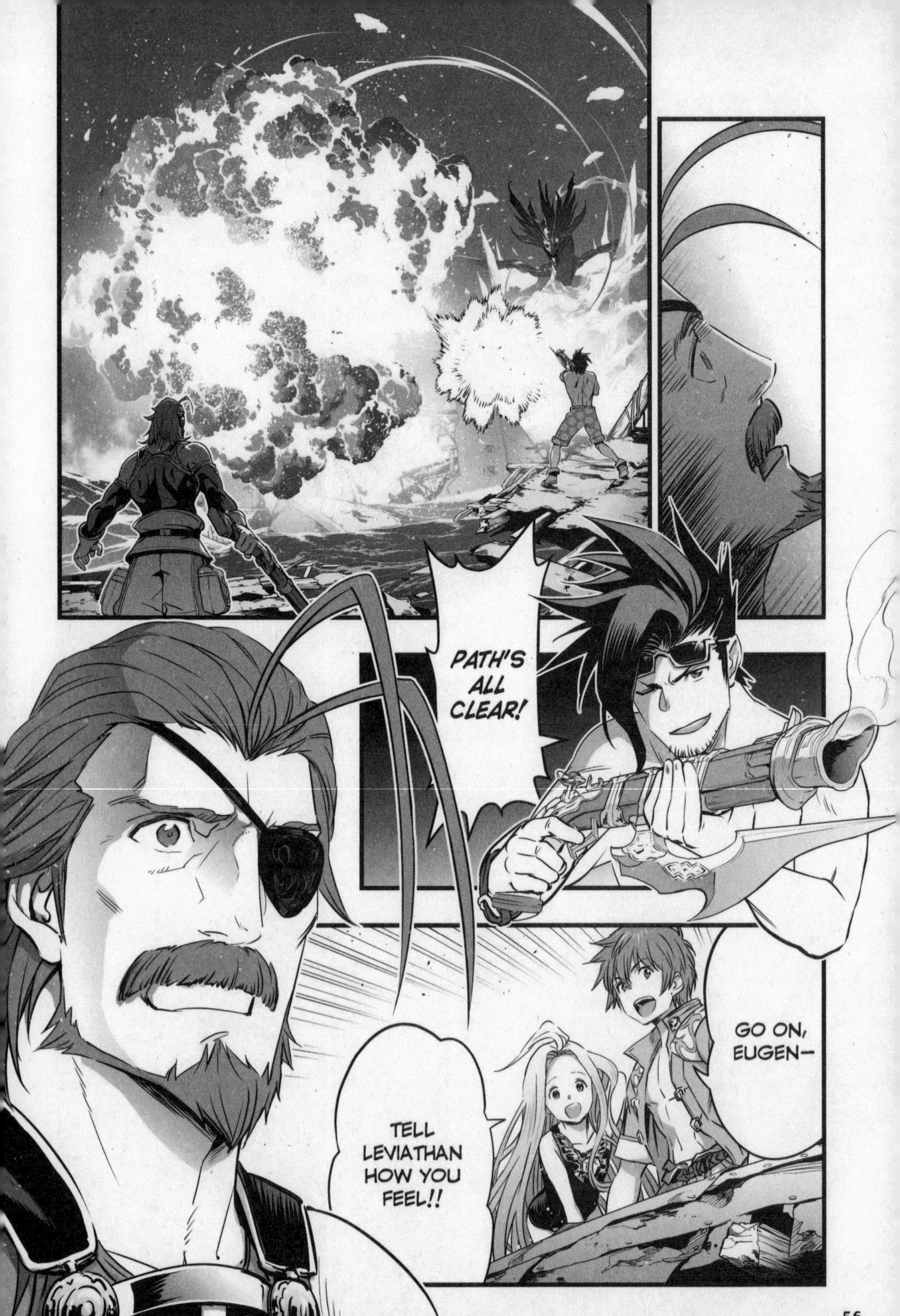
PATH'S ALL CLEAR!
GO ON, EUGEN—
TELL LEVIATHAN HOW YOU FEEL!!

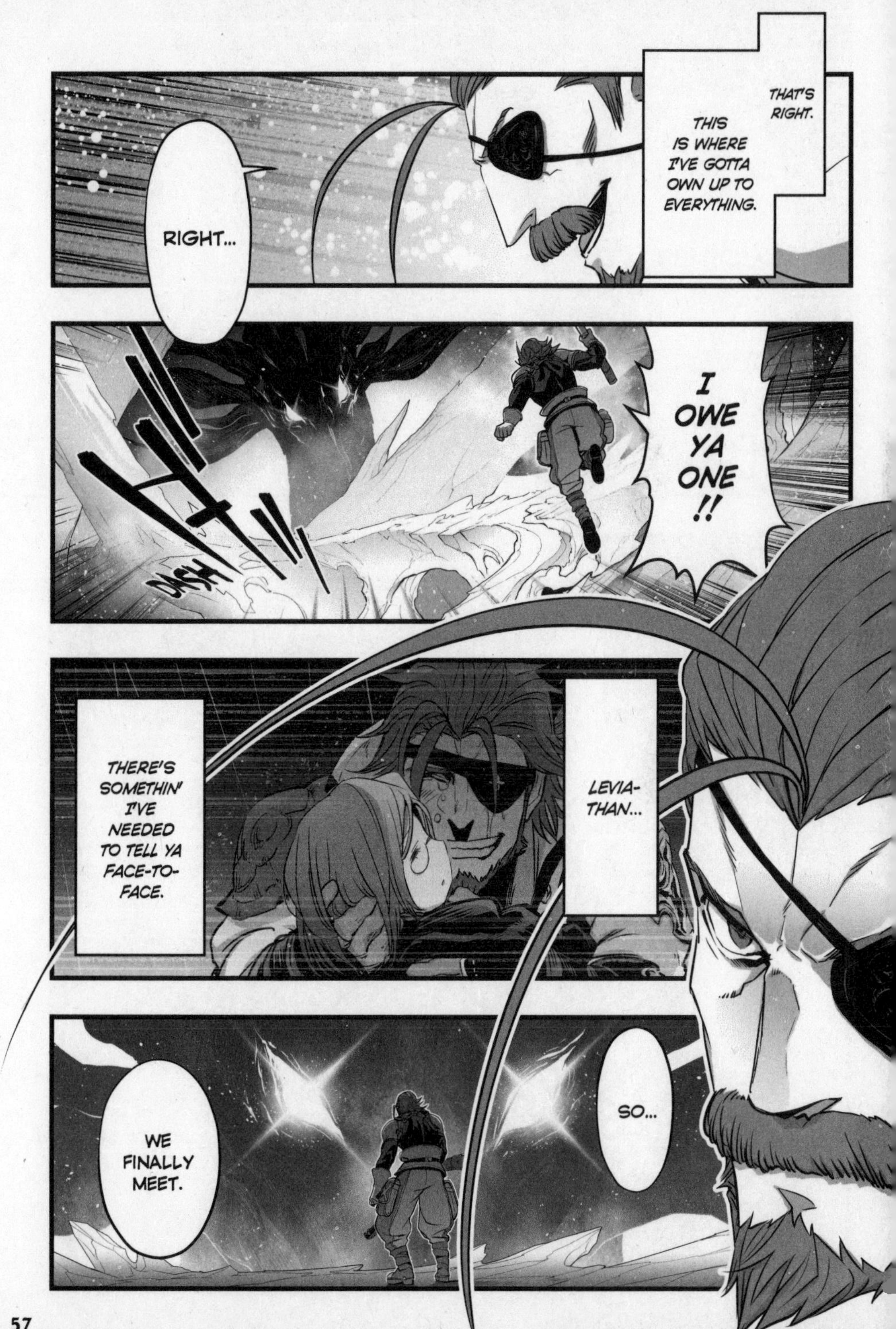
THAT'S RIGHT.
THIS IS WHERE I'VE GOTTA OWN UP TO EVERYTHING.
RIGHT...
I OWE YA ONE!!
DASH
LEVIA-THAN...
THERE'S SOMETHIN' I'VE NEEDED TO TELL YA FACE-TO-FACE.
SO...
WE FINALLY MEET.

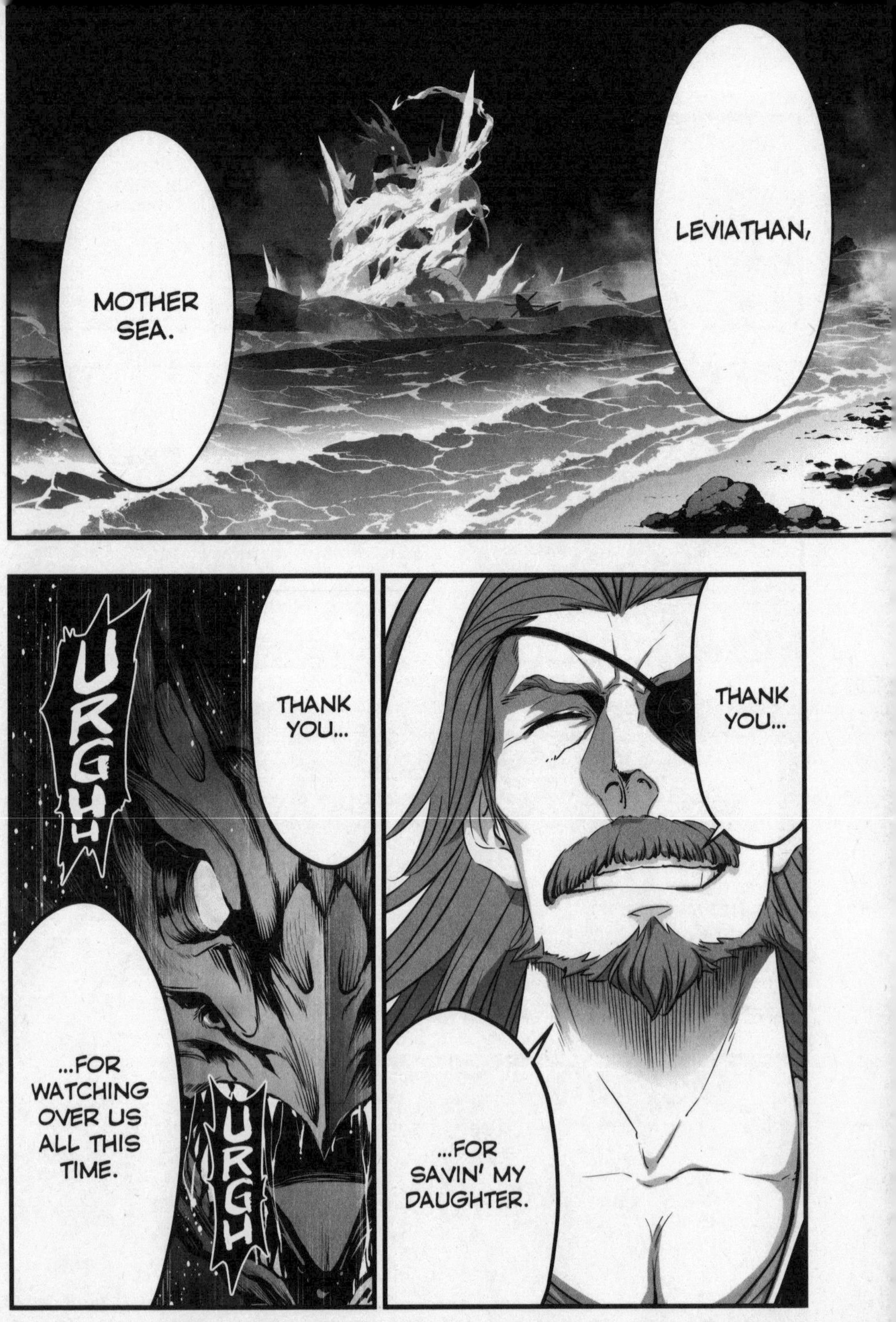
LEVIATHAN,
MOTHER SEA.
THANK YOU...
...FOR SAVIN' MY DAUGHTER.
URGH
THANK YOU...
...FOR WATCHING OVER US ALL THIS TIME.
URGH

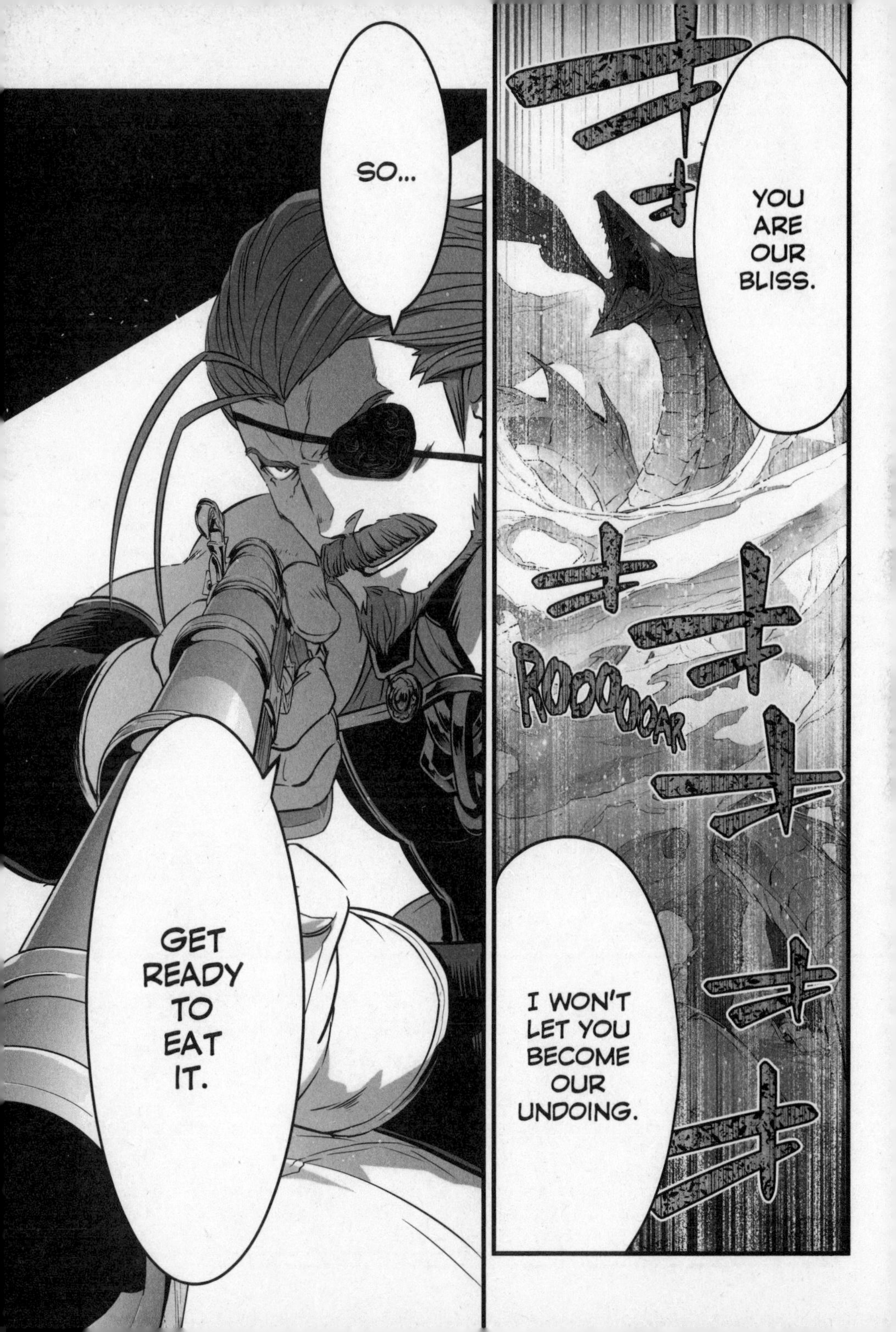
YOU ARE OUR BLISS.
ROOOOOAR
I WON'T LET YOU BECOME OUR UNDOING.
SO...
GET READY TO EAT IT.

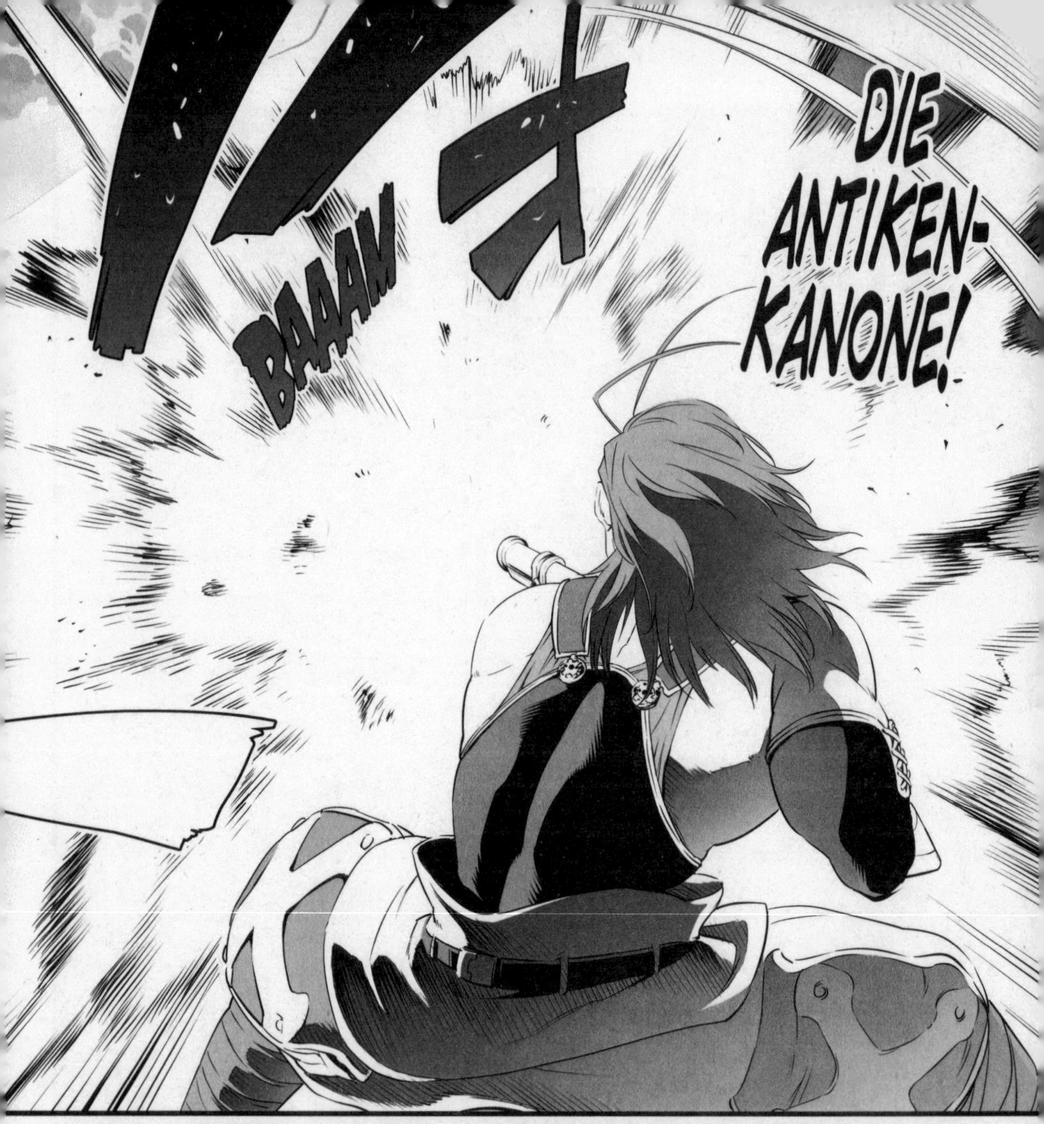
DIE ANTIKEN-KANONE!
BAAAM
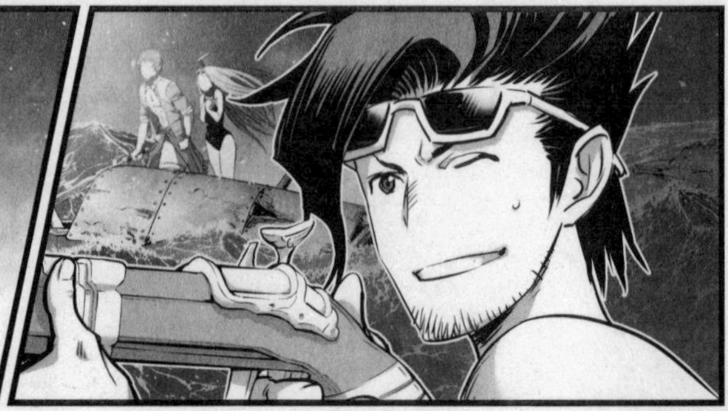
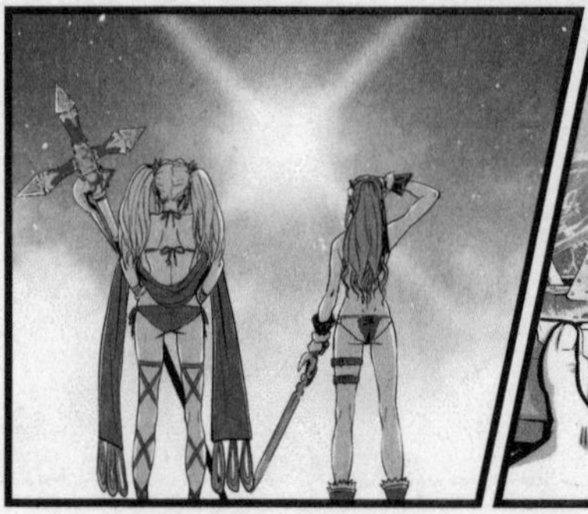

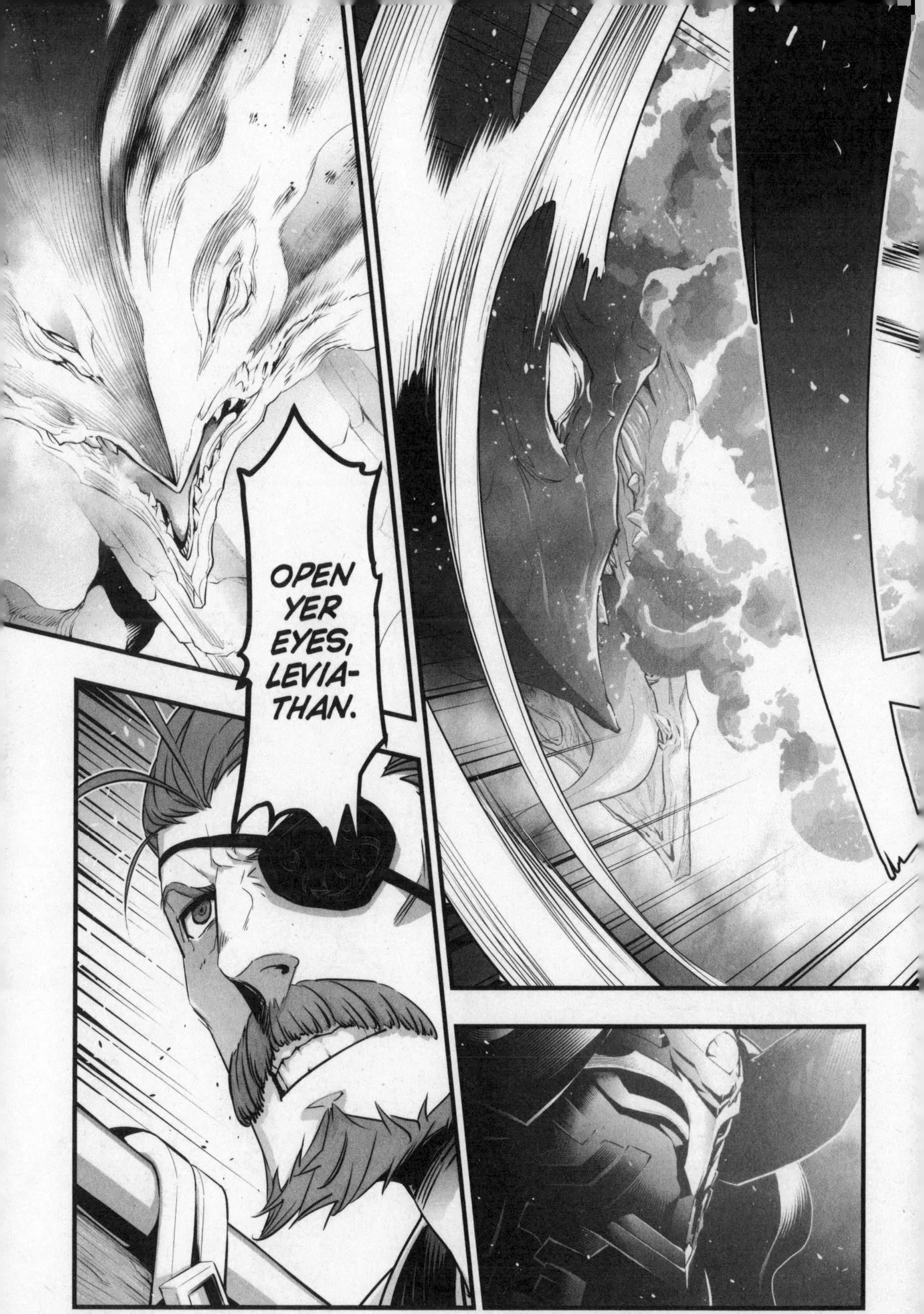
OPEN YER EYES, LEVIA- THAN.

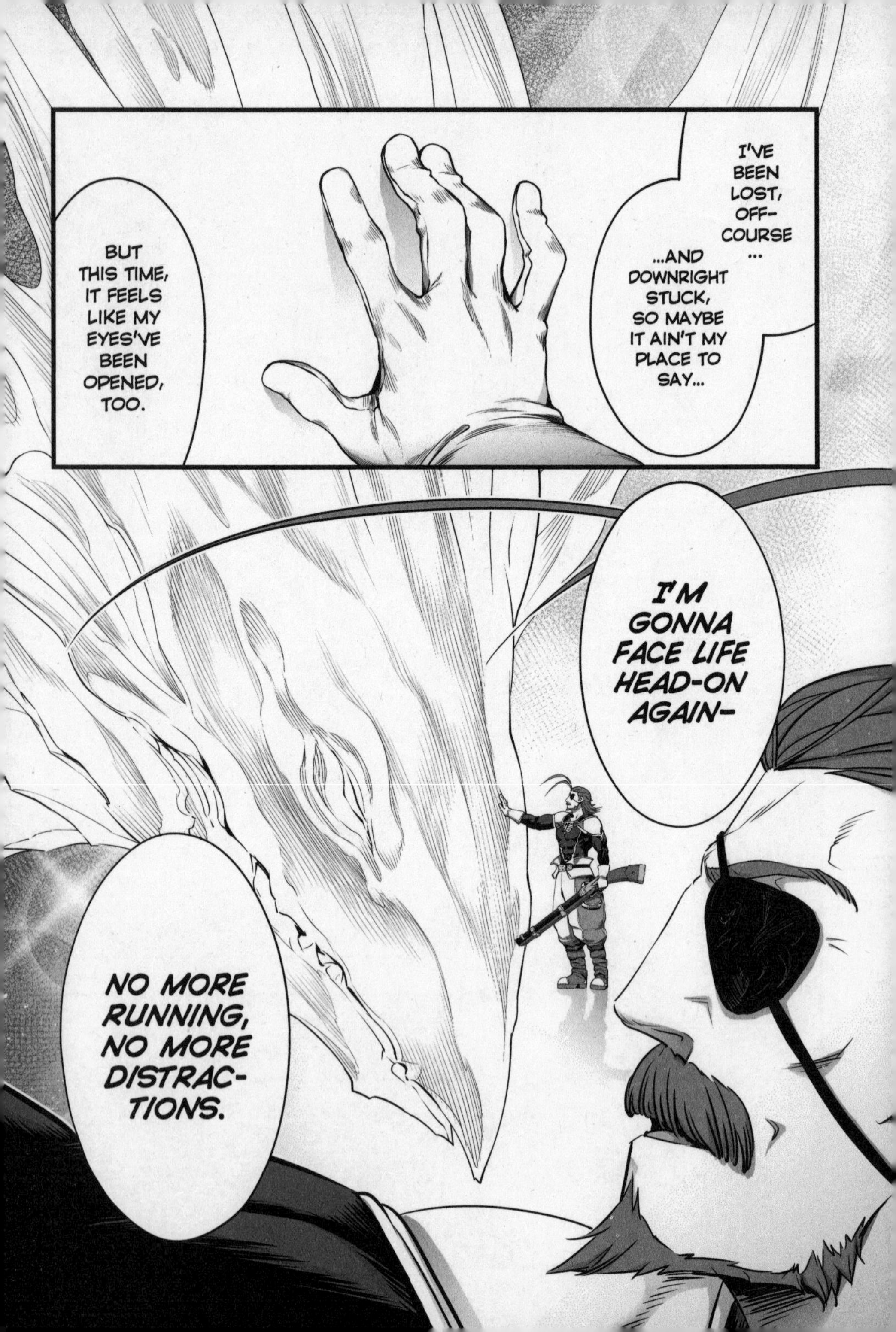
I'VE BEEN LOST, OFF-COURSE ...
...AND DOWNRIGHT STUCK, SO MAYBE IT AIN'T MY PLACE TO SAY...
BUT THIS TIME, IT FEELS LIKE MY EYES'VE BEEN OPENED, TOO.
I'M GONNA FACE LIFE HEAD-ON AGAIN-
NO MORE RUNNING, NO MORE DISTRAC-TIONS.

WELL, NOW IT'S ALL OVER.

I'M SORRY. IT MUST HAVE HURT, RIGHT?

COME...

LEVIATHAN.

IS SHE... ABSORBING LEVIATHAN'S POWER?!

THE HIGHER-UPS ARE GONNA GO NUTS WHEN THEY HEAR ABOUT THIS.

THERE'S A HUMAN WHO CAN DO THAT?!

DROOL...

APOLOGIES... BUT YOU'RE GOING TO HAVE TO GIVE ME THAT POWER.

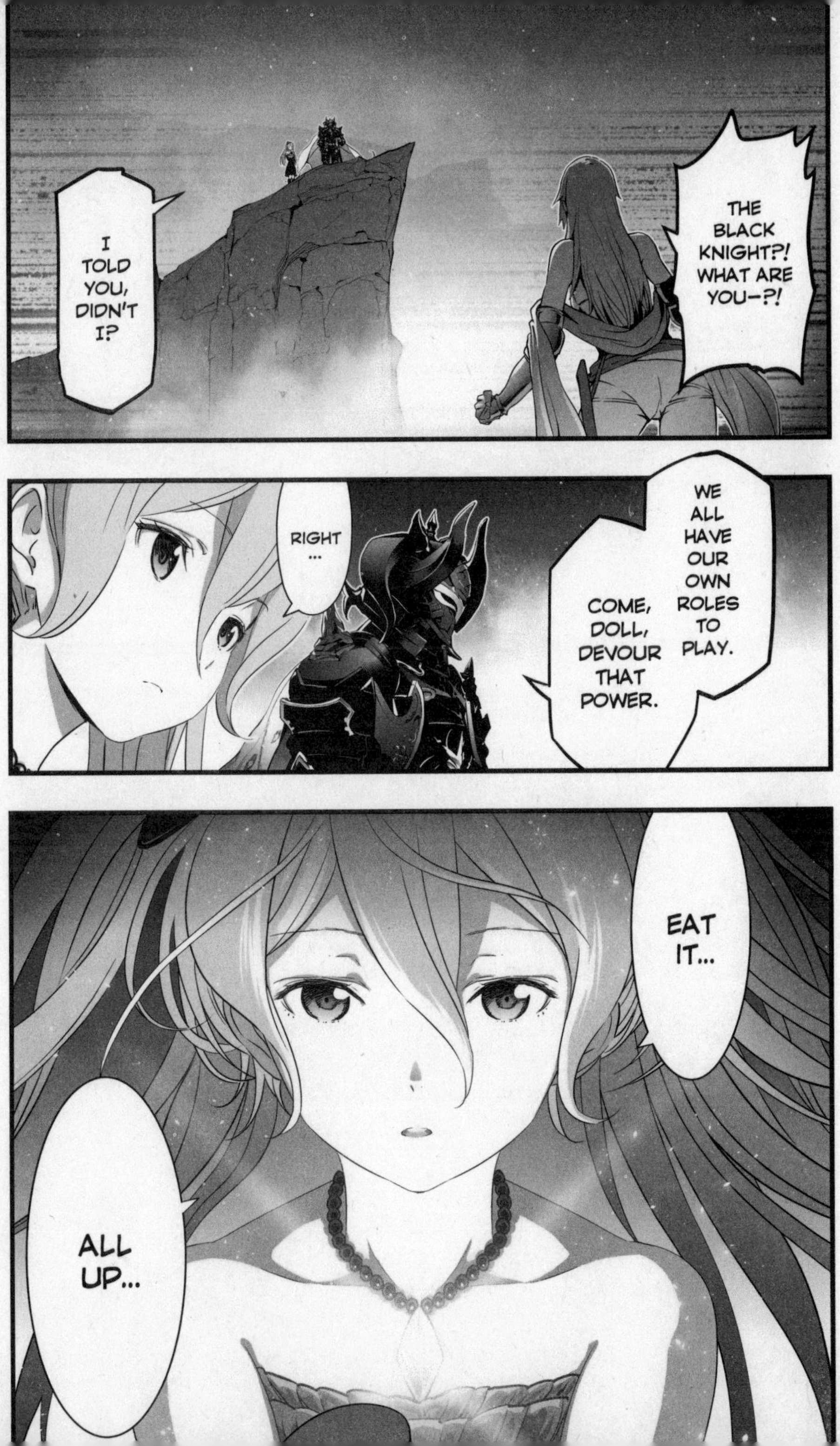
THE BLACK KNIGHT?! WHAT ARE YOU—?!
I TOLD YOU, DIDN'T I?
WE ALL HAVE OUR OWN ROLES TO PLAY.
COME, DOLL, DEVOUR THAT POWER.
RIGHT ...
EAT IT...
ALL UP...

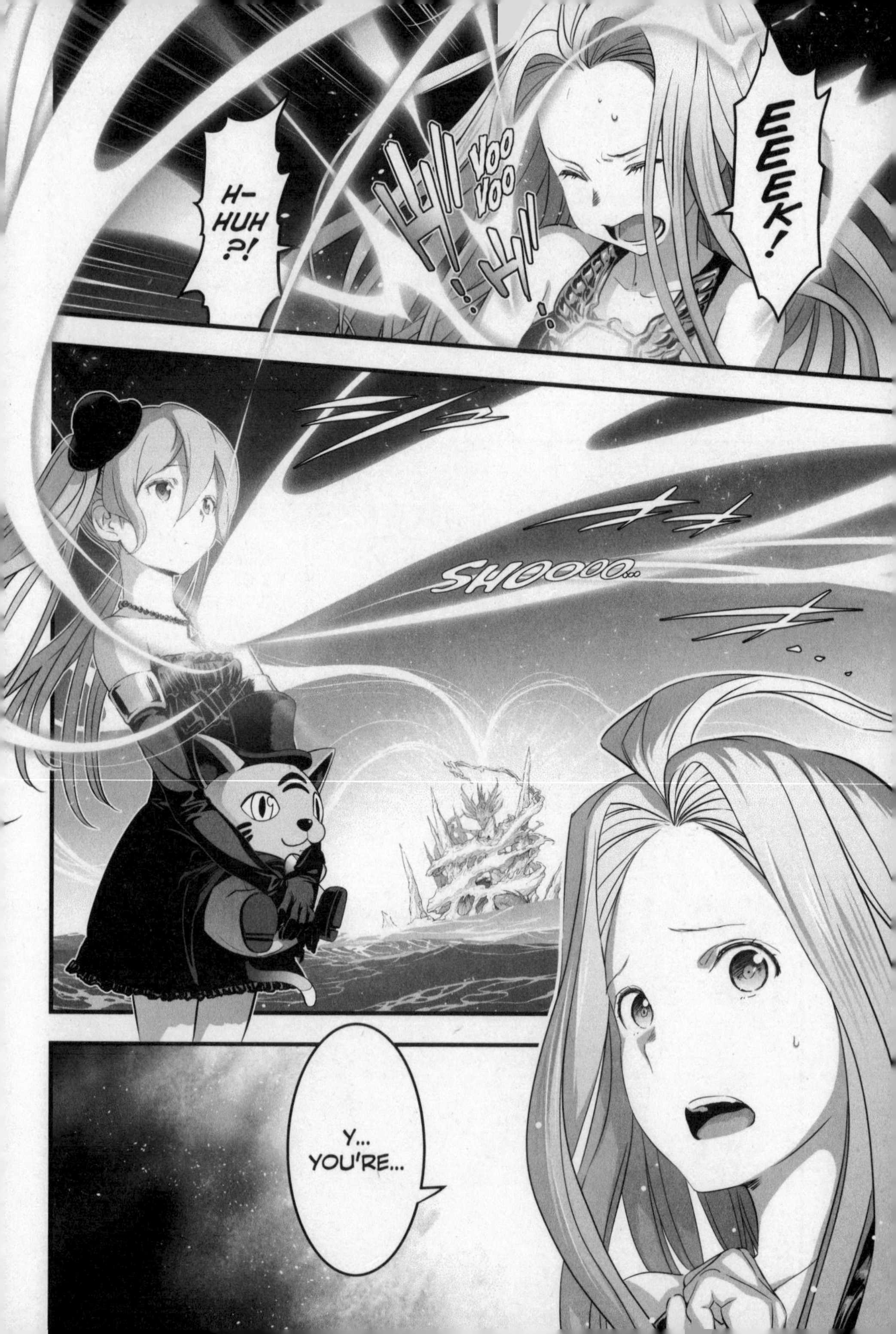
EEEK!
VOO VOO
H-HUH?!
SHOOOO...
Y... YOU'RE...

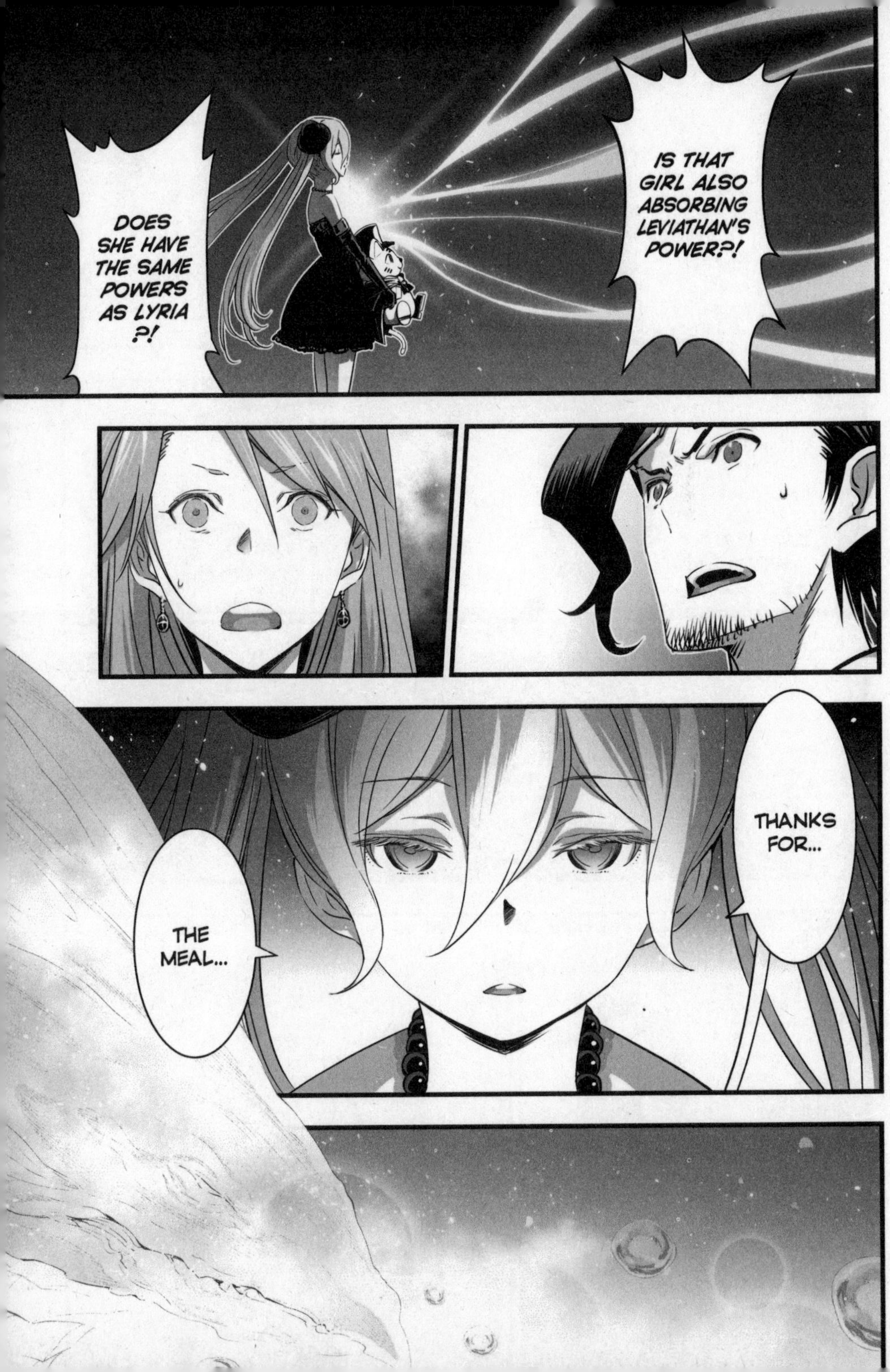
IS THAT GIRL ALSO ABSORBING LEVIATHAN'S POWER?!
DOES SHE HAVE THE SAME POWERS AS LYRIA ?!
THANKS FOR...
THE MEAL...

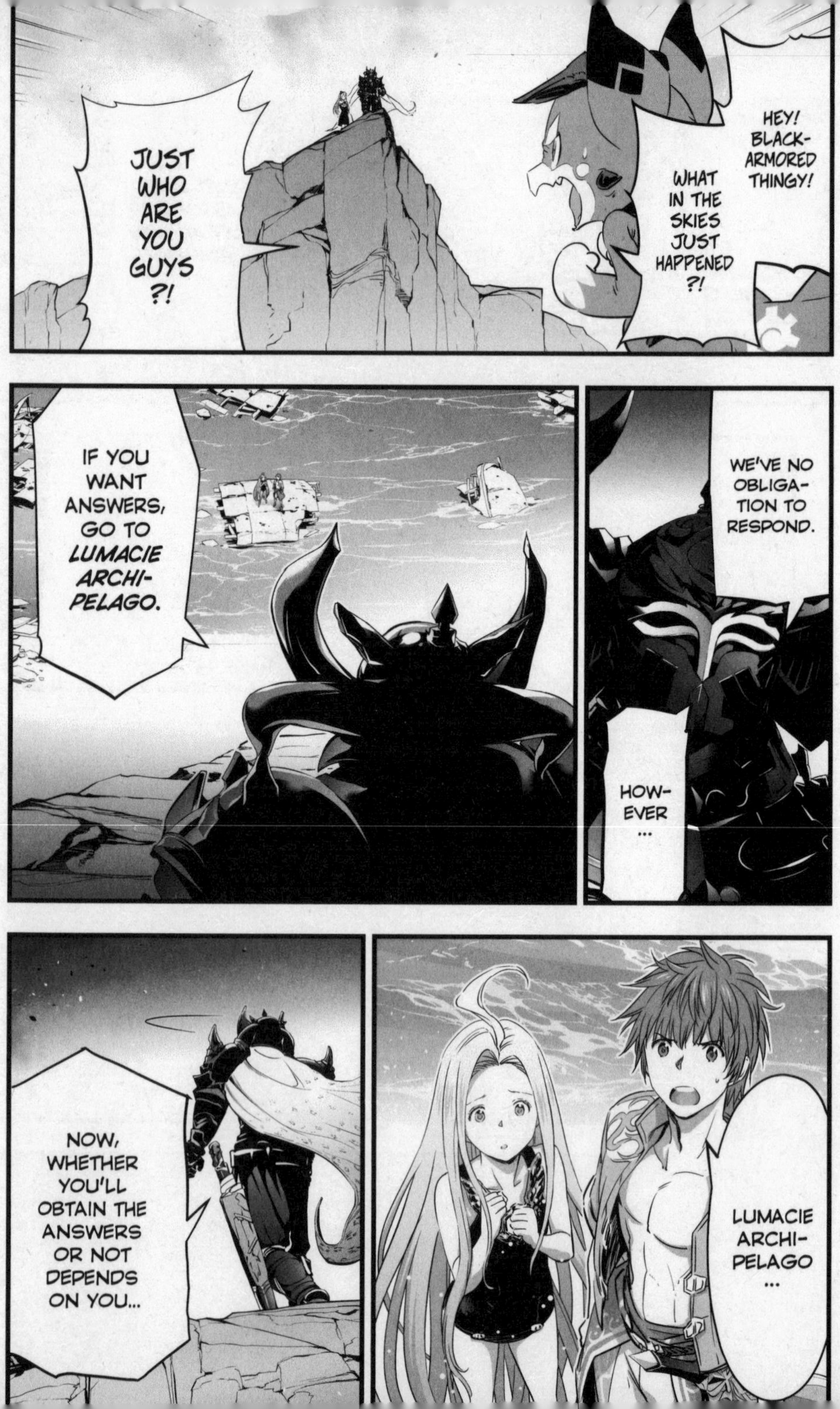
HEY! BLACK-ARMORED THINGY!
WHAT IN THE SKIES JUST HAPPENED ?!
JUST WHO ARE YOU GUYS ?!
WE'VE NO OBLIGATION TO RESPOND.
HOWEVER ...
IF YOU WANT ANSWERS, GO TO LUMACIE ARCHIPELAGO.
LUMACIE ARCHIPELAGO ...
NOW, WHETHER YOU'LL OBTAIN THE ANSWERS OR NOT DEPENDS ON YOU...

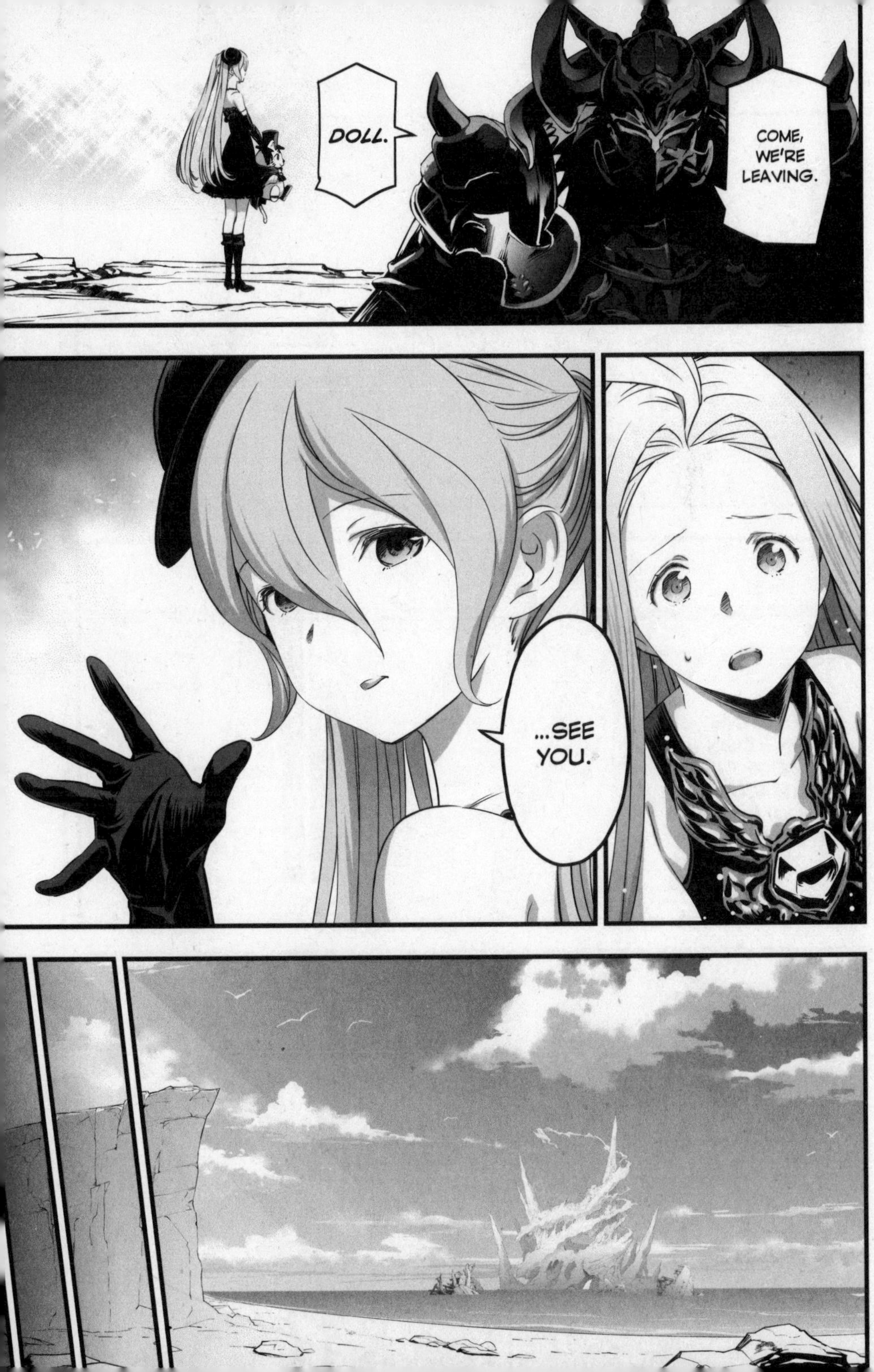
COME, WE'RE LEAVING.
DOLL.
...SEE YOU.

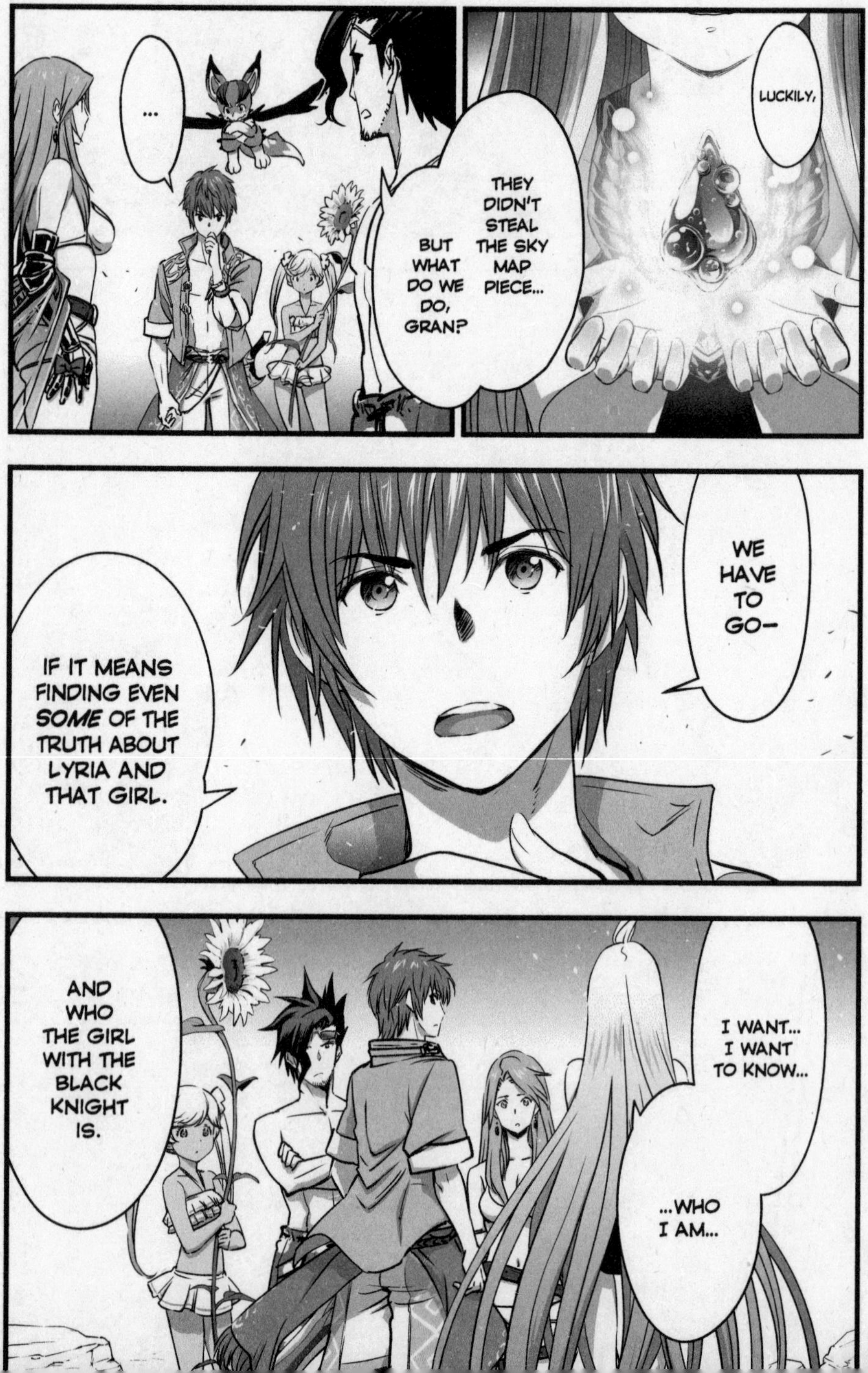
LUCKILY,
THEY DIDN'T STEAL THE SKY MAP PIECE...
BUT WHAT DO WE DO, GRAN?
...
WE HAVE TO GO—
IF IT MEANS FINDING EVEN *SOME* OF THE TRUTH ABOUT LYRIA AND THAT GIRL.
I WANT... I WANT TO KNOW...
...WHO I AM...
AND WHO THE GIRL WITH THE BLACK KNIGHT IS.

I'M SORRY FOR ACTING SO SELFISHLY,

BUT—

I DON'T WANT TO MISS THIS CHANCE...

...TO LEARN MORE ABOUT MYSELF.

THEN IT'S SETTLED.

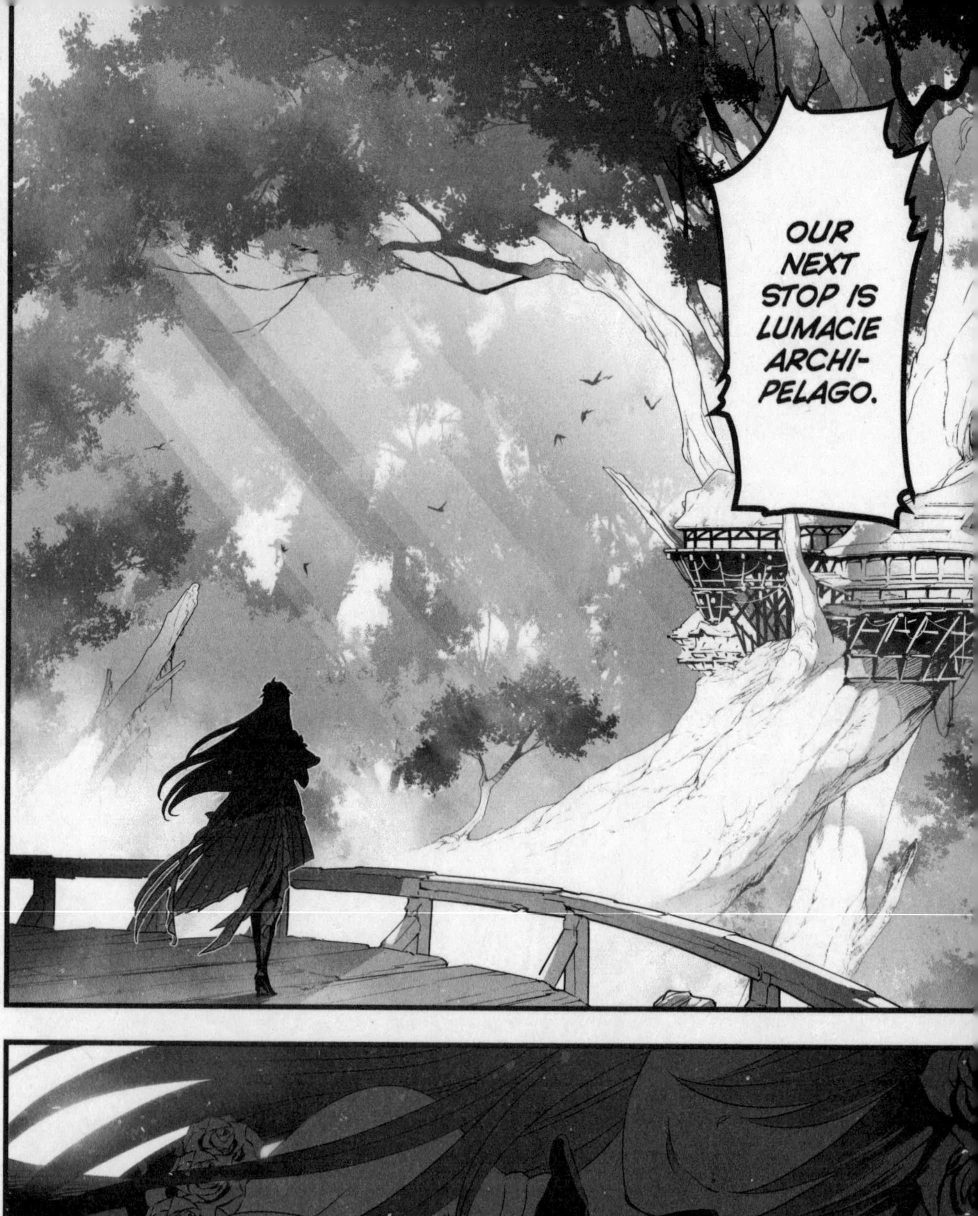
OUR NEXT STOP IS LUMACIE ARCHI-PELAGO.
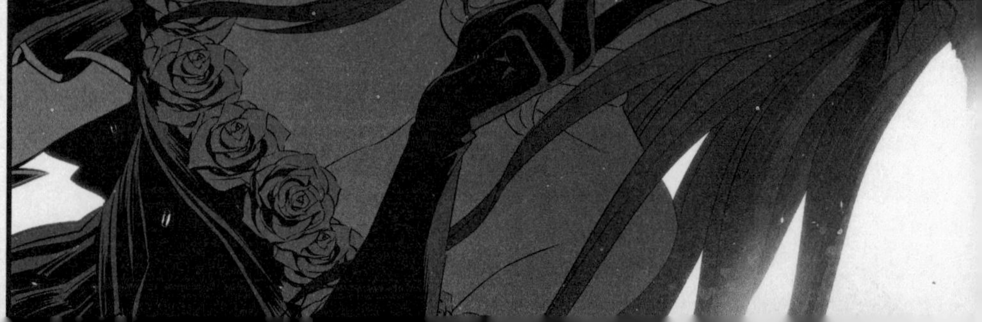

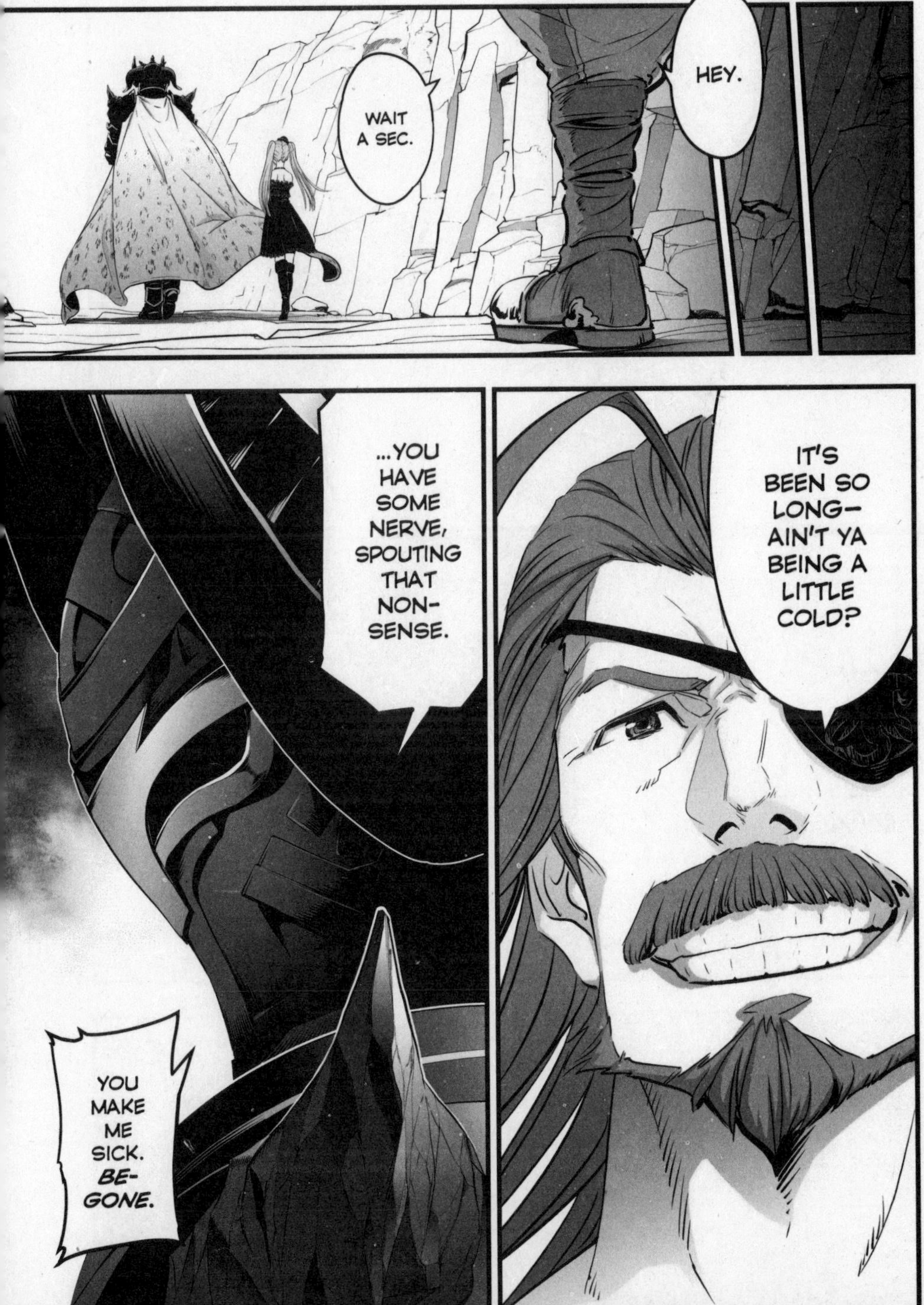
HEY.
WAIT A SEC.
IT'S BEEN SO LONG— AIN'T YA BEING A LITTLE COLD?
...YOU HAVE SOME NERVE, SPOUTING THAT NON-SENSE.
YOU MAKE ME SICK. *BE-GONE.*

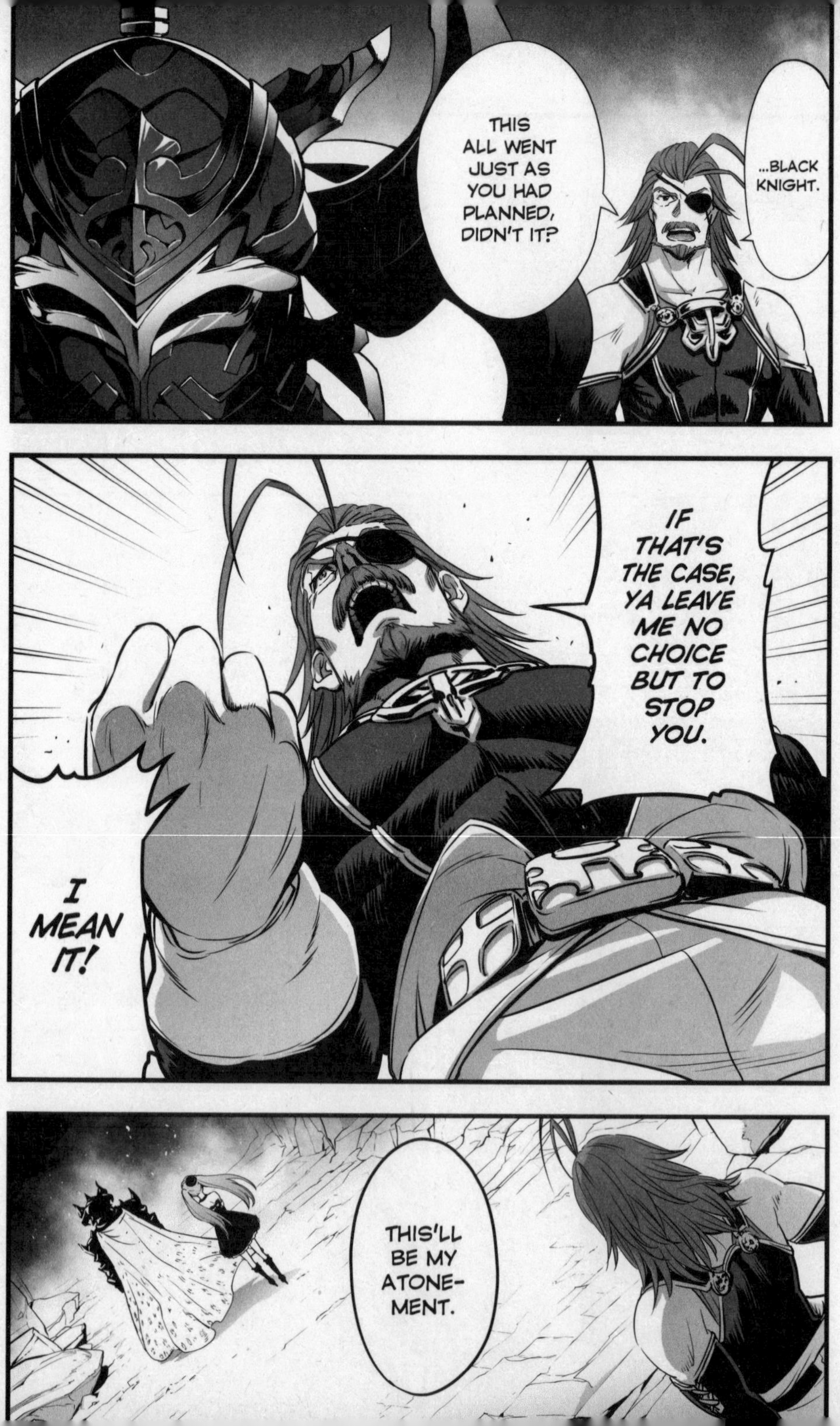
...BLACK KNIGHT.
THIS ALL WENT JUST AS YOU HAD PLANNED, DIDN'T IT?
IF THAT'S THE CASE, YA LEAVE ME NO CHOICE BUT TO STOP YOU.
I MEAN IT!
THIS'LL BE MY ATONE-MENT.

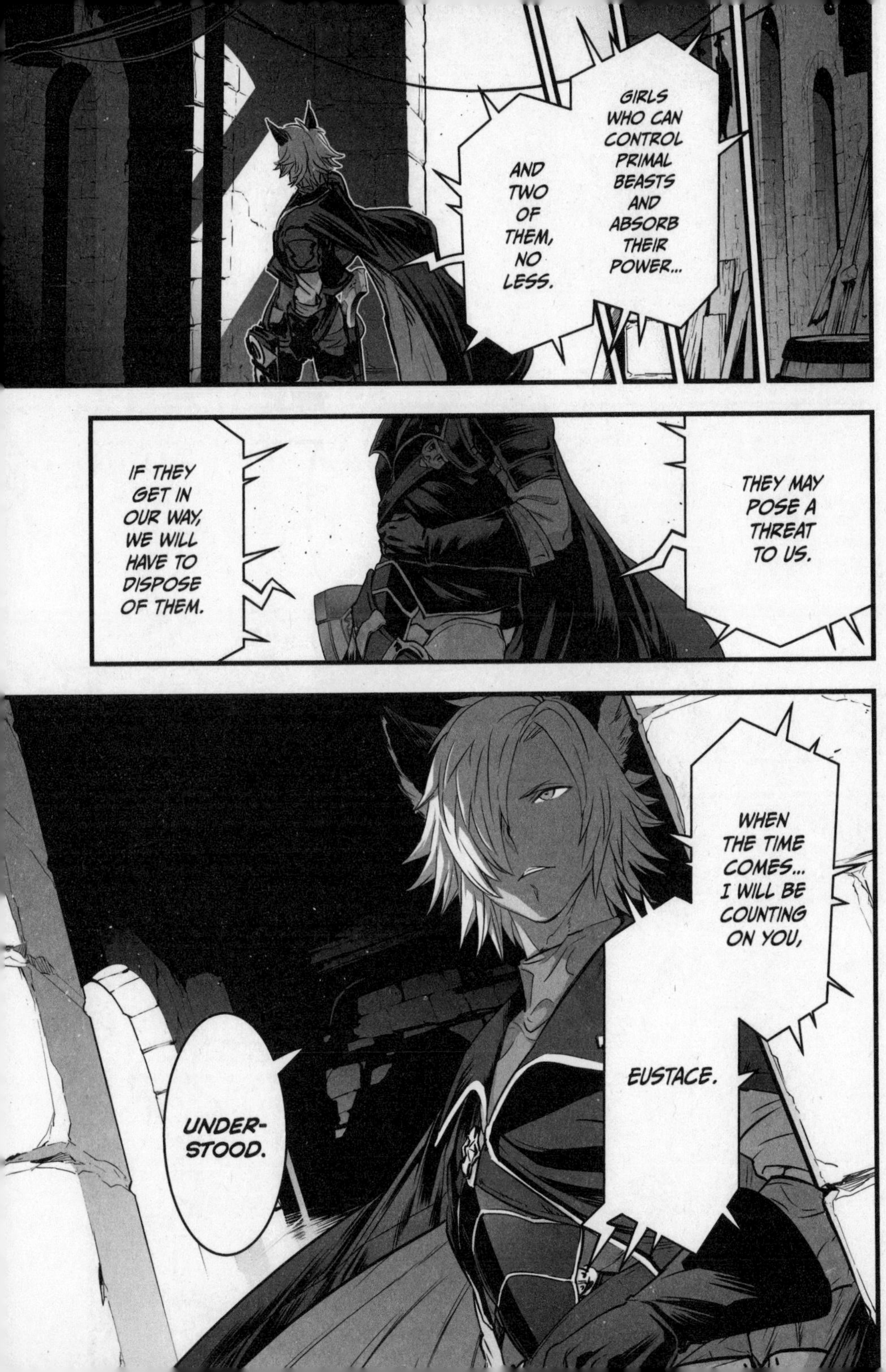
GIRLS WHO CAN CONTROL PRIMAL BEASTS AND ABSORB THEIR POWER...
AND TWO OF THEM, NO LESS.
THEY MAY POSE A THREAT TO US.
IF THEY GET IN OUR WAY, WE WILL HAVE TO DISPOSE OF THEM.
WHEN THE TIME COMES... I WILL BE COUNTING ON YOU,
EUSTACE.
UNDER-STOOD.

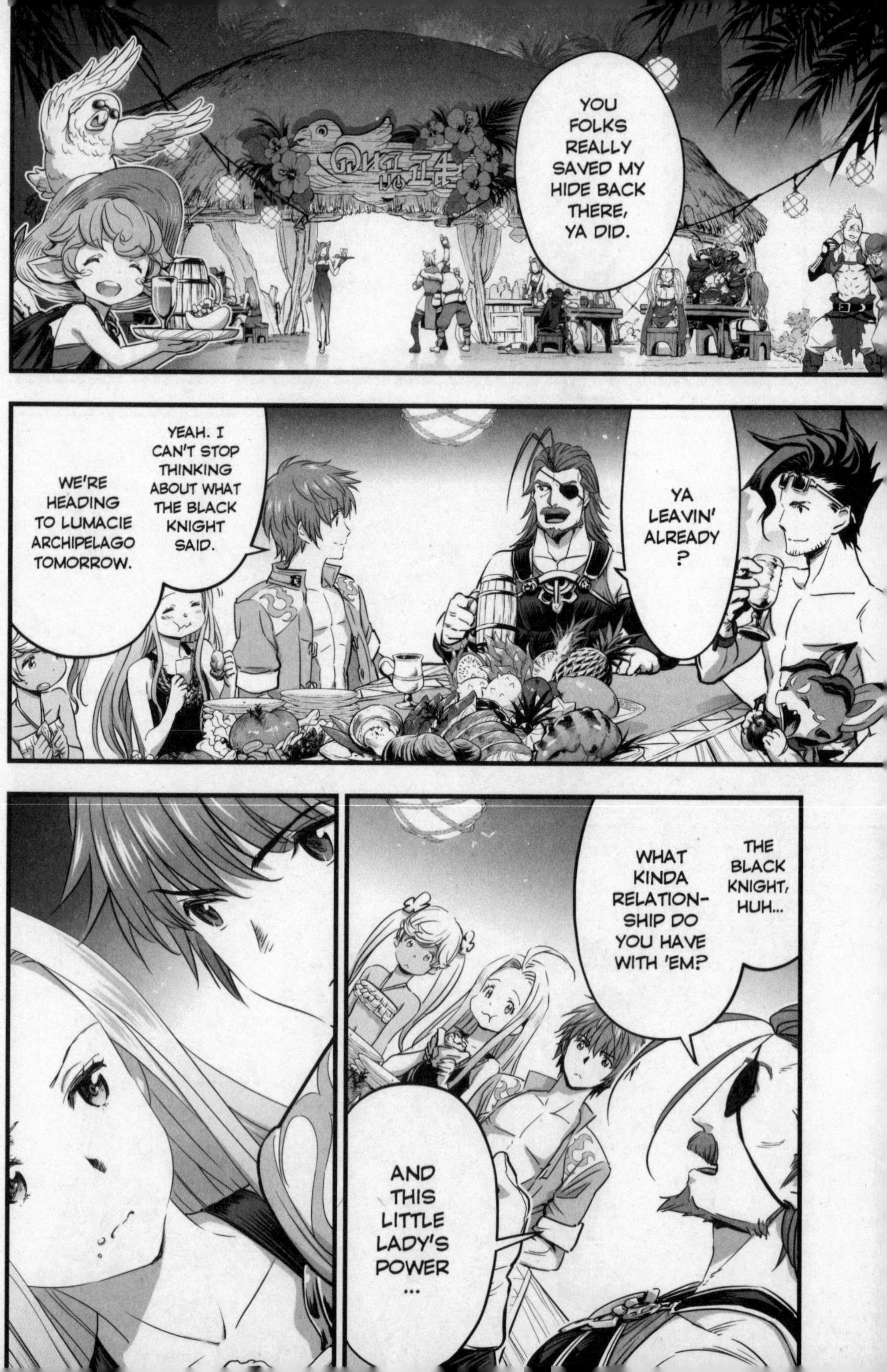
YOU FOLKS REALLY SAVED MY HIDE BACK THERE, YA DID.
YA LEAVIN' ALREADY?
YEAH. I CAN'T STOP THINKING ABOUT WHAT THE BLACK KNIGHT SAID.
WE'RE HEADING TO LUMACIE ARCHIPELAGO TOMORROW.
THE BLACK KNIGHT, HUH...
WHAT KINDA RELATION-SHIP DO YOU HAVE WITH 'EM?
AND THIS LITTLE LADY'S POWER...

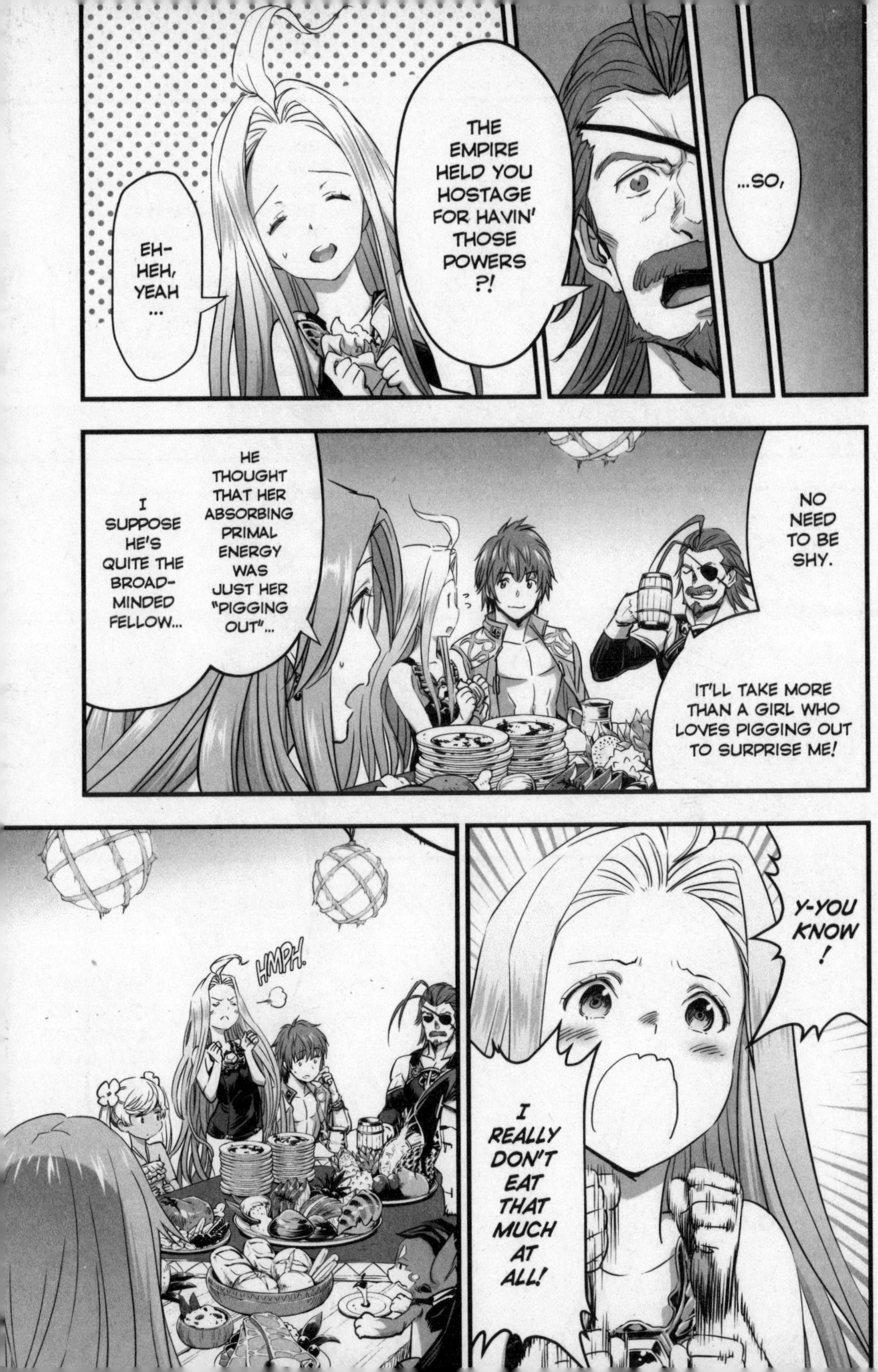
...SO,
THE EMPIRE HELD YOU HOSTAGE FOR HAVIN' THOSE POWERS?!
EH-HEH, YEAH...
NO NEED TO BE SHY.
IT'LL TAKE MORE THAN A GIRL WHO LOVES PIGGING OUT TO SURPRISE ME!
HE THOUGHT THAT HER ABSORBING PRIMAL ENERGY WAS JUST HER "PIGGING OUT"...
I SUPPOSE HE'S QUITE THE BROAD-MINDED FELLOW...
Y-YOU KNOW!
I REALLY DON'T EAT THAT MUCH AT ALL!
HMPH.

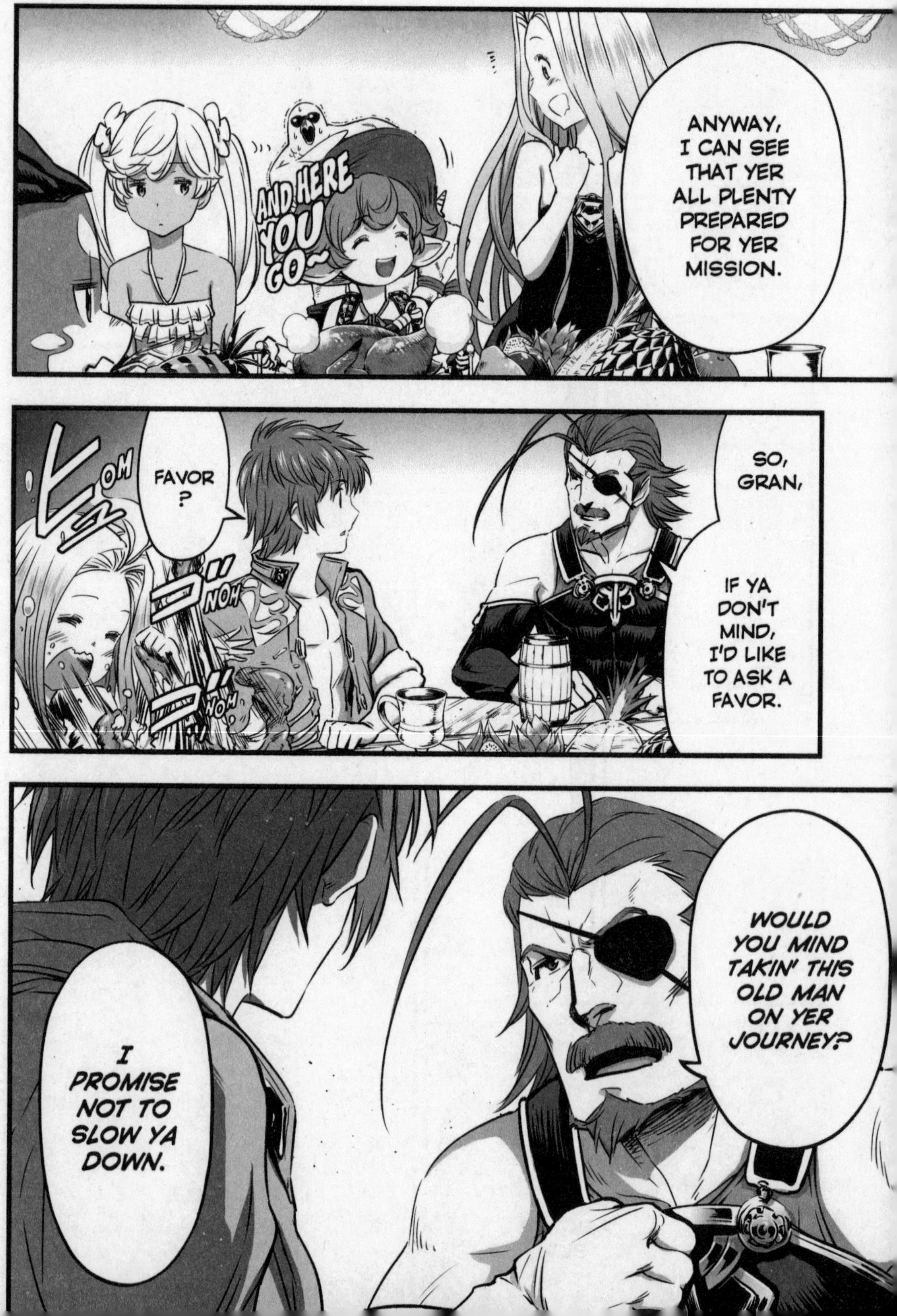
ANYWAY, I CAN SEE THAT YER ALL PLENTY PREPARED FOR YER MISSION.
AND HERE YOU GO~
SO, GRAN,
IF YA DON'T MIND, I'D LIKE TO ASK A FAVOR.
FAVOR?
OM
NOM
NOM
WOULD YOU MIND TAKIN' THIS OLD MAN ON YER JOURNEY?
I PROMISE NOT TO SLOW YA DOWN.

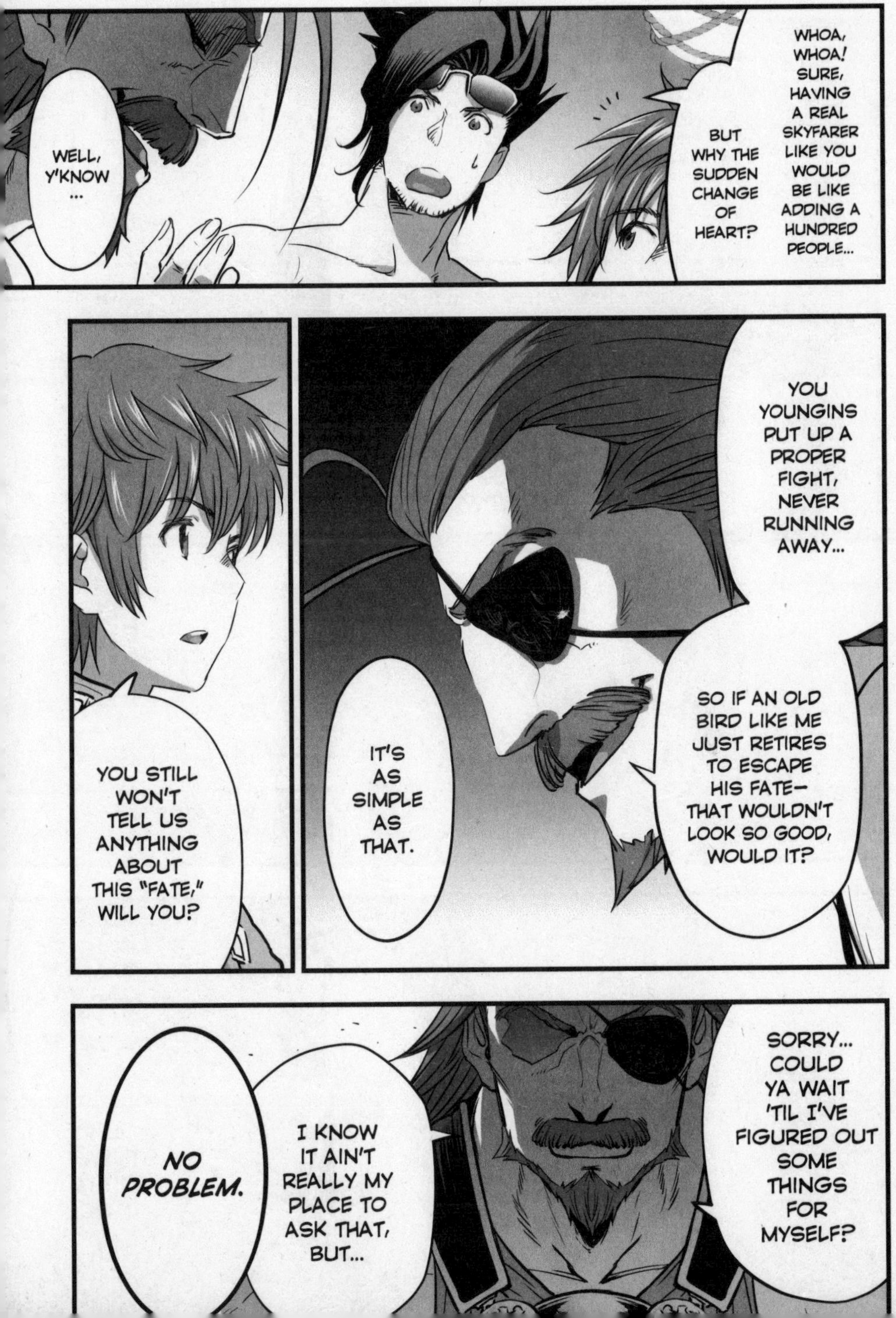
WHOA, WHOA! SURE, HAVING A REAL SKYFARER LIKE YOU WOULD BE LIKE ADDING A HUNDRED PEOPLE...
BUT WHY THE SUDDEN CHANGE OF HEART?
WELL, Y'KNOW ...
YOU YOUNGINS PUT UP A PROPER FIGHT, NEVER RUNNING AWAY...
SO IF AN OLD BIRD LIKE ME JUST RETIRES TO ESCAPE HIS FATE— THAT WOULDN'T LOOK SO GOOD, WOULD IT?
IT'S AS SIMPLE AS THAT.
YOU STILL WON'T TELL US ANYTHING ABOUT THIS "FATE," WILL YOU?
SORRY... COULD YA WAIT 'TIL I'VE FIGURED OUT SOME THINGS FOR MYSELF?
I KNOW IT AIN'T REALLY MY PLACE TO ASK THAT, BUT...
NO PROBLEM.

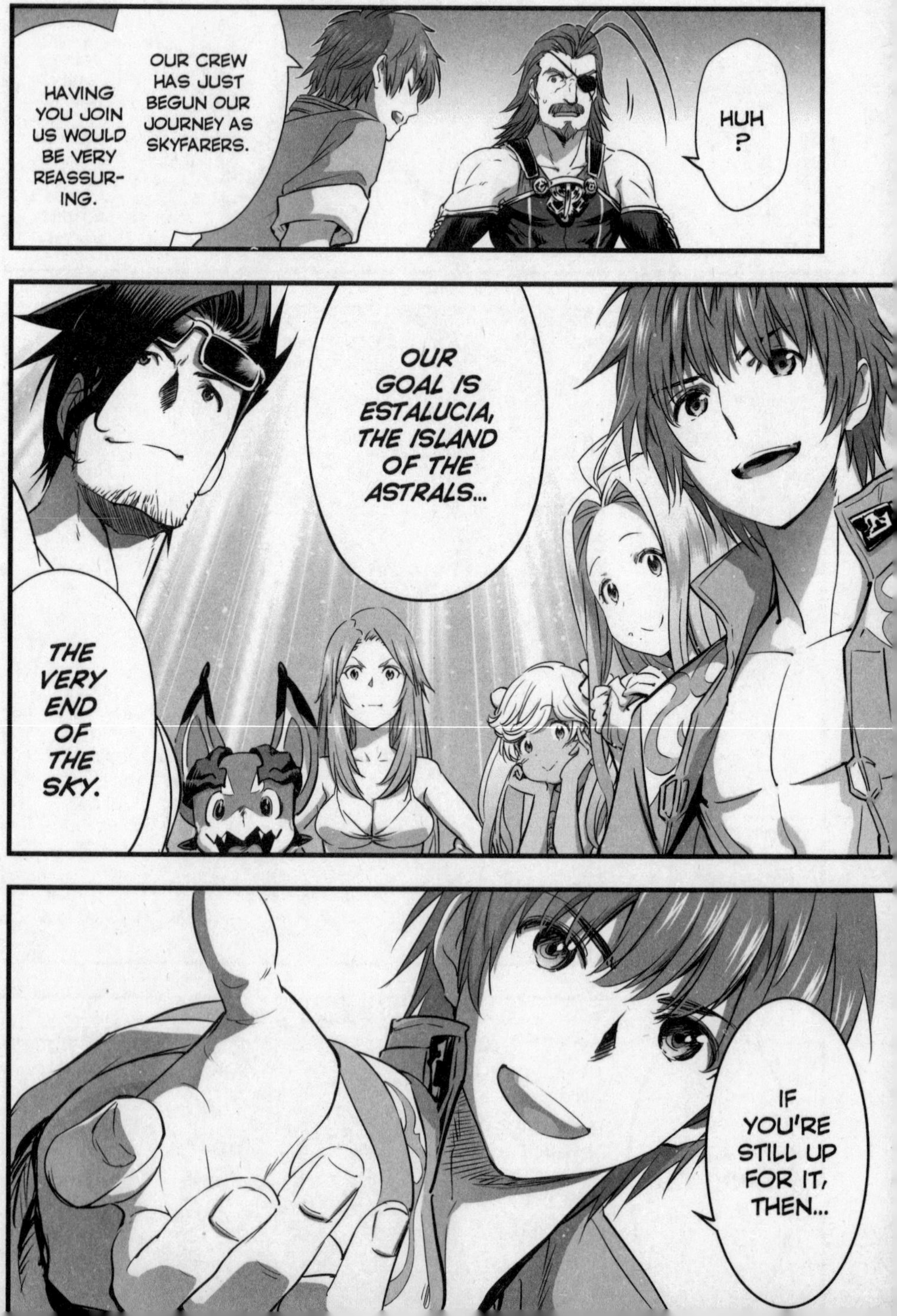
HUH?
OUR CREW HAS JUST BEGUN OUR JOURNEY AS SKYFARERS.
HAVING YOU JOIN US WOULD BE VERY REASSURING.
OUR GOAL IS ESTALUCIA, THE ISLAND OF THE ASTRALS...
THE VERY END OF THE SKY.
IF YOU'RE STILL UP FOR IT, THEN...

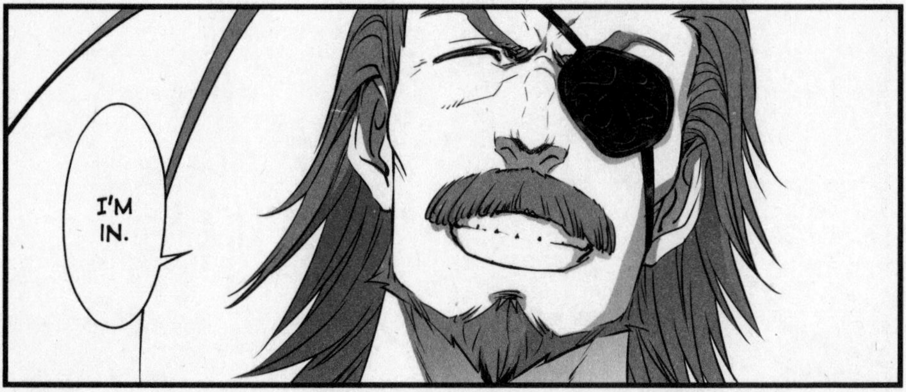
I'M IN.

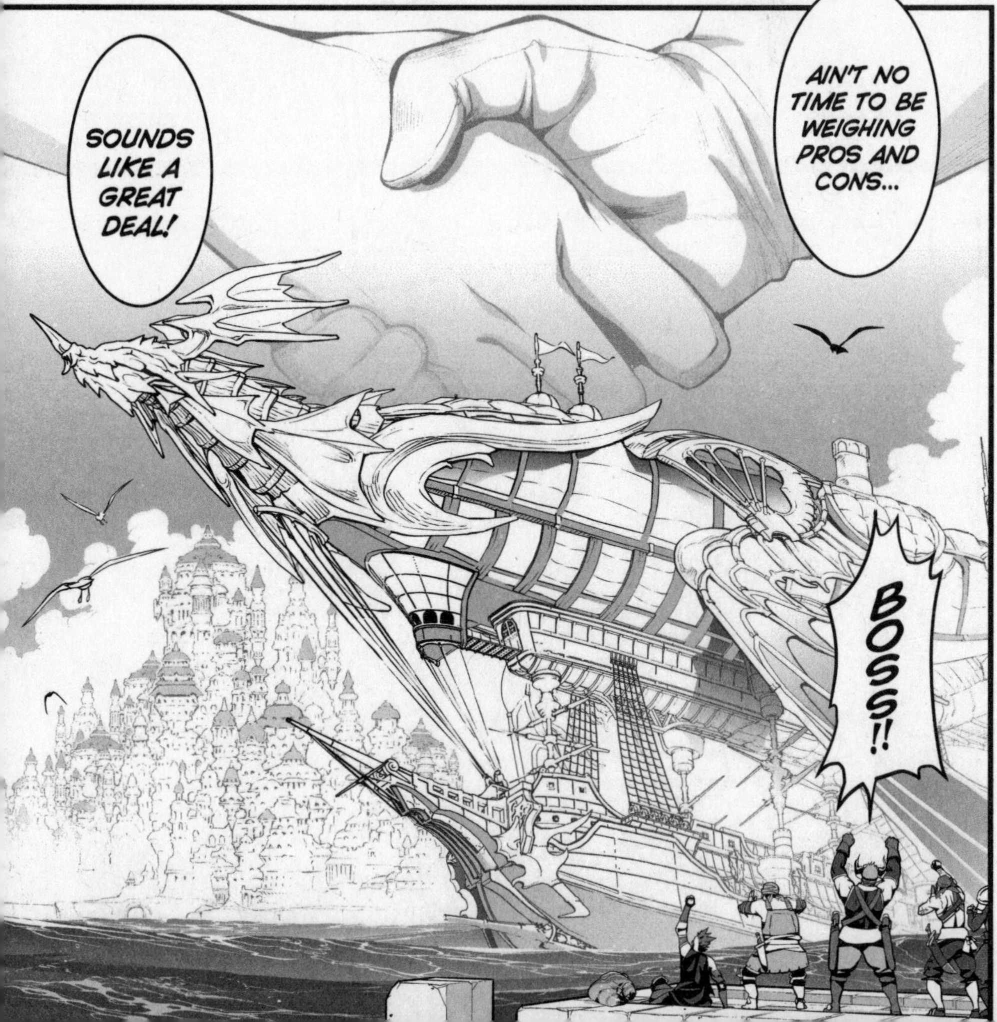
AIN'T NO TIME TO BE WEIGHING PROS AND CONS...
SOUNDS LIKE A GREAT DEAL!
BOSS!!

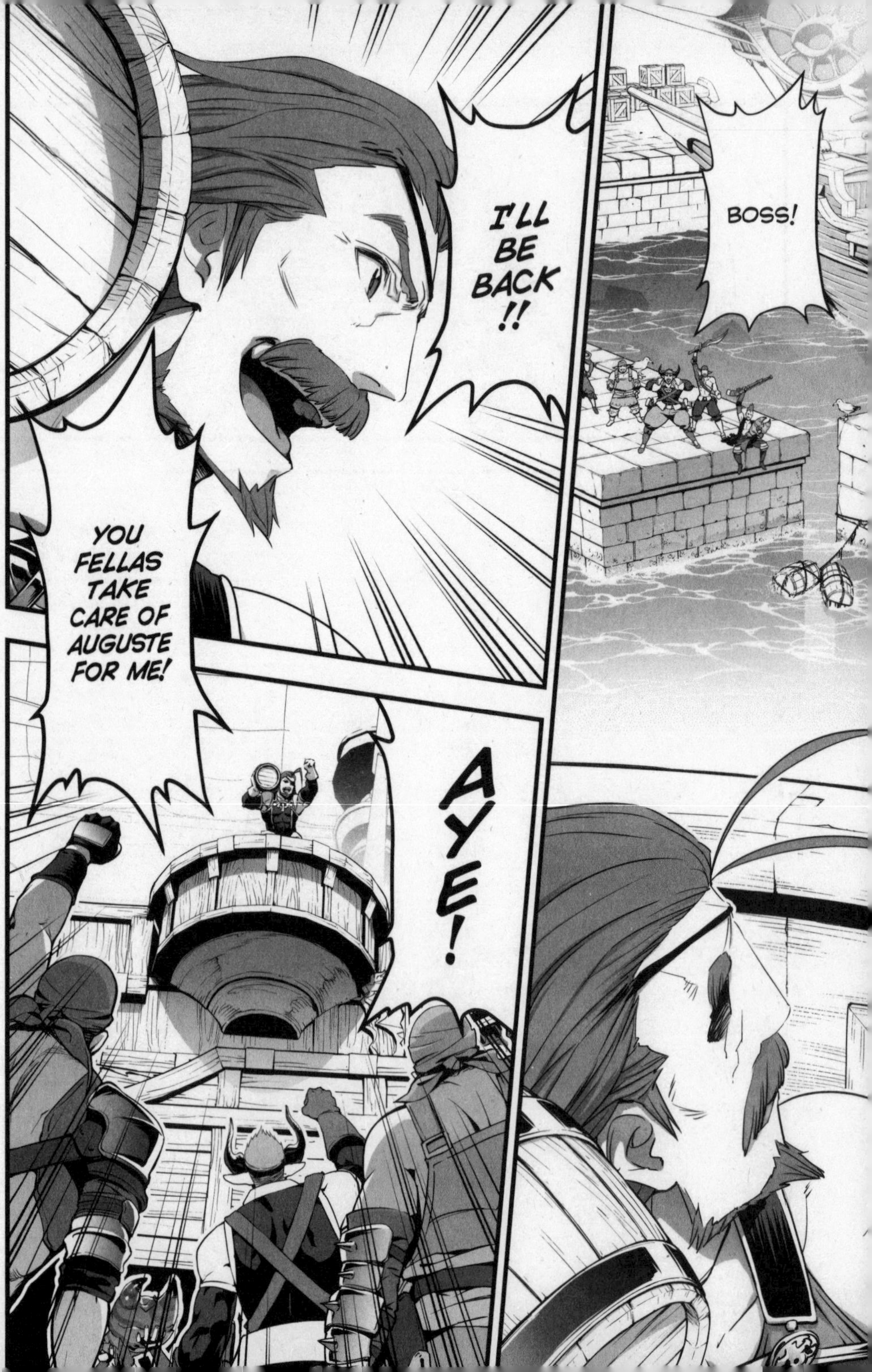

BOSS!
I'LL BE BACK!!
YOU FELLAS TAKE CARE OF AUGUSTE FOR ME!
AYE!

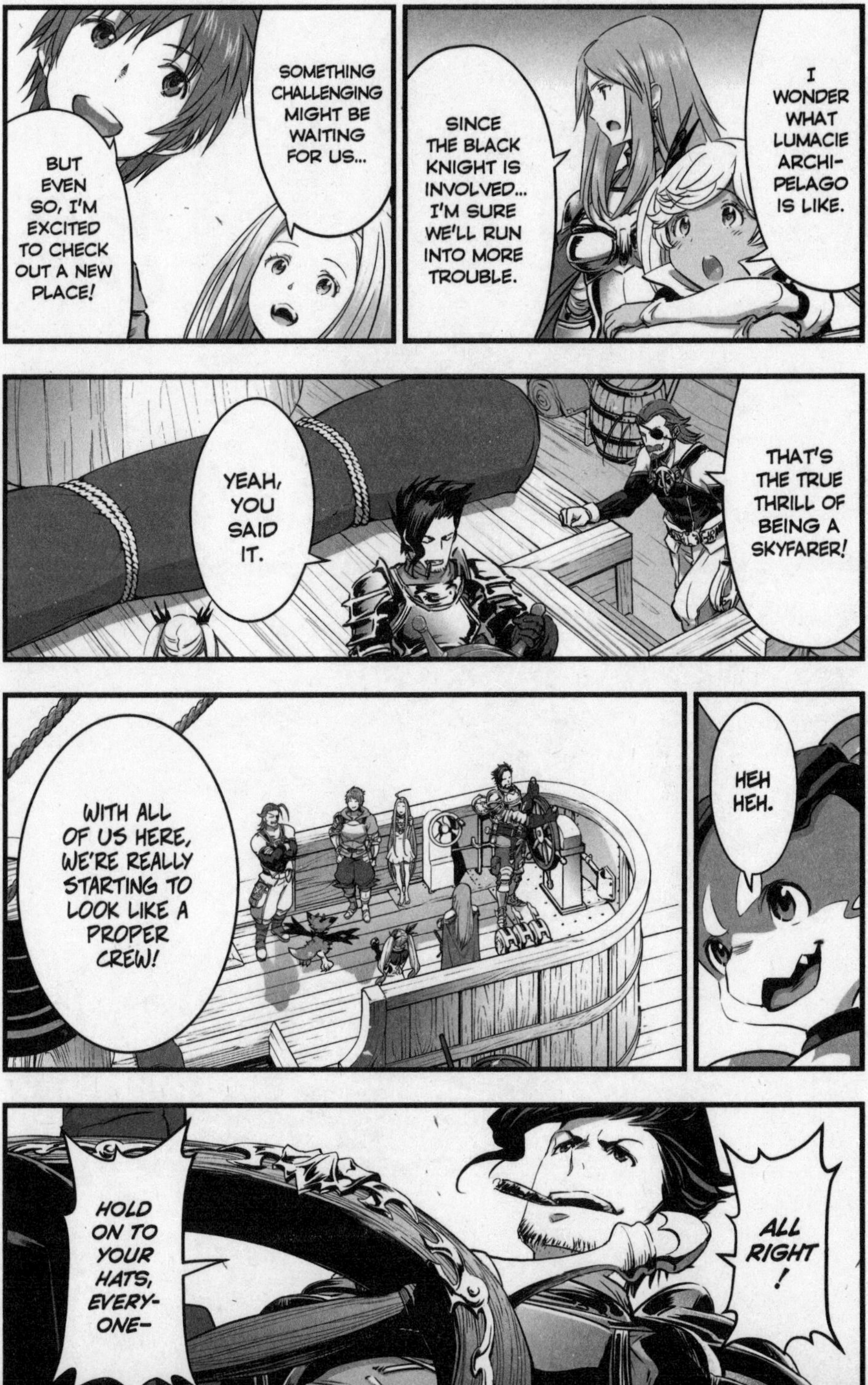
I WONDER WHAT LUMACIE ARCHIPELAGO IS LIKE.
SINCE THE BLACK KNIGHT IS INVOLVED... I'M SURE WE'LL RUN INTO MORE TROUBLE.
SOMETHING CHALLENGING MIGHT BE WAITING FOR US...
BUT EVEN SO, I'M EXCITED TO CHECK OUT A NEW PLACE!
THAT'S THE TRUE THRILL OF BEING A SKYFARER!
YEAH, YOU SAID IT.
HEH HEH.
WITH ALL OF US HERE, WE'RE REALLY STARTING TO LOOK LIKE A PROPER CREW!
ALL RIGHT!
HOLD ON TO YOUR HATS, EVERY-ONE-

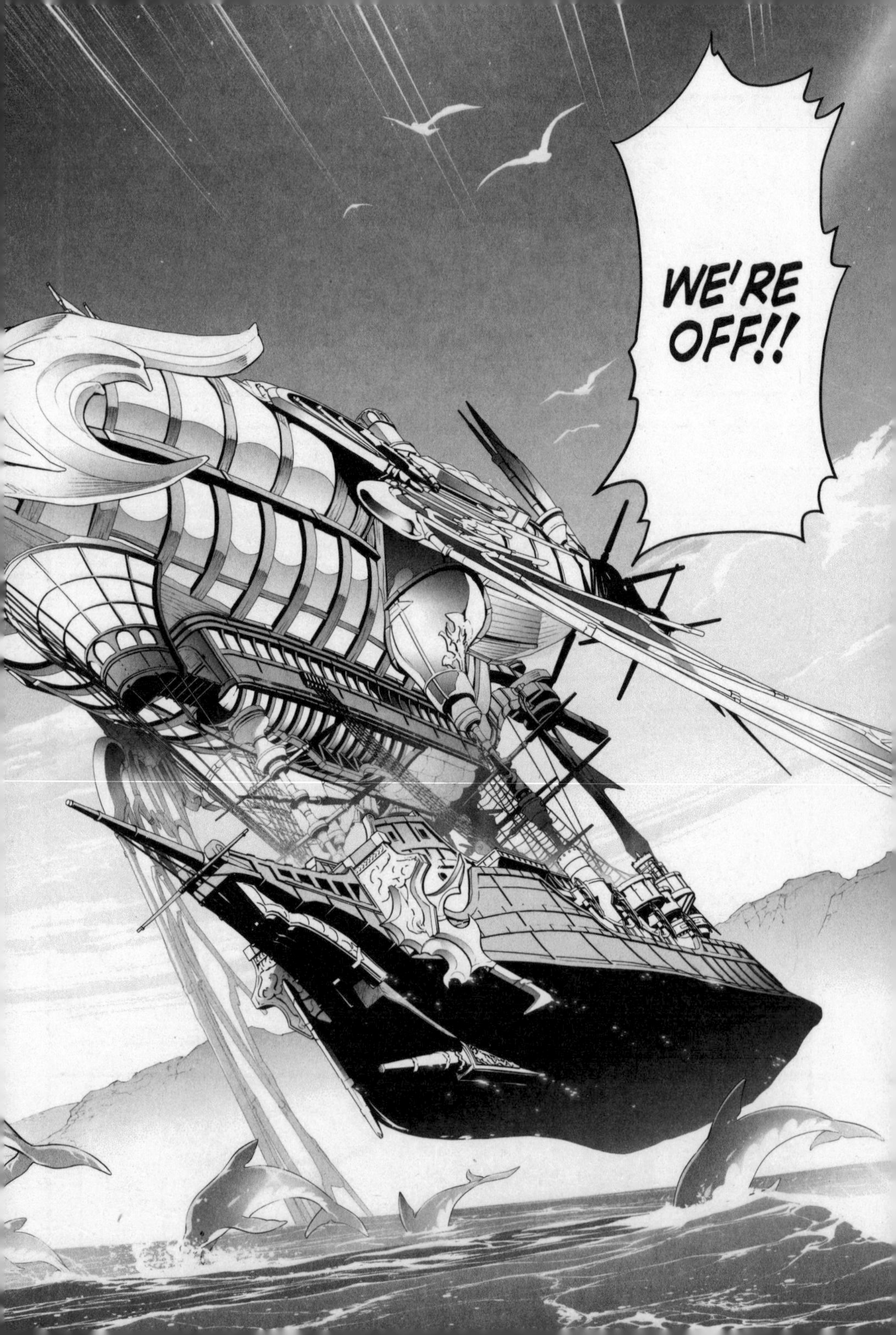
WE'RE OFF!!

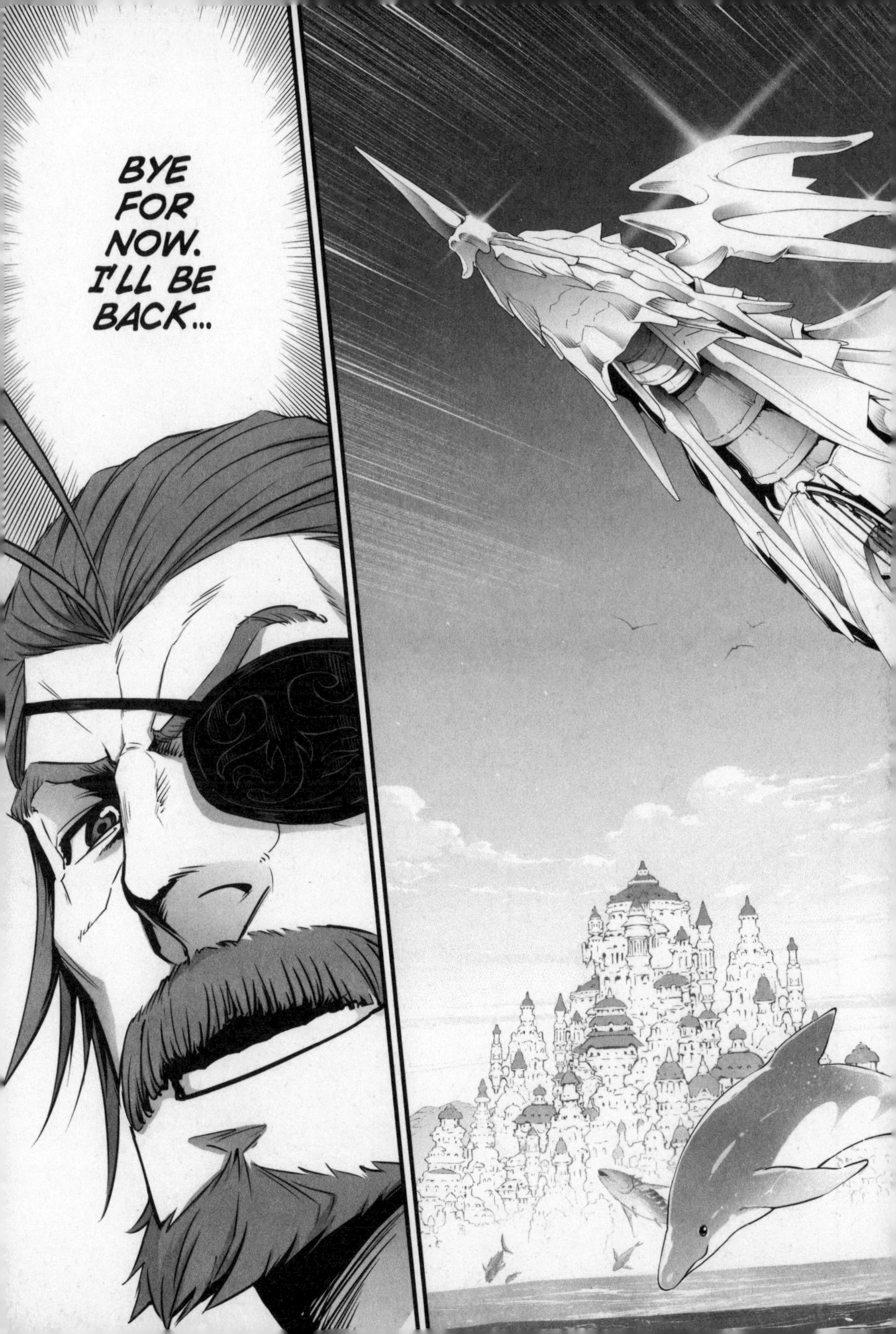
BYE FOR NOW. I'LL BE BACK...

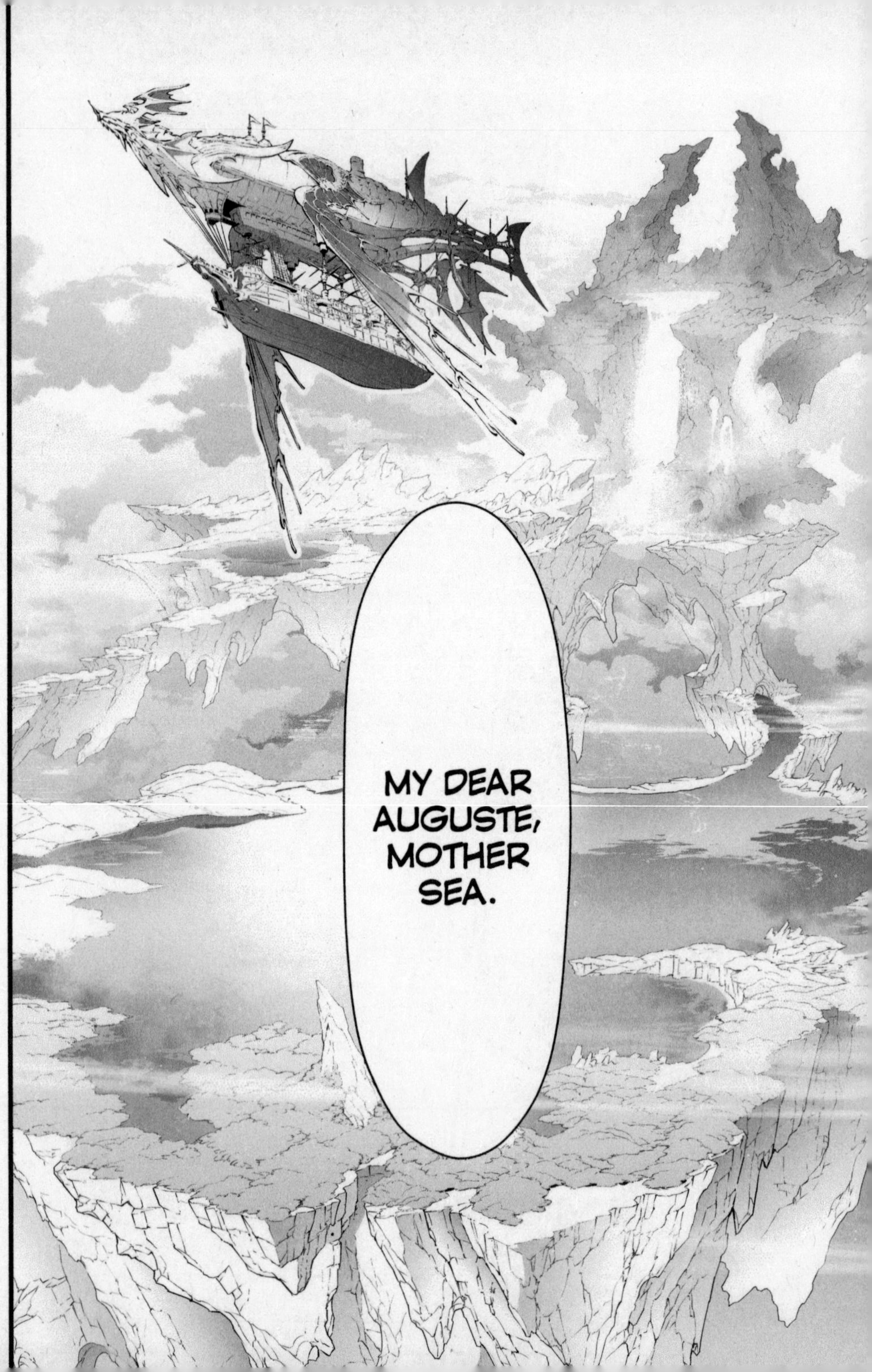
MY DEAR AUGUSTE, MOTHER SEA.

GRANBLUE FANTASY
グランブルーファンタジー

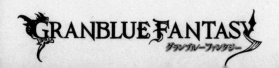

GRANBLUE FANTASY
グランブルーファンタジー

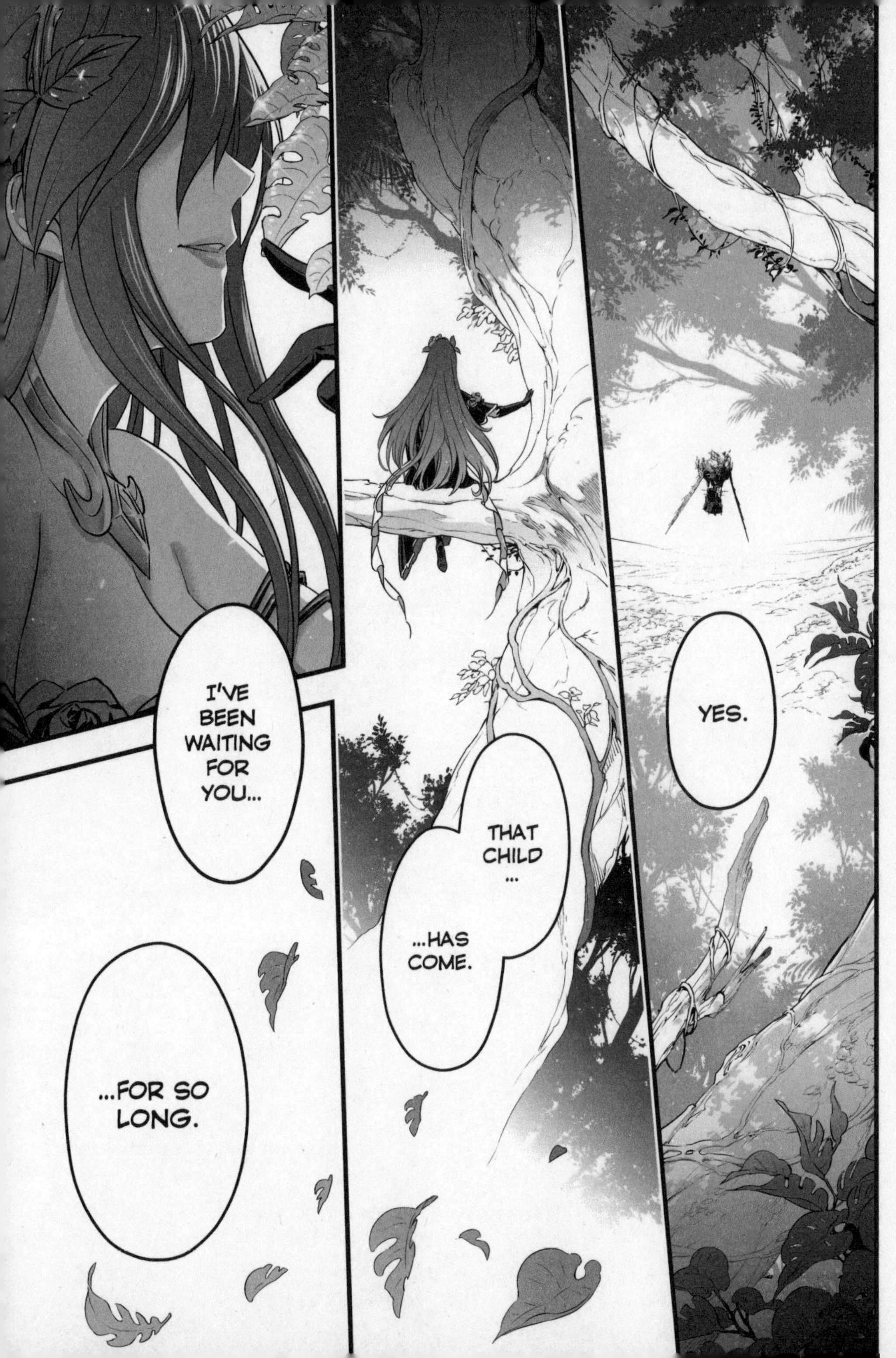
YES.
THAT CHILD ...
...HAS COME.
I'VE BEEN WAITING FOR YOU...
...FOR SO LONG.

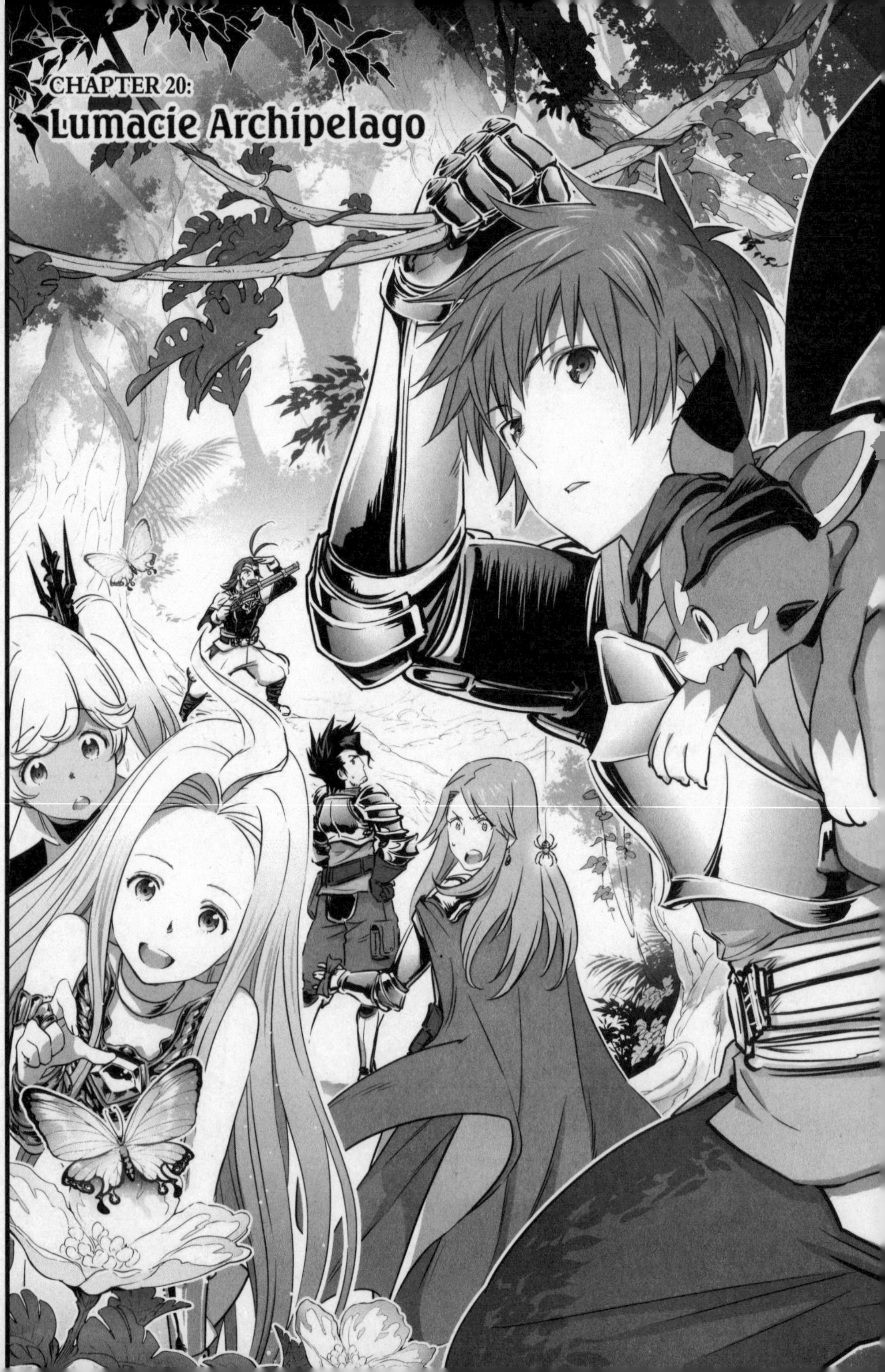
CHAPTER 20:
Lumacie Archipelago

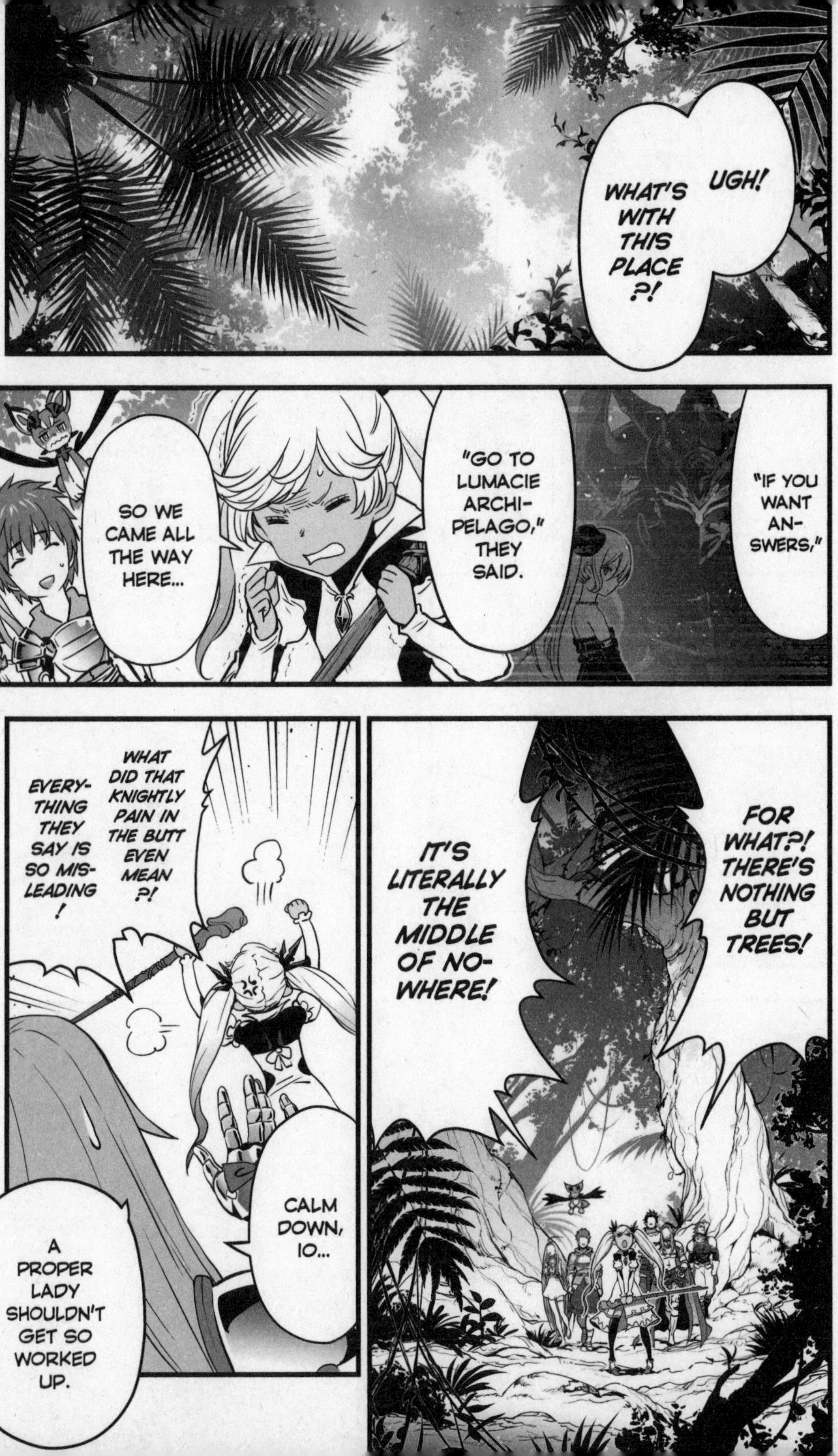
UGH! WHAT'S WITH THIS PLACE ?!
"IF YOU WANT ANSWERS,"
"GO TO LUMACIE ARCHIPELAGO," THEY SAID.
SO WE CAME ALL THE WAY HERE...
FOR WHAT?! THERE'S NOTHING BUT TREES!
IT'S LITERALLY THE MIDDLE OF NOWHERE!
WHAT DID THAT KNIGHTLY PAIN IN THE BUTT EVEN MEAN ?!
EVERYTHING THEY SAY IS SO MISLEADING !
CALM DOWN, IO...
A PROPER LADY SHOULDN'T GET SO WORKED UP.

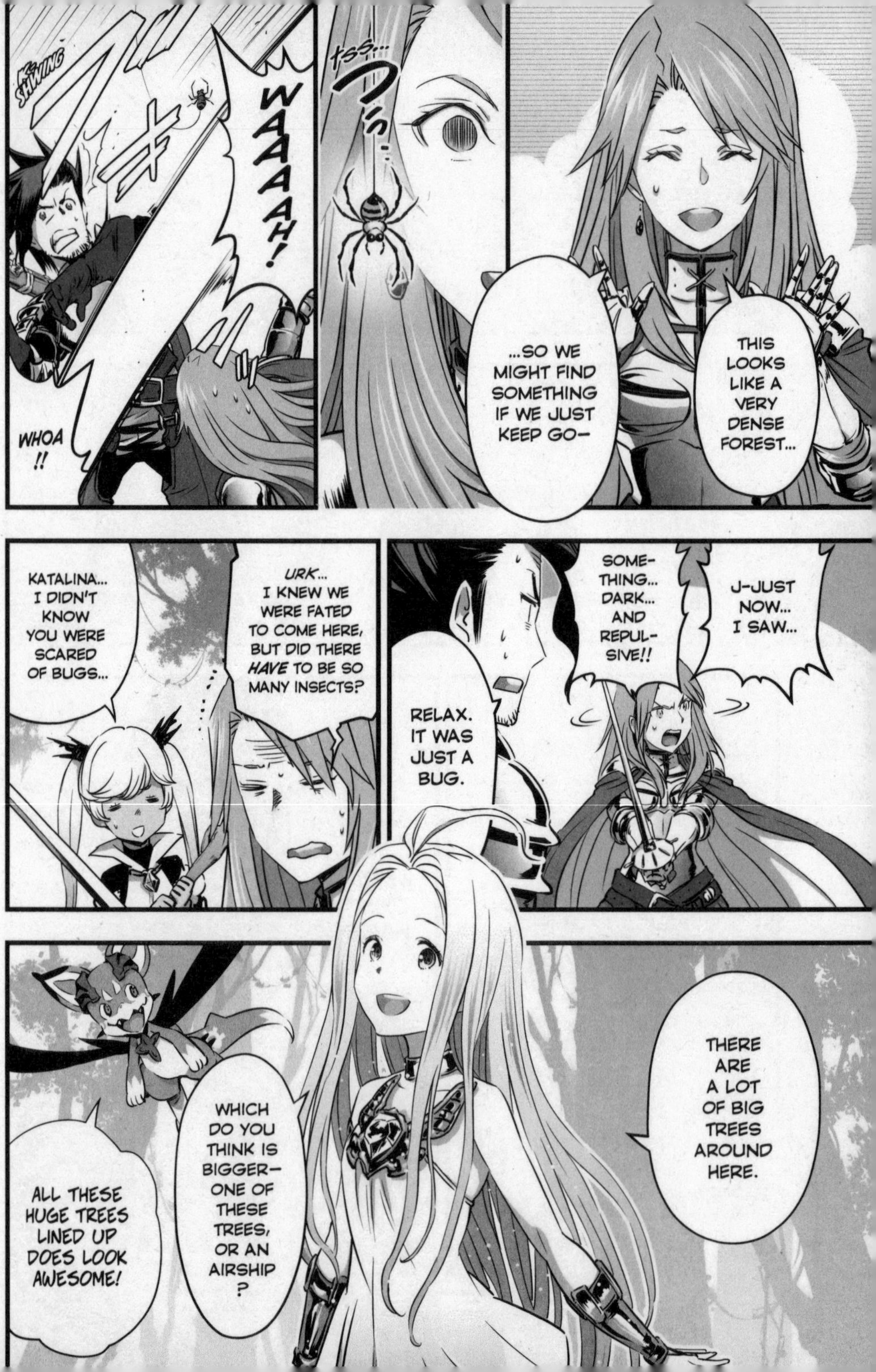
THIS LOOKS LIKE A VERY DENSE FOREST...
...SO WE MIGHT FIND SOMETHING IF WE JUST KEEP GO—
TSS...
K-SHWING
WAAAAAH!
WHOA !!
J-JUST NOW... I SAW...
SOME-THING... DARK... AND REPUL-SIVE!!
RELAX. IT WAS JUST A BUG.
URK... I KNEW WE WERE FATED TO COME HERE, BUT DID THERE *HAVE* TO BE SO MANY INSECTS?
KATALINA... I DIDN'T KNOW YOU WERE SCARED OF BUGS...
THERE ARE A LOT OF BIG TREES AROUND HERE.
WHICH DO YOU THINK IS BIGGER— ONE OF THESE TREES, OR AN AIRSHIP ?
ALL THESE HUGE TREES LINED UP DOES LOOK AWESOME!

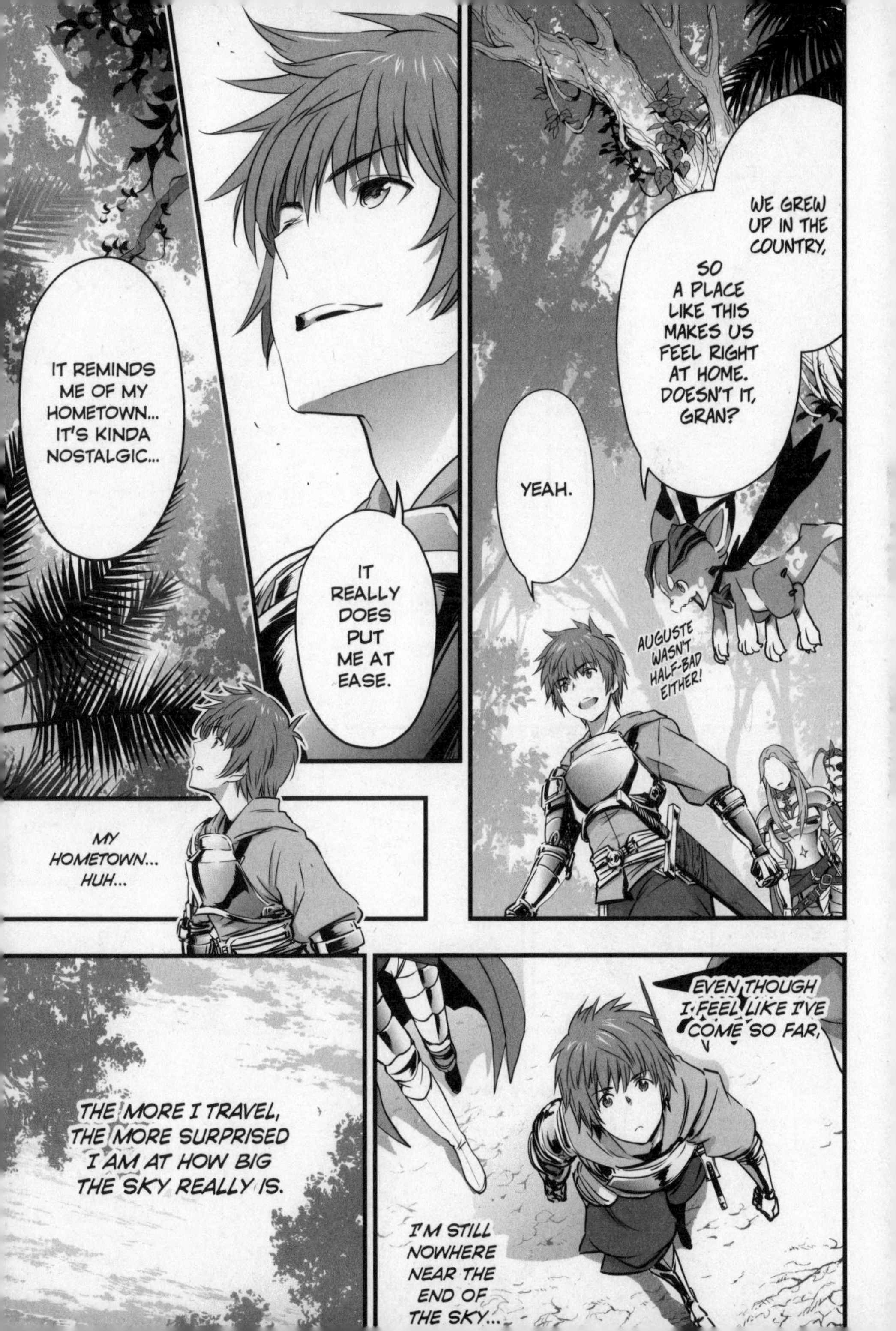
WE GREW UP IN THE COUNTRY,
SO A PLACE LIKE THIS MAKES US FEEL RIGHT AT HOME. DOESN'T IT, GRAN?
YEAH.
AUGUSTE WASN'T HALF-BAD EITHER!
IT REMINDS ME OF MY HOMETOWN... IT'S KINDA NOSTALGIC...
IT REALLY DOES PUT ME AT EASE.
MY HOMETOWN... HUH...
EVEN THOUGH I FEEL LIKE I'VE COME SO FAR,
I'M STILL NOWHERE NEAR THE END OF THE SKY...
THE MORE I TRAVEL, THE MORE SURPRISED I AM AT HOW BIG THE SKY REALLY IS.

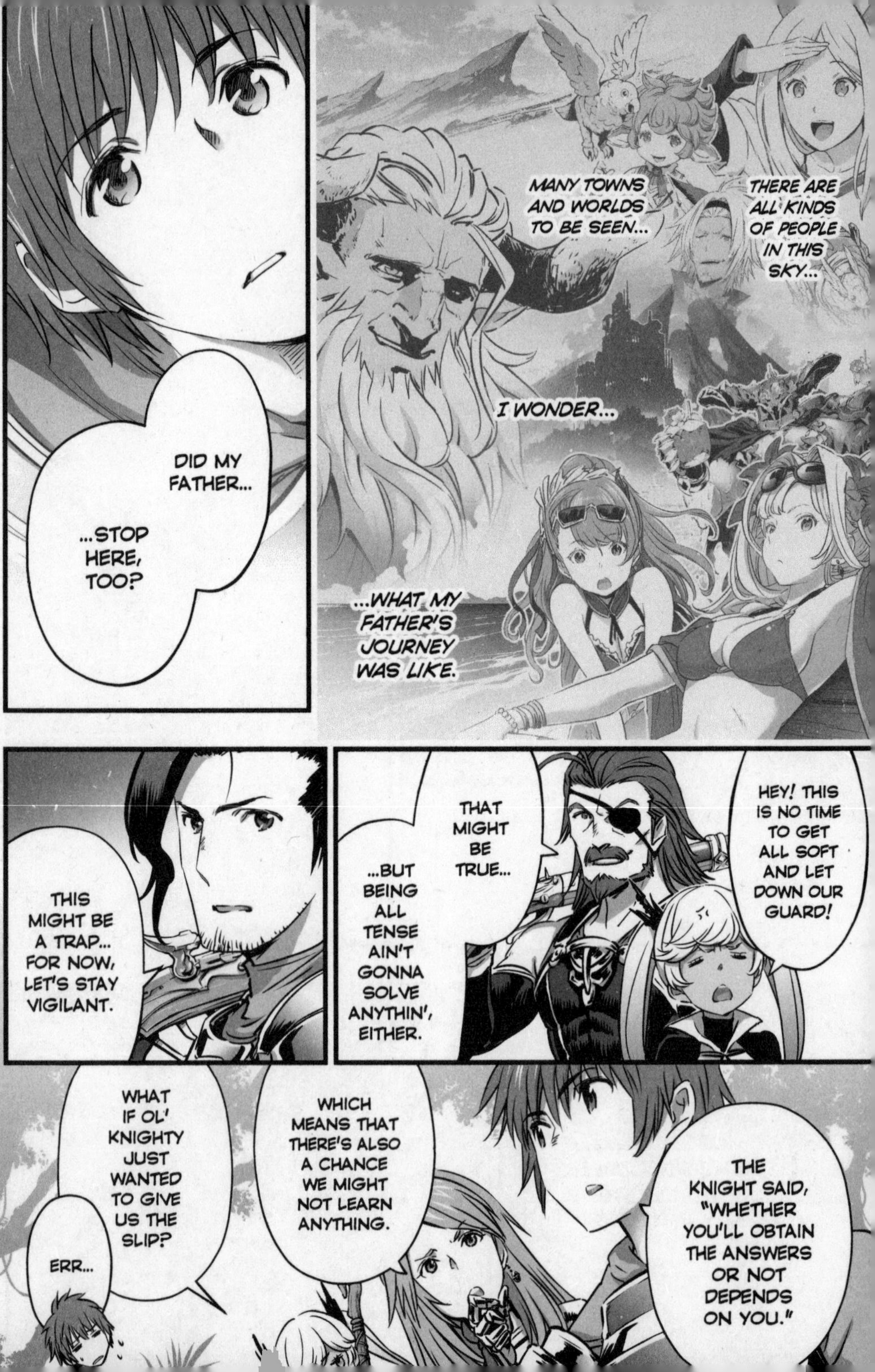
THERE ARE ALL KINDS OF PEOPLE IN THIS SKY...
MANY TOWNS AND WORLDS TO BE SEEN...
I WONDER...
...WHAT MY FATHER'S JOURNEY WAS LIKE.
DID MY FATHER...
...STOP HERE, TOO?
HEY! THIS IS NO TIME TO GET ALL SOFT AND LET DOWN OUR GUARD!
THAT MIGHT BE TRUE...
...BUT BEING ALL TENSE AIN'T GONNA SOLVE ANYTHIN', EITHER.
THIS MIGHT BE A TRAP... FOR NOW, LET'S STAY VIGILANT.
THE KNIGHT SAID, "WHETHER YOU'LL OBTAIN THE ANSWERS OR NOT DEPENDS ON YOU."
WHICH MEANS THAT THERE'S ALSO A CHANCE WE MIGHT NOT LEARN ANYTHING.
WHAT IF OL' KNIGHTY JUST WANTED TO GIVE US THE SLIP?
ERR...

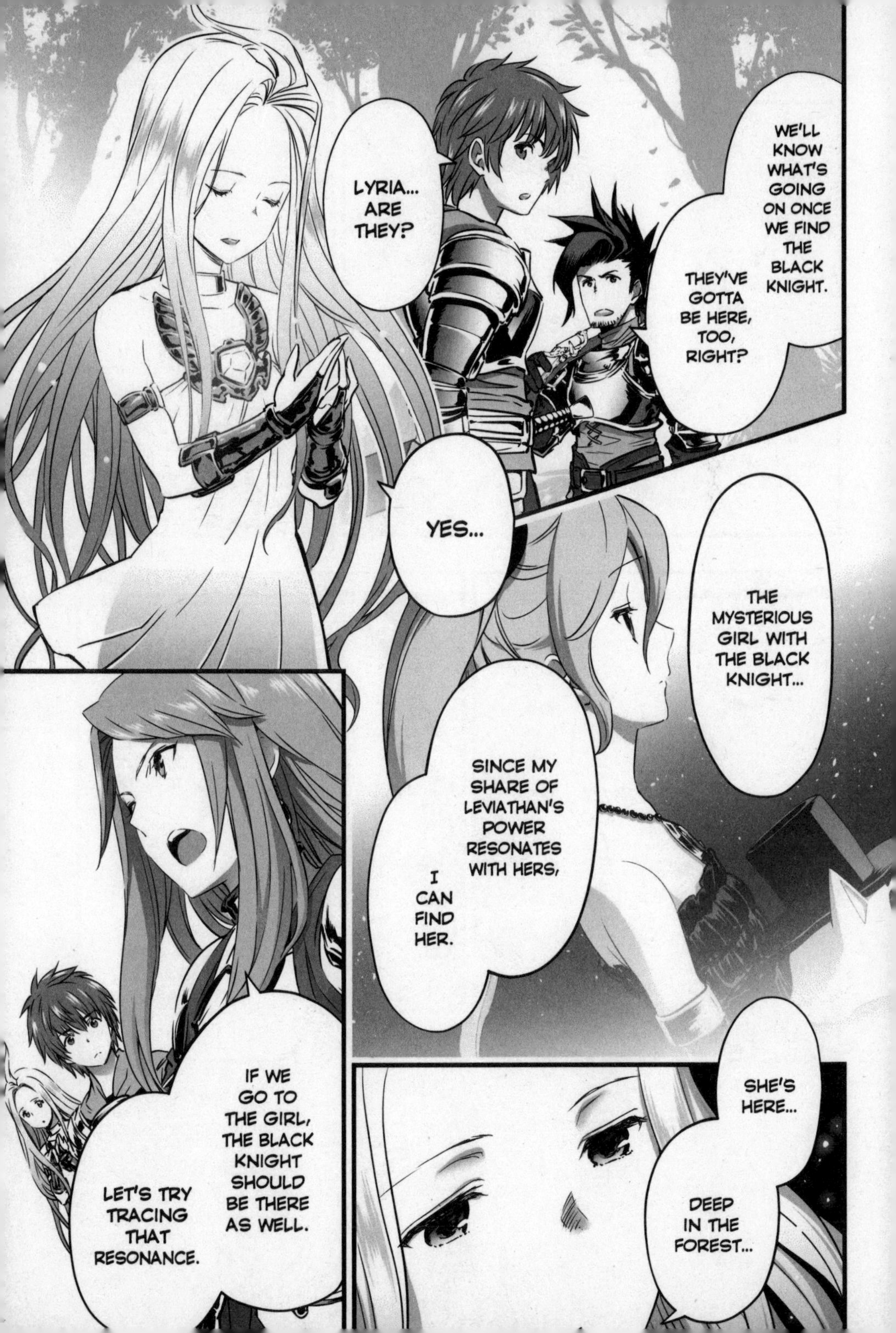
WE'LL KNOW WHAT'S GOING ON ONCE WE FIND THE BLACK KNIGHT.
THEY'VE GOTTA BE HERE, TOO, RIGHT?
LYRIA... ARE THEY?
YES...
THE MYSTERIOUS GIRL WITH THE BLACK KNIGHT...
SINCE MY SHARE OF LEVIATHAN'S POWER RESONATES WITH HERS,
I CAN FIND HER.
IF WE GO TO THE GIRL, THE BLACK KNIGHT SHOULD BE THERE AS WELL.
LET'S TRY TRACING THAT RESONANCE.
SHE'S HERE...
DEEP IN THE FOREST...

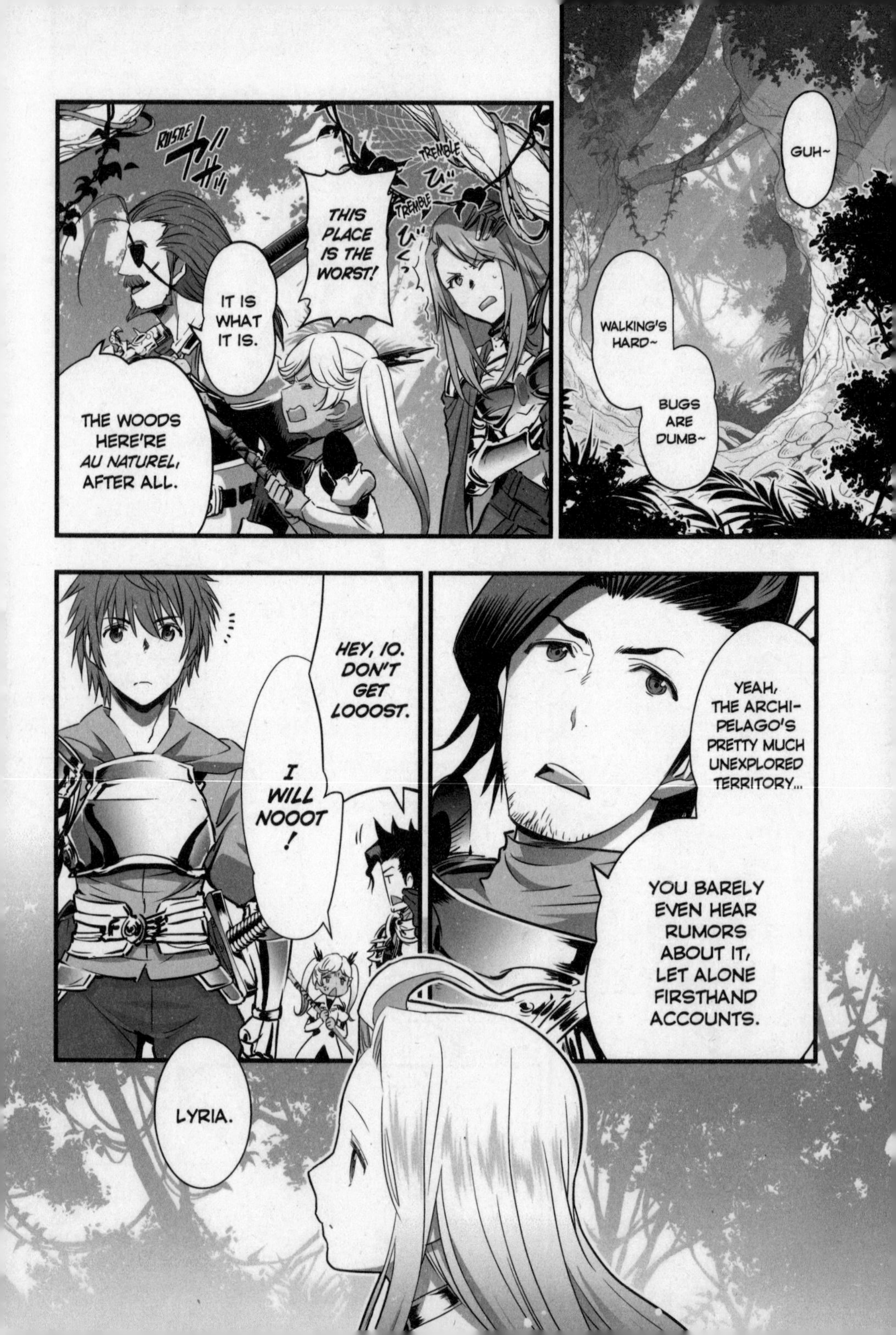
GUH~
WALKING'S HARD~
BUGS ARE DUMB~
TREMBLE
TREMBLE
THIS PLACE IS THE WORST!
RUSTLE
IT IS WHAT IT IS.
THE WOODS HERE'RE AU NATUREL, AFTER ALL.
YEAH, THE ARCHI-PELAGO'S PRETTY MUCH UNEXPLORED TERRITORY...
YOU BARELY EVEN HEAR RUMORS ABOUT IT, LET ALONE FIRSTHAND ACCOUNTS.
HEY, IO. DON'T GET LOOOST.
I WILL NOOOT!
...
LYRIA.

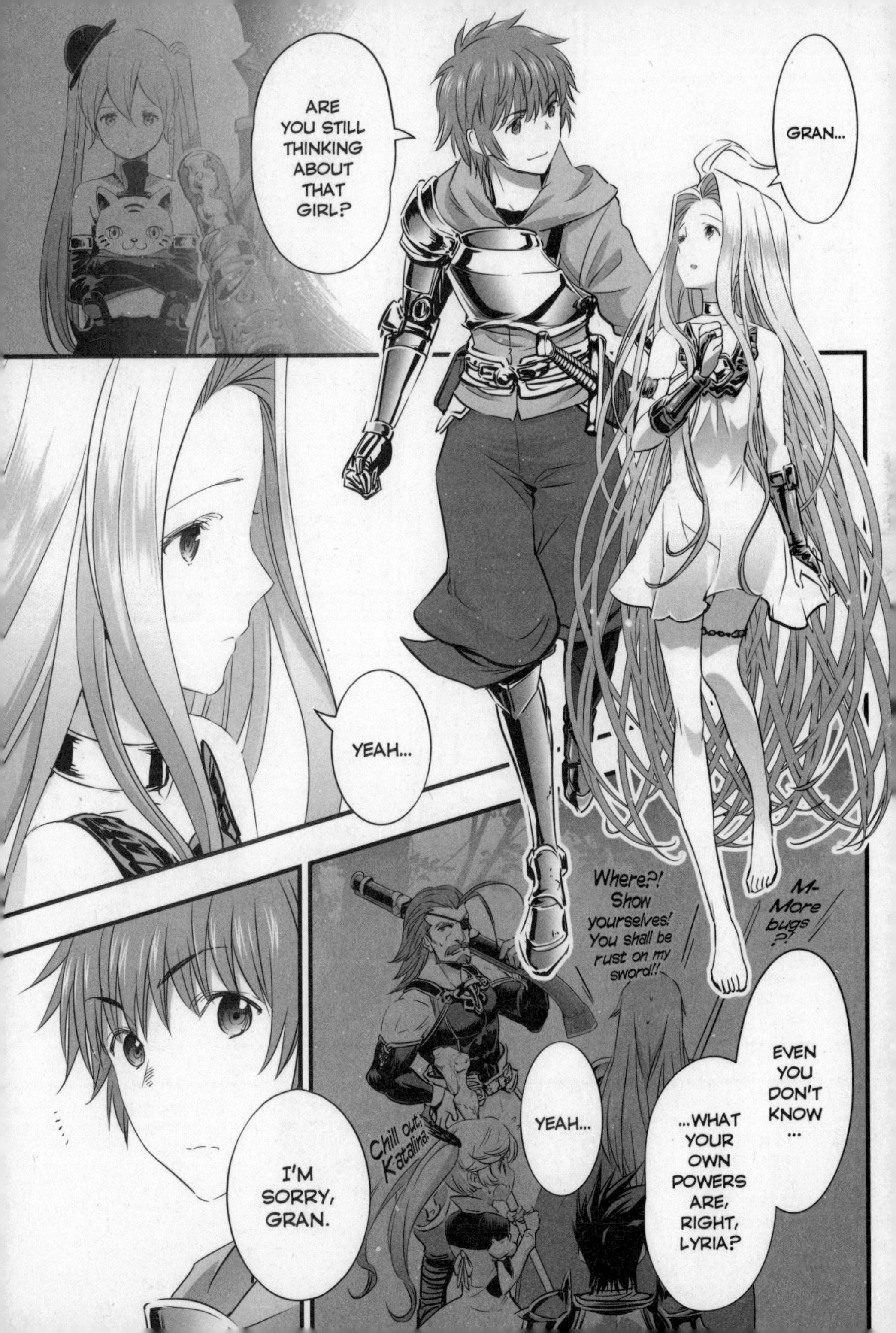
GRAN...
ARE YOU STILL THINKING ABOUT THAT GIRL?
YEAH...
M-More bugs?!
Where?! Show yourselves! You shall be rust on my sword!!
EVEN YOU DON'T KNOW ...
...WHAT YOUR OWN POWERS ARE, RIGHT, LYRIA?
YEAH...
Chill out, Katalina.
...
I'M SORRY, GRAN.

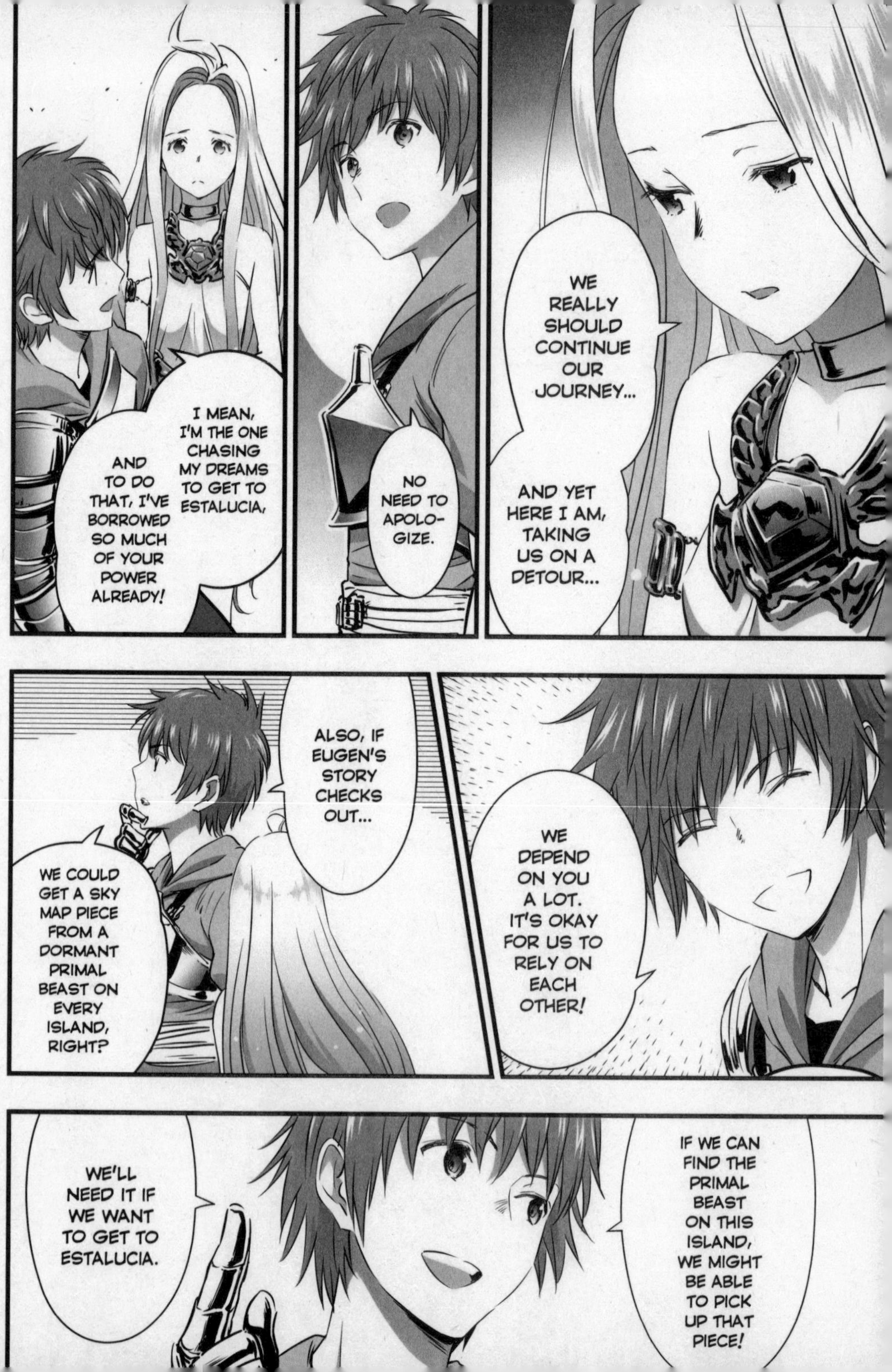
WE REALLY SHOULD CONTINUE OUR JOURNEY...
AND YET HERE I AM, TAKING US ON A DETOUR...
NO NEED TO APOLOGIZE.
I MEAN, I'M THE ONE CHASING MY DREAMS TO GET TO ESTALUCIA,
AND TO DO THAT, I'VE BORROWED SO MUCH OF YOUR POWER ALREADY!
WE DEPEND ON YOU A LOT. IT'S OKAY FOR US TO RELY ON EACH OTHER!
ALSO, IF EUGEN'S STORY CHECKS OUT...
WE COULD GET A SKY MAP PIECE FROM A DORMANT PRIMAL BEAST ON EVERY ISLAND, RIGHT?
IF WE CAN FIND THE PRIMAL BEAST ON THIS ISLAND, WE MIGHT BE ABLE TO PICK UP THAT PIECE!
WE'LL NEED IT IF WE WANT TO GET TO ESTALUCIA.

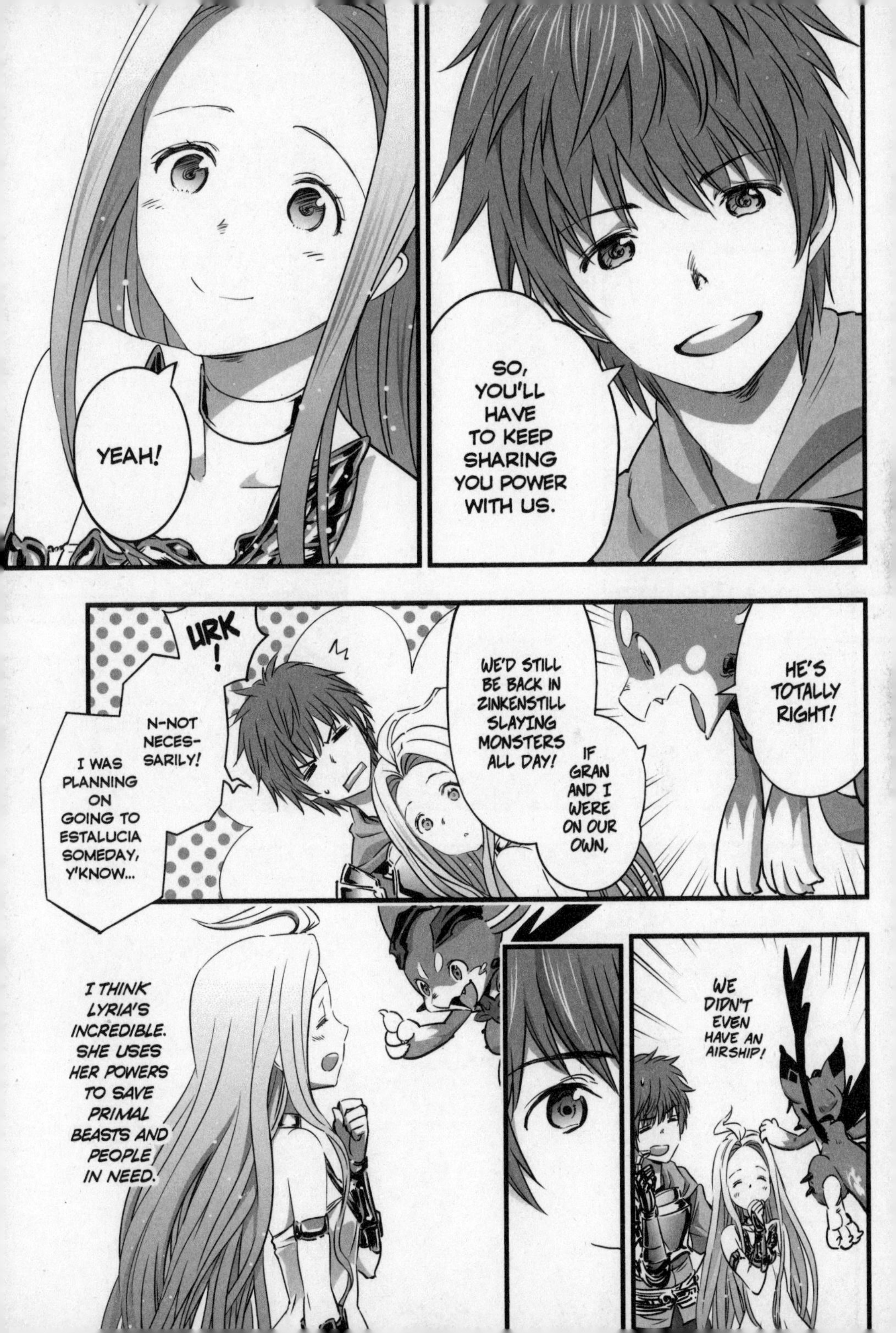
SO, YOU'LL HAVE TO KEEP SHARING YOU POWER WITH US.
YEAH!
HE'S TOTALLY RIGHT!
IF GRAN AND I WERE ON OUR OWN,
WE'D STILL BE BACK IN ZINKENSTILL SLAYING MONSTERS ALL DAY!
URK!
N-NOT NECES-SARILY!
I WAS PLANNING ON GOING TO ESTALUCIA SOMEDAY, Y'KNOW...
WE DIDN'T EVEN HAVE AN AIRSHIP!
I THINK LYRIA'S INCREDIBLE. SHE USES HER POWERS TO SAVE PRIMAL BEASTS AND PEOPLE IN NEED.

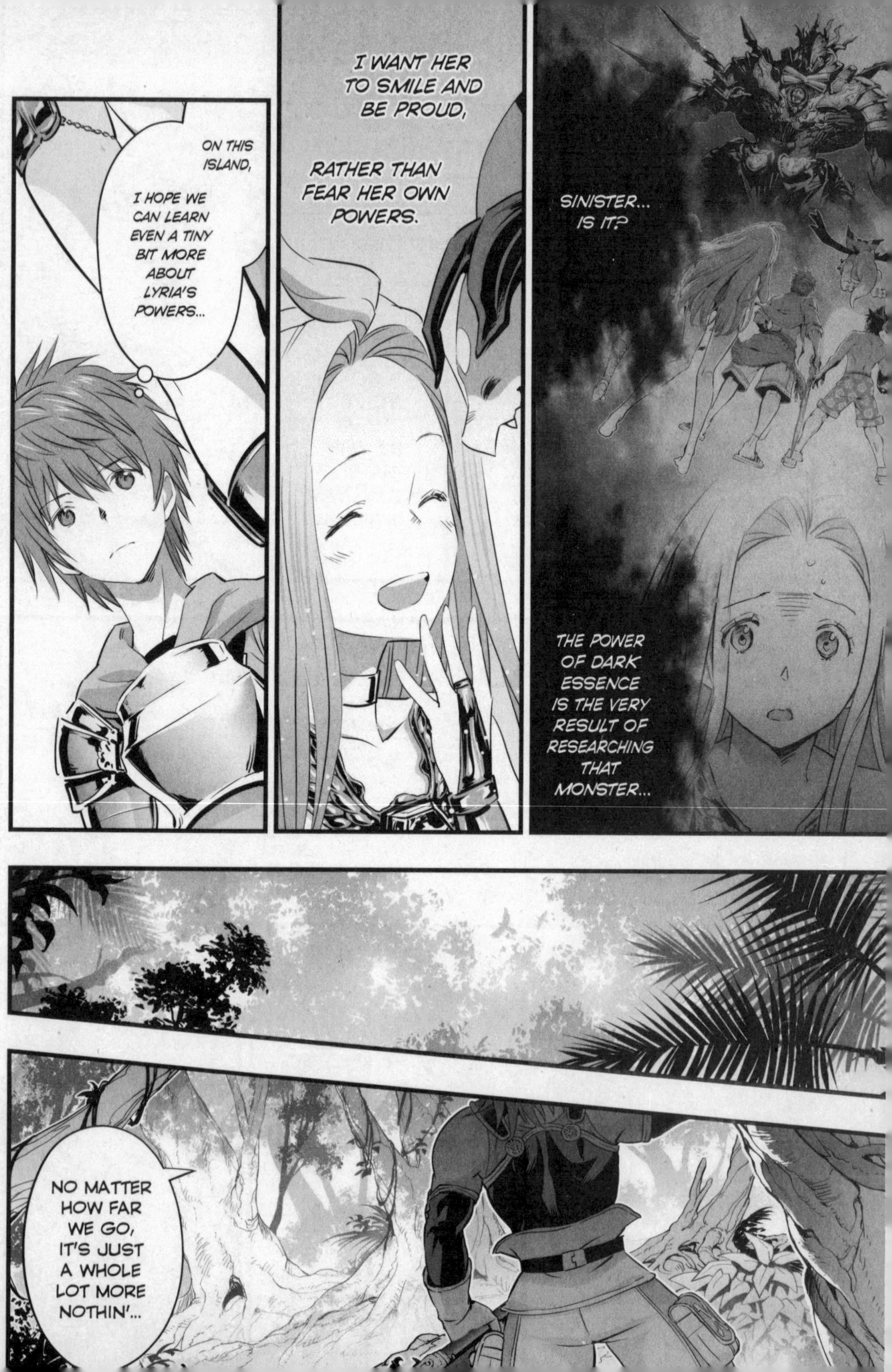
SINISTER... IS IT?
THE POWER OF DARK ESSENCE IS THE VERY RESULT OF RESEARCHING THAT MONSTER...
I WANT HER TO SMILE AND BE PROUD,
RATHER THAN FEAR HER OWN POWERS.
ON THIS ISLAND, I HOPE WE CAN LEARN EVEN A TINY BIT MORE ABOUT LYRIA'S POWERS...
NO MATTER HOW FAR WE GO, IT'S JUST A WHOLE LOT MORE NOTHIN'...

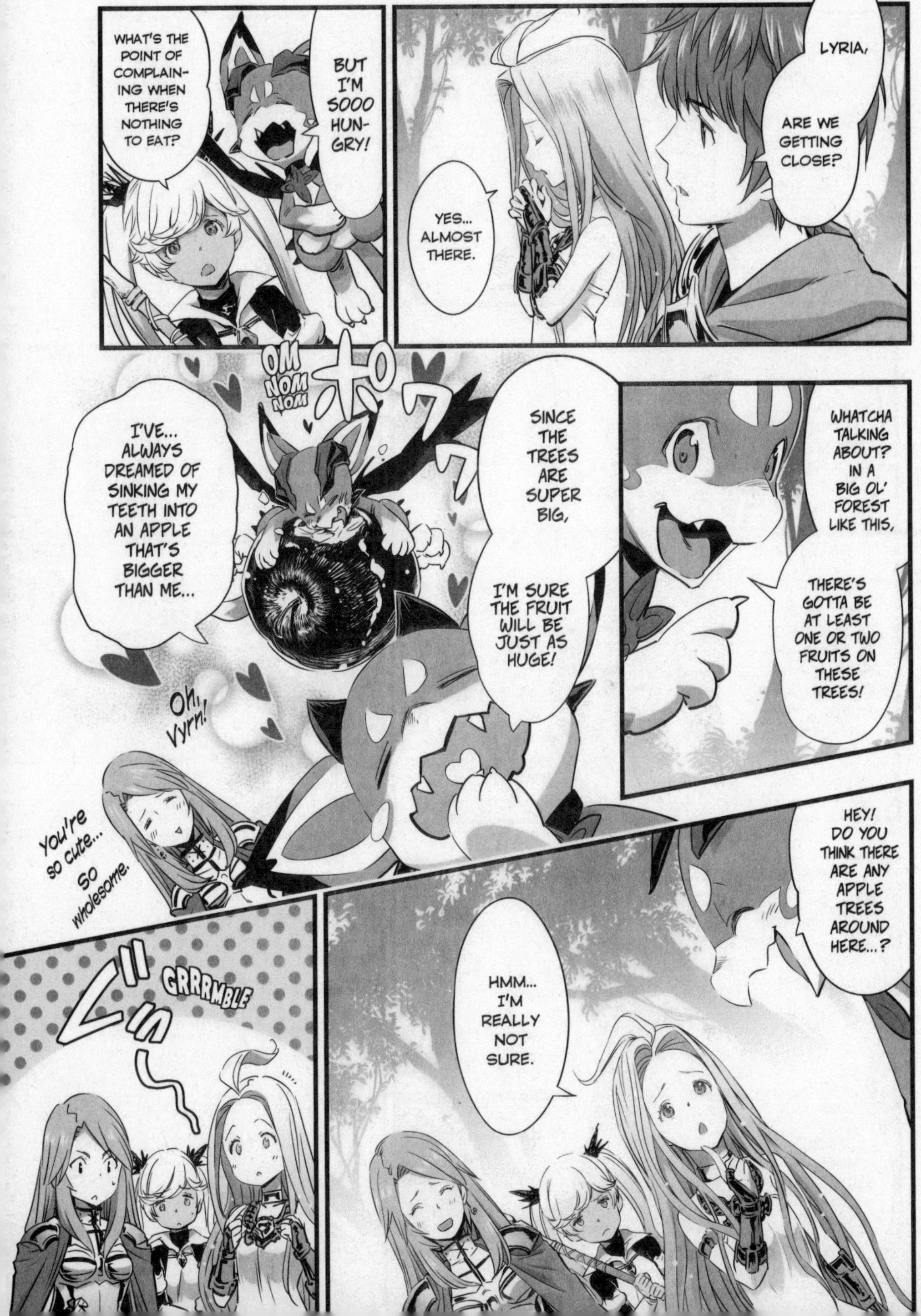
LYRIA,
ARE WE GETTING CLOSE?
YES... ALMOST THERE.
BUT I'M SOOO HUNGRY!
WHAT'S THE POINT OF COMPLAINING WHEN THERE'S NOTHING TO EAT?
WHATCHA TALKING ABOUT? IN A BIG OL' FOREST LIKE THIS,
THERE'S GOTTA BE AT LEAST ONE OR TWO FRUITS ON THESE TREES!
SINCE THE TREES ARE SUPER BIG,
I'M SURE THE FRUIT WILL BE JUST AS HUGE!
OM NOM NOM
I'VE... ALWAYS DREAMED OF SINKING MY TEETH INTO AN APPLE THAT'S BIGGER THAN ME...
Oh, Vyrn!
You're so cute... So wholesome.
HEY! DO YOU THINK THERE ARE ANY APPLE TREES AROUND HERE...?
HMM... I'M REALLY NOT SURE.
GRRRMBLE

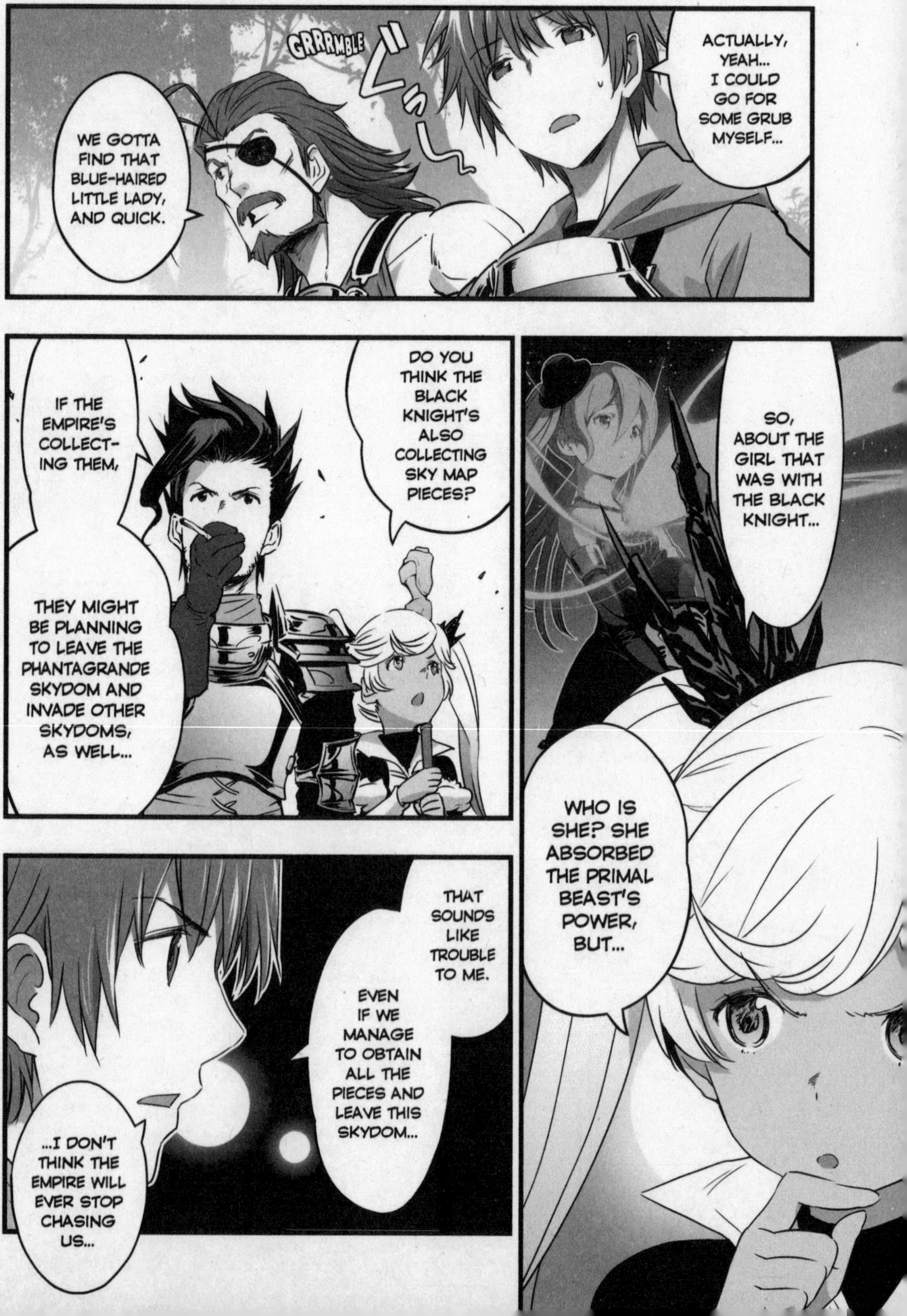
ACTUALLY, YEAH... I COULD GO FOR SOME GRUB MYSELF...
GRRRMBLE
WE GOTTA FIND THAT BLUE-HAIRED LITTLE LADY, AND QUICK.
SO, ABOUT THE GIRL THAT WAS WITH THE BLACK KNIGHT...
WHO IS SHE? SHE ABSORBED THE PRIMAL BEAST'S POWER, BUT...
DO YOU THINK THE BLACK KNIGHT'S ALSO COLLECTING SKY MAP PIECES?
IF THE EMPIRE'S COLLECT-ING THEM,
THEY MIGHT BE PLANNING TO LEAVE THE PHANTAGRANDE SKYDOM AND INVADE OTHER SKYDOMS, AS WELL...
THAT SOUNDS LIKE TROUBLE TO ME.
EVEN IF WE MANAGE TO OBTAIN ALL THE PIECES AND LEAVE THIS SKYDOM...
...I DON'T THINK THE EMPIRE WILL EVER STOP CHASING US...

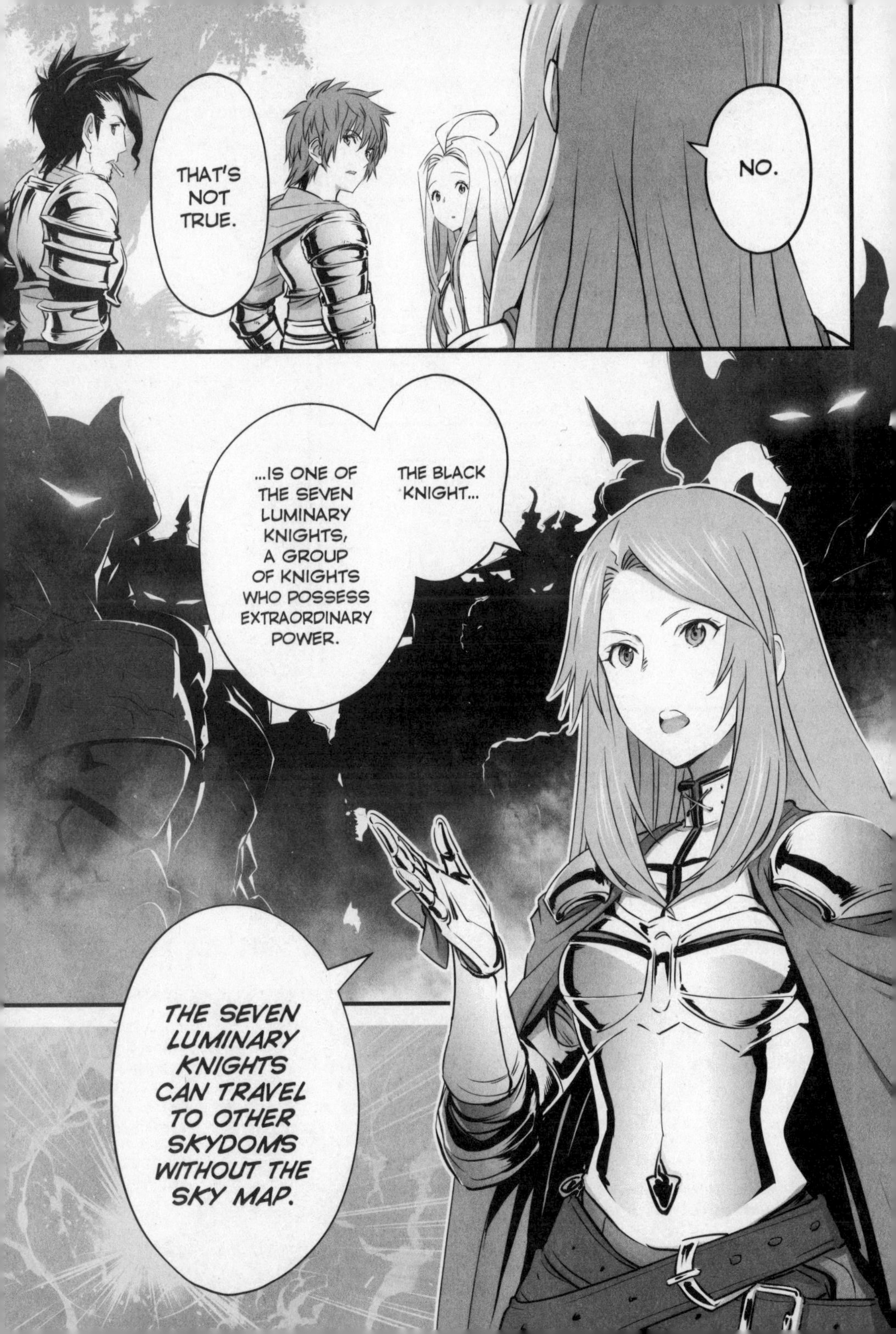
NO.
THAT'S NOT TRUE.
THE BLACK KNIGHT...
...IS ONE OF THE SEVEN LUMINARY KNIGHTS, A GROUP OF KNIGHTS WHO POSSESS EXTRAORDINARY POWER.
THE SEVEN LUMINARY KNIGHTS CAN TRAVEL TO OTHER SKYDOMS WITHOUT THE SKY MAP.

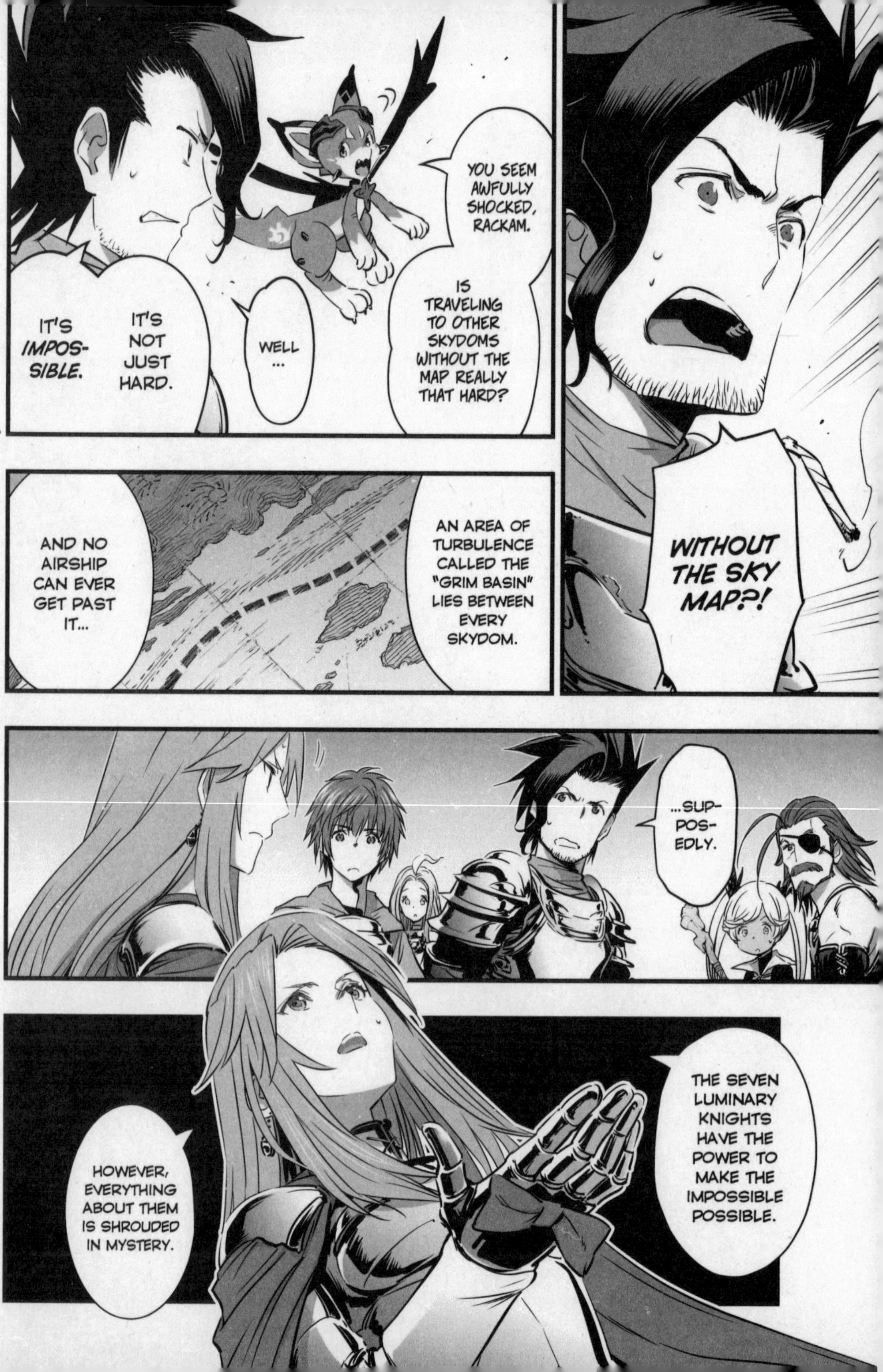
WITHOUT THE SKY MAP?!
YOU SEEM AWFULLY SHOCKED, RACKAM.
IS TRAVELING TO OTHER SKYDOMS WITHOUT THE MAP REALLY THAT HARD?
WELL ...
IT'S NOT JUST HARD.
IT'S *IMPOSSIBLE*.
AN AREA OF TURBULENCE CALLED THE "GRIM BASIN" LIES BETWEEN EVERY SKYDOM.
AND NO AIRSHIP CAN EVER GET PAST IT...
...SUPPOSEDLY.
THE SEVEN LUMINARY KNIGHTS HAVE THE POWER TO MAKE THE IMPOSSIBLE POSSIBLE.
HOWEVER, EVERYTHING ABOUT THEM IS SHROUDED IN MYSTERY.

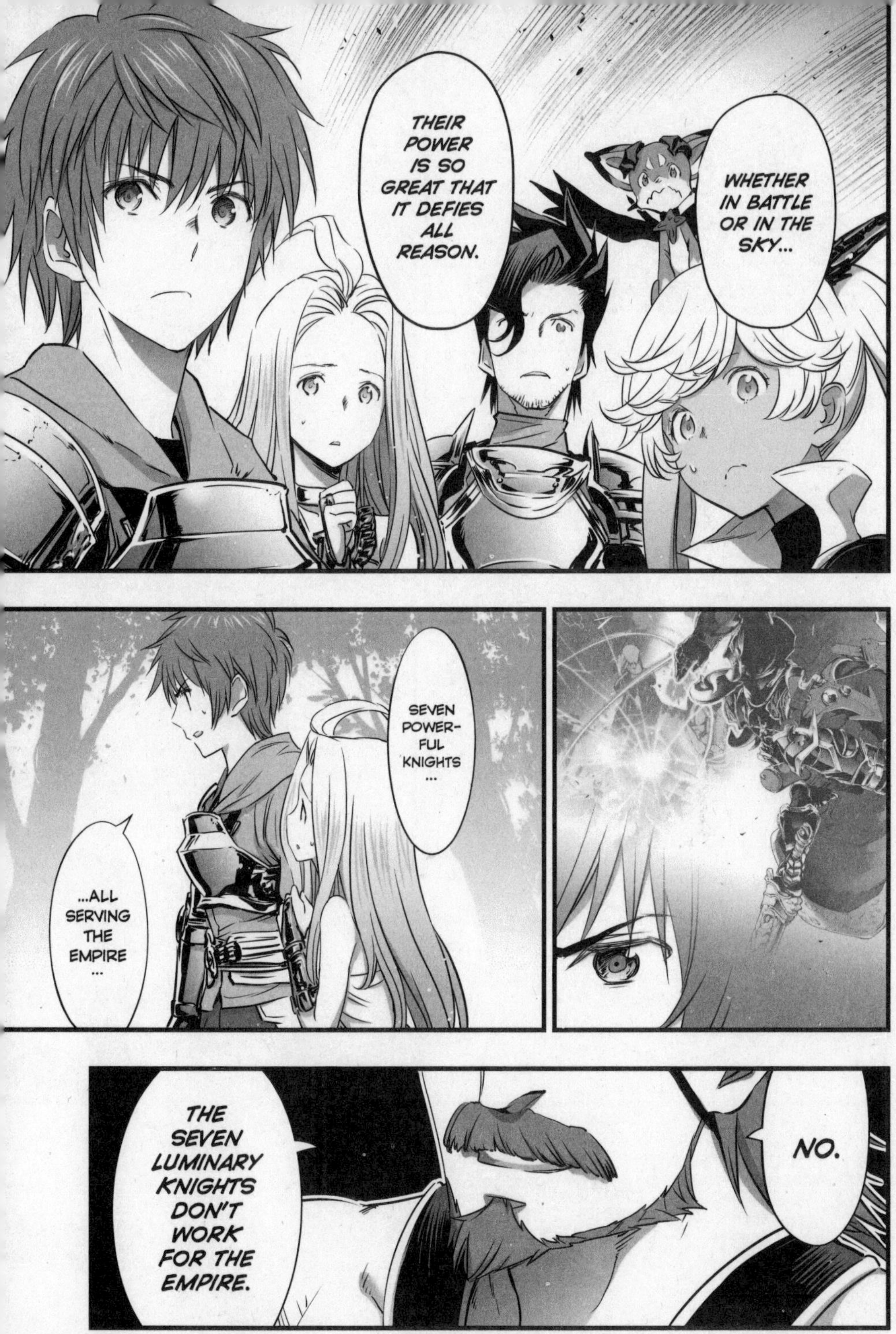

WHETHER IN BATTLE OR IN THE SKY...
THEIR POWER IS SO GREAT THAT IT DEFIES ALL REASON.
SEVEN POWER-FUL KNIGHTS...
...ALL SERVING THE EMPIRE...
NO.
THE SEVEN LUMINARY KNIGHTS DON'T WORK FOR THE EMPIRE.

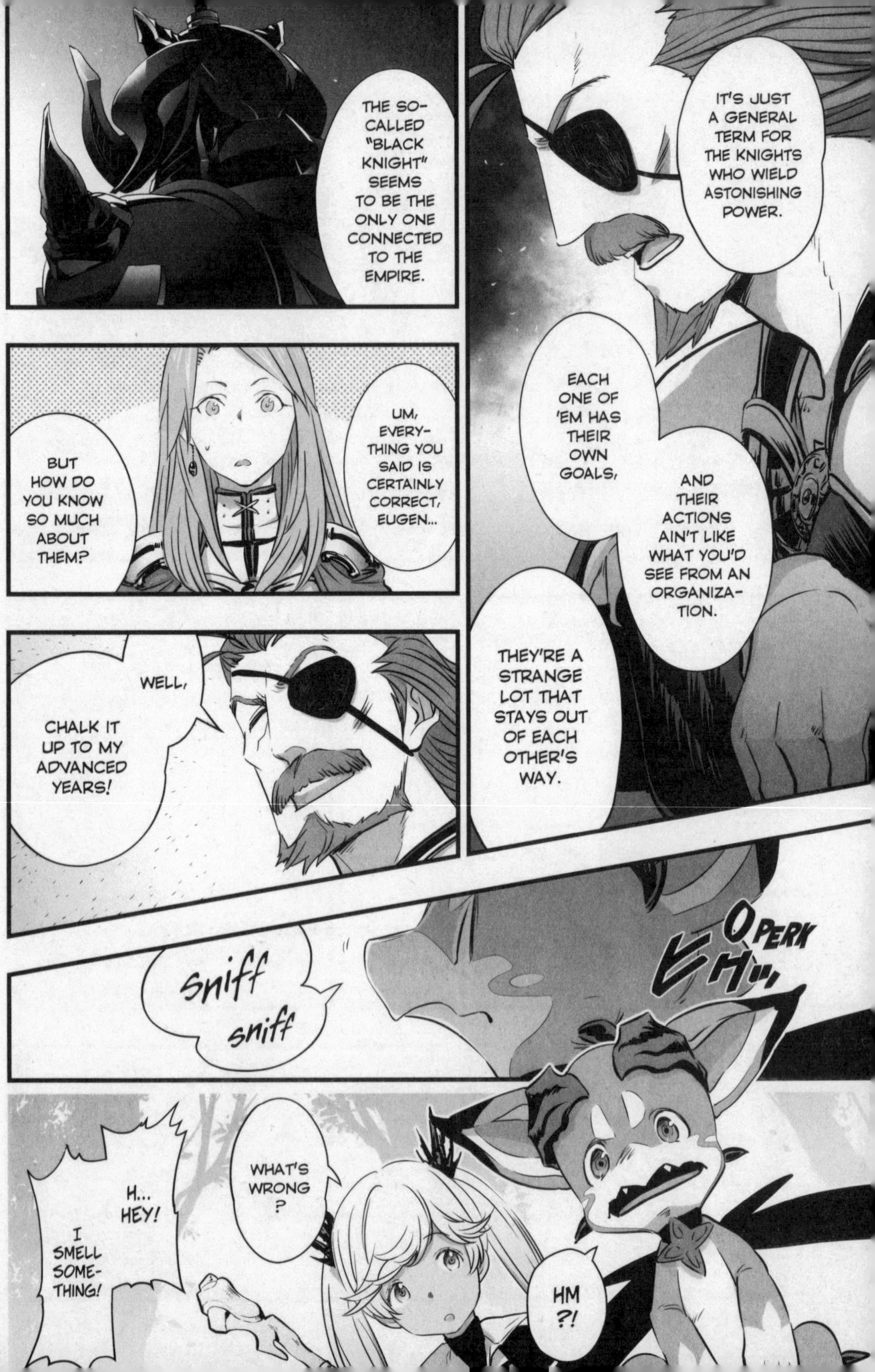
IT'S JUST A GENERAL TERM FOR THE KNIGHTS WHO WIELD ASTONISHING POWER.
EACH ONE OF 'EM HAS THEIR OWN GOALS,
AND THEIR ACTIONS AIN'T LIKE WHAT YOU'D SEE FROM AN ORGANIZA-TION.
THEY'RE A STRANGE LOT THAT STAYS OUT OF EACH OTHER'S WAY.
THE SO-CALLED "BLACK KNIGHT" SEEMS TO BE THE ONLY ONE CONNECTED TO THE EMPIRE.
UM, EVERY-THING YOU SAID IS CERTAINLY CORRECT, EUGEN...
BUT HOW DO YOU KNOW SO MUCH ABOUT THEM?
WELL,
CHALK IT UP TO MY ADVANCED YEARS!
PERK
sniff sniff
HM ?!
WHAT'S WRONG ?
H... HEY!
I SMELL SOME-THING!

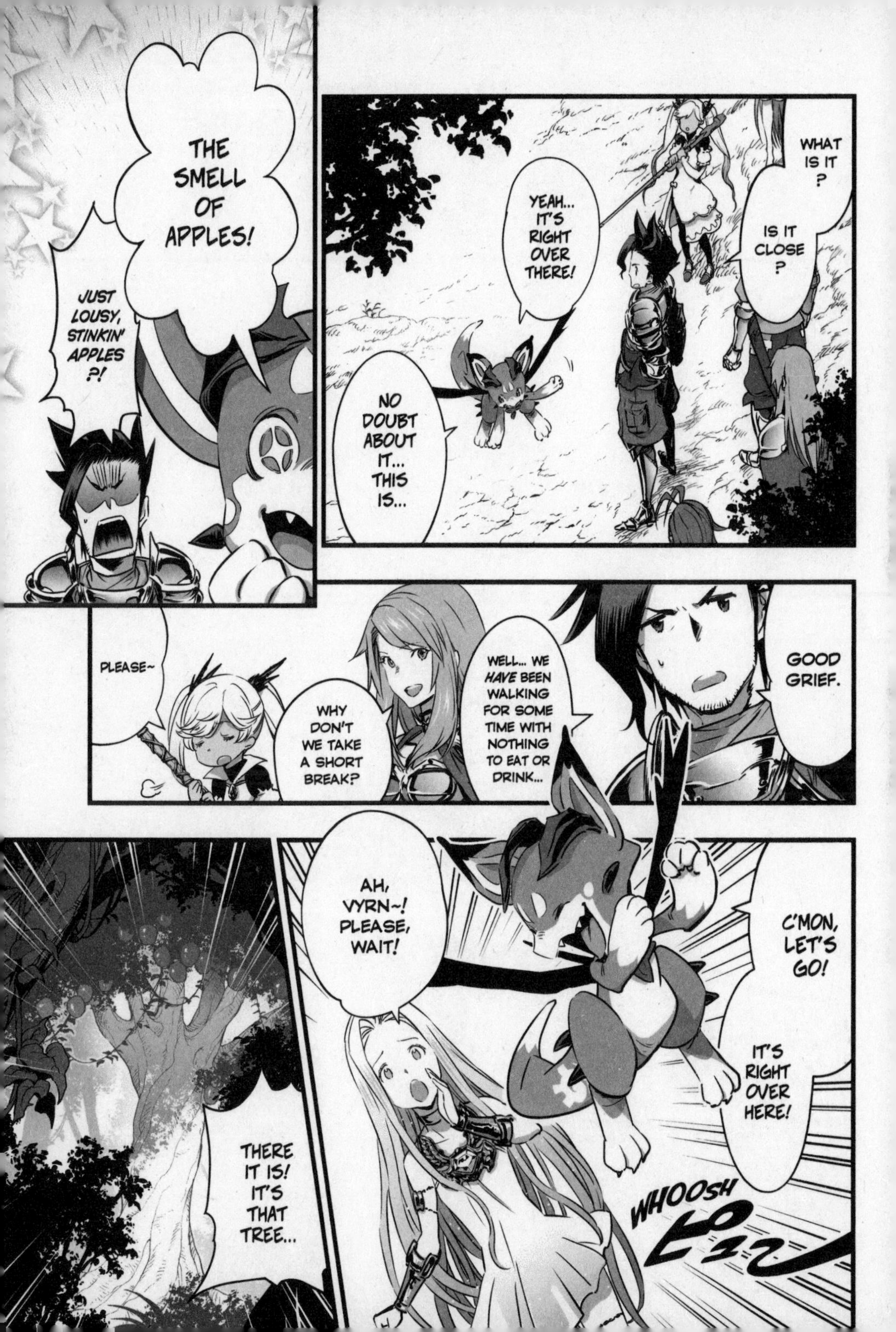
WHAT IS IT? IS IT CLOSE?
YEAH... IT'S RIGHT OVER THERE!
NO DOUBT ABOUT IT... THIS IS...
THE SMELL OF APPLES!
JUST LOUSY, STINKIN' APPLES?!
GOOD GRIEF.
WELL... WE *HAVE* BEEN WALKING FOR SOME TIME WITH NOTHING TO EAT OR DRINK...
WHY DON'T WE TAKE A SHORT BREAK?
PLEASE~
C'MON, LET'S GO!
IT'S RIGHT OVER HERE!
AH, VYRN~! PLEASE, WAIT!
WHOOSH
THERE IT IS! IT'S THAT TREE...

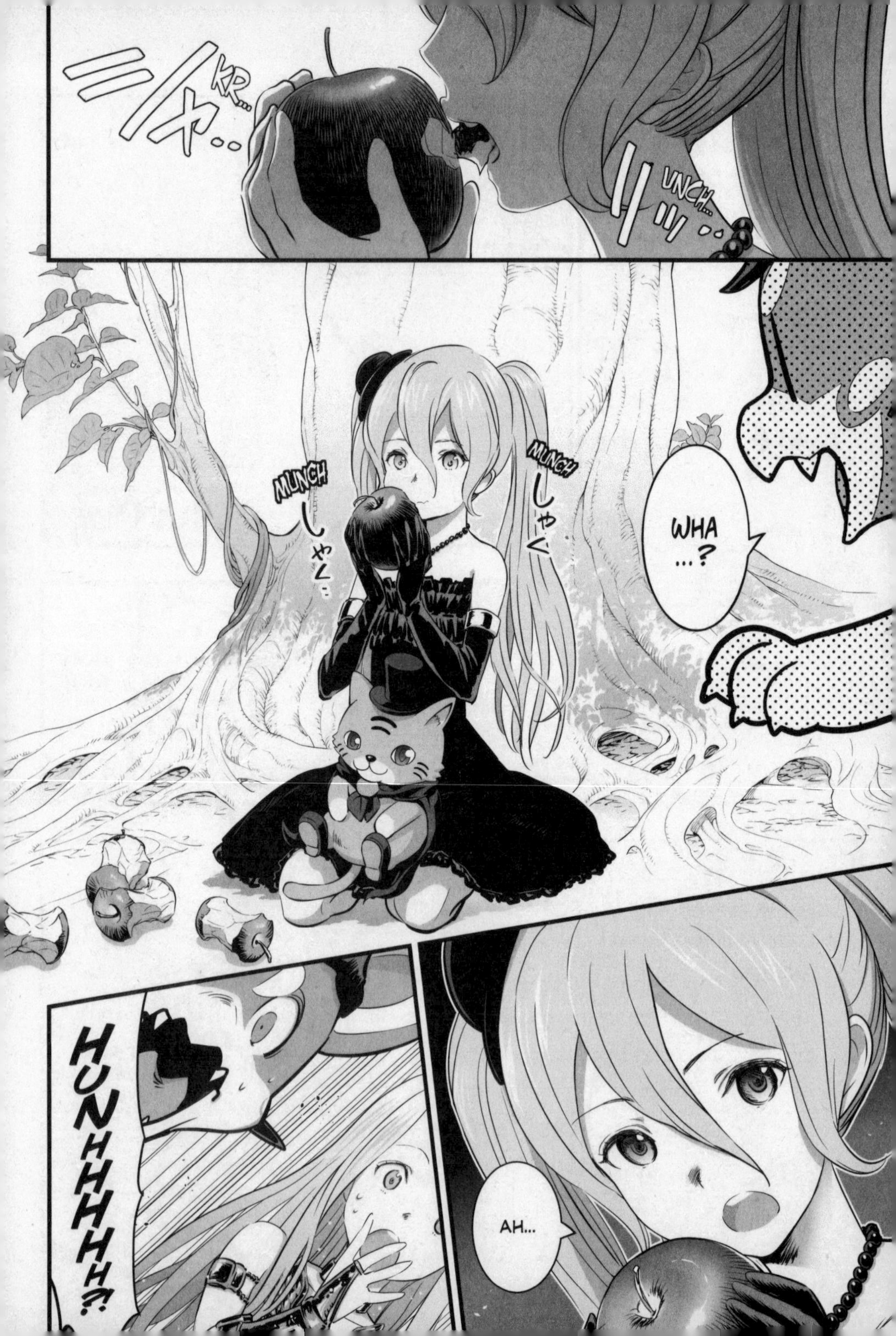
KR...
UNCH...
MUNCH
MUNCH
WHA ...?
AH...
HUNHHHHHH?!

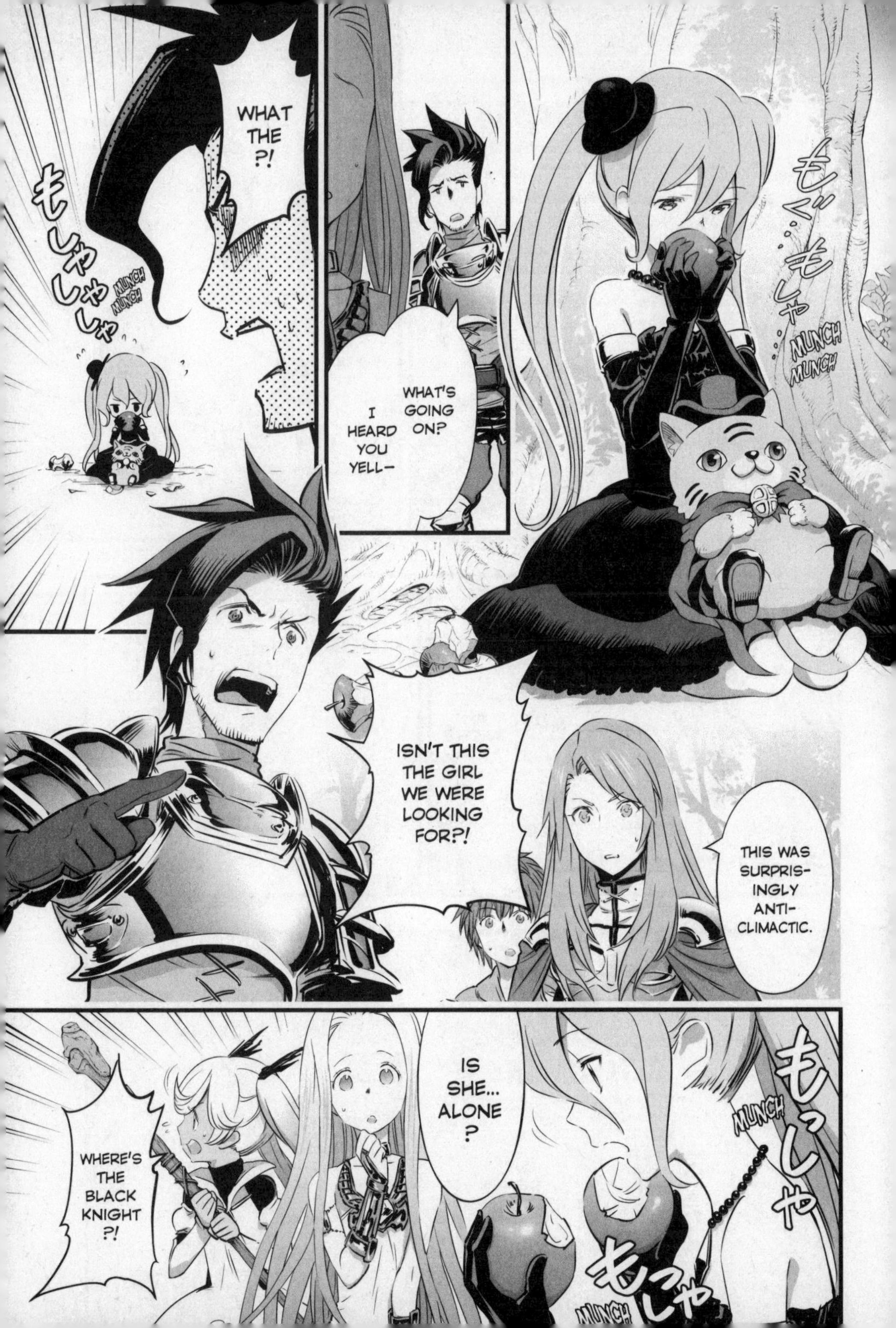
もぐ…もしゃ
MUNCH MUNCH
WHAT'S GOING ON?
I HEARD YOU YELL—
WHAT THE ?!
もしゃしゃしゃ
MUNCH MUNCH
ISN'T THIS THE GIRL WE WERE LOOKING FOR?!
THIS WAS SURPRIS-INGLY ANTI-CLIMACTIC.
もっしゃ
MUNCH
IS SHE... ALONE ?
WHERE'S THE BLACK KNIGHT ?!
もっしゃ
MUNCH

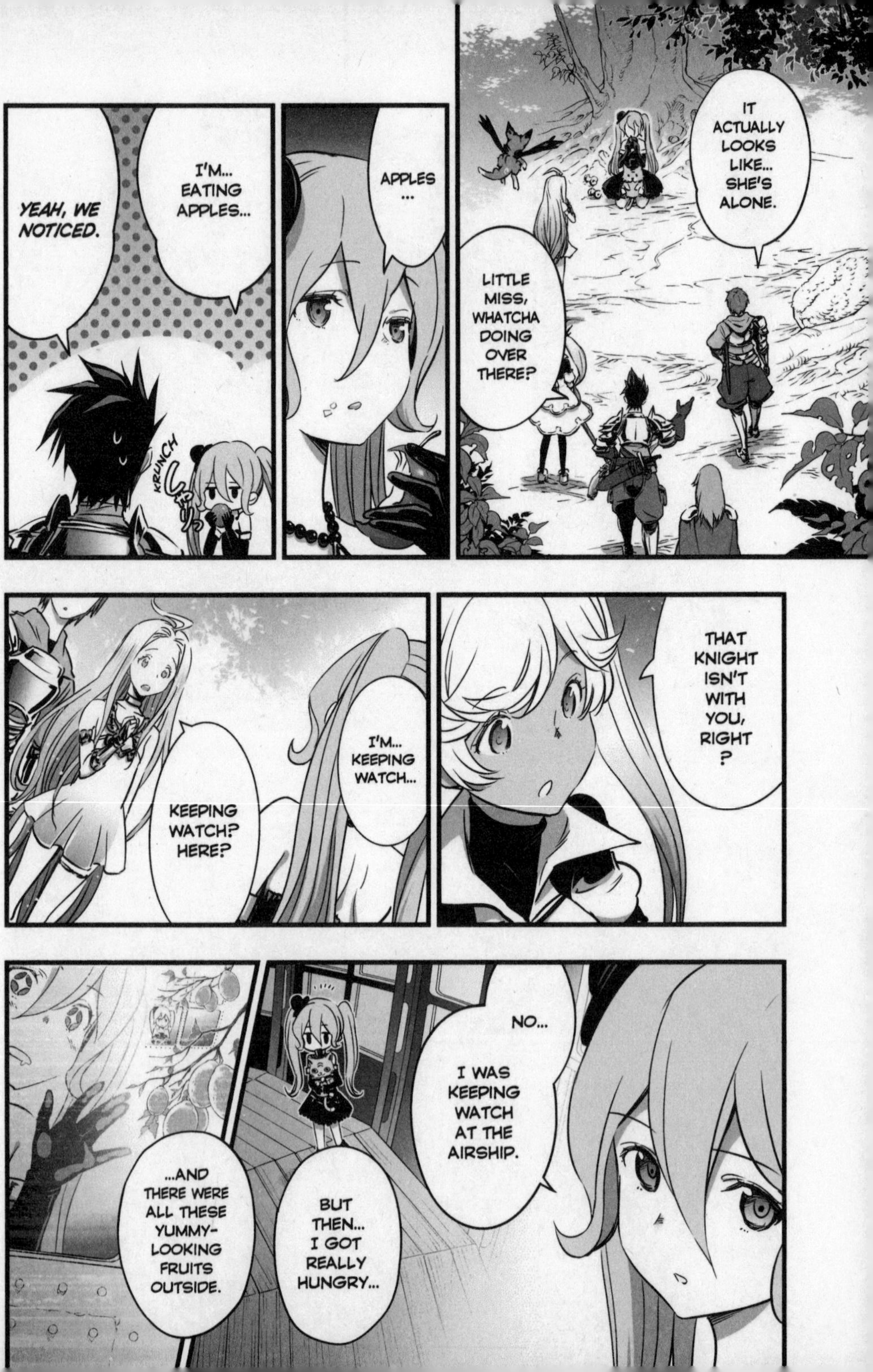
IT ACTUALLY LOOKS LIKE... SHE'S ALONE.
LITTLE MISS, WHATCHA DOING OVER THERE?
APPLES ...
I'M... EATING APPLES...
YEAH, WE NOTICED.
KRUNCH
THAT KNIGHT ISN'T WITH YOU, RIGHT?
I'M... KEEPING WATCH...
KEEPING WATCH? HERE?
NO...
I WAS KEEPING WATCH AT THE AIRSHIP.
BUT THEN... I GOT REALLY HUNGRY...
...AND THERE WERE ALL THESE YUMMY-LOOKING FRUITS OUTSIDE.

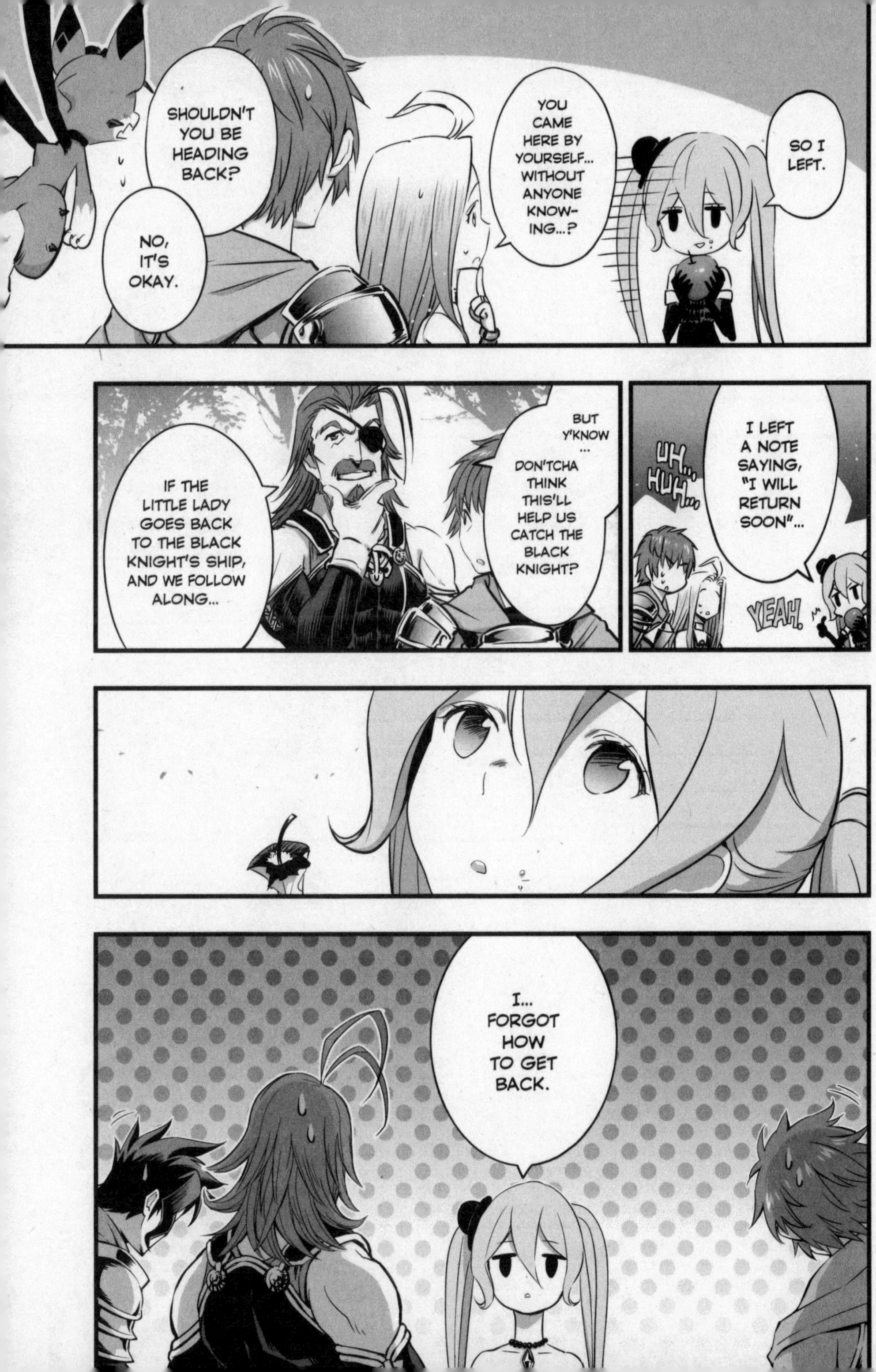
SO I LEFT.
YOU CAME HERE BY YOURSELF... WITHOUT ANYONE KNOWING...?
SHOULDN'T YOU BE HEADING BACK?
NO, IT'S OKAY.
I LEFT A NOTE SAYING, "I WILL RETURN SOON"...
UH... HUH...
YEAH.
BUT Y'KNOW ...
DON'TCHA THINK THIS'LL HELP US CATCH THE BLACK KNIGHT?
IF THE LITTLE LADY GOES BACK TO THE BLACK KNIGHT'S SHIP, AND WE FOLLOW ALONG...
I... FORGOT HOW TO GET BACK.

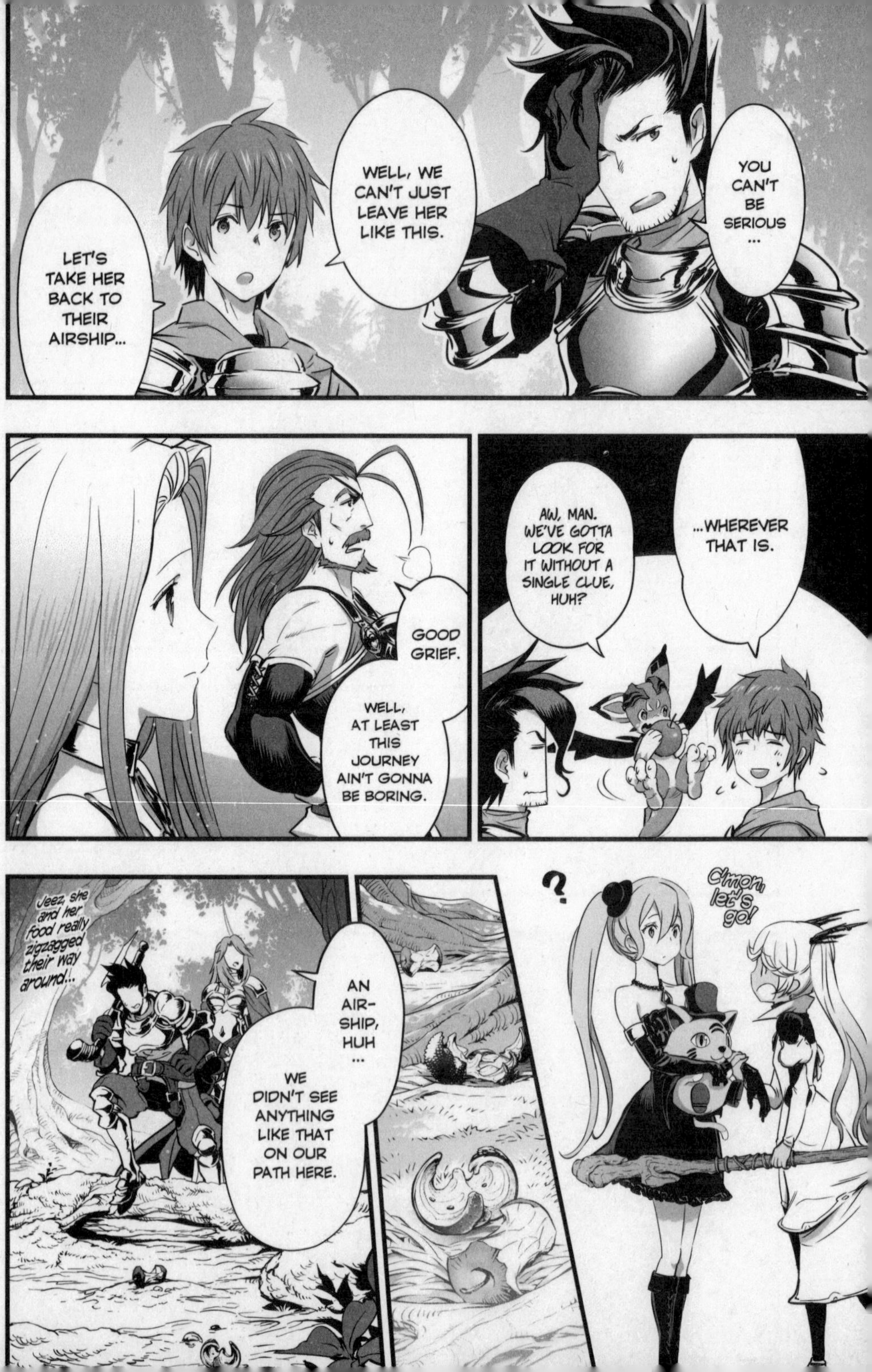
YOU CAN'T BE SERIOUS ...
WELL, WE CAN'T JUST LEAVE HER LIKE THIS.
LET'S TAKE HER BACK TO THEIR AIRSHIP...
...WHEREVER THAT IS.
AW, MAN. WE'VE GOTTA LOOK FOR IT WITHOUT A SINGLE CLUE, HUH?
GOOD GRIEF.
WELL, AT LEAST THIS JOURNEY AIN'T GONNA BE BORING.
C'mon, let's go!
?
AN AIR-SHIP, HUH ...
WE DIDN'T SEE ANYTHING LIKE THAT ON OUR PATH HERE.
Jeez, she and her food really zigzagged their way around!!...

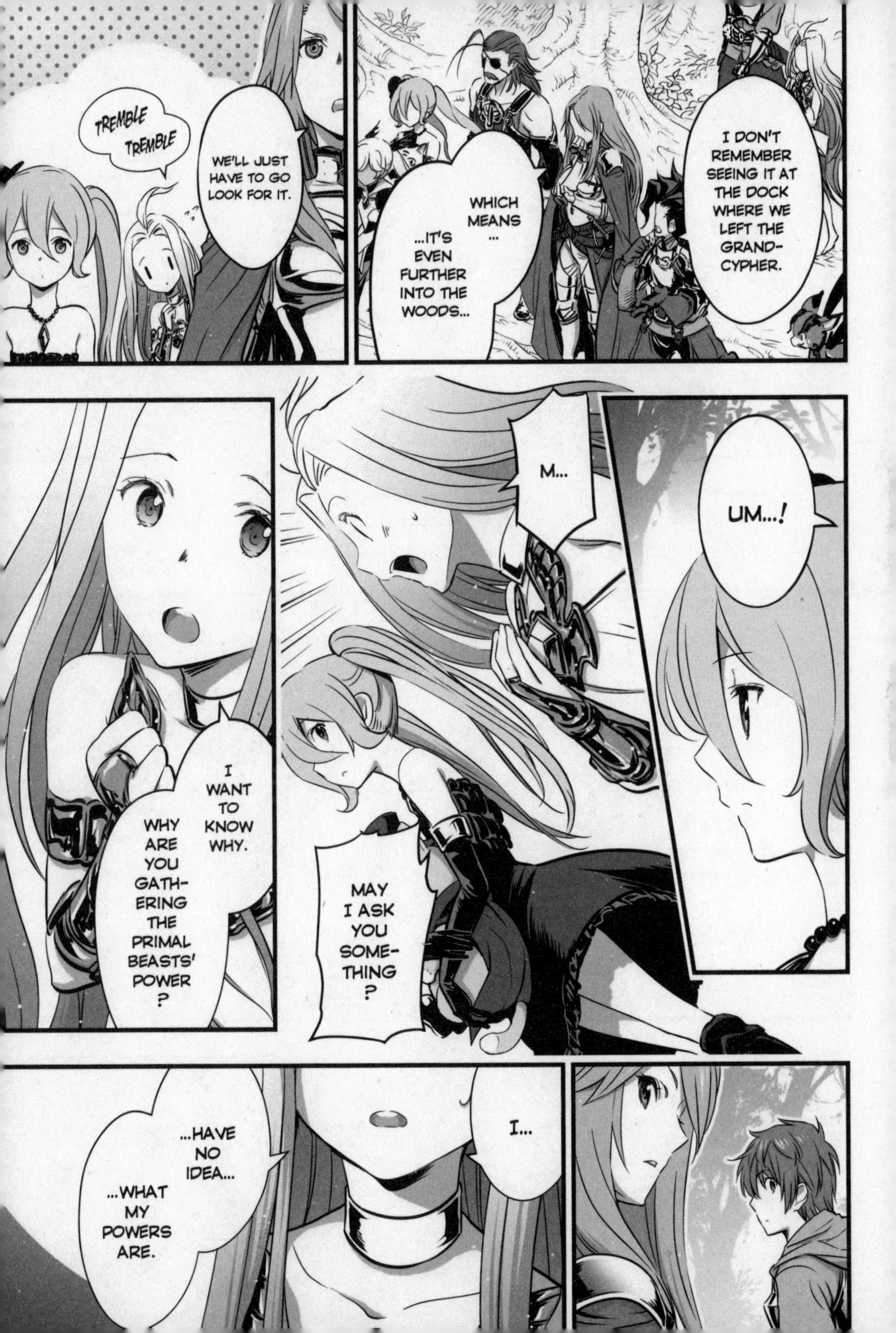
I DON'T REMEMBER SEEING IT AT THE DOCK WHERE WE LEFT THE GRAND-CYPHER.
WHICH MEANS ...
...IT'S EVEN FURTHER INTO THE WOODS...
WE'LL JUST HAVE TO GO LOOK FOR IT.
TREMBLE TREMBLE
UM...!
M...
MAY I ASK YOU SOMETHING?
I WANT TO KNOW WHY.
WHY ARE YOU GATHERING THE PRIMAL BEASTS' POWER?
I...
...HAVE NO IDEA...
...WHAT MY POWERS ARE.

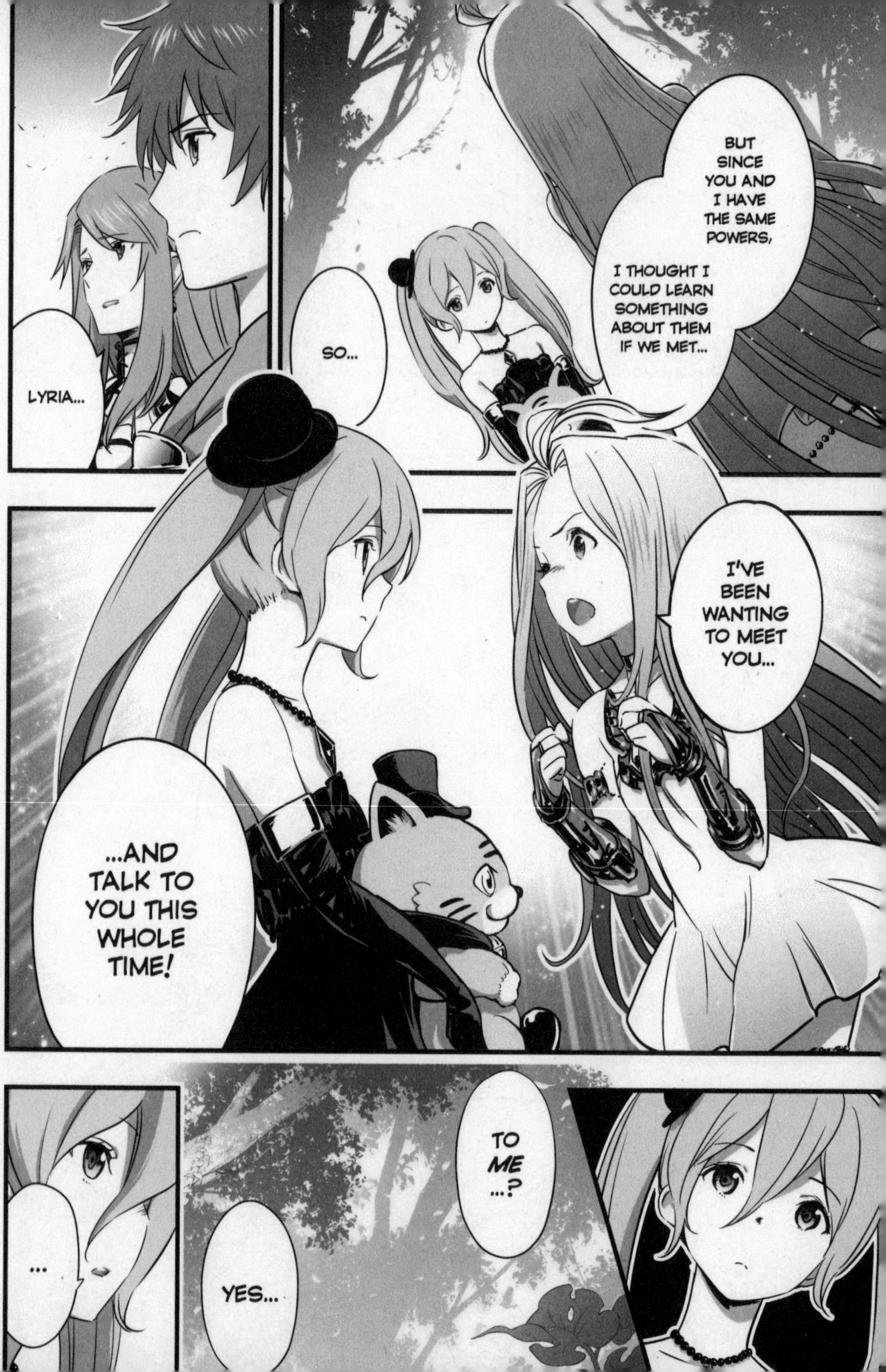
BUT SINCE YOU AND I HAVE THE SAME POWERS,
I THOUGHT I COULD LEARN SOMETHING ABOUT THEM IF WE MET...
SO...
LYRIA...
I'VE BEEN WANTING TO MEET YOU...
...AND TALK TO YOU THIS WHOLE TIME!
TO *ME*...?
YES...
...

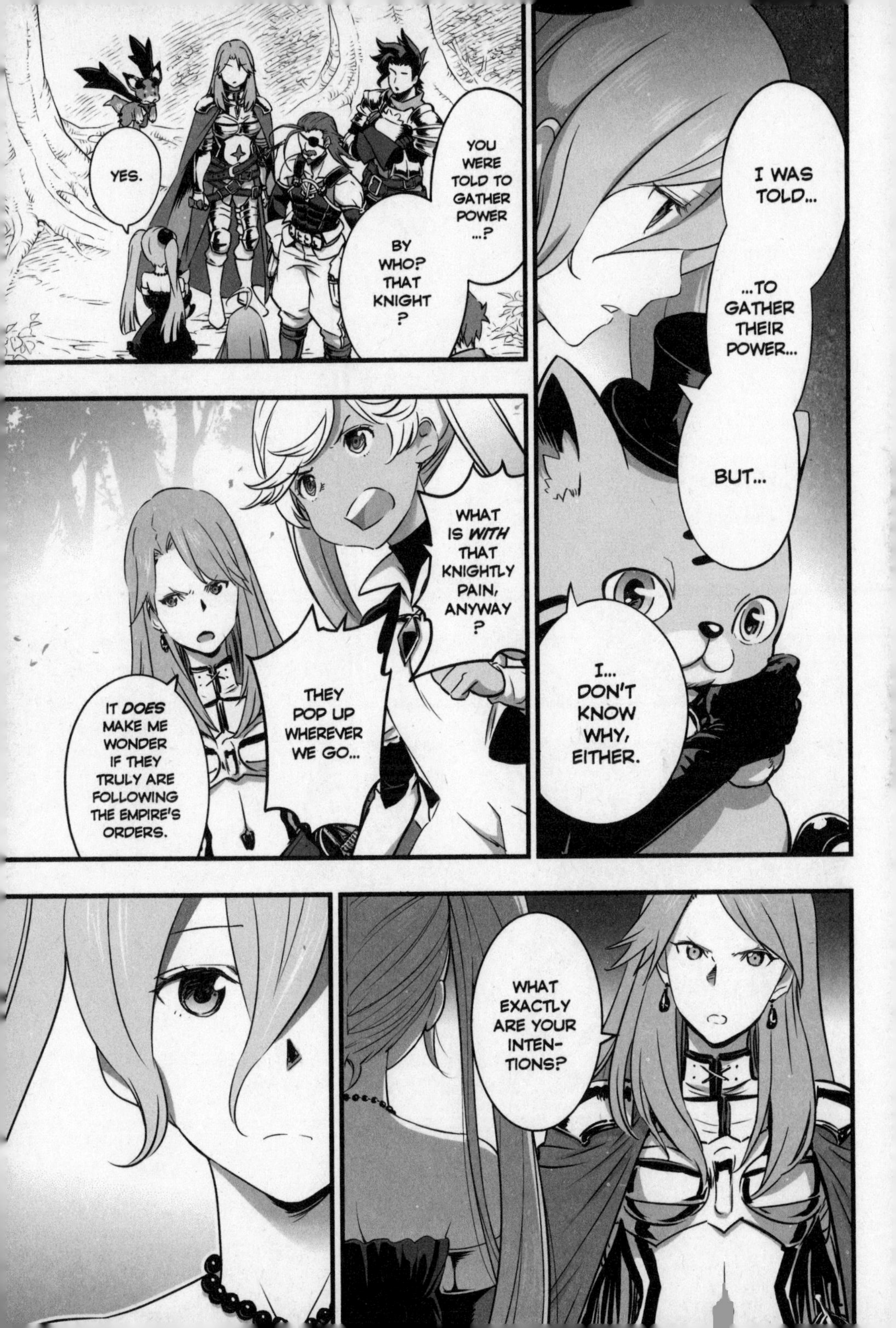
I WAS TOLD...
...TO GATHER THEIR POWER...
BUT...
I... DON'T KNOW WHY, EITHER.
YOU WERE TOLD TO GATHER POWER ...?
BY WHO? THAT KNIGHT?
YES.
WHAT IS *WITH* THAT KNIGHTLY PAIN, ANYWAY?
THEY POP UP WHEREVER WE GO...
IT *DOES* MAKE ME WONDER IF THEY TRULY ARE FOLLOWING THE EMPIRE'S ORDERS.
WHAT EXACTLY ARE YOUR INTEN-TIONS?

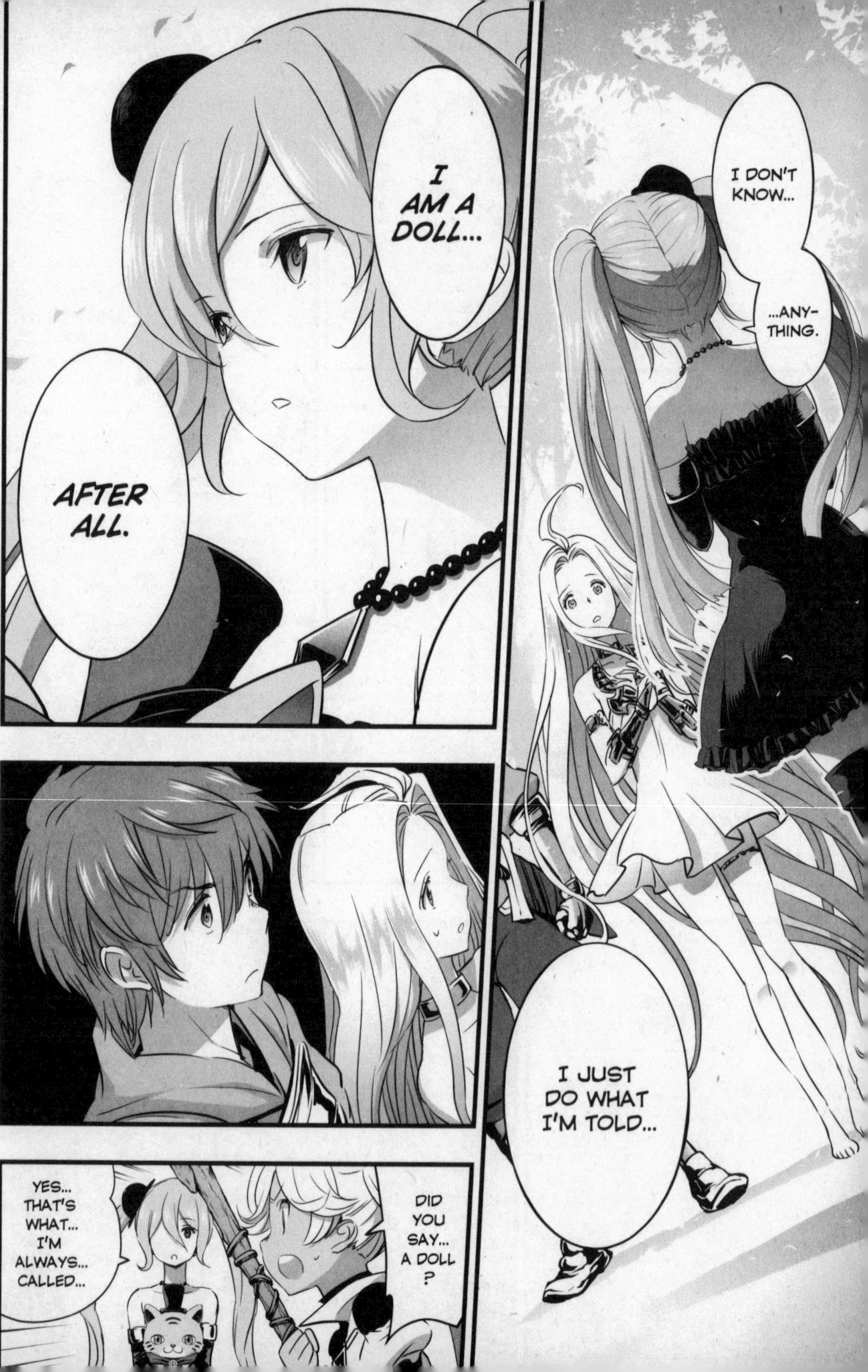
I DON'T KNOW...
...ANY-THING.
I JUST DO WHAT I'M TOLD...
I AM A DOLL...
AFTER ALL.
DID YOU SAY... A DOLL?
YES... THAT'S WHAT... I'M ALWAYS... CALLED...

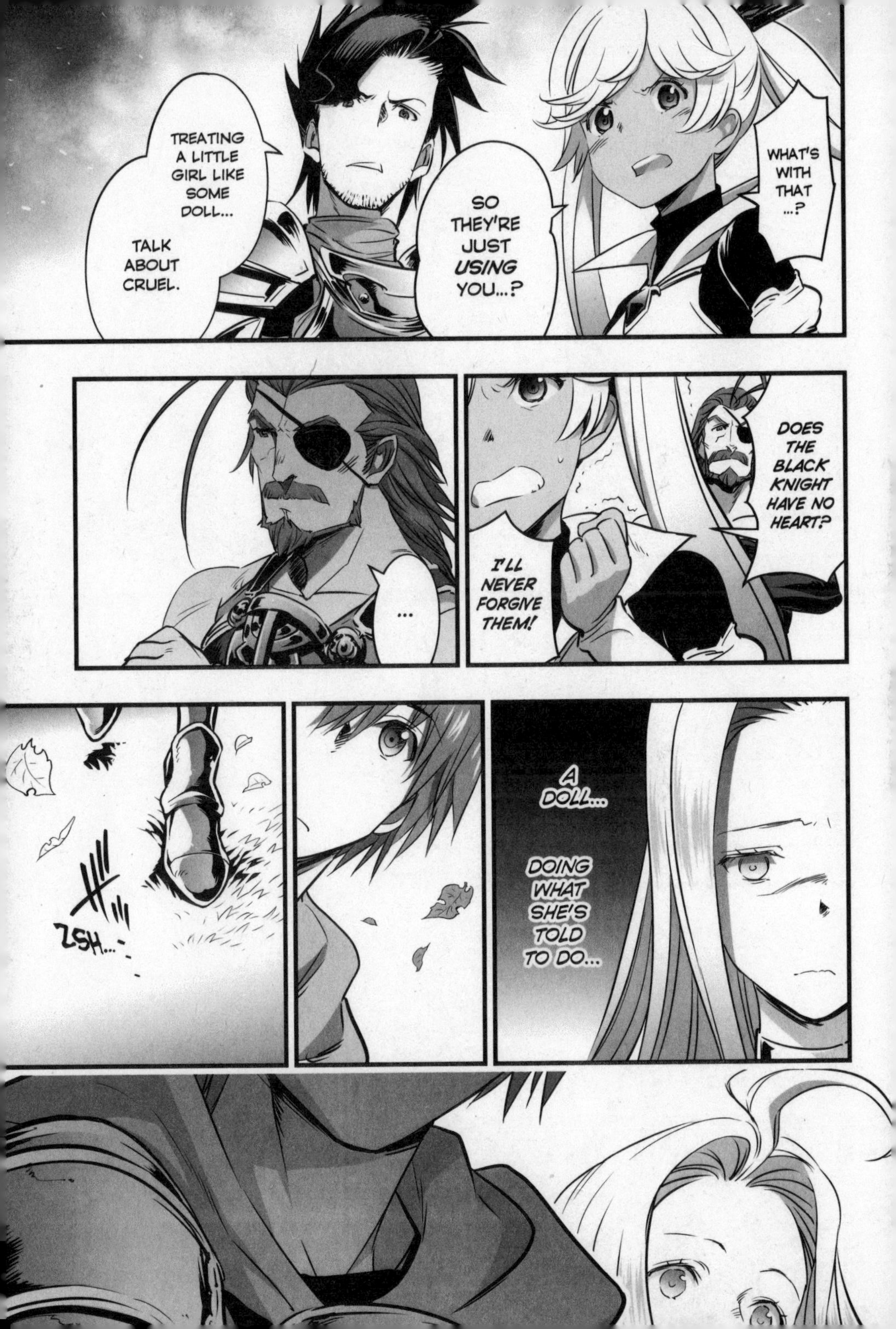
WHAT'S WITH THAT ...?
SO THEY'RE JUST *USING* YOU...?
TREATING A LITTLE GIRL LIKE SOME DOLL...
TALK ABOUT CRUEL.
DOES THE BLACK KNIGHT HAVE NO HEART?
I'LL NEVER FORGIVE THEM!
...
A DOLL...
DOING WHAT SHE'S TOLD TO DO...
ZSH...

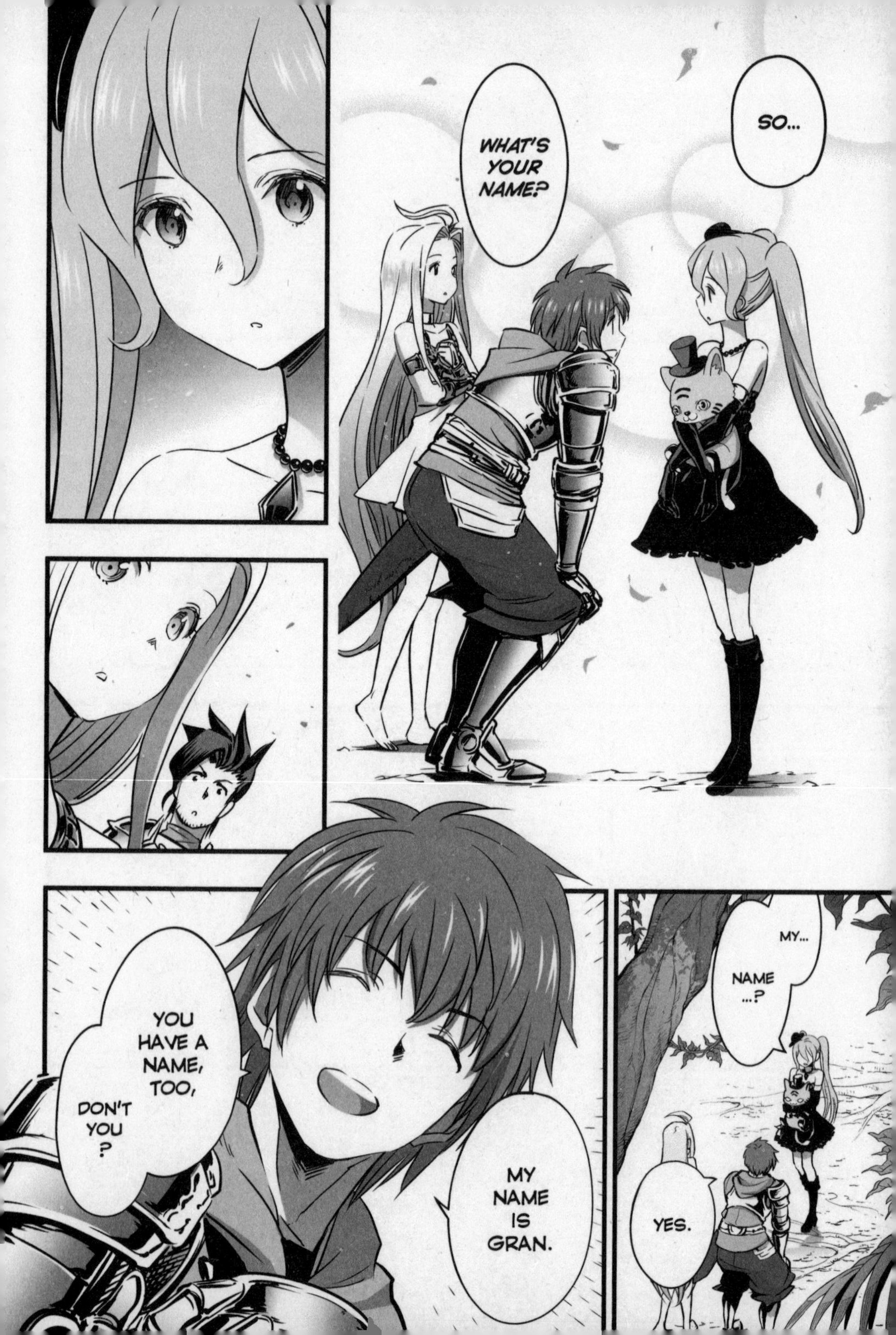
SO...
WHAT'S YOUR NAME?
MY... NAME ...?
YES.
MY NAME IS GRAN.
YOU HAVE A NAME, TOO, DON'T YOU?

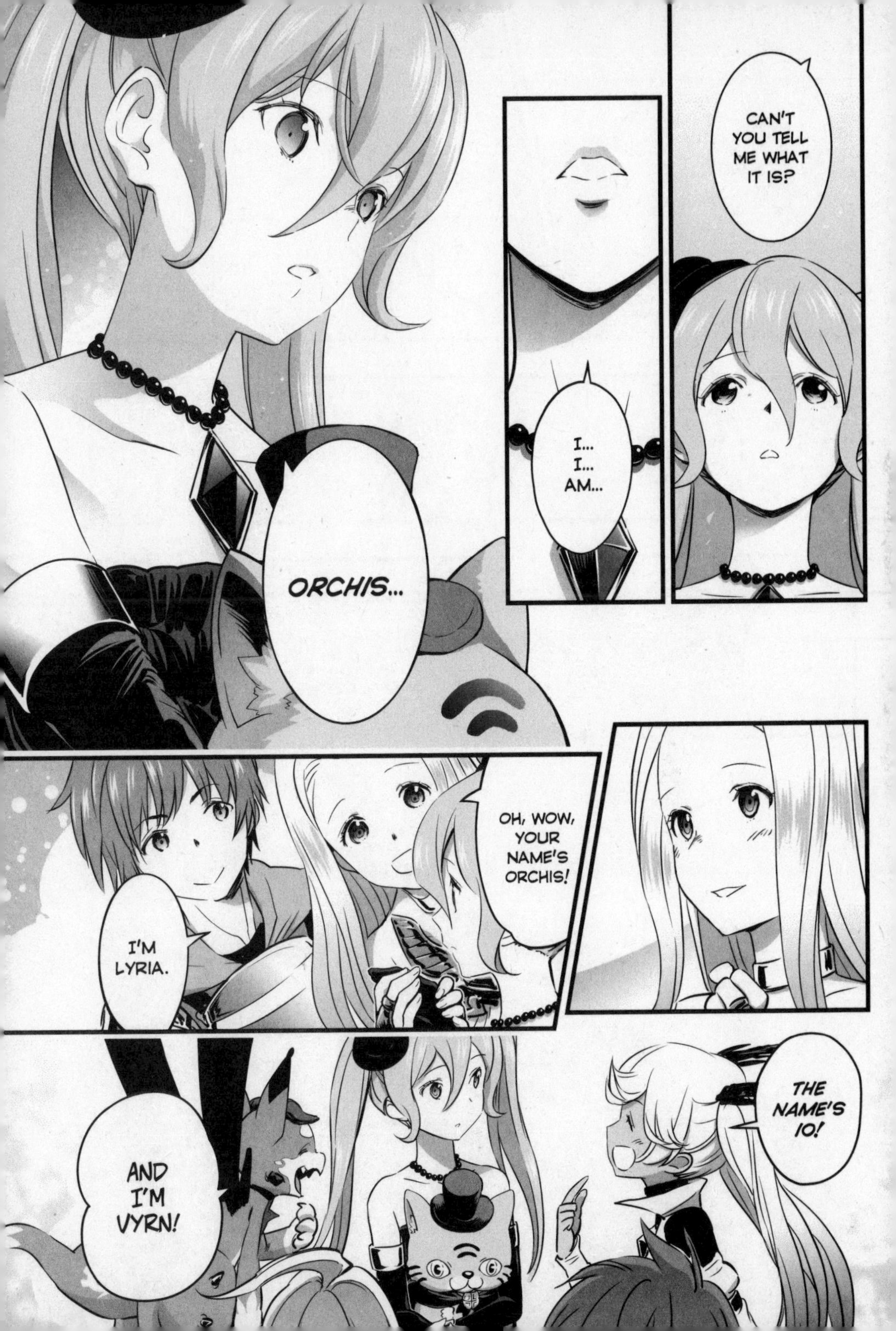
CAN'T YOU TELL ME WHAT IT IS?
I... I... AM...
ORCHIS...
OH, WOW, YOUR NAME'S ORCHIS!
I'M LYRIA.
THE NAME'S IO!
AND I'M VYRN!

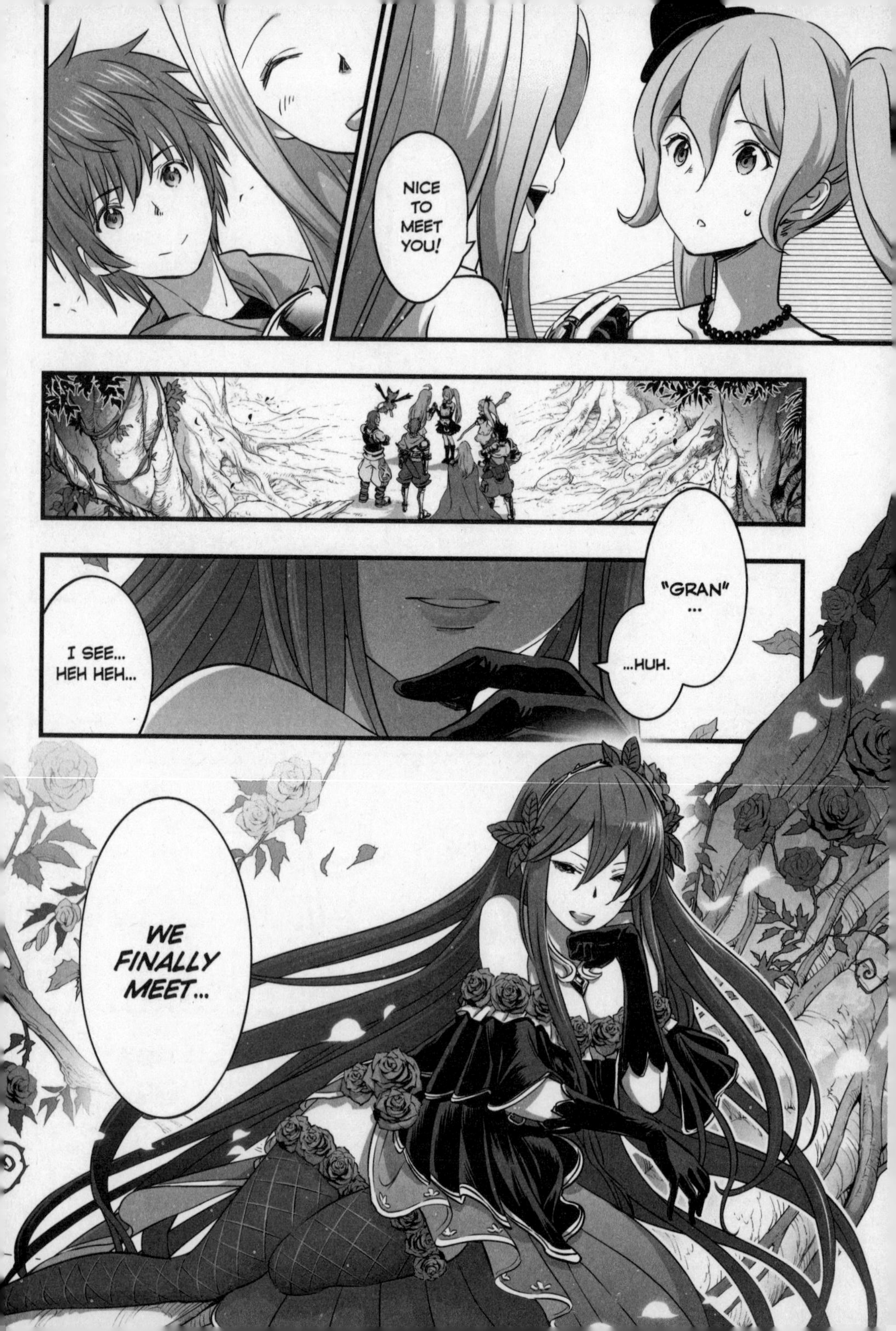
NICE TO MEET YOU!
"GRAN" ...
...HUH.
I SEE... HEH HEH...
WE FINALLY MEET...

GRANBLUE FANTASY
グランブルーファンタジー

GRANBLUE FANTASY
グランブルーファンタジー

CHAPTER 28: Rosetta

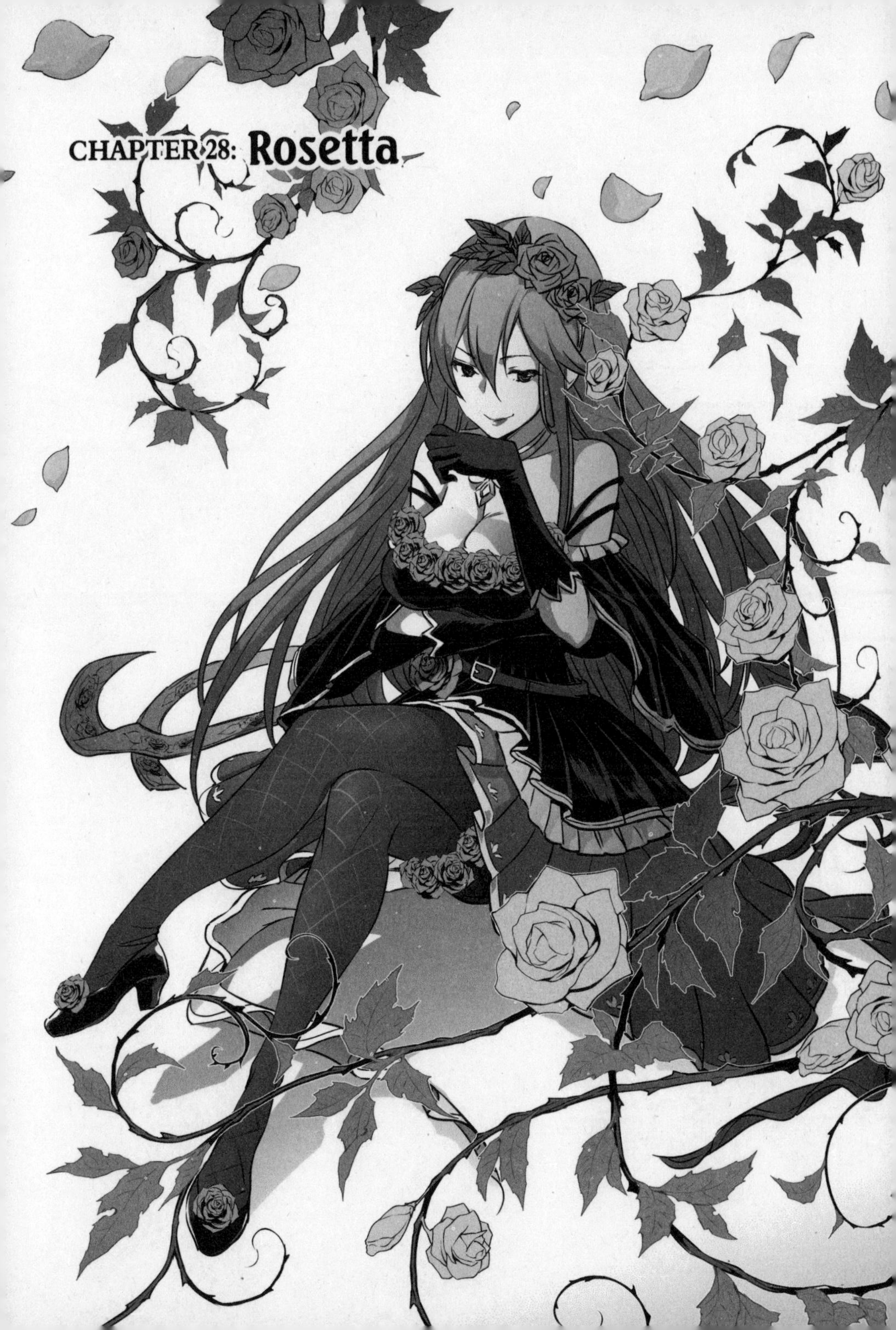

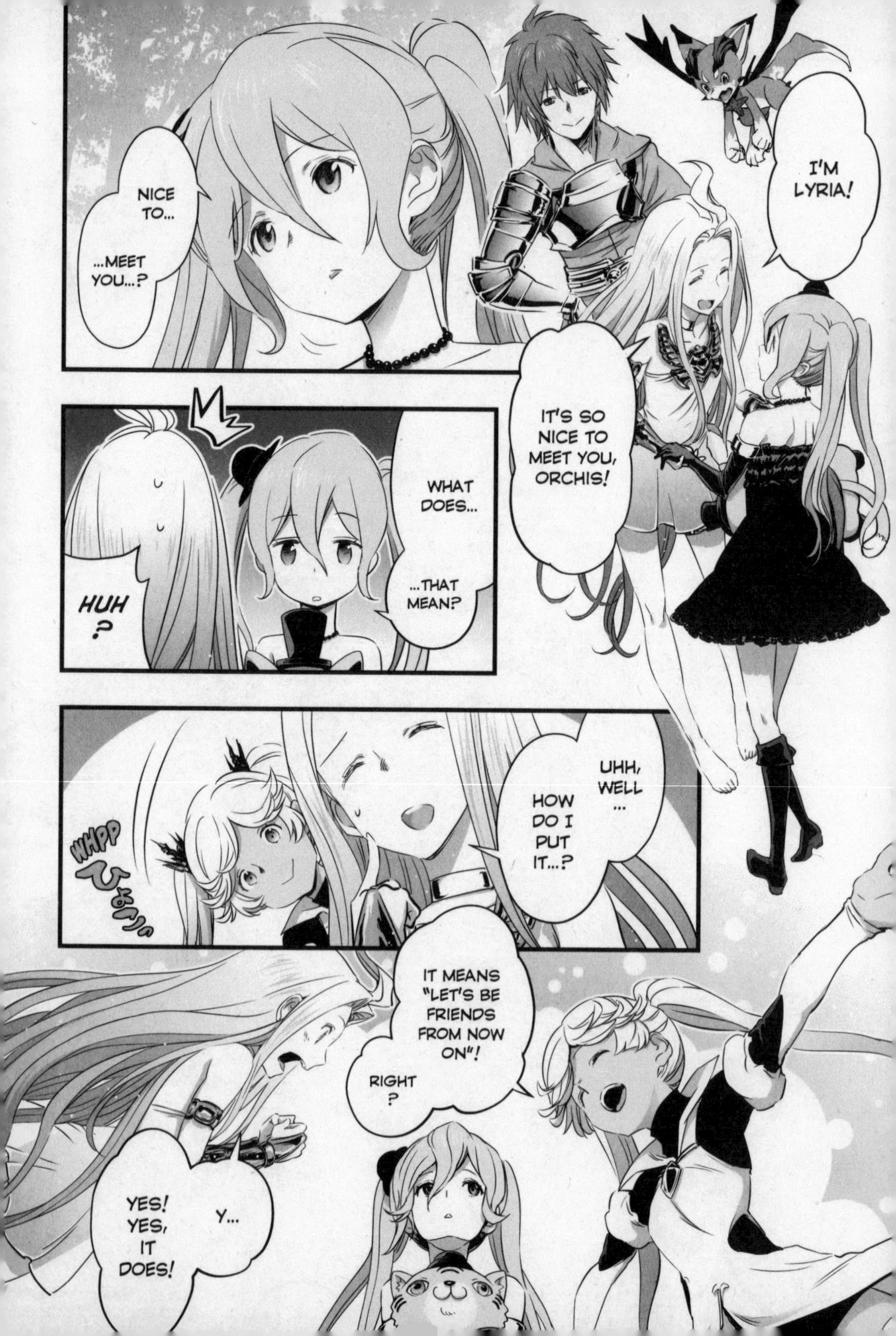
I'M LYRIA!
IT'S SO NICE TO MEET YOU, ORCHIS!
NICE TO...
...MEET YOU...?
WHAT DOES...
...THAT MEAN?
HUH?
UHH, WELL...
HOW DO I PUT IT...?
WHPP
IT MEANS "LET'S BE FRIENDS FROM NOW ON"!
RIGHT?
Y...
YES! YES, IT DOES!

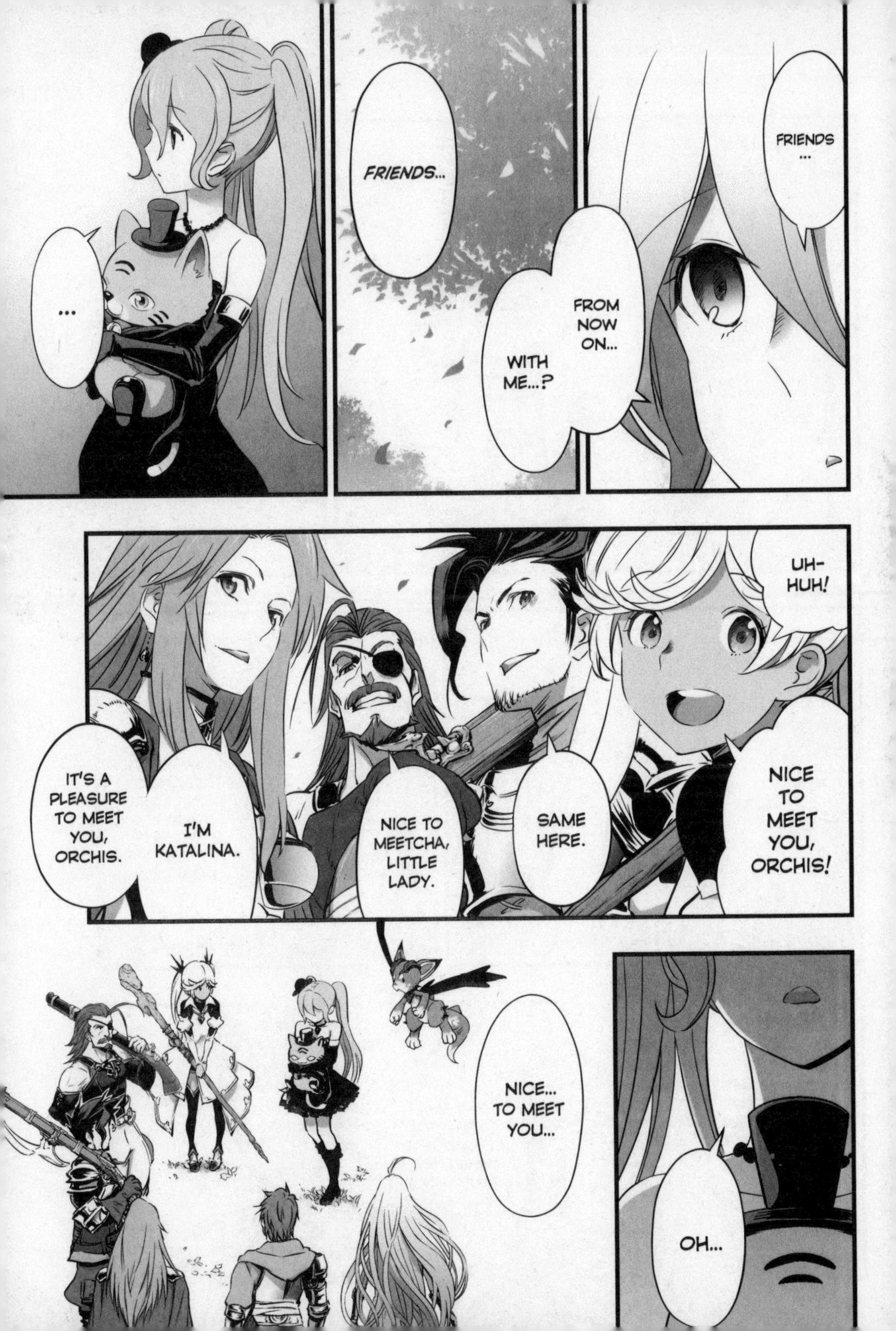
FRIENDS ...
FROM NOW ON...
WITH ME...?
FRIENDS...
...
UH-HUH!
NICE TO MEET YOU, ORCHIS!
SAME HERE.
NICE TO MEETCHA, LITTLE LADY.
I'M KATALINA.
IT'S A PLEASURE TO MEET YOU, ORCHIS.
OH...
NICE... TO MEET YOU...

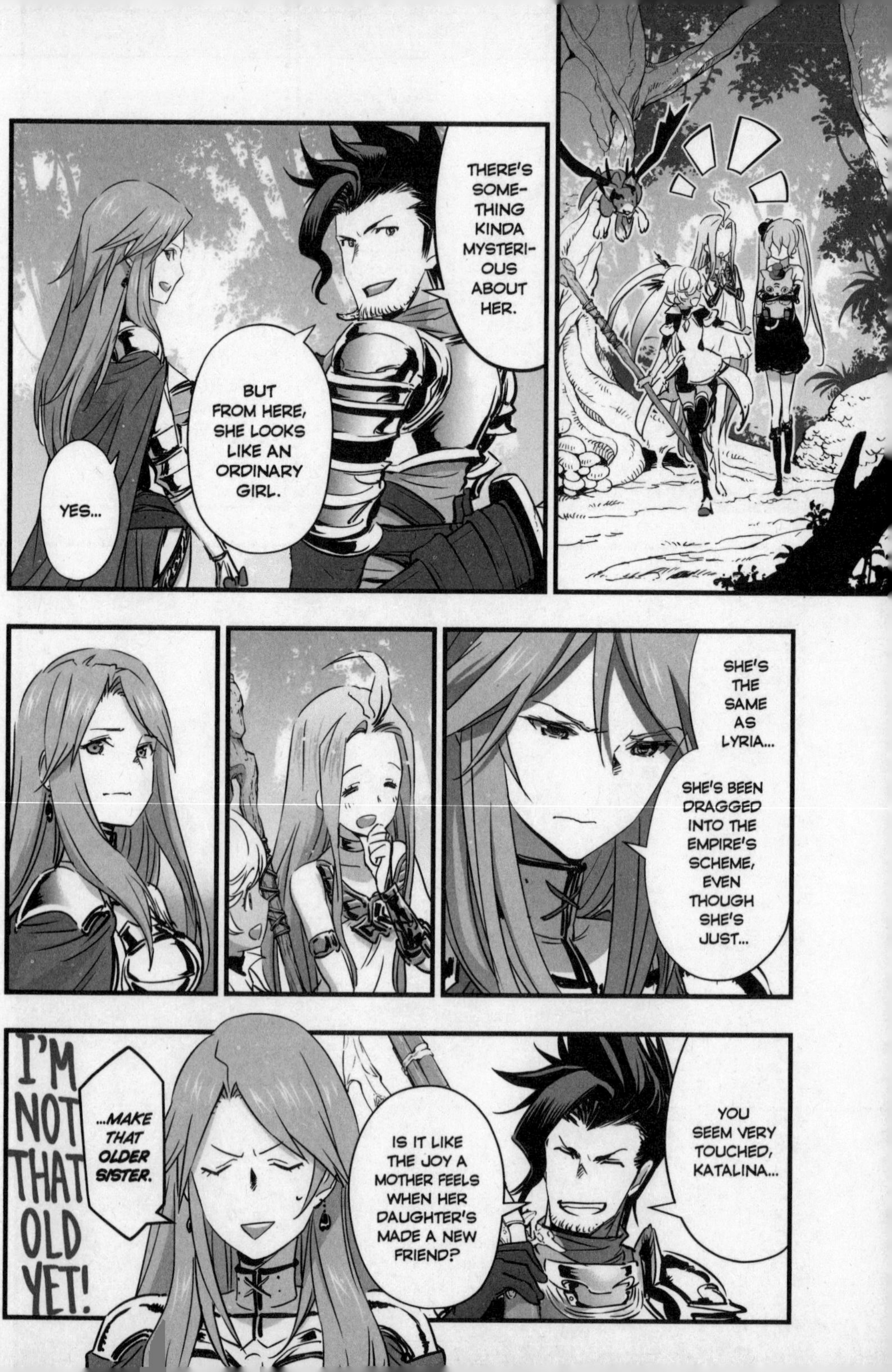
THERE'S SOME-THING KINDA MYSTERI-OUS ABOUT HER.
BUT FROM HERE, SHE LOOKS LIKE AN ORDINARY GIRL.
YES...
SHE'S THE SAME AS LYRIA...
SHE'S BEEN DRAGGED INTO THE EMPIRE'S SCHEME, EVEN THOUGH SHE'S JUST...
YOU SEEM VERY TOUCHED, KATALINA...
IS IT LIKE THE JOY A MOTHER FEELS WHEN HER DAUGHTER'S MADE A NEW FRIEND?
...MAKE THAT OLDER SISTER.
I'M NOT THAT OLD YET!

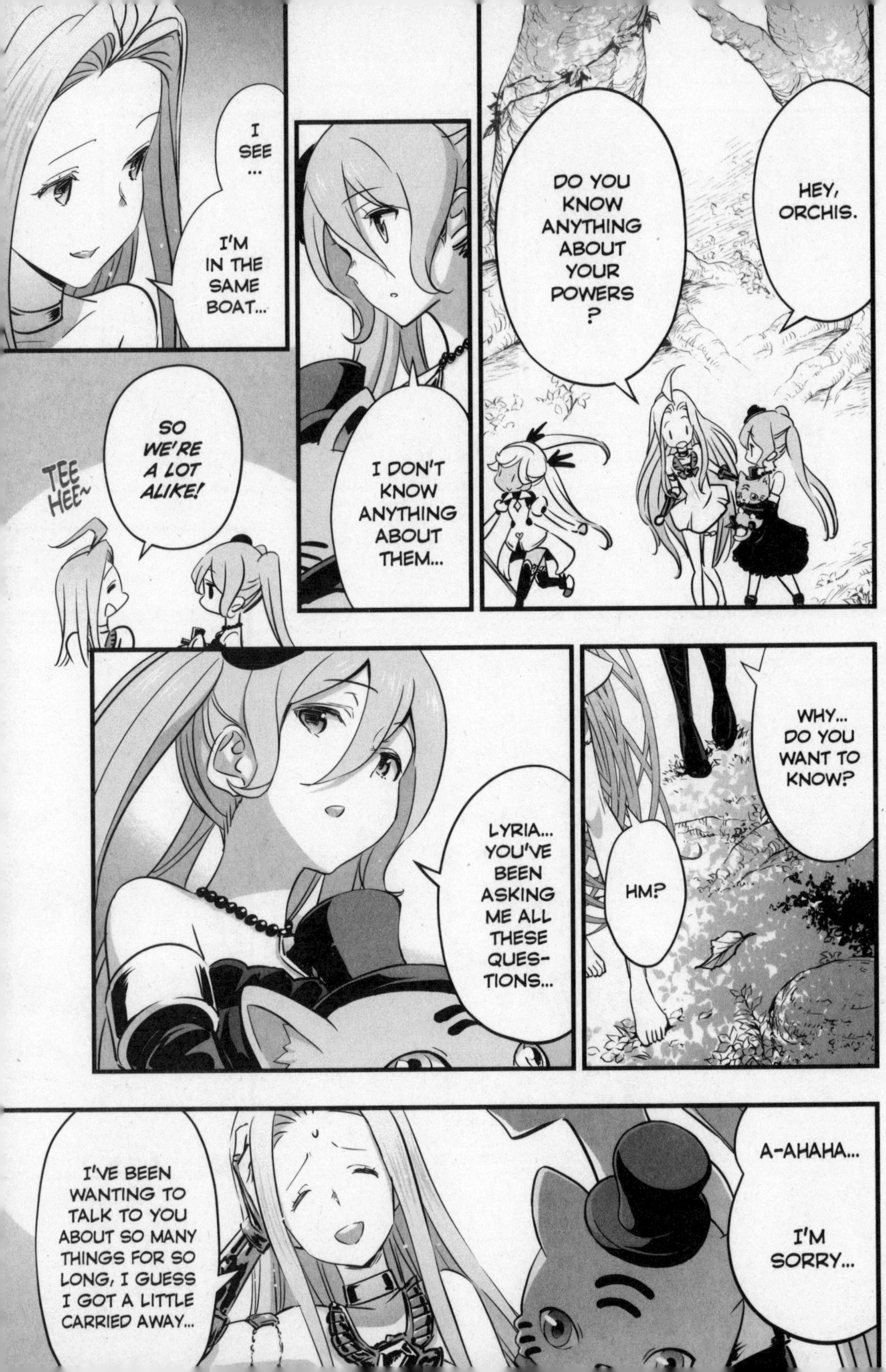
HEY, ORCHIS.
DO YOU KNOW ANYTHING ABOUT YOUR POWERS?
I DON'T KNOW ANYTHING ABOUT THEM...
I SEE...
I'M IN THE SAME BOAT...
SO WE'RE A LOT ALIKE!
TEE HEE~
WHY... DO YOU WANT TO KNOW?
HM?
LYRIA... YOU'VE BEEN ASKING ME ALL THESE QUES-TIONS...
A-AHAHA...
I'M SORRY...
I'VE BEEN WANTING TO TALK TO YOU ABOUT SO MANY THINGS FOR SO LONG, I GUESS I GOT A LITTLE CARRIED AWAY...

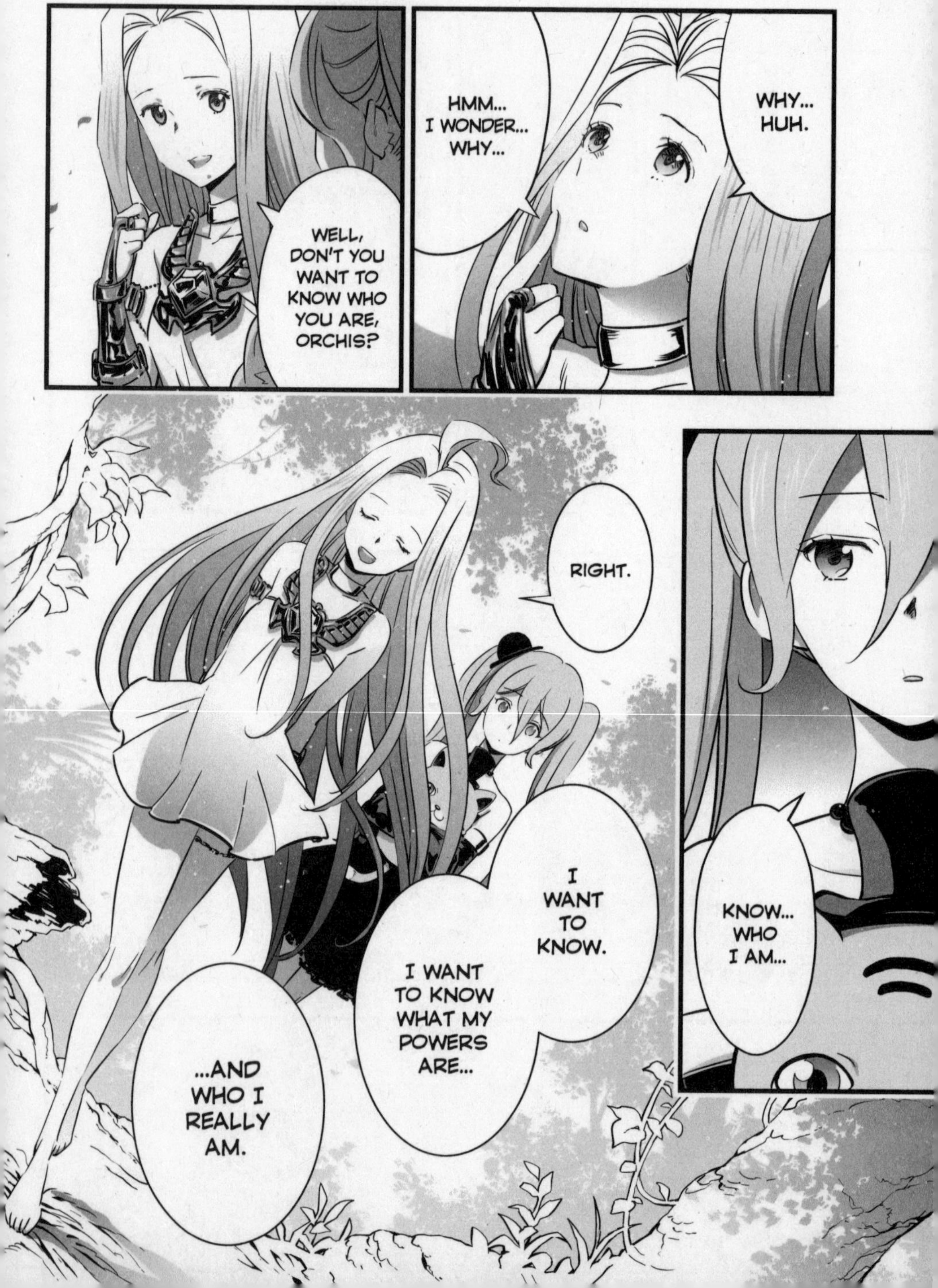
WHY... HUH.
HMM... I WONDER... WHY...
WELL, DON'T YOU WANT TO KNOW WHO YOU ARE, ORCHIS?
KNOW... WHO I AM...
RIGHT.
I WANT TO KNOW.
I WANT TO KNOW WHAT MY POWERS ARE...
...AND WHO I REALLY AM.

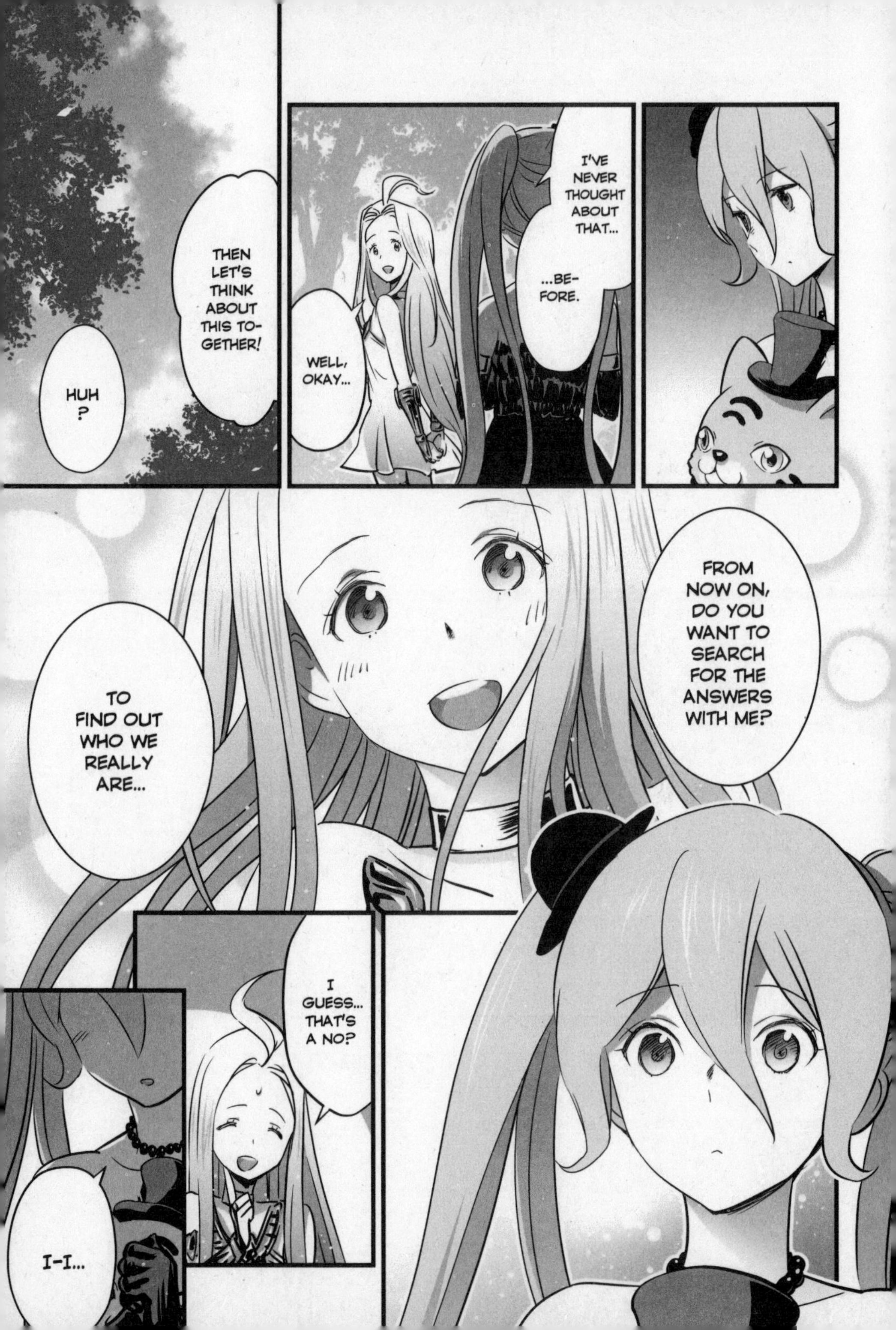
I'VE NEVER THOUGHT ABOUT THAT...
...BE-FORE.
WELL, OKAY...
THEN LET'S THINK ABOUT THIS TO-GETHER!
HUH?
FROM NOW ON, DO YOU WANT TO SEARCH FOR THE ANSWERS WITH ME?
TO FIND OUT WHO WE REALLY ARE...
I GUESS... THAT'S A NO?
I-I...

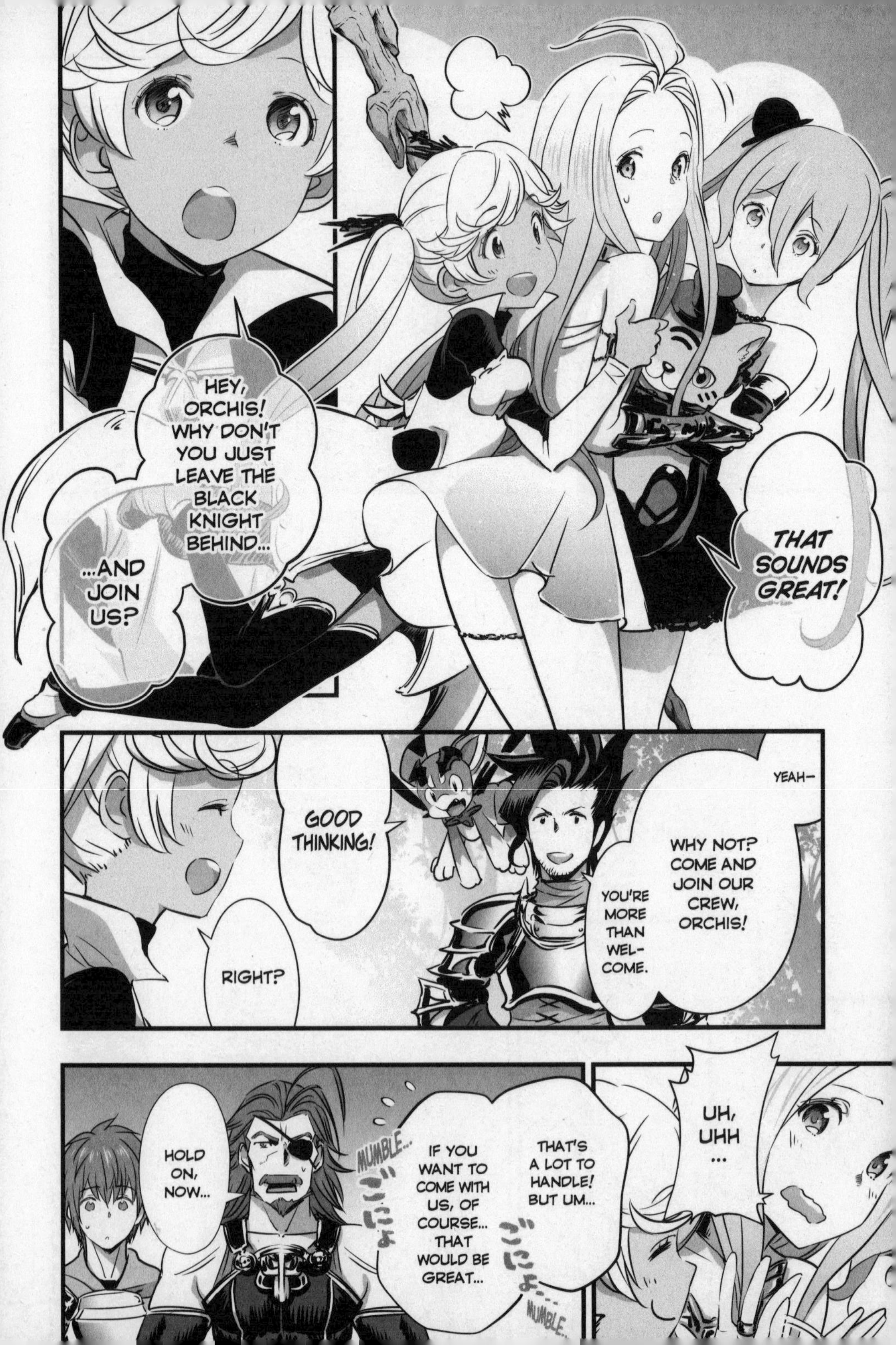
HEY, ORCHIS! WHY DON'T YOU JUST LEAVE THE BLACK KNIGHT BEHIND...
...AND JOIN US?
THAT SOUNDS GREAT!
YEAH—
WHY NOT? COME AND JOIN OUR CREW, ORCHIS!
YOU'RE MORE THAN WEL-COME.
GOOD THINKING!
RIGHT?
UH, UHH ...
THAT'S A LOT TO HANDLE! BUT UM...
IF YOU WANT TO COME WITH US, OF COURSE... THAT WOULD BE GREAT...
MUMBLE...
ごにょ
ごによ...
MUMBLE...
HOLD ON, NOW...

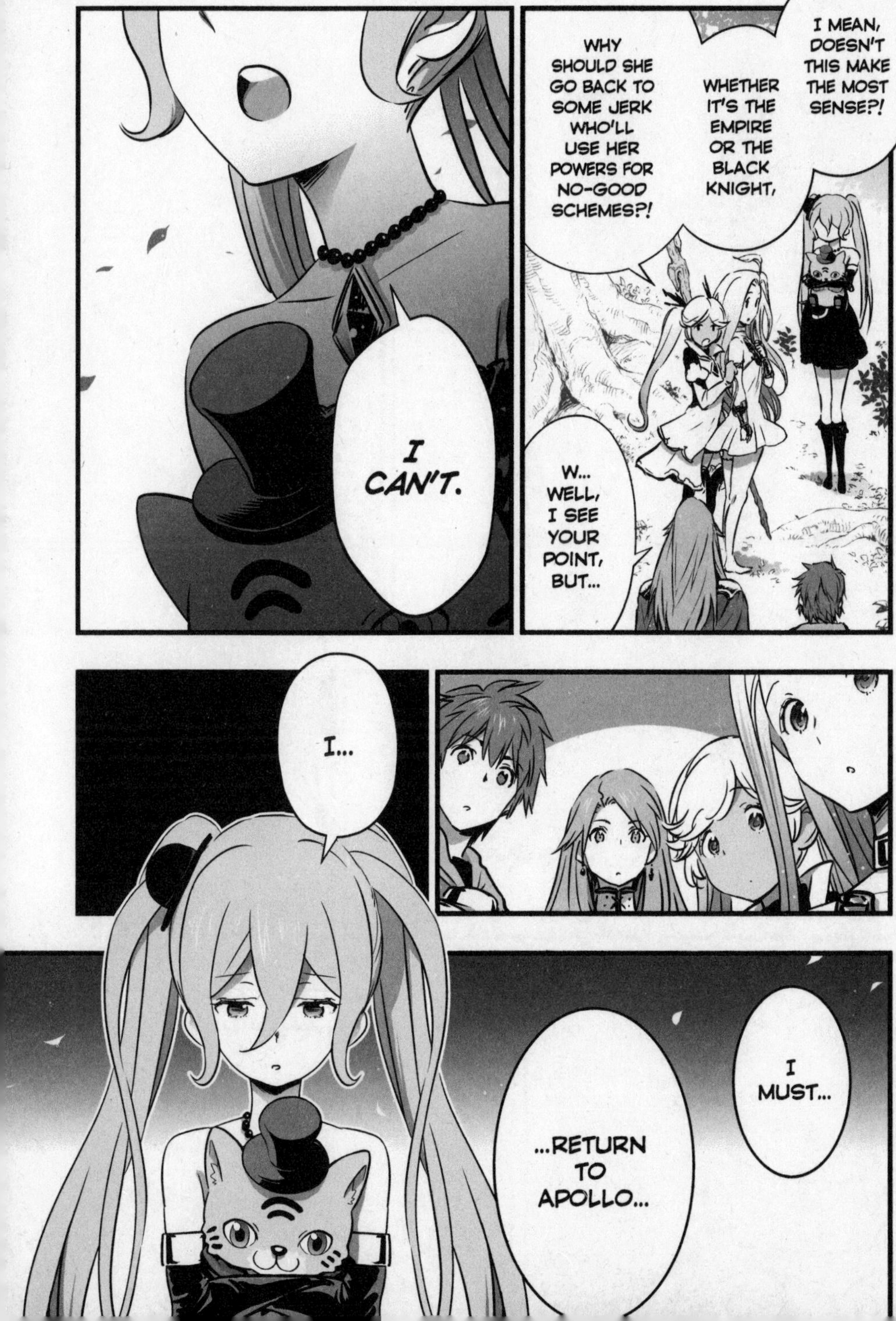
I MEAN, DOESN'T THIS MAKE THE MOST SENSE?!
WHETHER IT'S THE EMPIRE OR THE BLACK KNIGHT,
WHY SHOULD SHE GO BACK TO SOME JERK WHO'LL USE HER POWERS FOR NO-GOOD SCHEMES?!
W... WELL, I SEE YOUR POINT, BUT...
I CAN'T.
I...
I MUST...
...RETURN TO APOLLO...

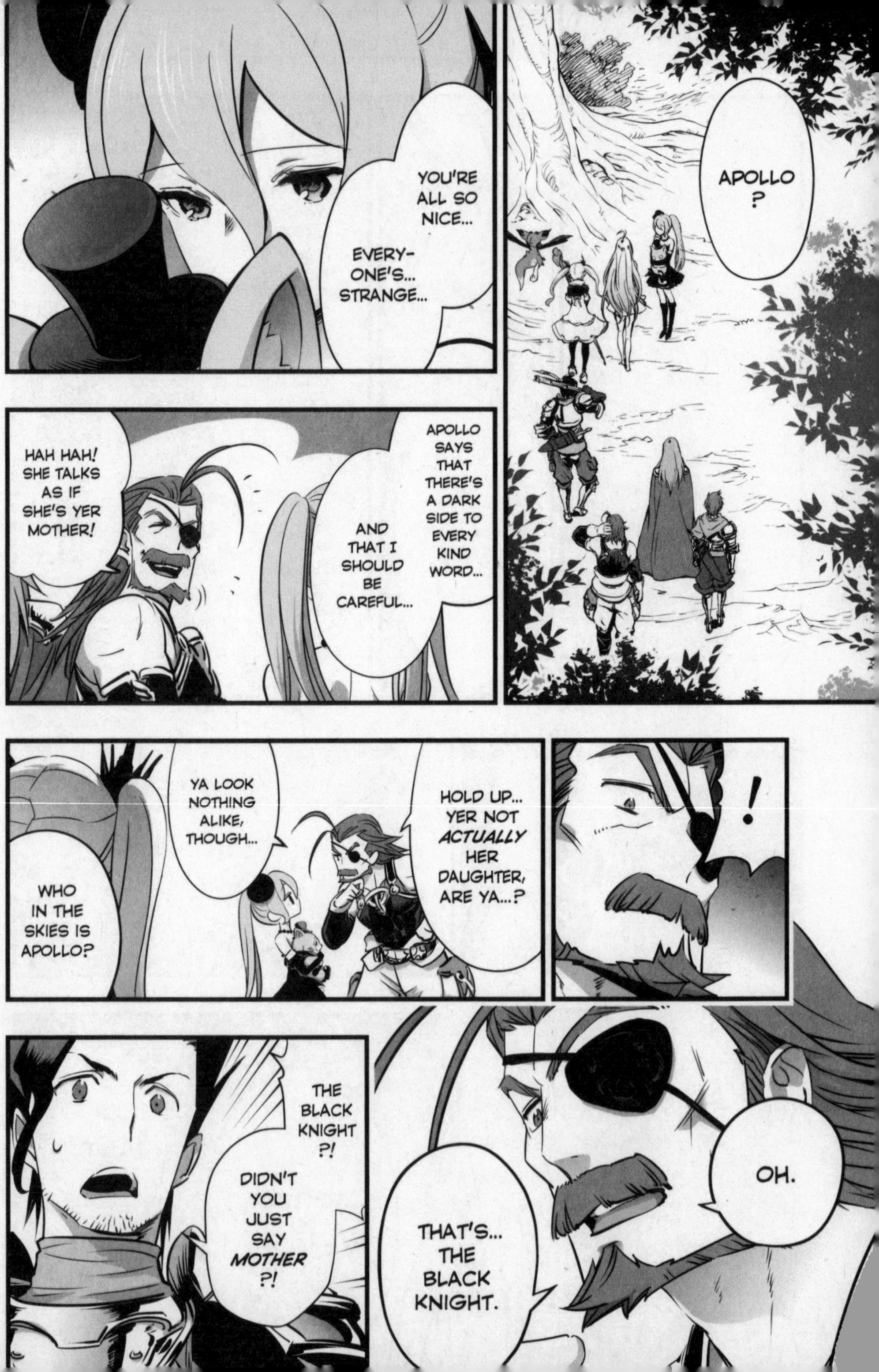
APOLLO?
YOU'RE ALL SO NICE...
EVERY-ONE'S... STRANGE...
APOLLO SAYS THAT THERE'S A DARK SIDE TO EVERY KIND WORD...
AND THAT I SHOULD BE CAREFUL...
HAH HAH! SHE TALKS AS IF SHE'S YER MOTHER!
!
HOLD UP... YER NOT *ACTUALLY* HER DAUGHTER, ARE YA...?
YA LOOK NOTHING ALIKE, THOUGH...
WHO IN THE SKIES IS APOLLO?
OH.
THAT'S... THE BLACK KNIGHT.
THE BLACK KNIGHT?!
DIDN'T YOU JUST SAY *MOTHER*?!

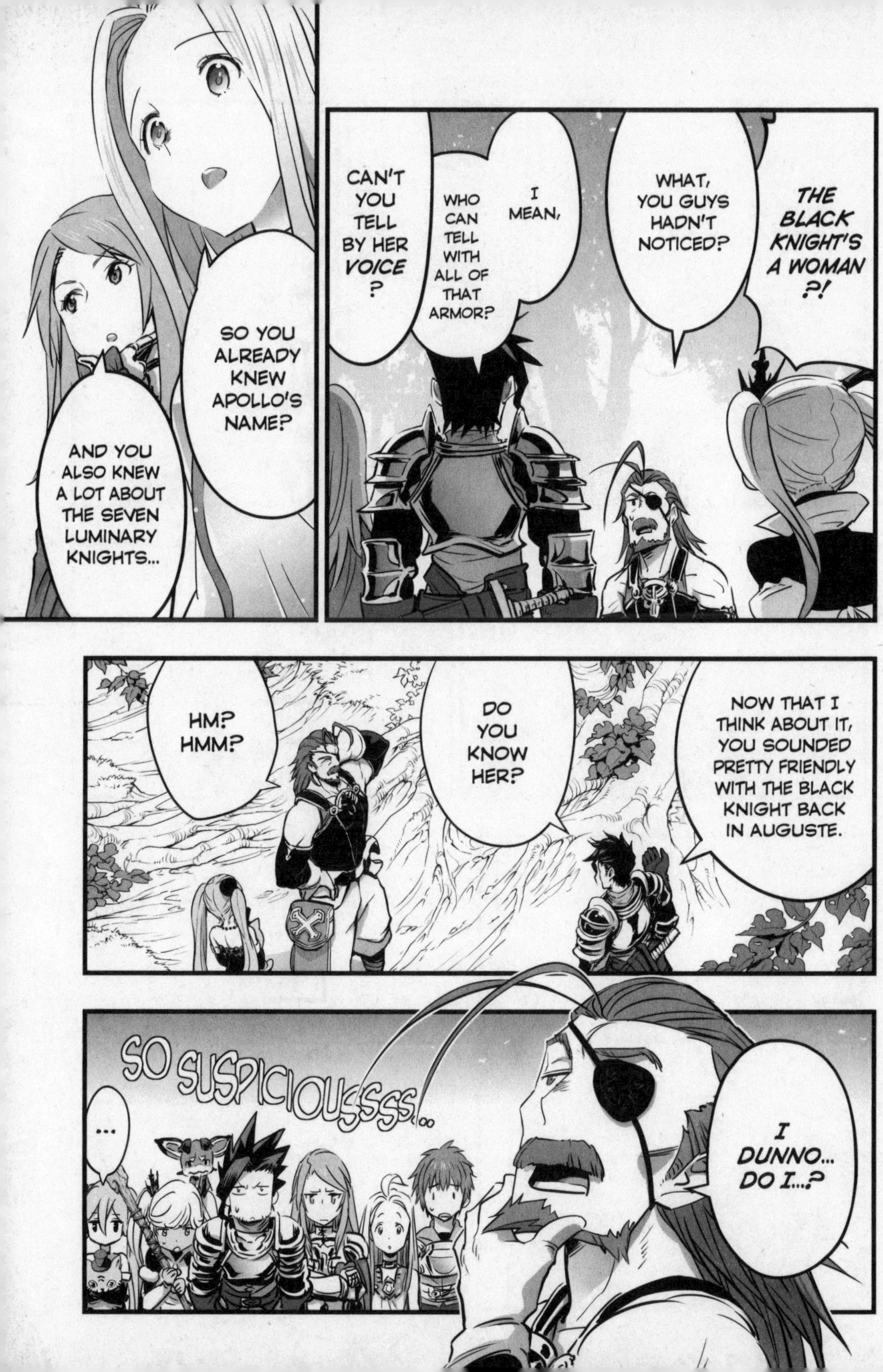
THE BLACK KNIGHT'S A WOMAN?!
WHAT, YOU GUYS HADN'T NOTICED?
I MEAN,
WHO CAN TELL WITH ALL OF THAT ARMOR?
CAN'T YOU TELL BY HER VOICE?
SO YOU ALREADY KNEW APOLLO'S NAME?
AND YOU ALSO KNEW A LOT ABOUT THE SEVEN LUMINARY KNIGHTS...
NOW THAT I THINK ABOUT IT, YOU SOUNDED PRETTY FRIENDLY WITH THE BLACK KNIGHT BACK IN AUGUSTE.
DO YOU KNOW HER?
HM? HMM?
I DUNNO... DO I...?
SO SUSPICIOUSSSSS...
...

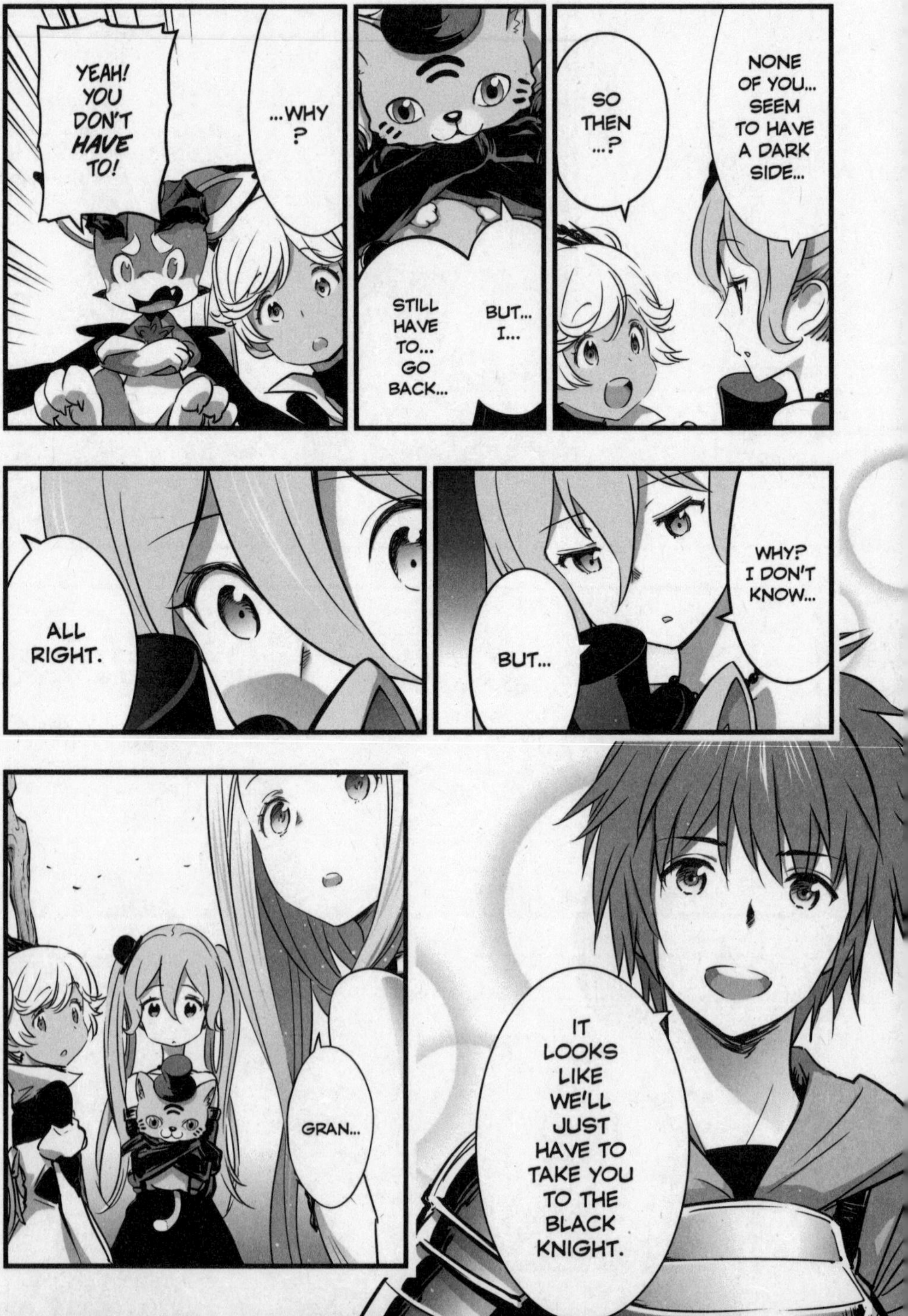
NONE OF YOU... SEEM TO HAVE A DARK SIDE...
SO THEN ...?
BUT... I...
STILL HAVE TO... GO BACK...
...WHY ?
YEAH! YOU DON'T *HAVE* TO!
WHY? I DON'T KNOW...
BUT...
ALL RIGHT.
IT LOOKS LIKE WE'LL JUST HAVE TO TAKE YOU TO THE BLACK KNIGHT.
GRAN...

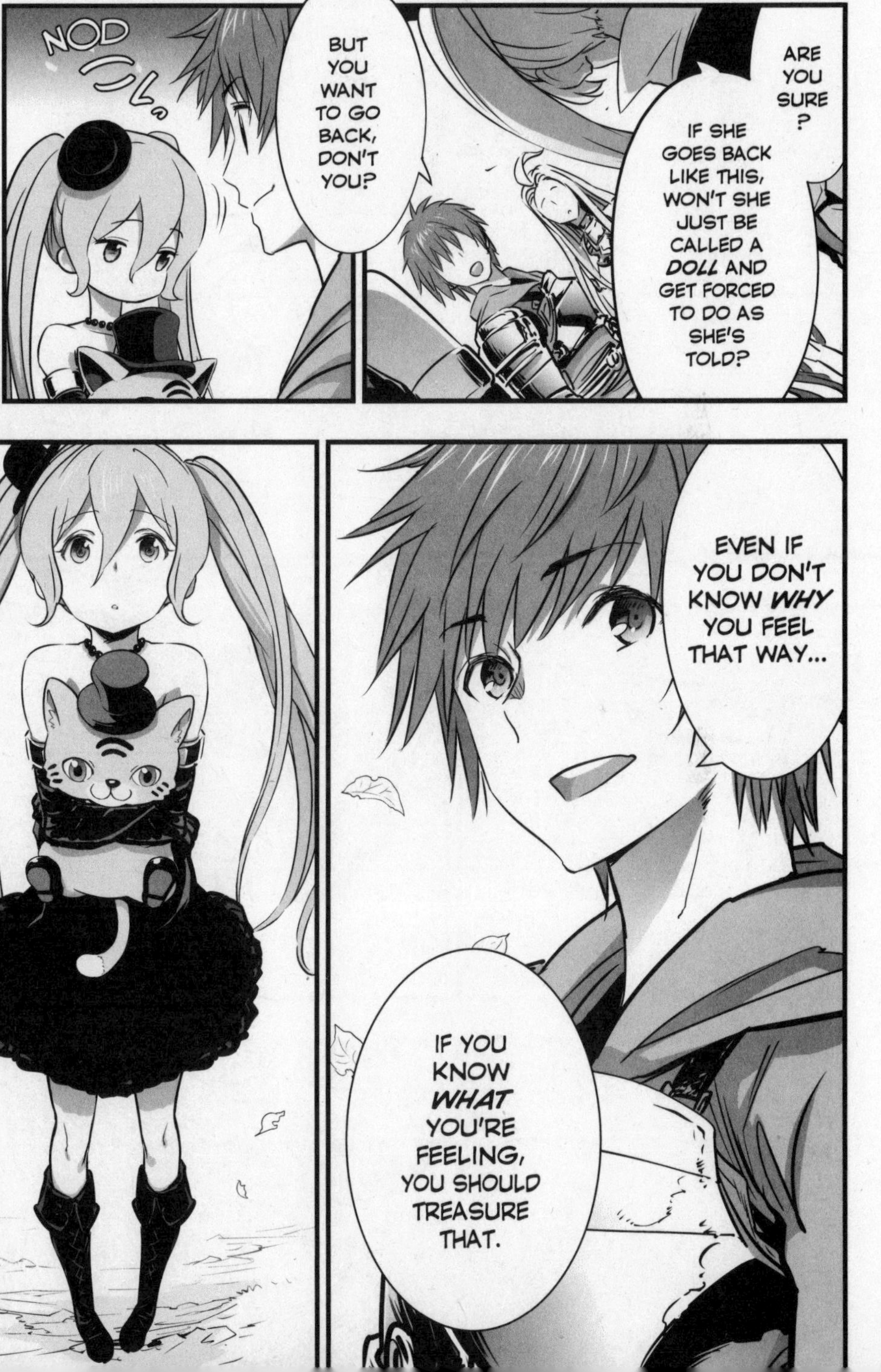
ARE YOU SURE?
IF SHE GOES BACK LIKE THIS, WON'T SHE JUST BE CALLED A *DOLL* AND GET FORCED TO DO AS SHE'S TOLD?
NOD
BUT YOU WANT TO GO BACK, DON'T YOU?
EVEN IF YOU DON'T KNOW *WHY* YOU FEEL THAT WAY...
IF YOU KNOW *WHAT* YOU'RE FEELING, YOU SHOULD TREASURE THAT.

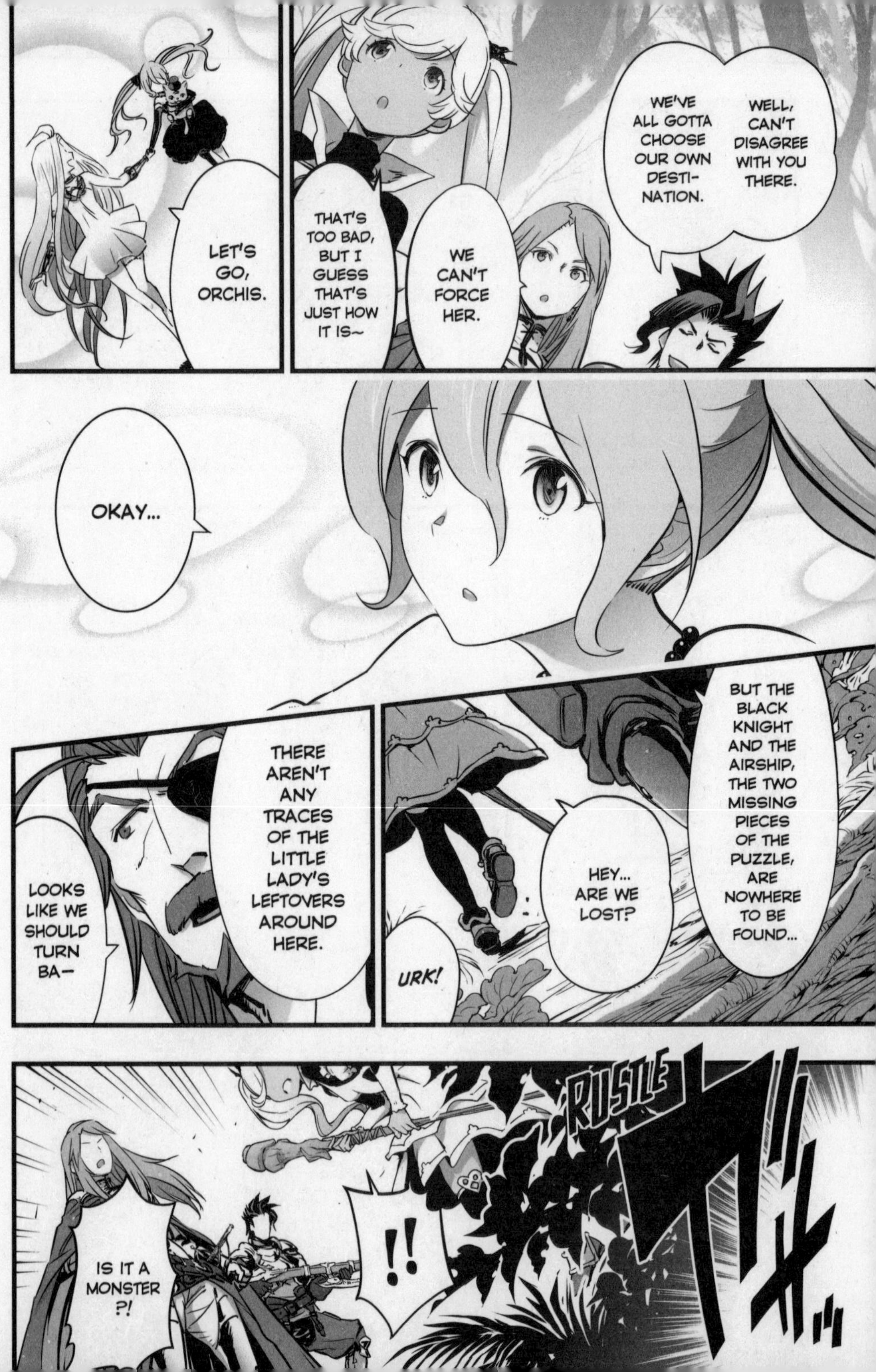
WELL, CAN'T DISAGREE WITH YOU THERE.
WE'VE ALL GOTTA CHOOSE OUR OWN DESTINATION.
WE CAN'T FORCE HER.
THAT'S TOO BAD, BUT I GUESS THAT'S JUST HOW IT IS~
LET'S GO, ORCHIS.
OKAY...
BUT THE BLACK KNIGHT AND THE AIRSHIP, THE TWO MISSING PIECES OF THE PUZZLE, ARE NOWHERE TO BE FOUND...
HEY... ARE WE LOST?
URK!
THERE AREN'T ANY TRACES OF THE LITTLE LADY'S LEFTOVERS AROUND HERE.
LOOKS LIKE WE SHOULD TURN BA—
RUSTLE
!!
IS IT A MONSTER?!

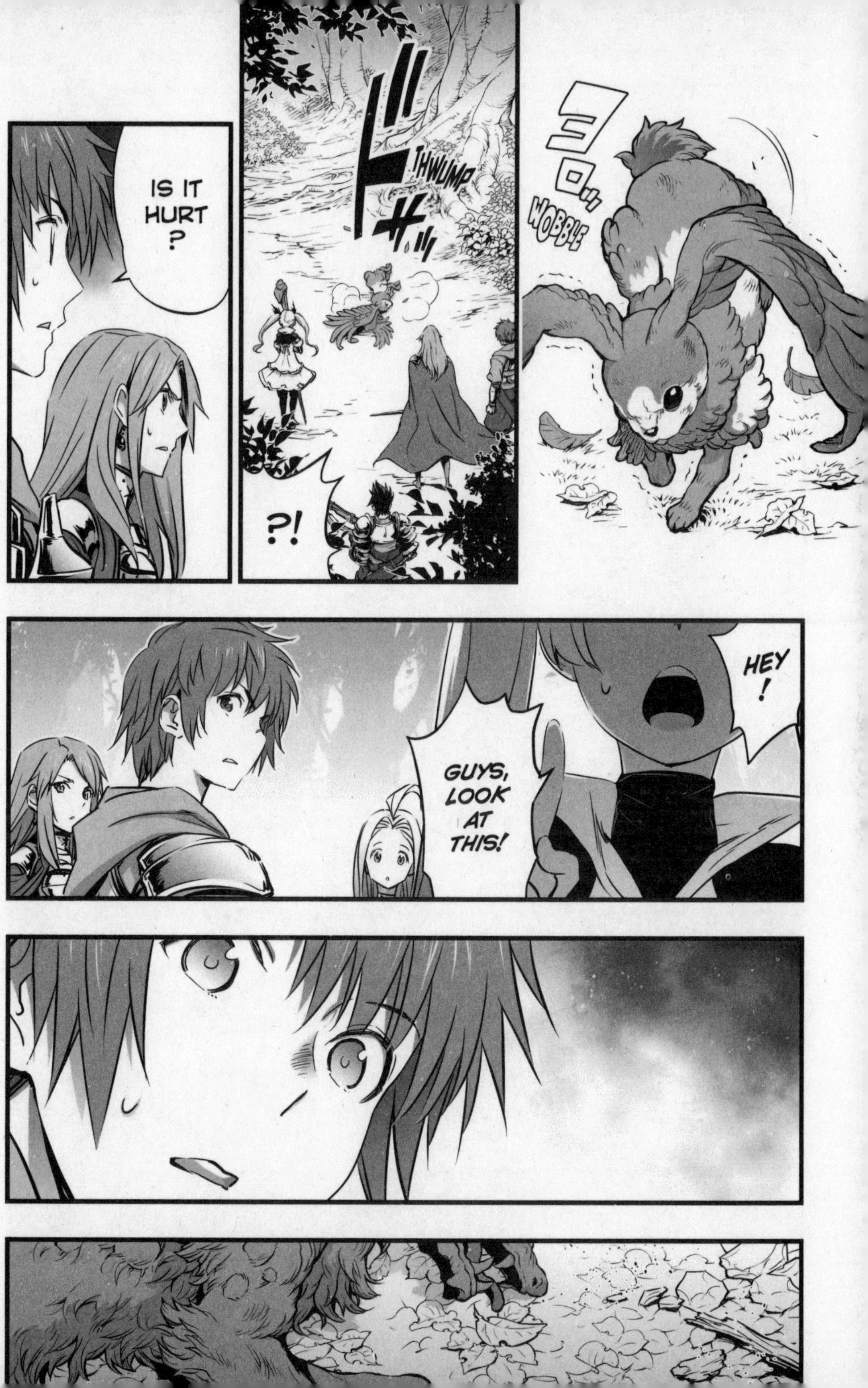
WOBBLE
THWUMP
?!
IS IT HURT?
HEY!
GUYS, LOOK AT THIS!

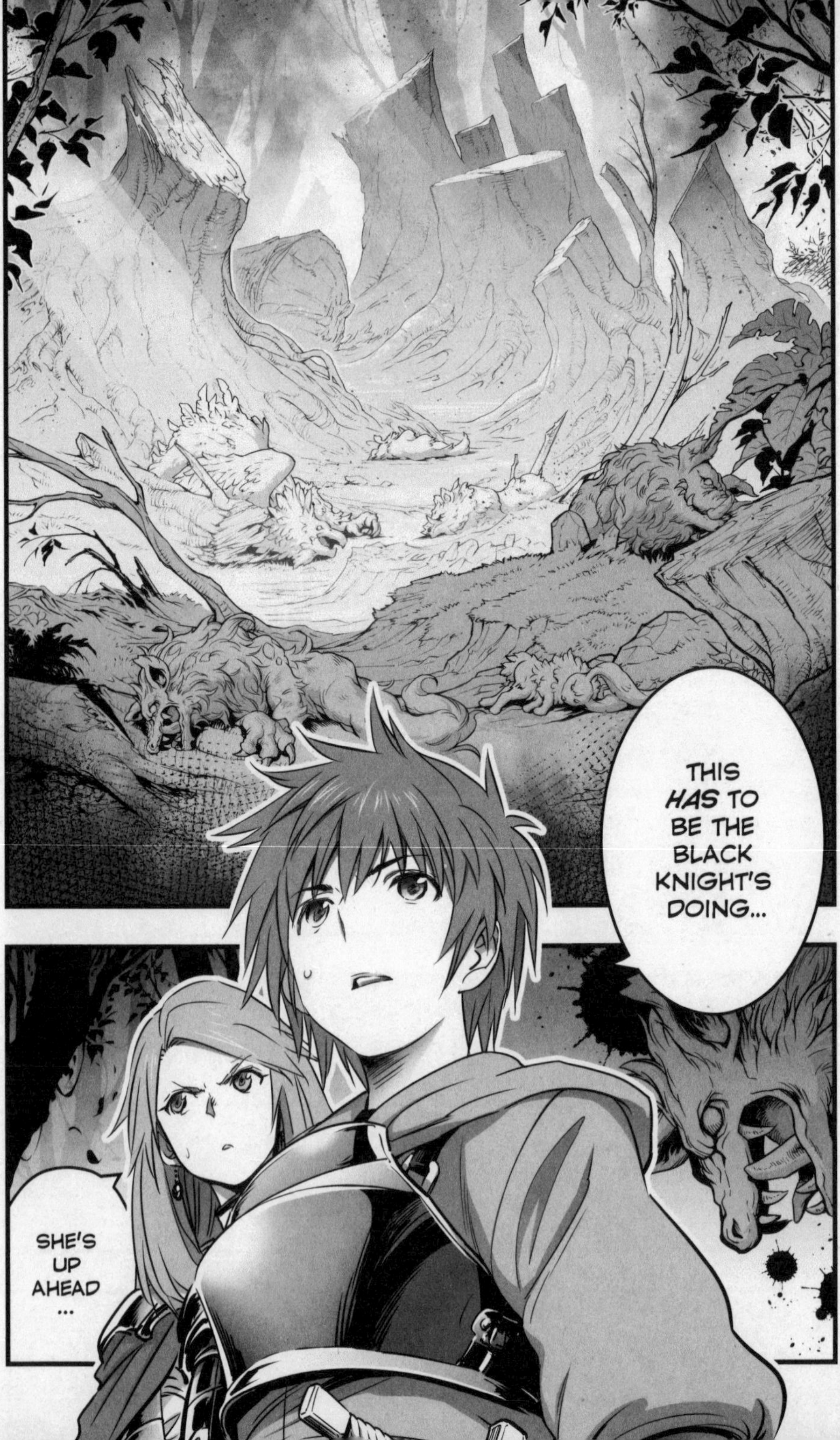
THIS HAS TO BE THE BLACK KNIGHT'S DOING...
SHE'S UP AHEAD ...

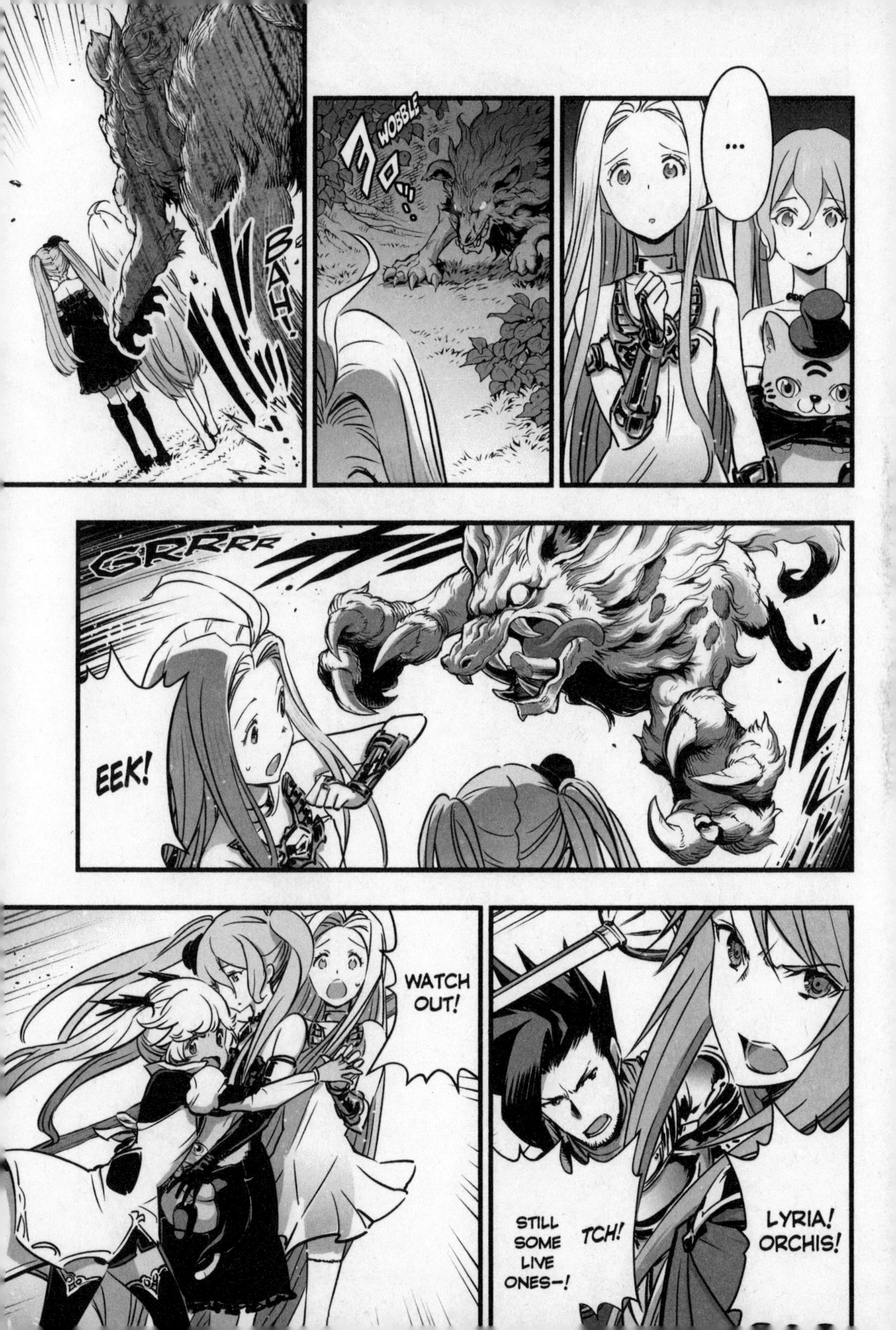
...
WOBBLE
BAH!
GRRRR
EEK!
LYRIA! ORCHIS!
TCH!
STILL SOME LIVE ONES—!
WATCH OUT!

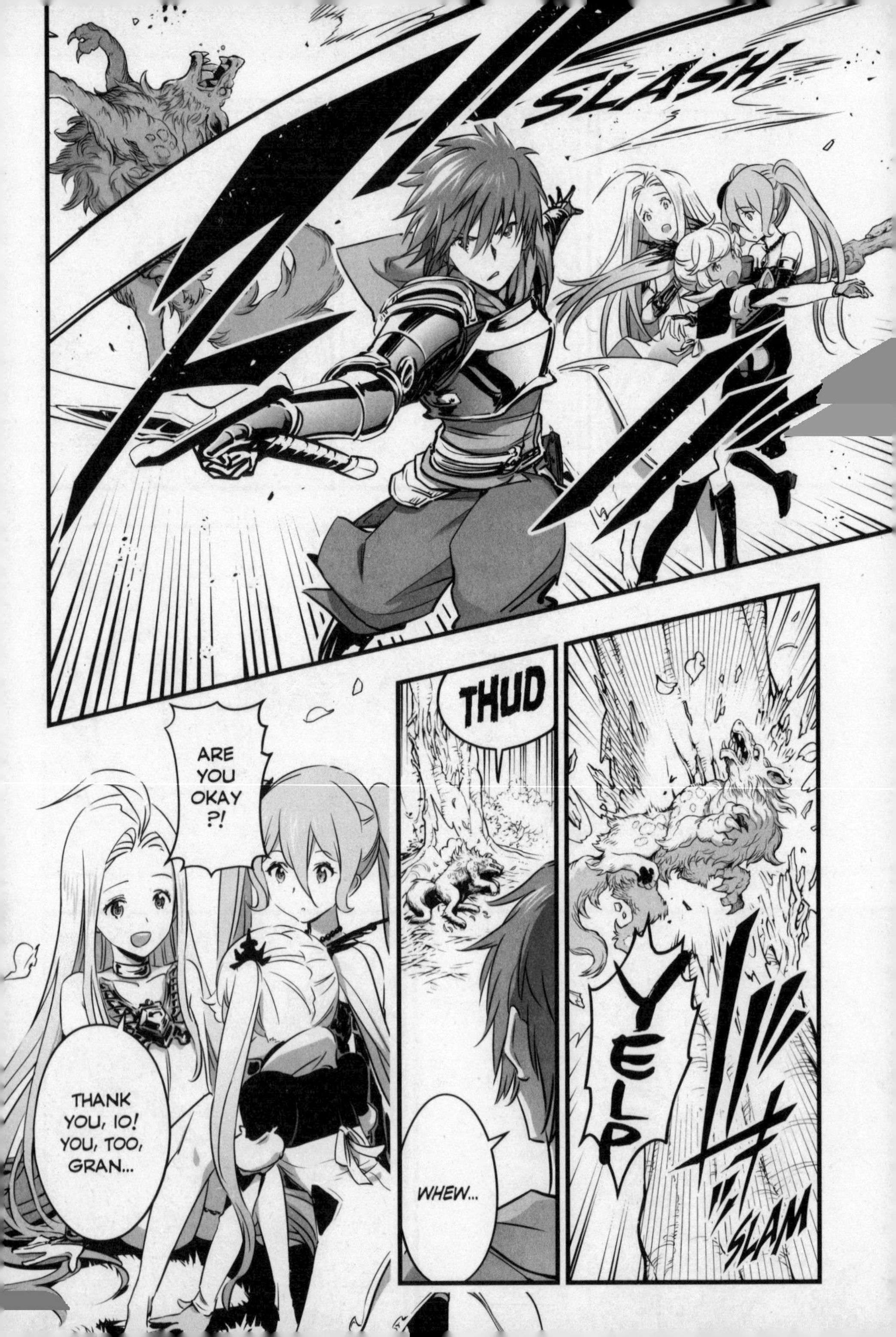
SLASH
YELP
SLAM
THUD
WHEW...
ARE YOU OKAY?!
THANK YOU, IO! YOU, TOO, GRAN...

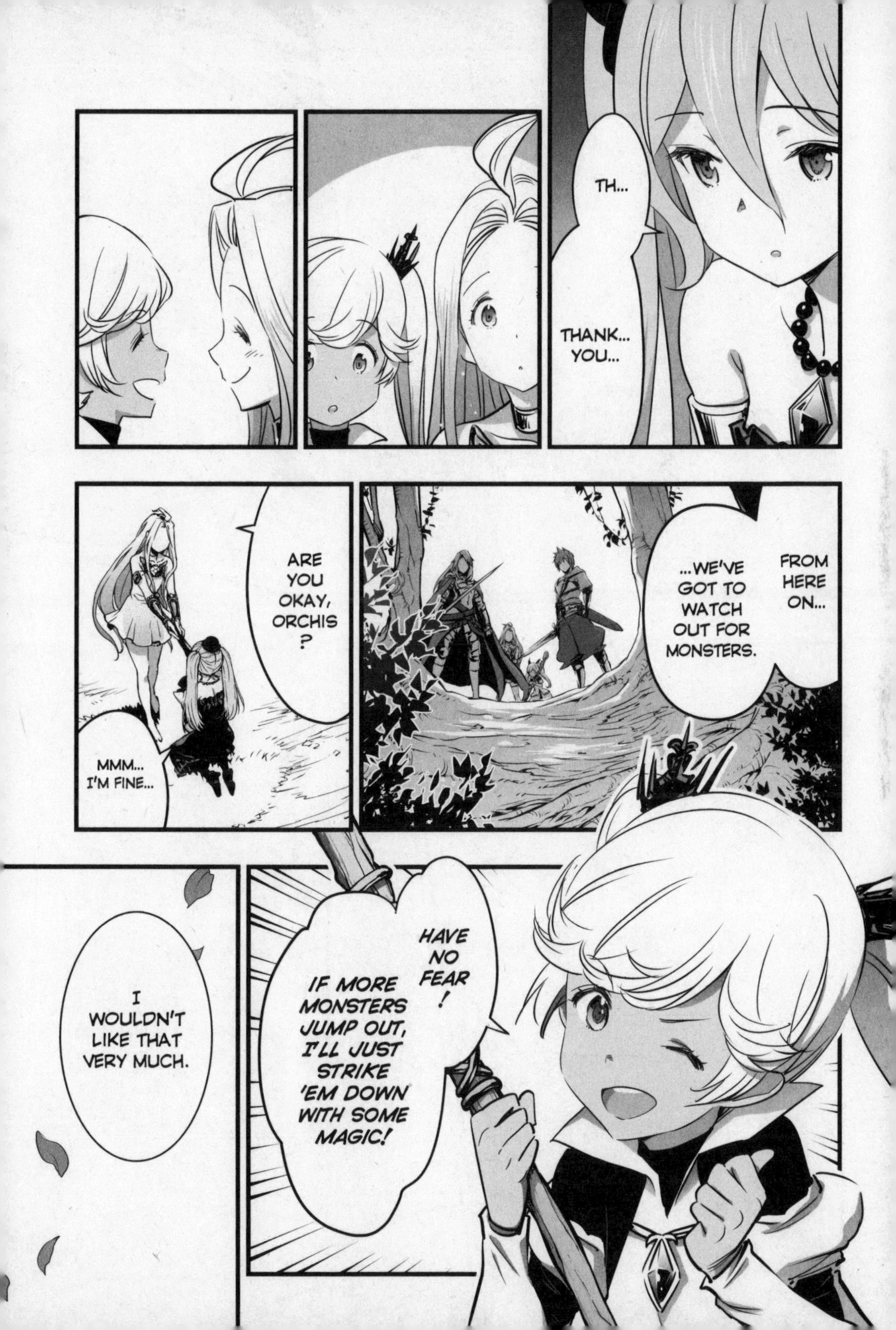
TH...
THANK... YOU...
FROM HERE ON...
...WE'VE GOT TO WATCH OUT FOR MONSTERS.
ARE YOU OKAY, ORCHIS?
MMM... I'M FINE...
HAVE NO FEAR!
IF MORE MONSTERS JUMP OUT, I'LL JUST STRIKE 'EM DOWN WITH SOME MAGIC!
I WOULDN'T LIKE THAT VERY MUCH.

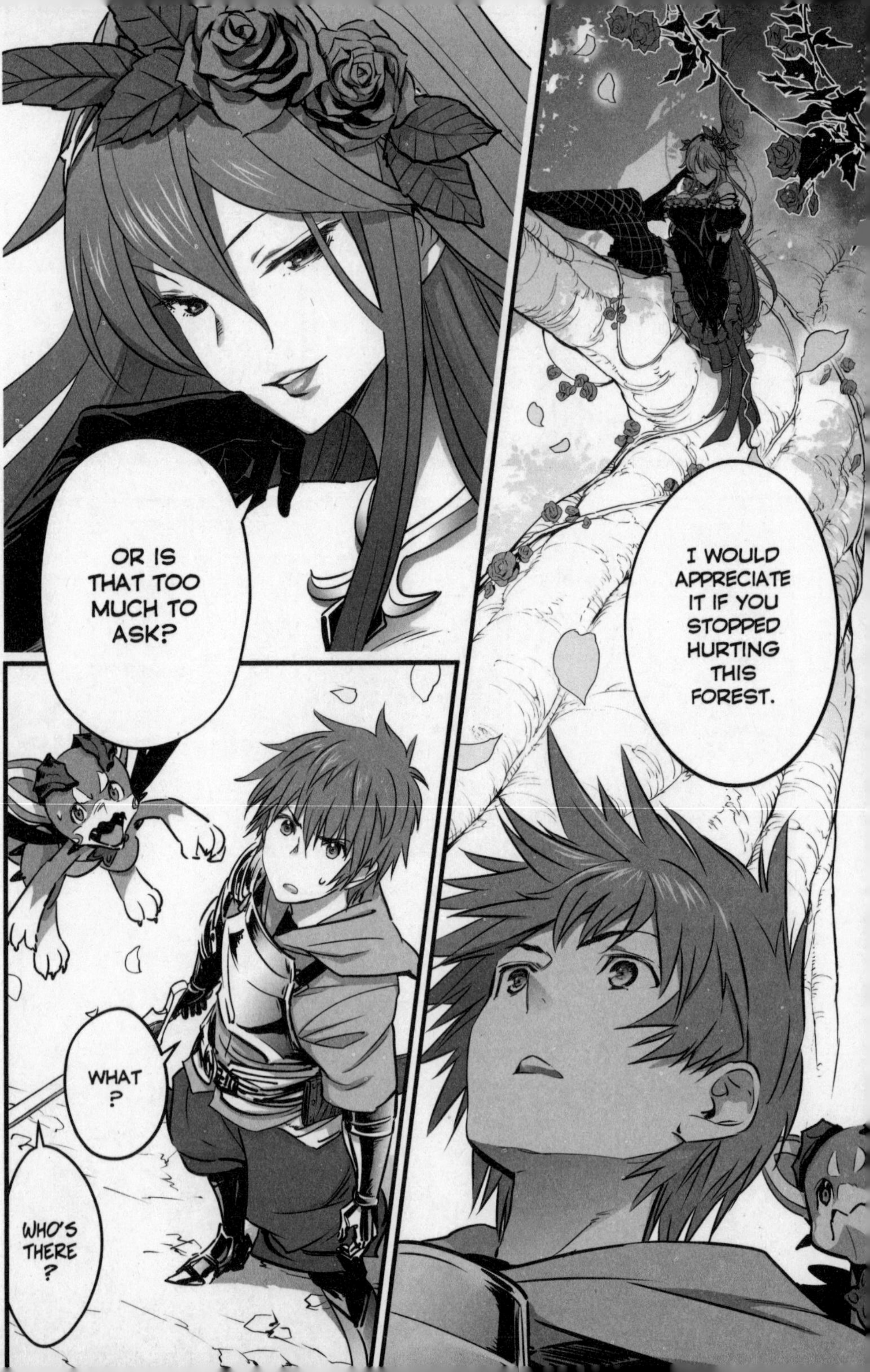
I WOULD APPRECIATE IT IF YOU STOPPED HURTING THIS FOREST.
OR IS THAT TOO MUCH TO ASK?
WHAT?
WHO'S THERE?

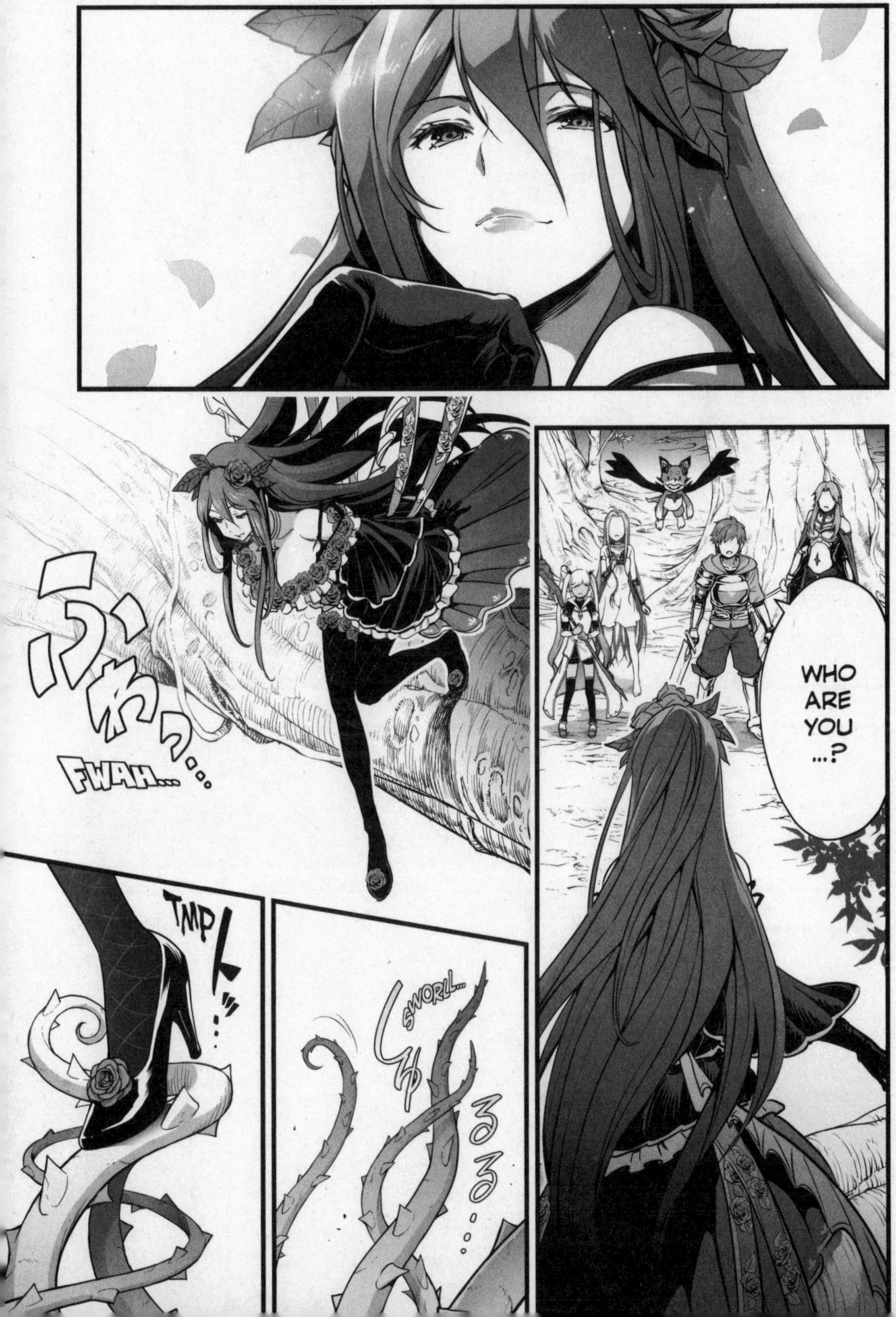
WHO ARE YOU ...?
ふわっ...
FWAH...
しゅるる...
SWORL...
トッ...
TMP

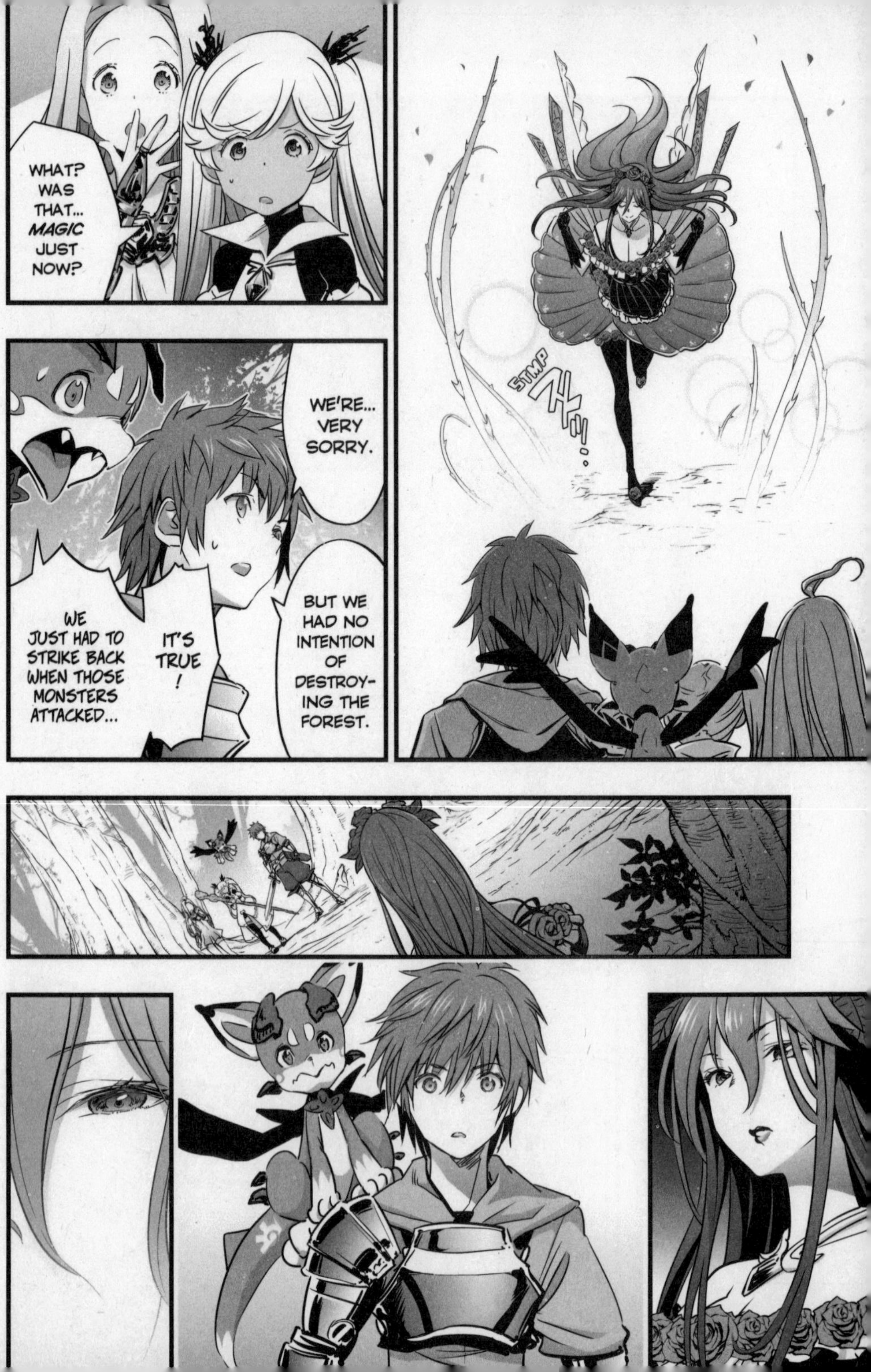
STMP
WHAT? WAS THAT... *MAGIC* JUST NOW?
WE'RE... VERY SORRY.
BUT WE HAD NO INTENTION OF DESTROY-ING THE FOREST.
IT'S TRUE!
WE JUST HAD TO STRIKE BACK WHEN THOSE MONSTERS ATTACKED...

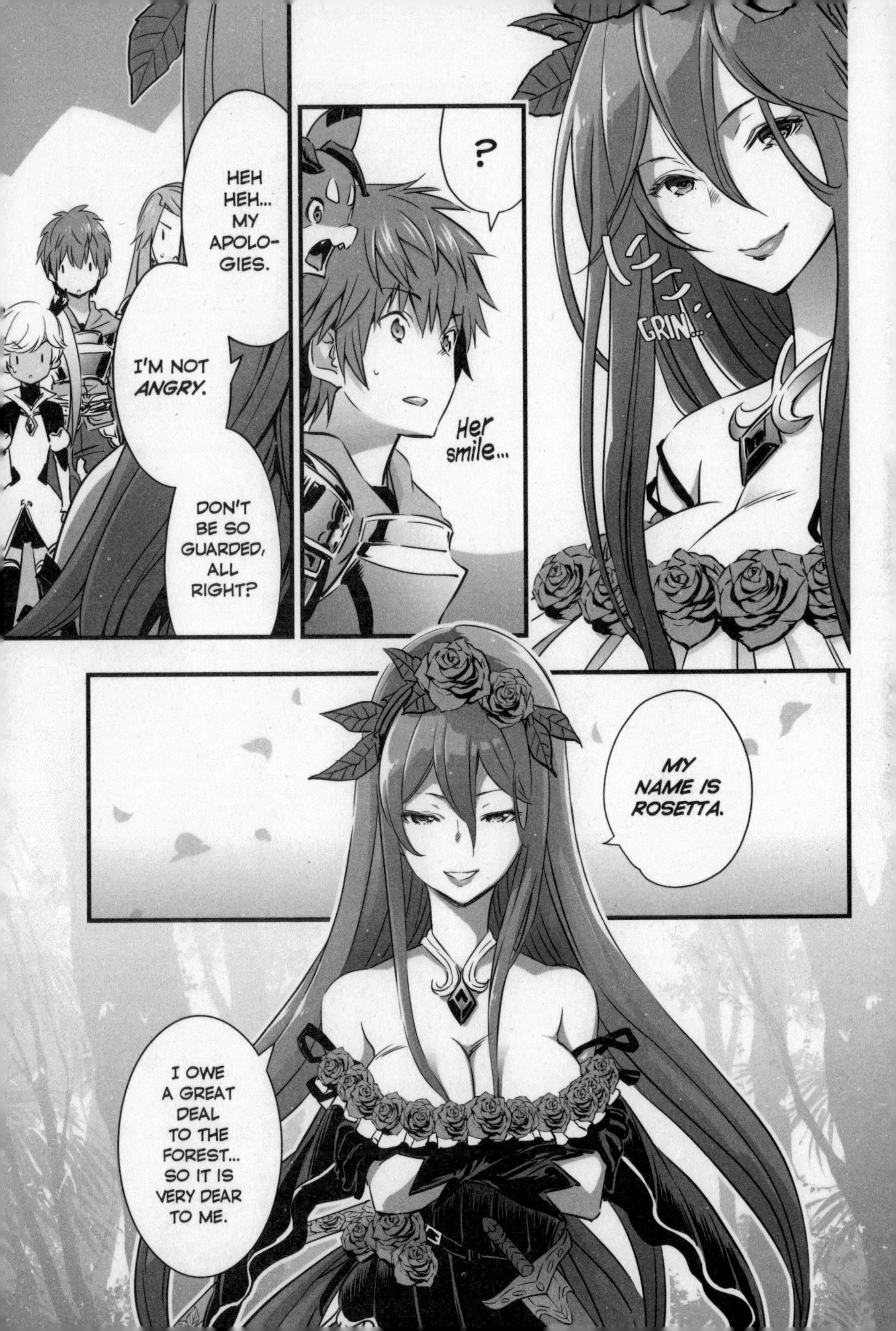
GRIN...
?
Her smile...
HEH HEH... MY APOLOGIES.
I'M NOT *ANGRY*.
DON'T BE SO GUARDED, ALL RIGHT?
MY NAME IS ROSETTA.
I OWE A GREAT DEAL TO THE FOREST... SO IT IS VERY DEAR TO ME.

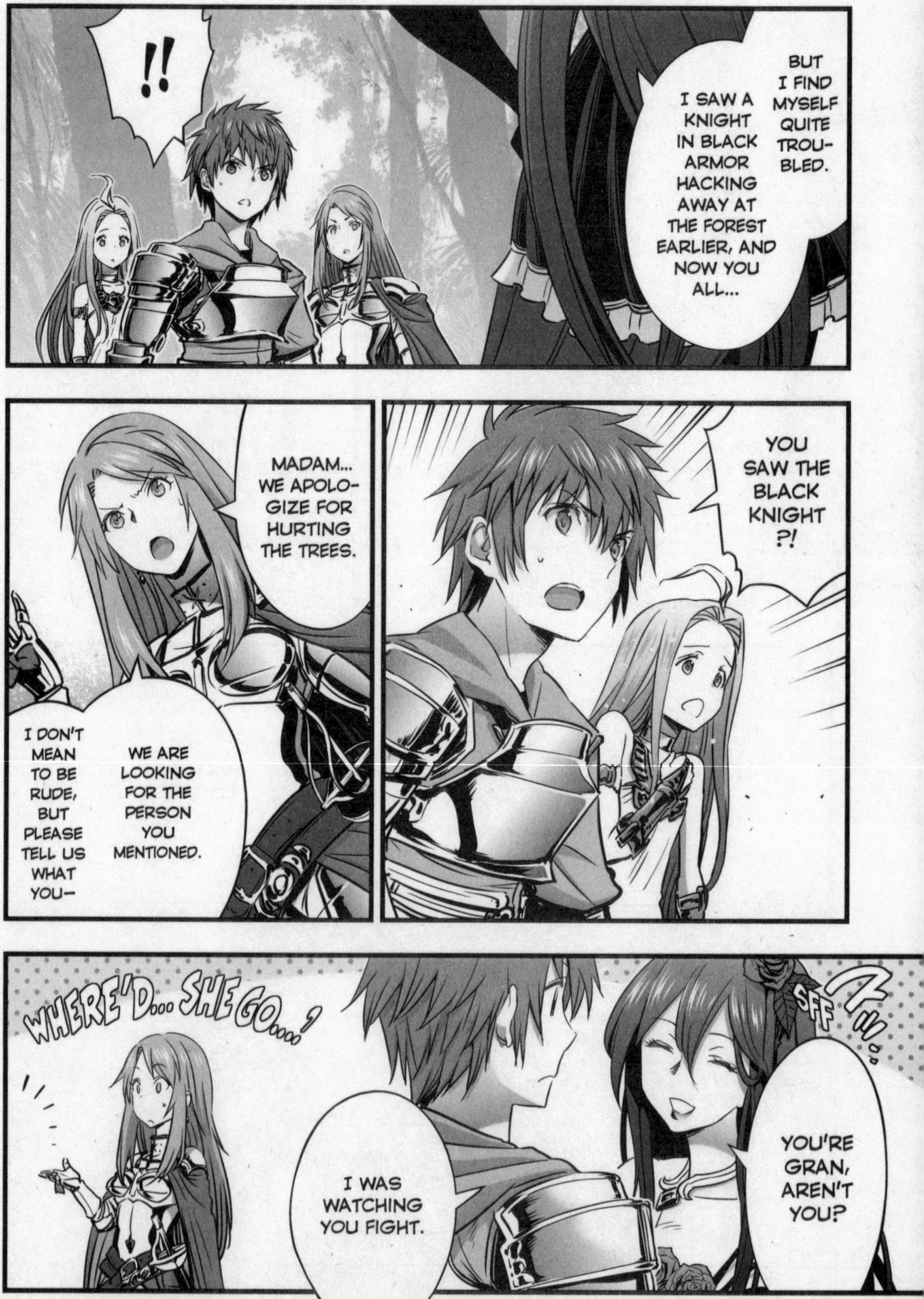
BUT I FIND MYSELF QUITE TROU-BLED.
I SAW A KNIGHT IN BLACK ARMOR HACKING AWAY AT THE FOREST EARLIER, AND NOW YOU ALL...
!!
YOU SAW THE BLACK KNIGHT?!
MADAM... WE APOLO-GIZE FOR HURTING THE TREES.
WE ARE LOOKING FOR THE PERSON YOU MENTIONED.
I DON'T MEAN TO BE RUDE, BUT PLEASE TELL US WHAT YOU—
SFF
YOU'RE GRAN, AREN'T YOU?
I WAS WATCHING YOU FIGHT.
WHERE'D... SHE GO...?

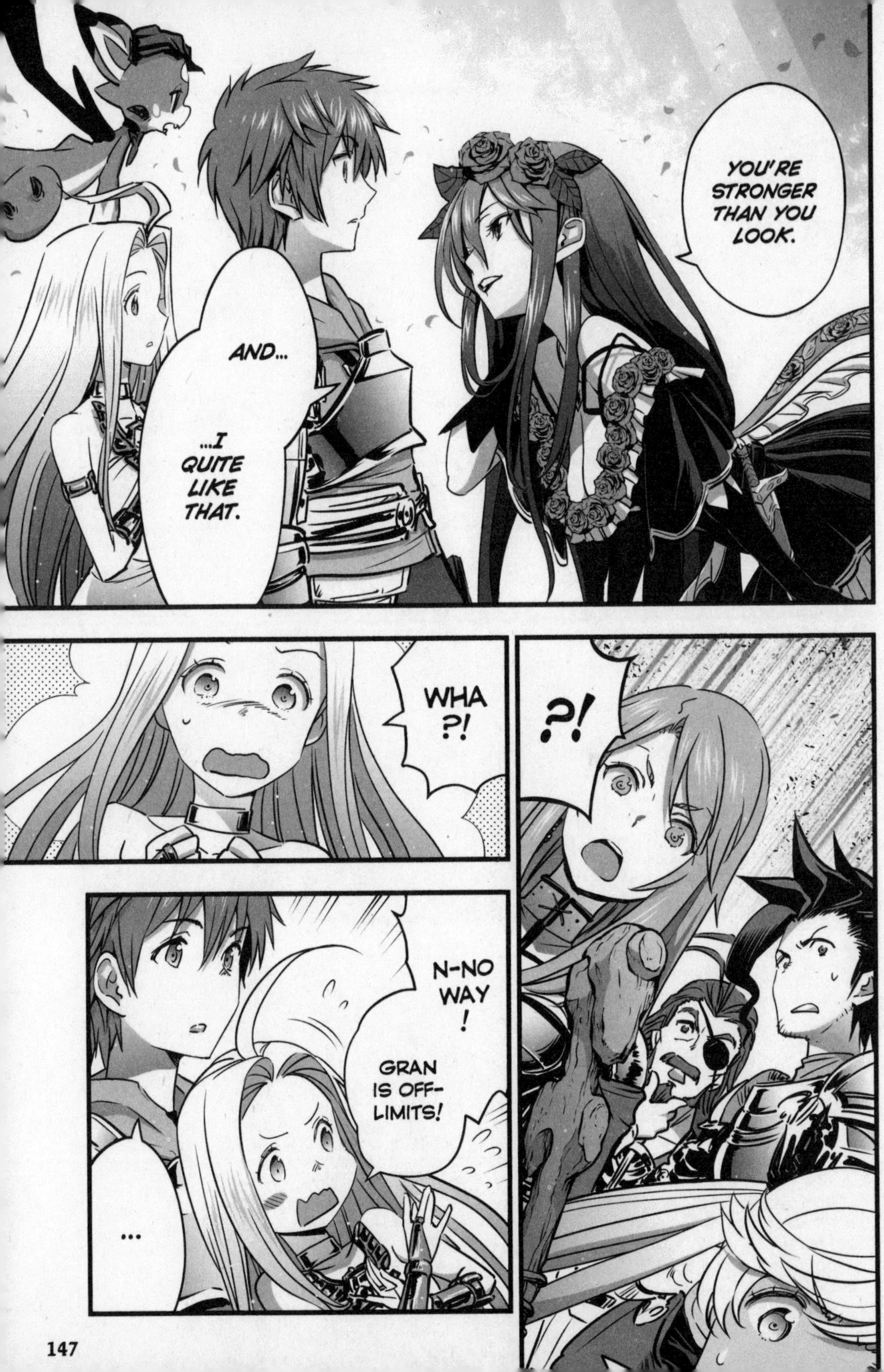

YOU'RE STRONGER THAN YOU LOOK.
AND...
...I QUITE LIKE THAT.
?!
WHA ?!
N-NO WAY !
GRAN IS OFF-LIMITS!
...

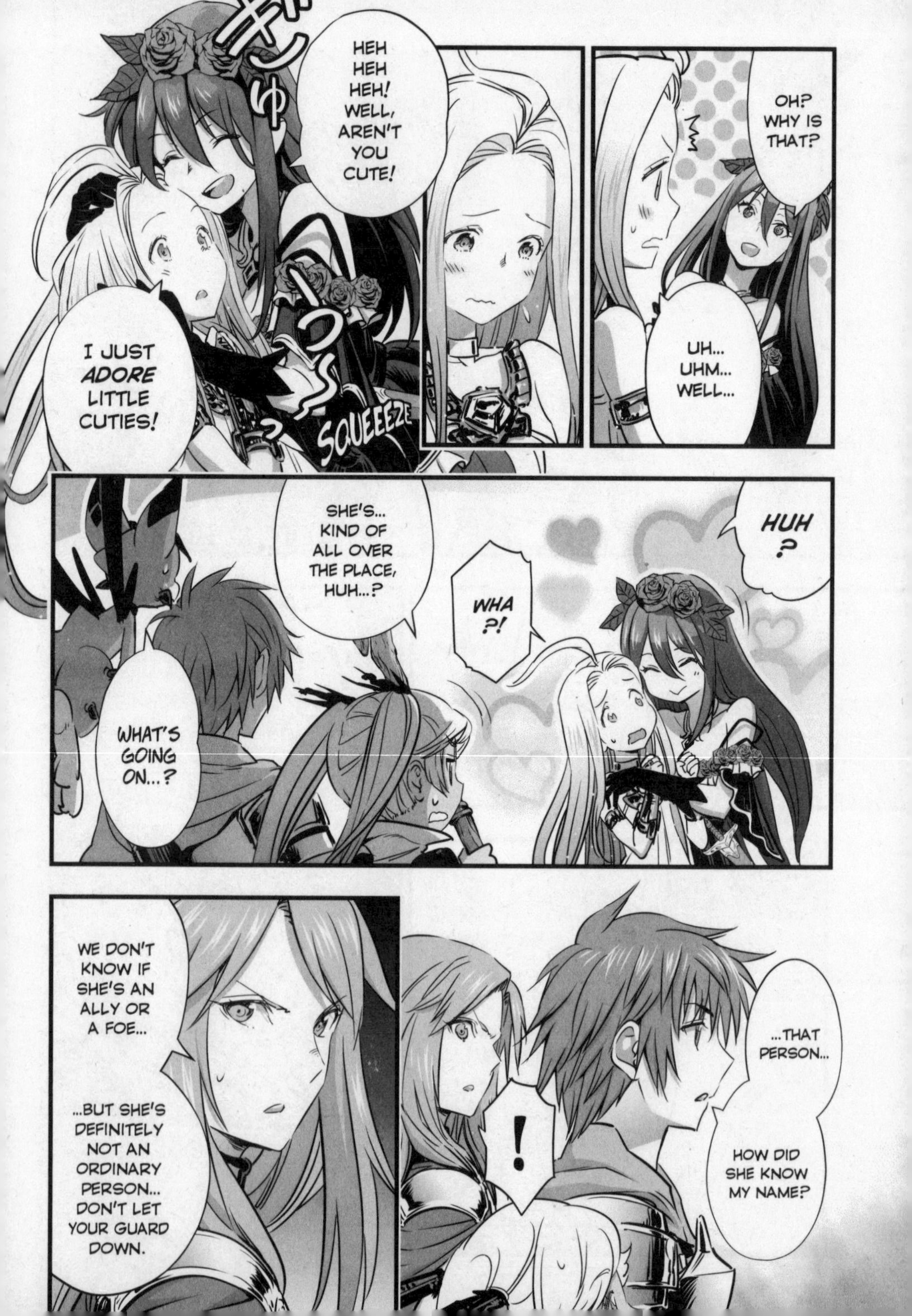
OH? WHY IS THAT?
UH... UHM... WELL...
ぎゅ
HEH HEH HEH! WELL, AREN'T YOU CUTE!
I JUST ADORE LITTLE CUTIES!
SQUEEEZE
HUH?
WHA?!
SHE'S... KIND OF ALL OVER THE PLACE, HUH...?
WHAT'S GOING ON...?
...THAT PERSON...
HOW DID SHE KNOW MY NAME?
!
WE DON'T KNOW IF SHE'S AN ALLY OR A FOE...
...BUT SHE'S DEFINITELY NOT AN ORDINARY PERSON... DON'T LET YOUR GUARD DOWN.

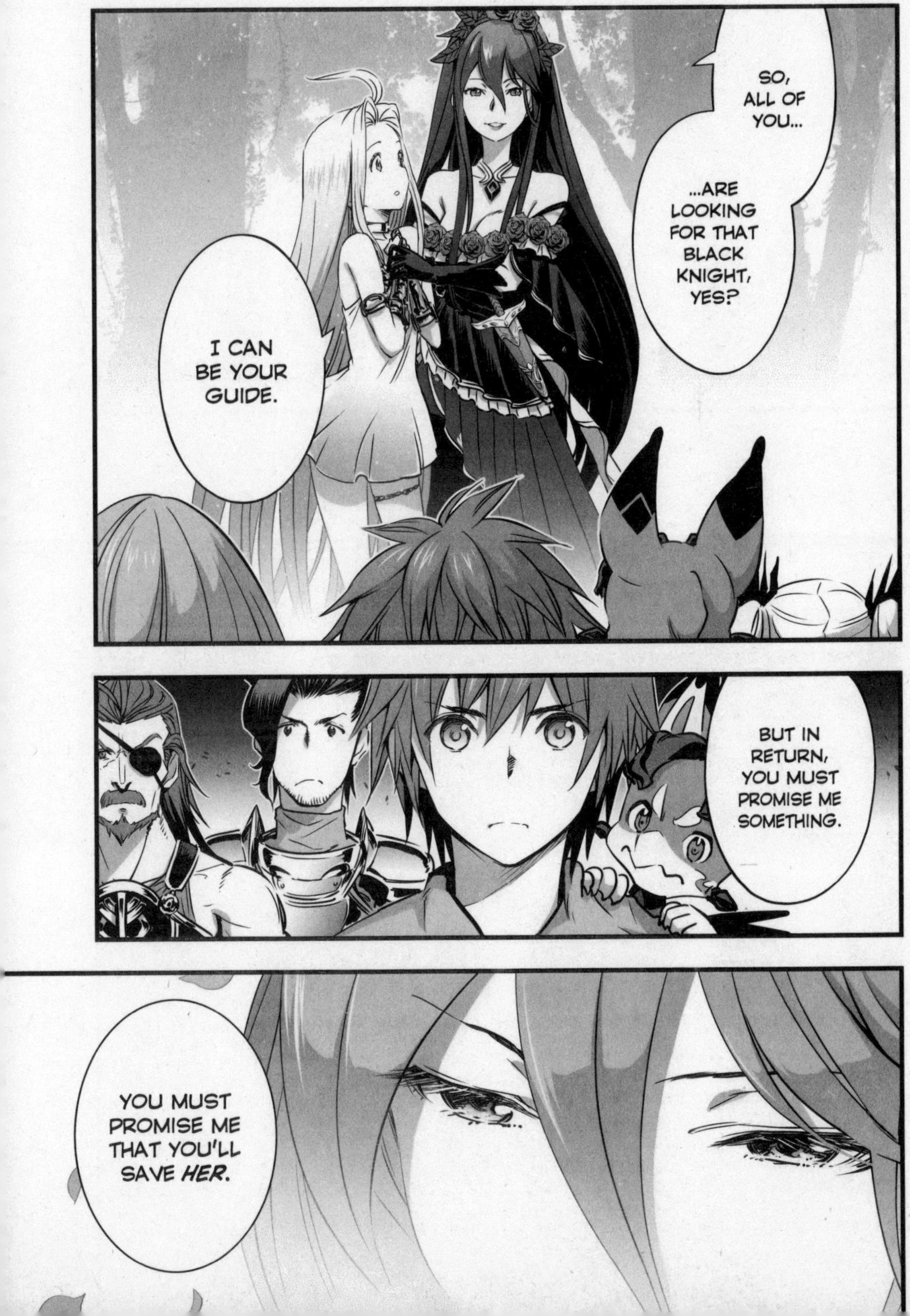
SO, ALL OF YOU...
...ARE LOOKING FOR THAT BLACK KNIGHT, YES?
I CAN BE YOUR GUIDE.
BUT IN RETURN, YOU MUST PROMISE ME SOMETHING.
YOU MUST PROMISE ME THAT YOU'LL SAVE *HER*.

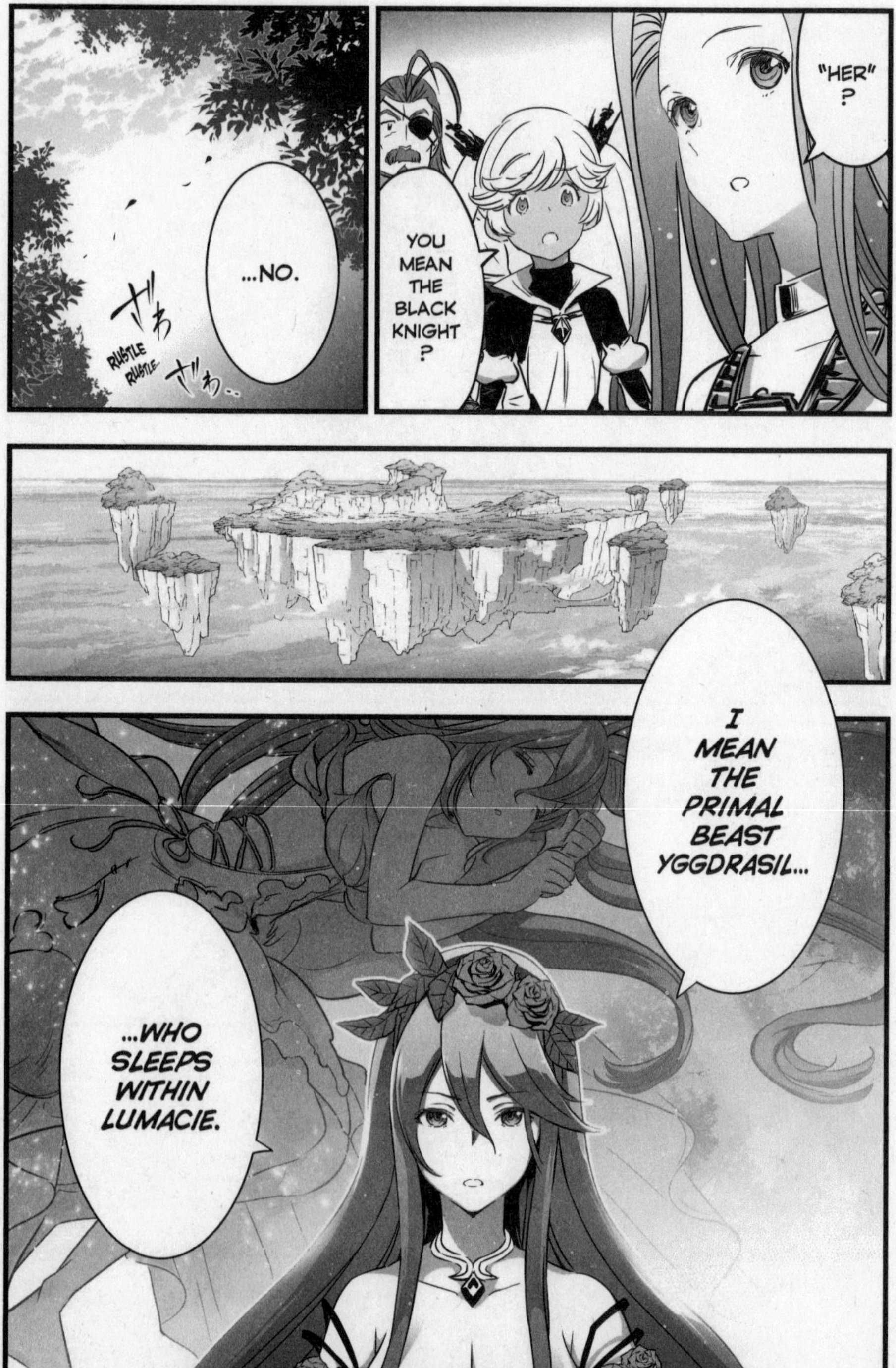
"HER"?
YOU MEAN THE BLACK KNIGHT?
...NO.
ざわ
RUSTLE RUSTLE
ざわ..
I MEAN THE PRIMAL BEAST YGGDRASIL...
...WHO SLEEPS WITHIN LUMACIE.

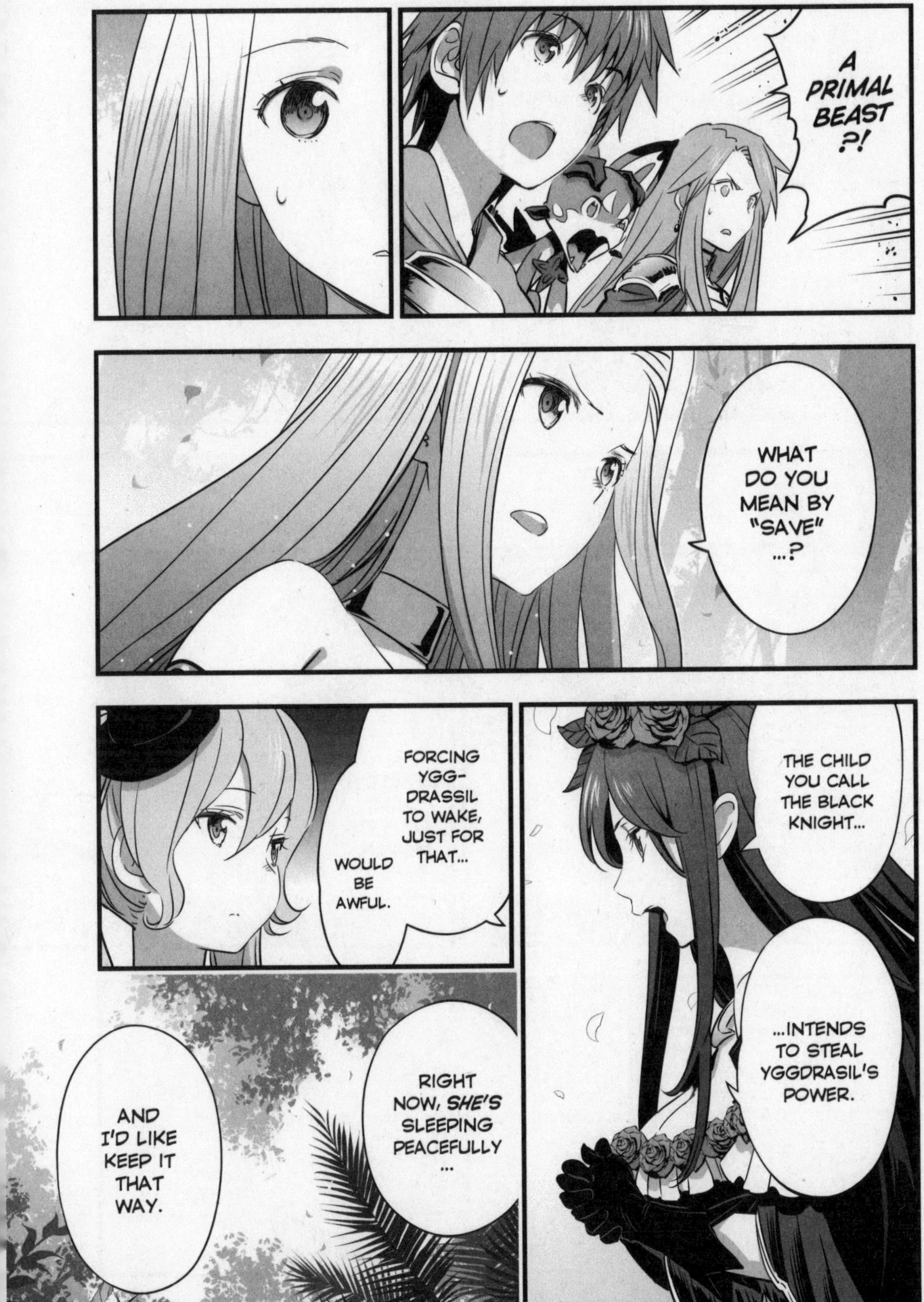
A PRIMAL BEAST ?!
WHAT DO YOU MEAN BY "SAVE" ...?
THE CHILD YOU CALL THE BLACK KNIGHT...
...INTENDS TO STEAL YGGDRASIL'S POWER.
FORCING YGG-DRASSIL TO WAKE, JUST FOR THAT...
WOULD BE AWFUL.
RIGHT NOW, *SHE'S* SLEEPING PEACEFULLY ...
AND I'D LIKE KEEP IT THAT WAY.

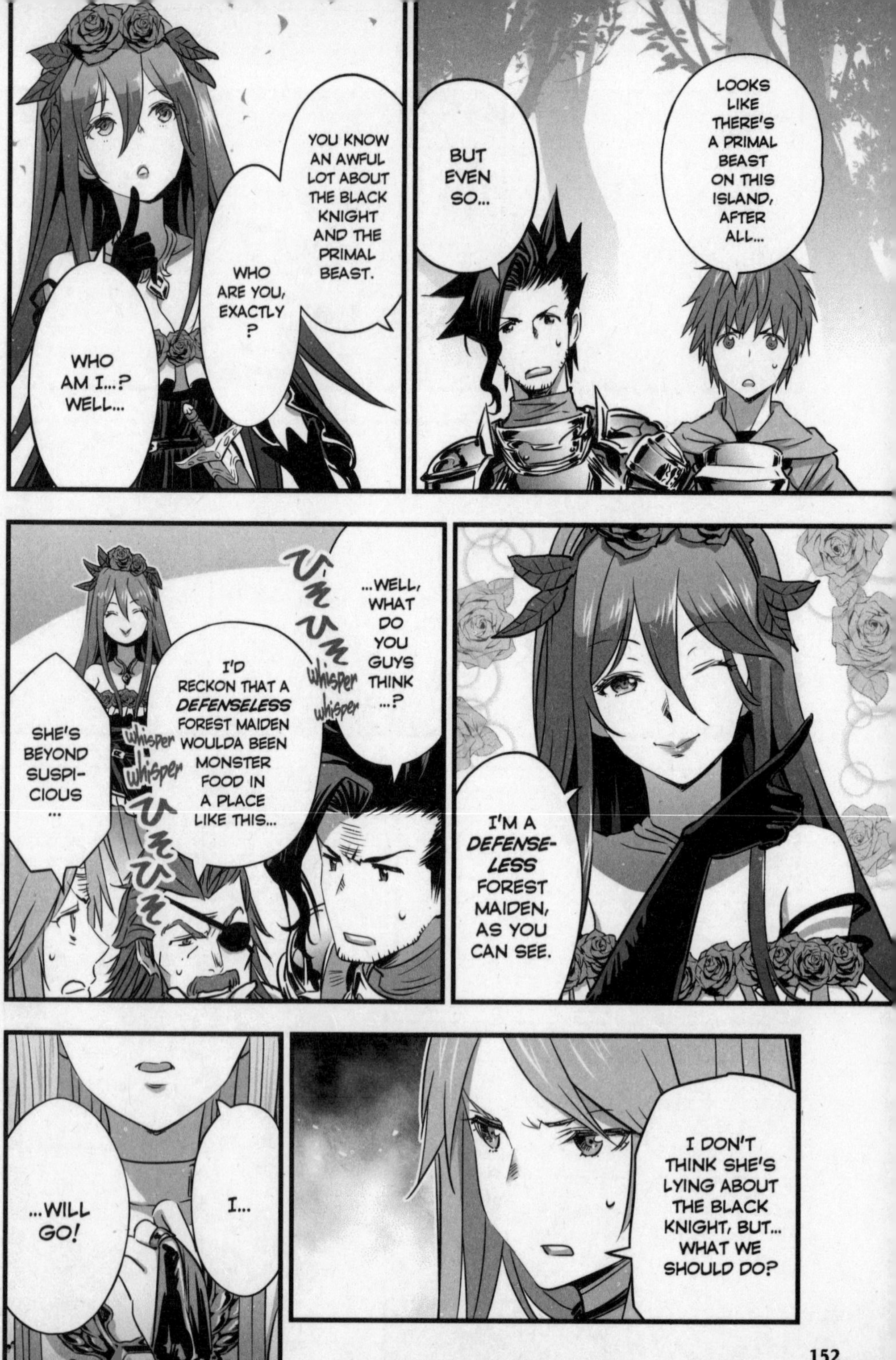
LOOKS LIKE THERE'S A PRIMAL BEAST ON THIS ISLAND, AFTER ALL...
BUT EVEN SO...
YOU KNOW AN AWFUL LOT ABOUT THE BLACK KNIGHT AND THE PRIMAL BEAST.
WHO ARE YOU, EXACTLY?
WHO AM I...? WELL...
I'M A *DEFENSELESS* FOREST MAIDEN, AS YOU CAN SEE.
...WELL, WHAT DO YOU GUYS THINK...?
ひそひそ whisper whisper
I'D RECKON THAT A *DEFENSELESS* FOREST MAIDEN WOULDA BEEN MONSTER FOOD IN A PLACE LIKE THIS...
whisper whisper ひそひそ
SHE'S BEYOND SUSPICIOUS...
I DON'T THINK SHE'S LYING ABOUT THE BLACK KNIGHT, BUT... WHAT WE SHOULD DO?
I...
...WILL GO!

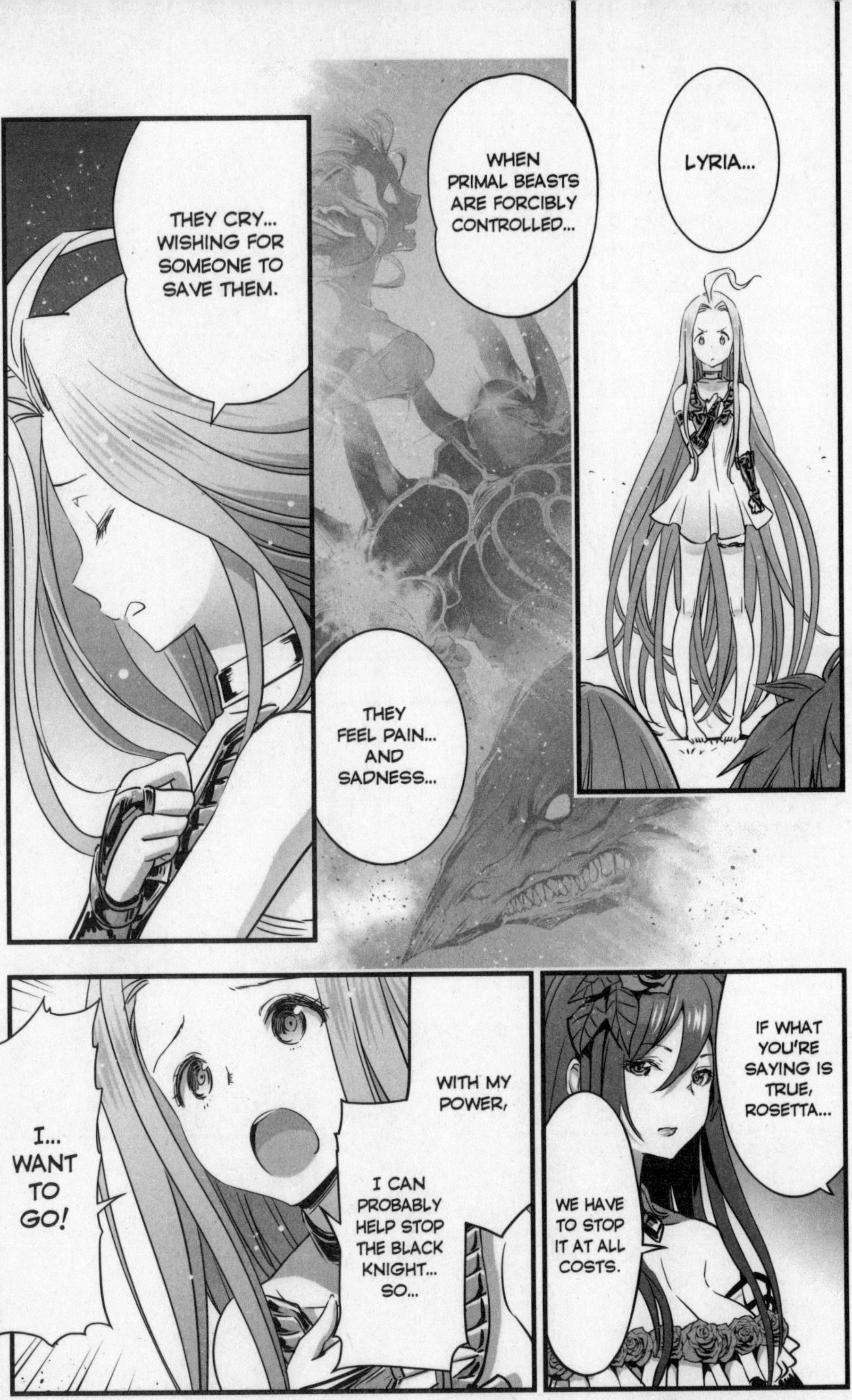

LYRIA...
WHEN PRIMAL BEASTS ARE FORCIBLY CONTROLLED...
THEY FEEL PAIN... AND SADNESS...
THEY CRY... WISHING FOR SOMEONE TO SAVE THEM.
IF WHAT YOU'RE SAYING IS TRUE, ROSETTA...
WE HAVE TO STOP IT AT ALL COSTS.
WITH MY POWER,
I CAN PROBABLY HELP STOP THE BLACK KNIGHT... SO...
I... WANT TO GO!

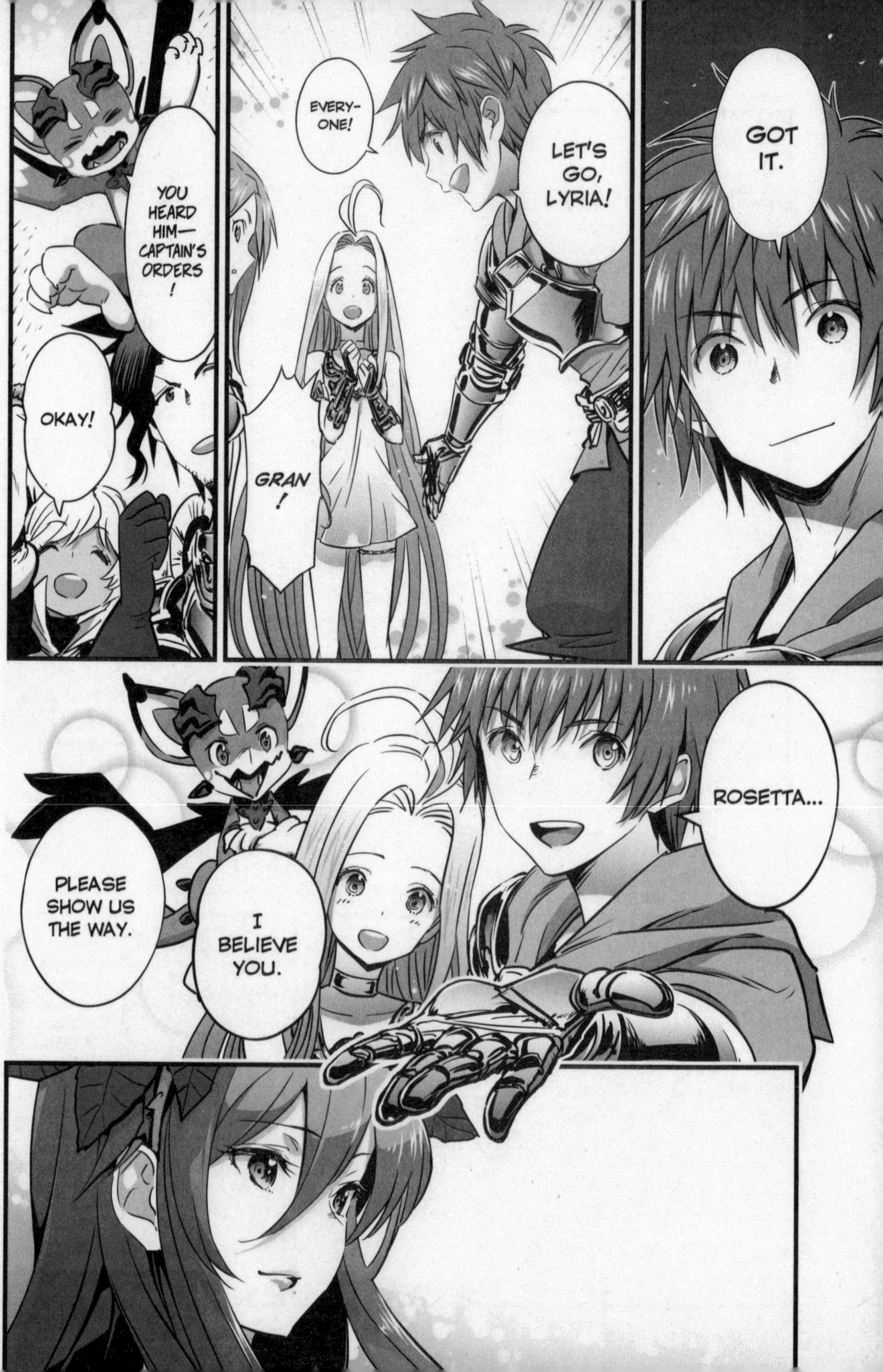
GOT IT.
LET'S GO, LYRIA!
EVERY-ONE!
GRAN!
YOU HEARD HIM—CAPTAIN'S ORDERS!
OKAY!
ROSETTA...
I BELIEVE YOU.
PLEASE SHOW US THE WAY.

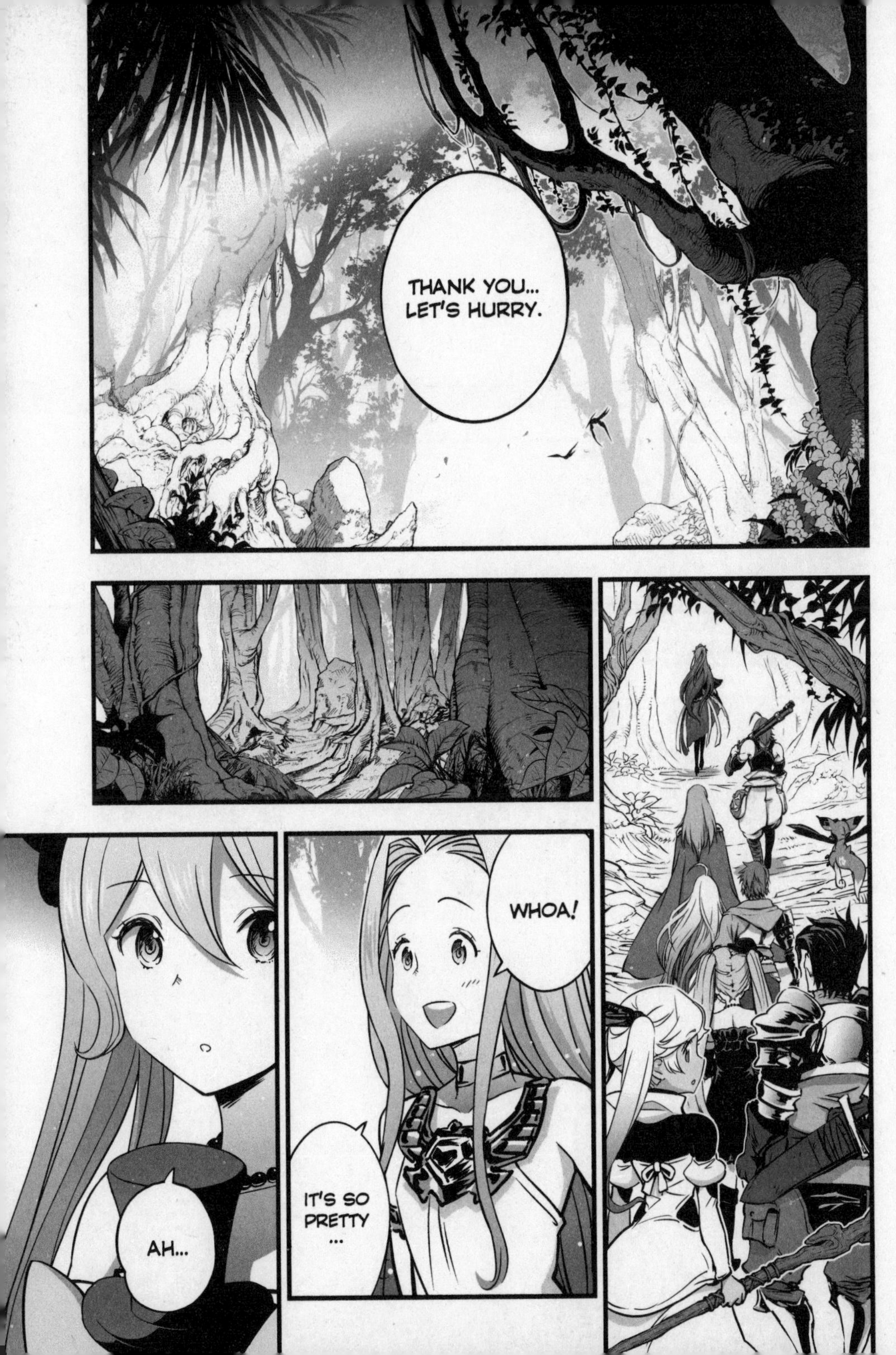
THANK YOU... LET'S HURRY.
WHOA!
IT'S SO PRETTY ...
AH...

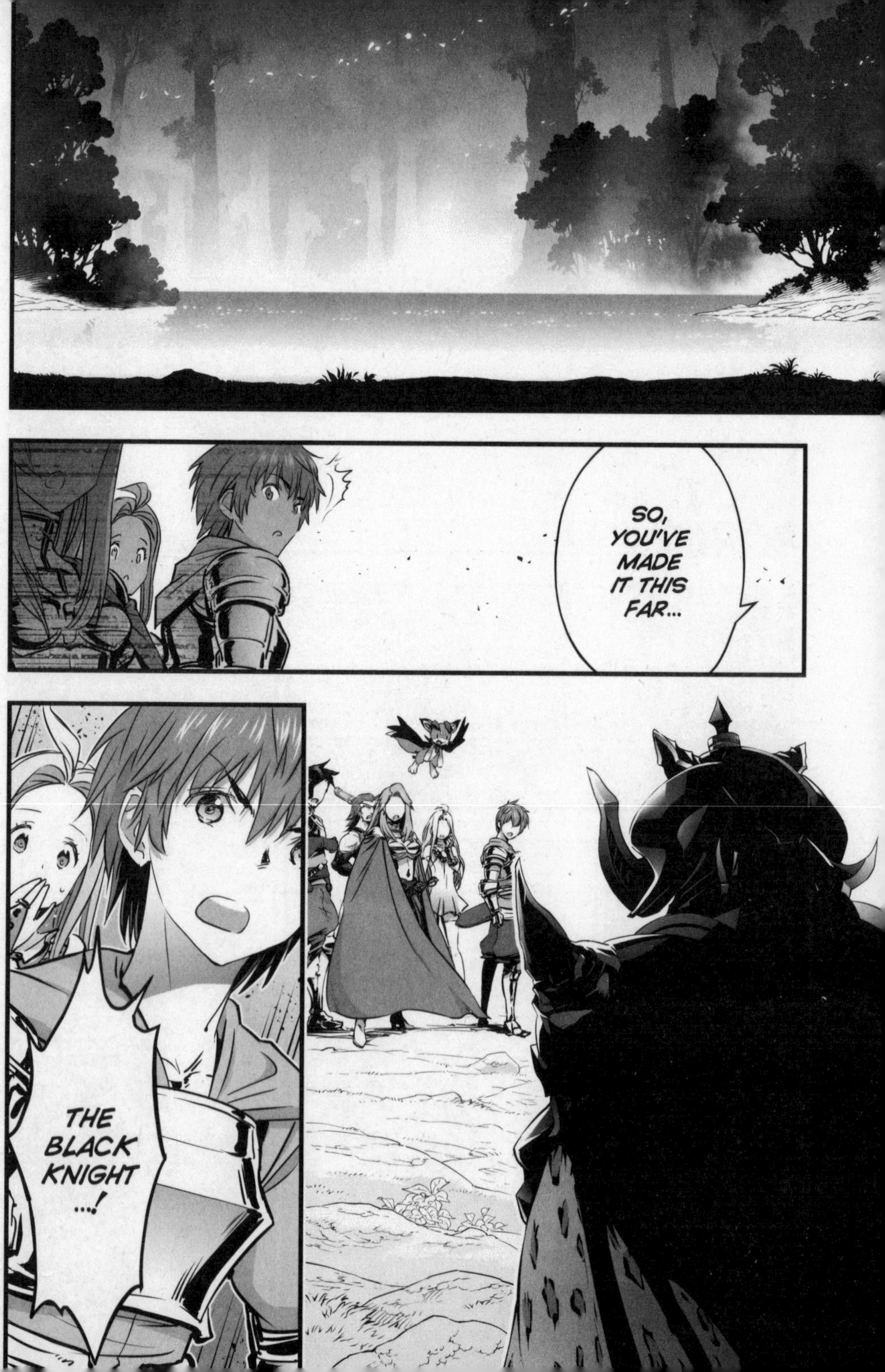
SO, YOU'VE MADE IT THIS FAR...
THE BLACK KNIGHT ...!

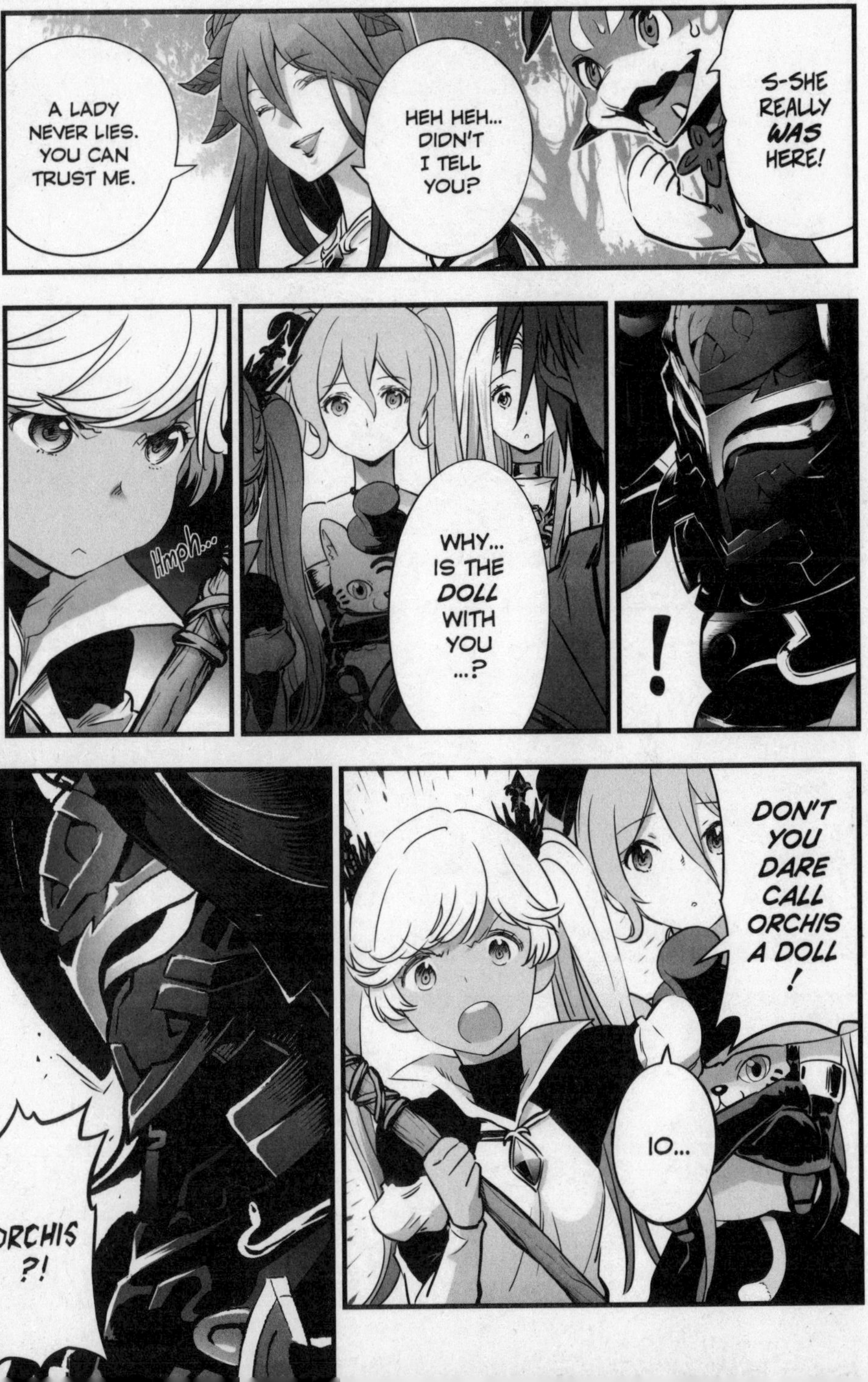
S-SHE REALLY WAS HERE!
HEH HEH... DIDN'T I TELL YOU?
A LADY NEVER LIES. YOU CAN TRUST ME.
!
WHY... IS THE DOLL WITH YOU ...?
Hmph...
DON'T YOU DARE CALL ORCHIS A DOLL!
IO...
ORCHIS?!

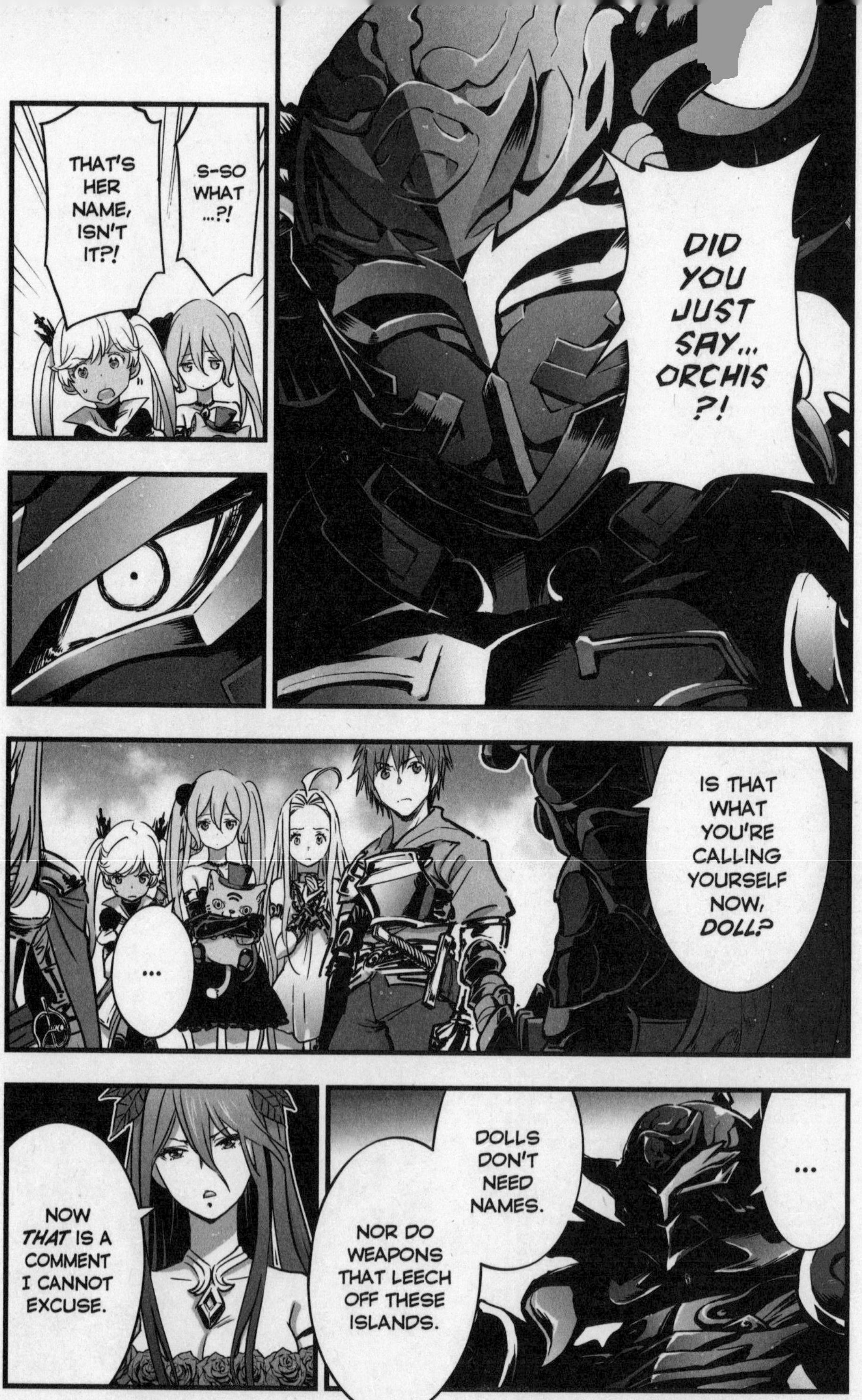
DID YOU JUST SAY... ORCHIS?!
S-SO WHAT ...?!
THAT'S HER NAME, ISN'T IT?!
IS THAT WHAT YOU'RE CALLING YOURSELF NOW, DOLL?
...
...
DOLLS DON'T NEED NAMES.
NOR DO WEAPONS THAT LEECH OFF THESE ISLANDS.
NOW THAT IS A COMMENT I CANNOT EXCUSE.

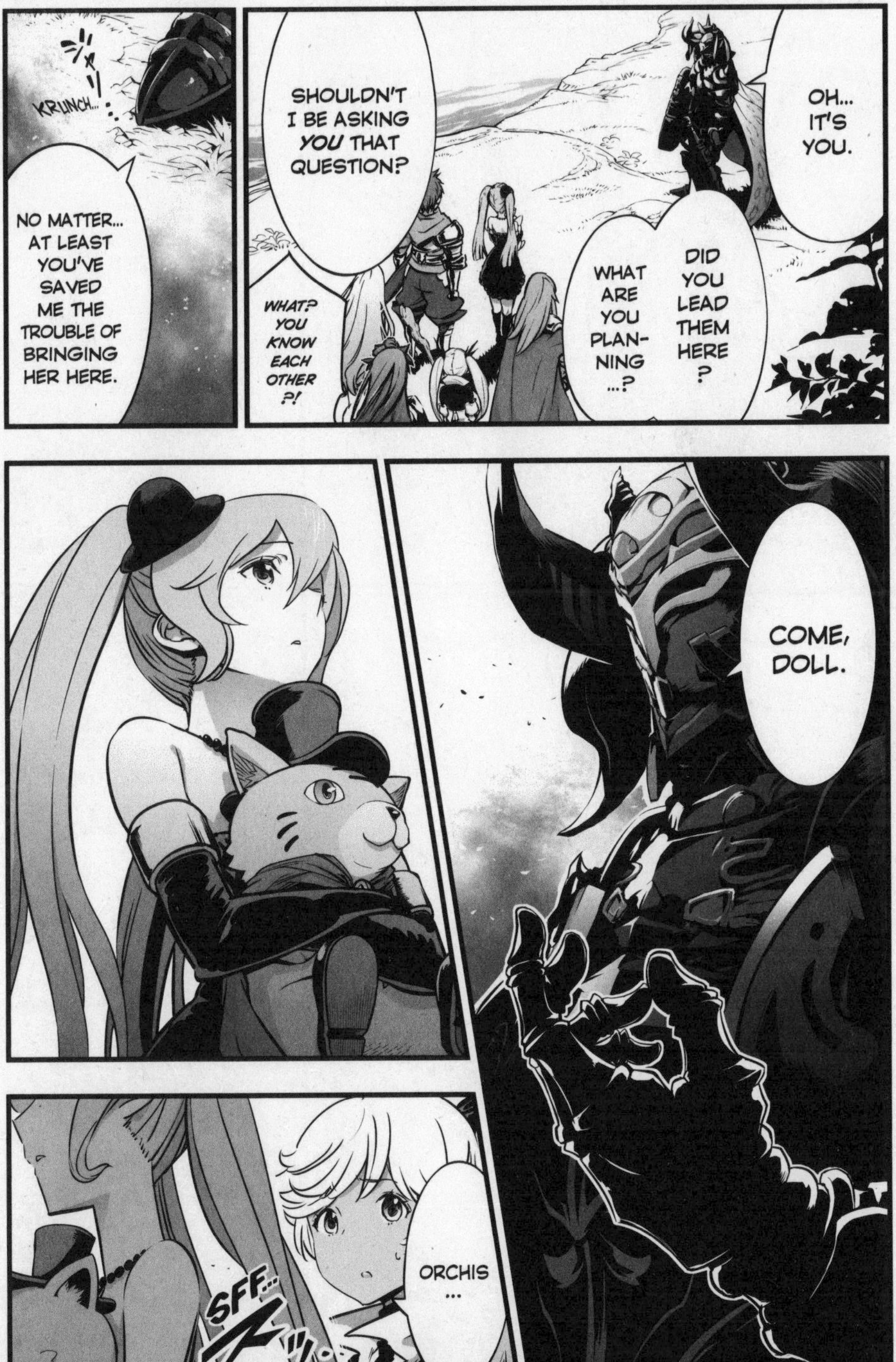
OH... IT'S YOU.
DID YOU LEAD THEM HERE?
WHAT ARE YOU PLANNING...?
SHOULDN'T I BE ASKING YOU THAT QUESTION?
WHAT? YOU KNOW EACH OTHER?!
KRUNCH...
NO MATTER... AT LEAST YOU'VE SAVED ME THE TROUBLE OF BRINGING HER HERE.
COME, DOLL.
ORCHIS...
SFF...

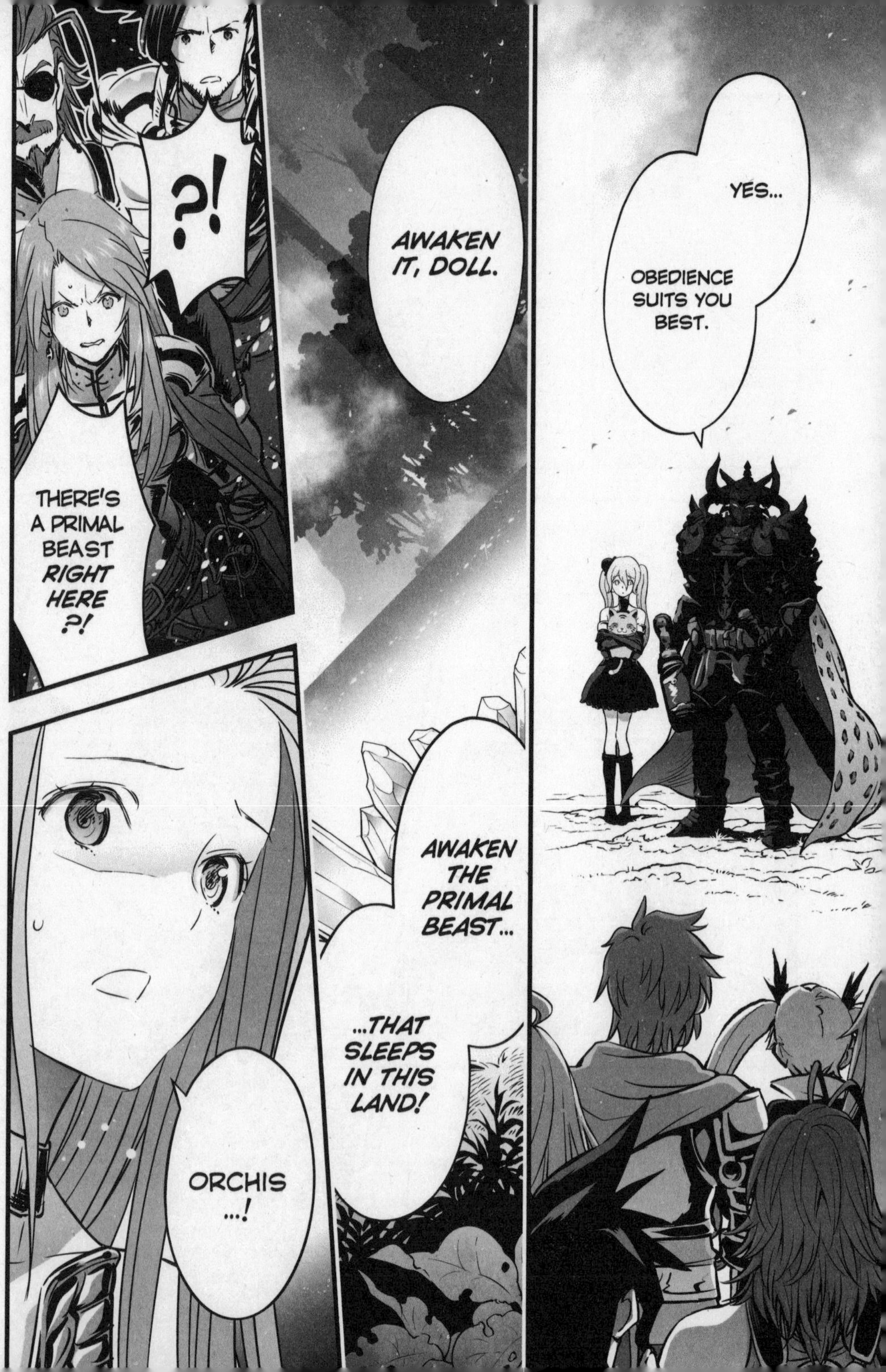

YES...
OBEDIENCE SUITS YOU BEST.
AWAKEN IT, DOLL.
?!
THERE'S A PRIMAL BEAST RIGHT HERE?!
AWAKEN THE PRIMAL BEAST...
...THAT SLEEPS IN THIS LAND!
ORCHIS...!

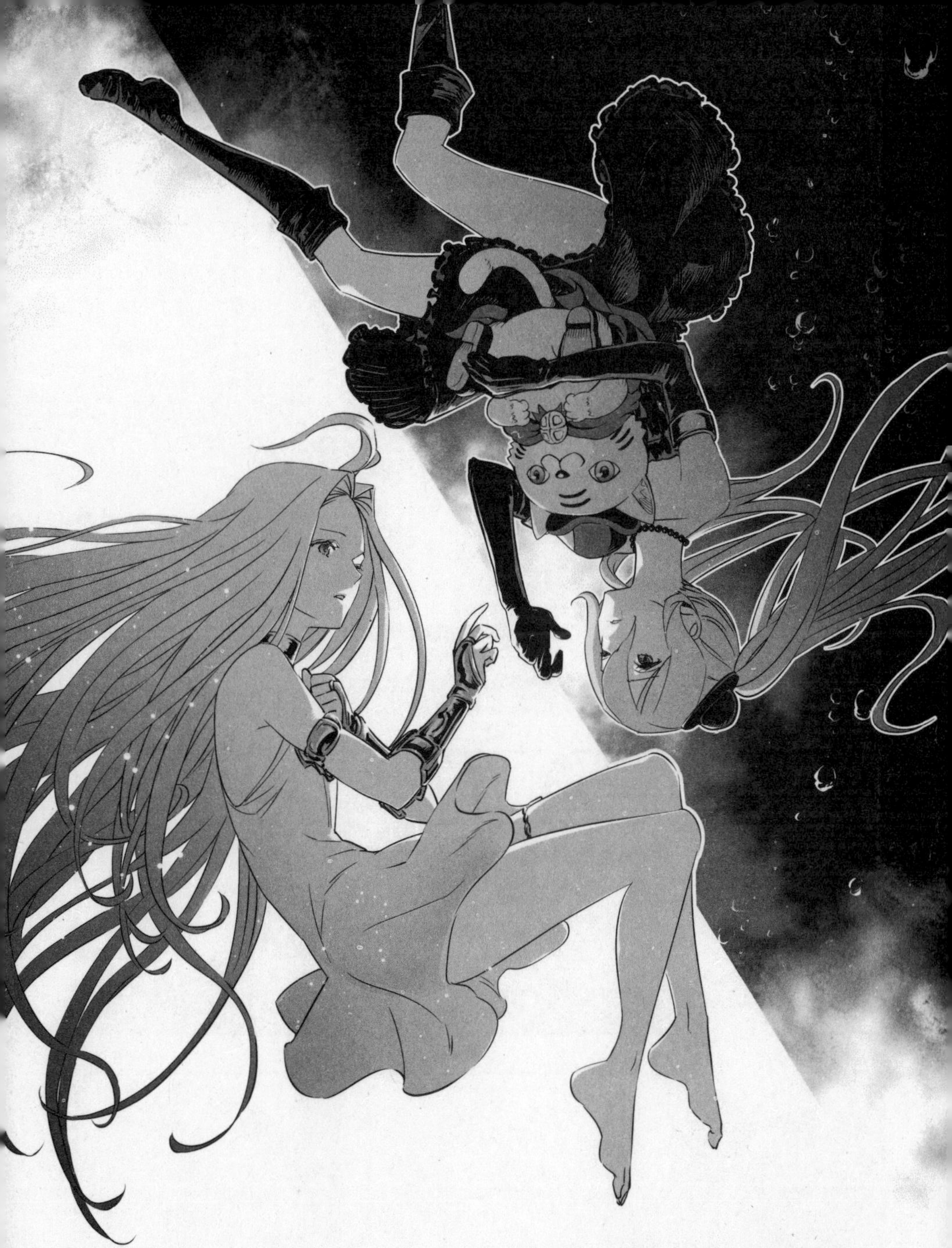

CHAPTER 29: Missed Connection

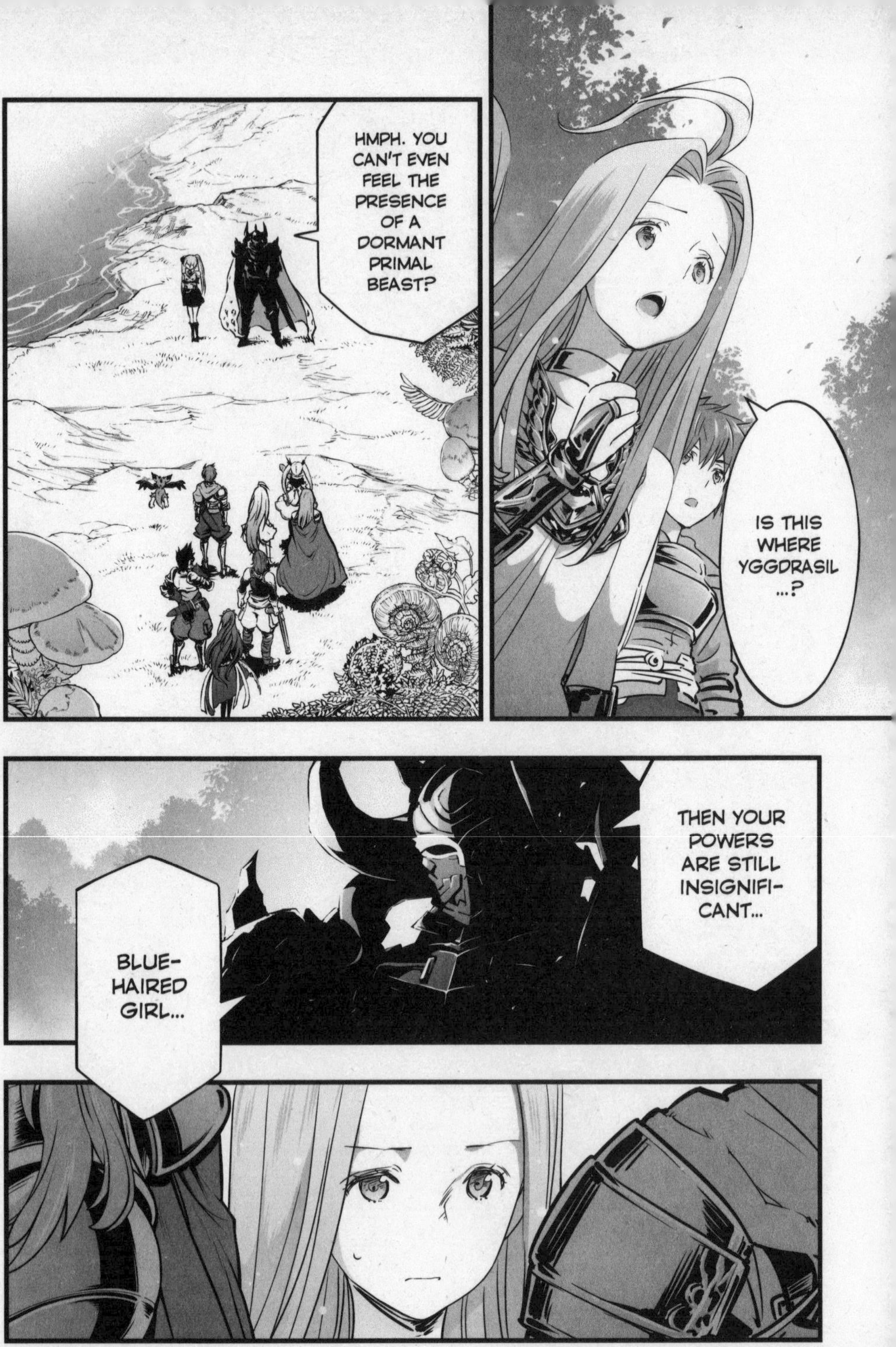
IS THIS WHERE YGGDRASIL ...?
HMPH. YOU CAN'T EVEN FEEL THE PRESENCE OF A DORMANT PRIMAL BEAST?
THEN YOUR POWERS ARE STILL INSIGNIFI-CANT...
BLUE-HAIRED GIRL...

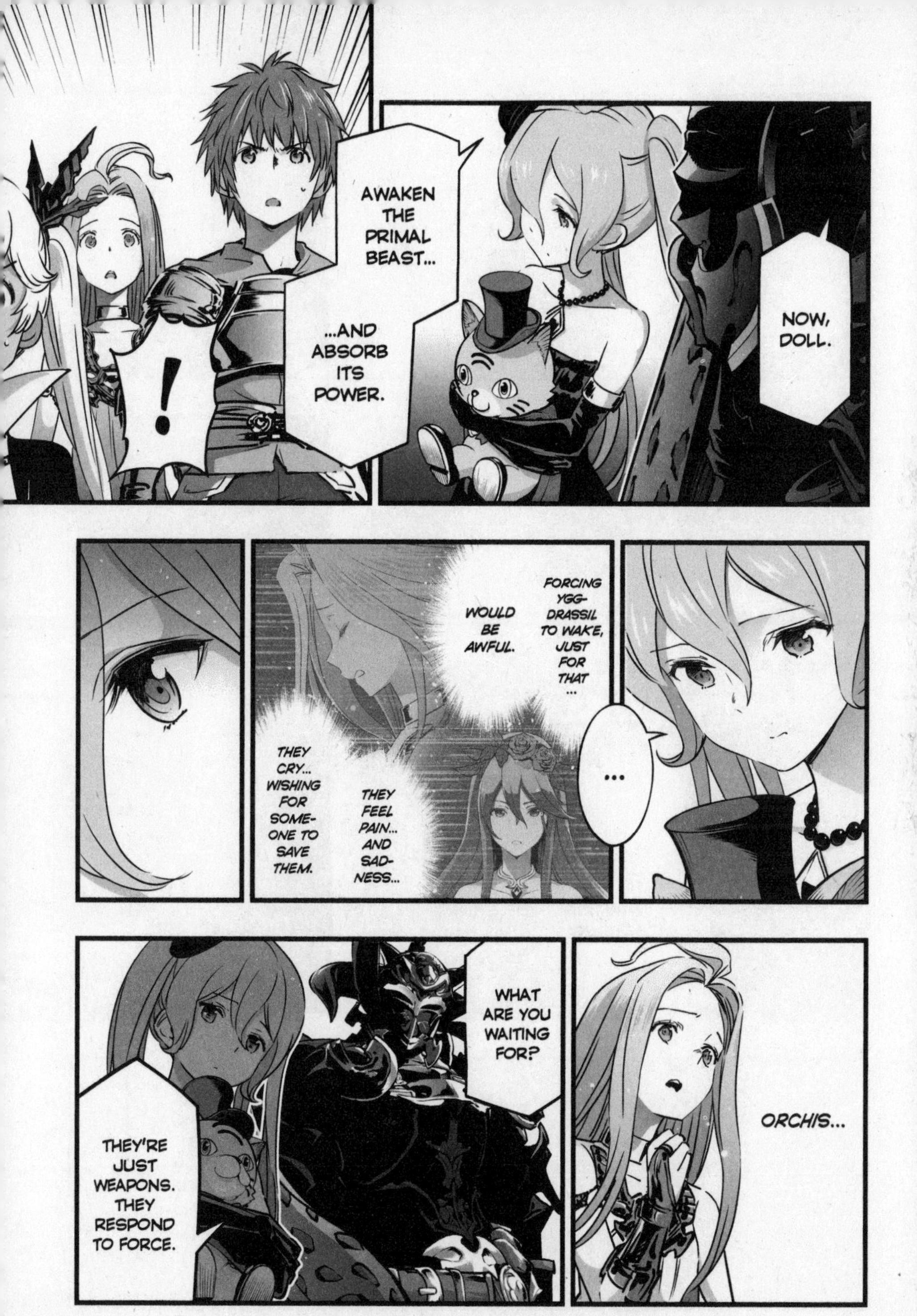
NOW, DOLL.
AWAKEN THE PRIMAL BEAST...
...AND ABSORB ITS POWER.
!
...
FORCING YGG-DRASSIL TO WAKE, JUST FOR THAT...
WOULD BE AWFUL.
THEY FEEL PAIN... AND SAD-NESS...
THEY CRY... WISHING FOR SOME-ONE TO SAVE THEM.
ORCHIS...
WHAT ARE YOU WAITING FOR?
THEY'RE JUST WEAPONS. THEY RESPOND TO FORCE.

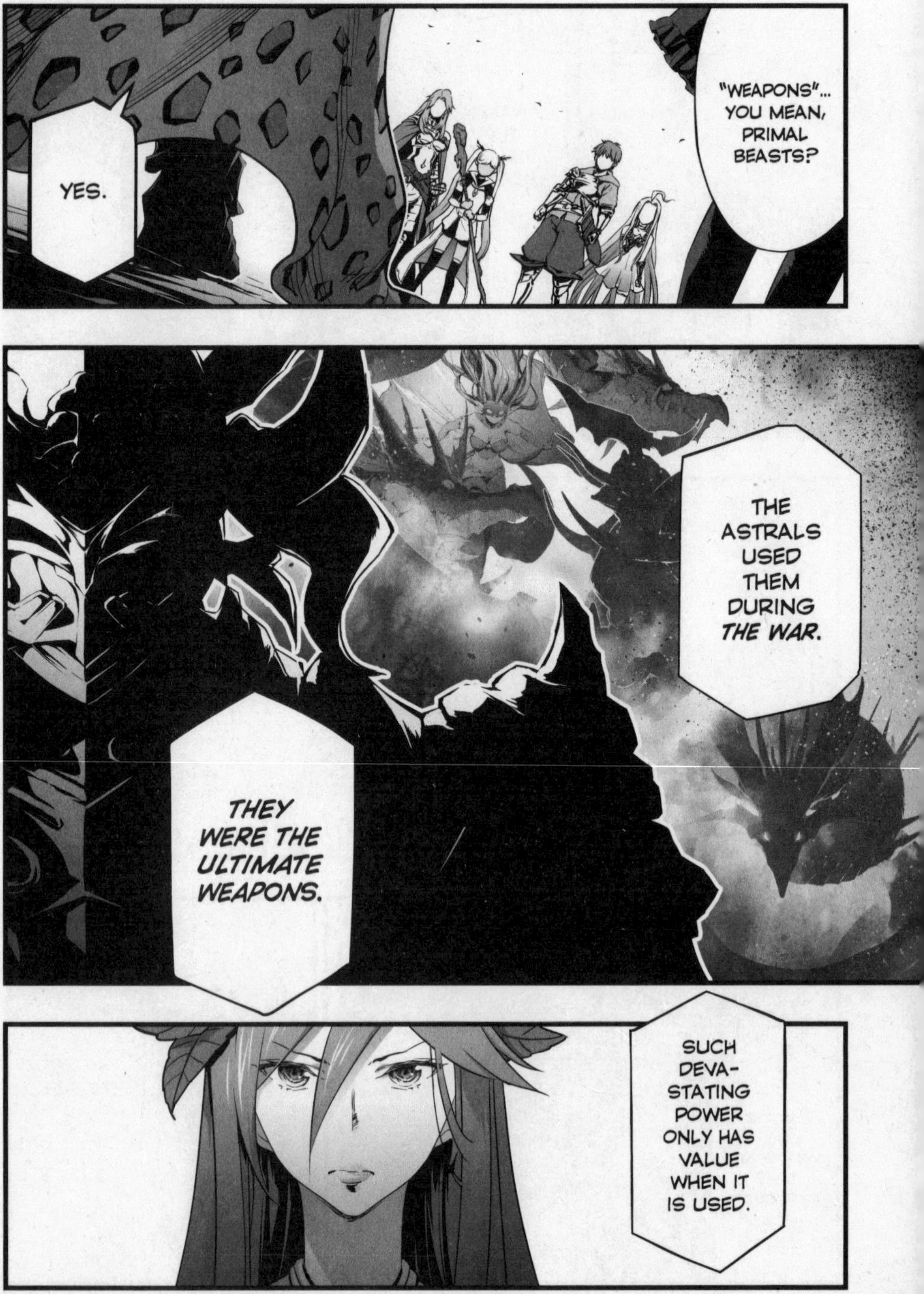
"WEAPONS"... YOU MEAN, PRIMAL BEASTS?
YES.
THE ASTRALS USED THEM DURING *THE WAR*.
THEY WERE THE ULTIMATE WEAPONS.
SUCH DEVA-STATING POWER ONLY HAS VALUE WHEN IT IS USED.

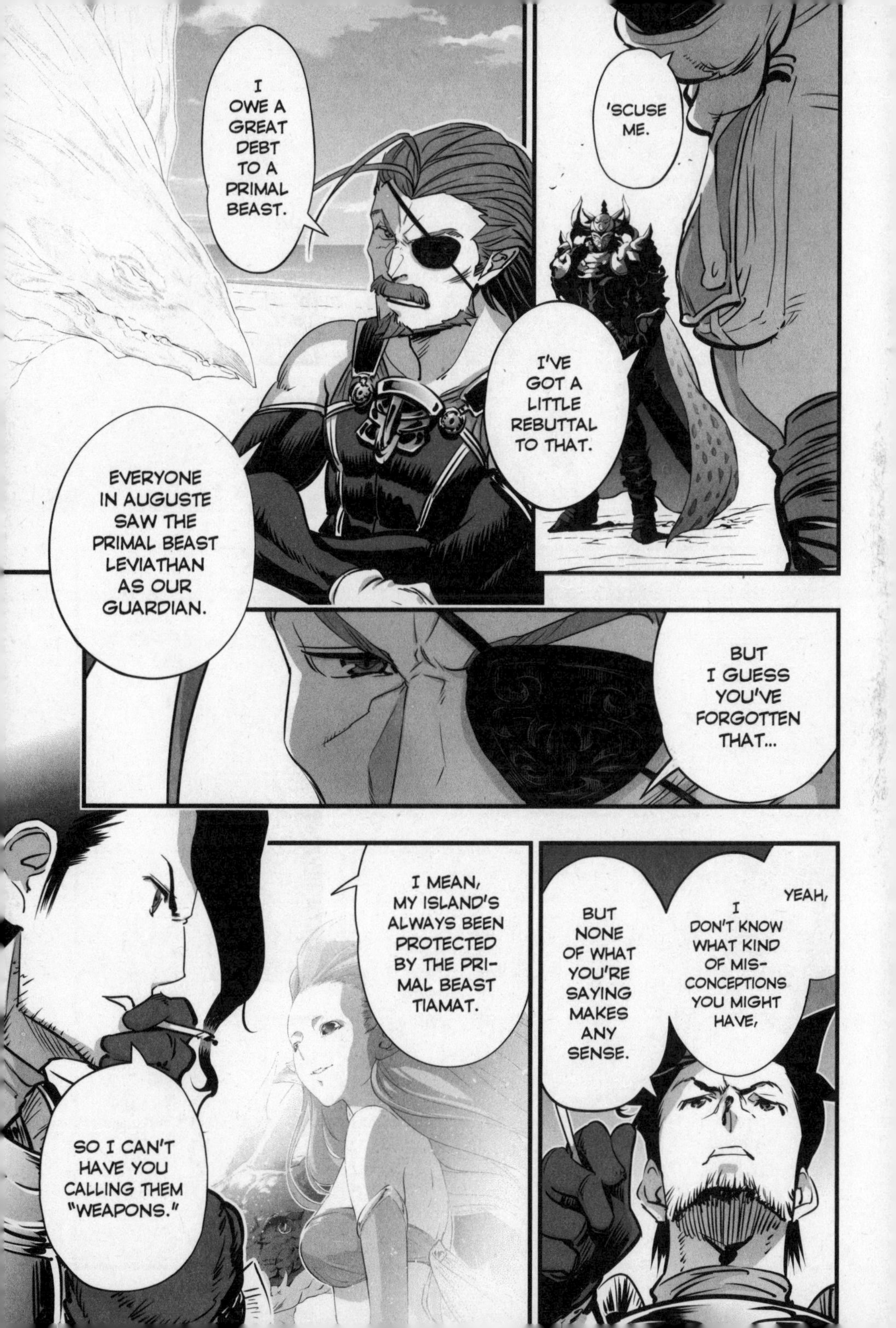
'SCUSE ME.
I'VE GOT A LITTLE REBUTTAL TO THAT.
I OWE A GREAT DEBT TO A PRIMAL BEAST.
EVERYONE IN AUGUSTE SAW THE PRIMAL BEAST LEVIATHAN AS OUR GUARDIAN.
BUT I GUESS YOU'VE FORGOTTEN THAT...
YEAH, I DON'T KNOW WHAT KIND OF MIS-CONCEPTIONS YOU MIGHT HAVE,
BUT NONE OF WHAT YOU'RE SAYING MAKES ANY SENSE.
I MEAN, MY ISLAND'S ALWAYS BEEN PROTECTED BY THE PRI-MAL BEAST TIAMAT.
SO I CAN'T HAVE YOU CALLING THEM "WEAPONS."

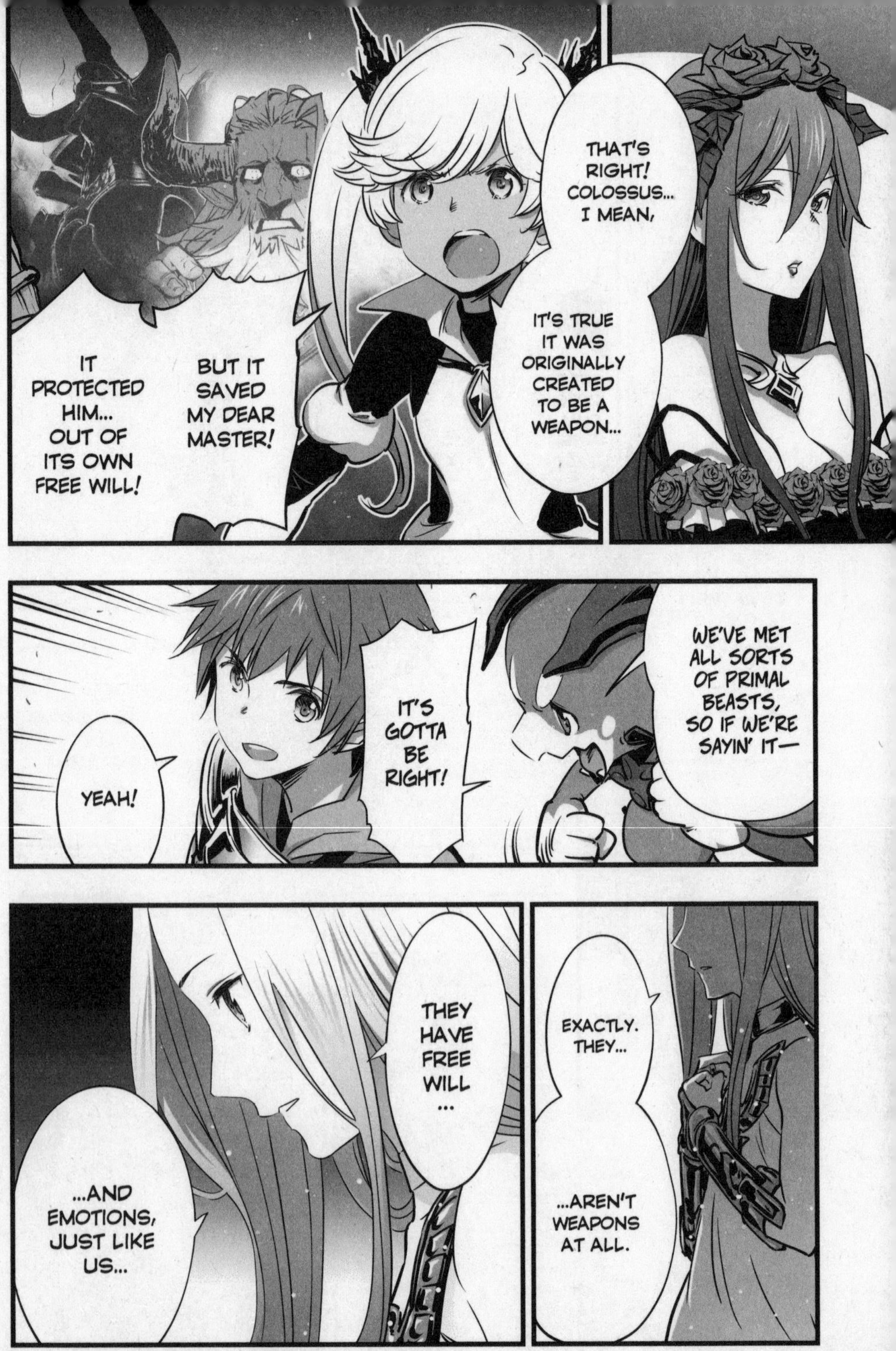
THAT'S RIGHT! COLOSSUS... I MEAN,
IT'S TRUE IT WAS ORIGINALLY CREATED TO BE A WEAPON...
BUT IT SAVED MY DEAR MASTER!
IT PROTECTED HIM... OUT OF ITS OWN FREE WILL!
WE'VE MET ALL SORTS OF PRIMAL BEASTS, SO IF WE'RE SAYIN' IT—
IT'S GOTTA BE RIGHT!
YEAH!
EXACTLY. THEY...
...AREN'T WEAPONS AT ALL.
THEY HAVE FREE WILL ...
...AND EMOTIONS, JUST LIKE US...

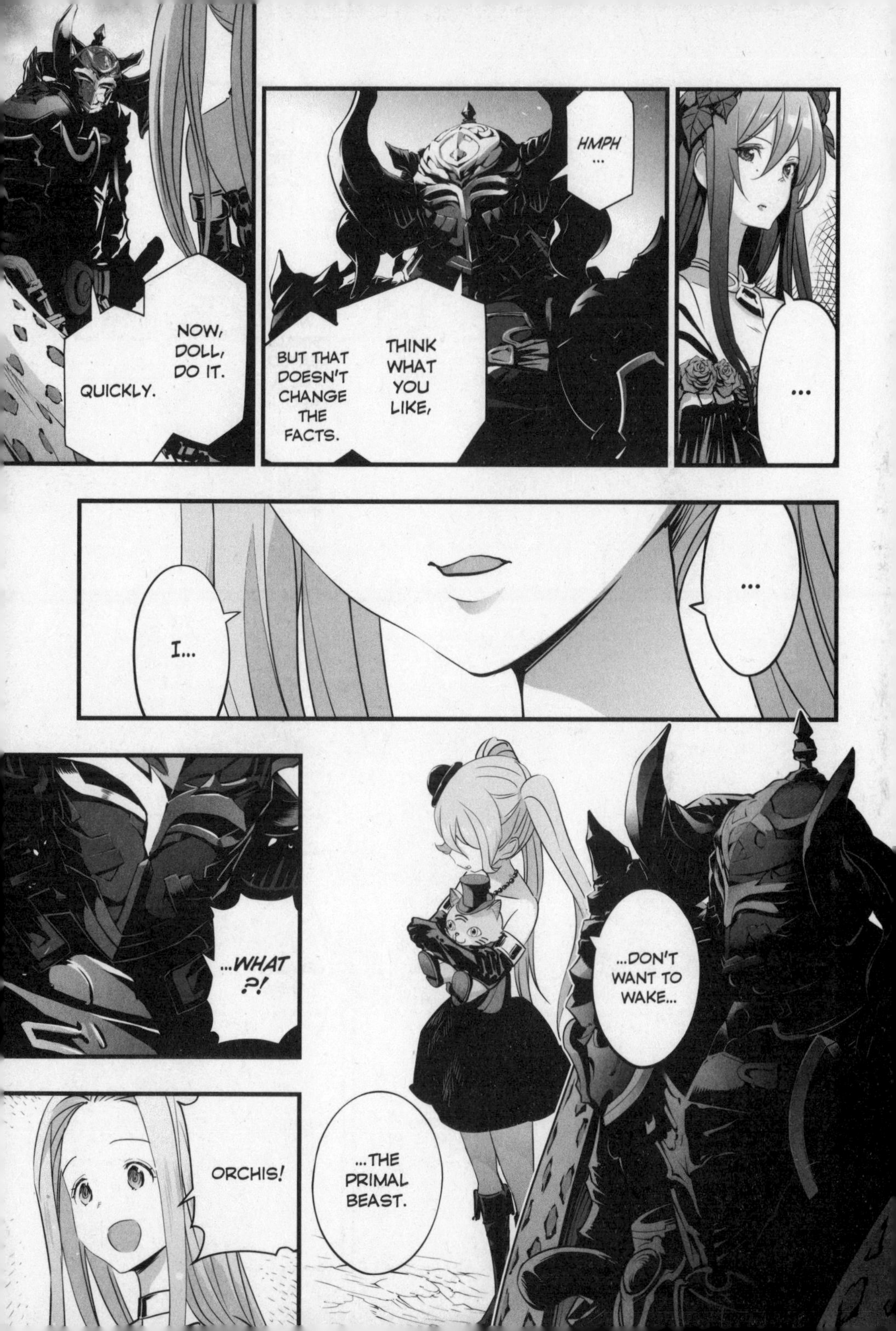
...
HMPH ...
THINK WHAT YOU LIKE,
BUT THAT DOESN'T CHANGE THE FACTS.
NOW, DOLL, DO IT.
QUICKLY.
...
I...
...DON'T WANT TO WAKE...
...THE PRIMAL BEAST.
...WHAT ?!
ORCHIS!

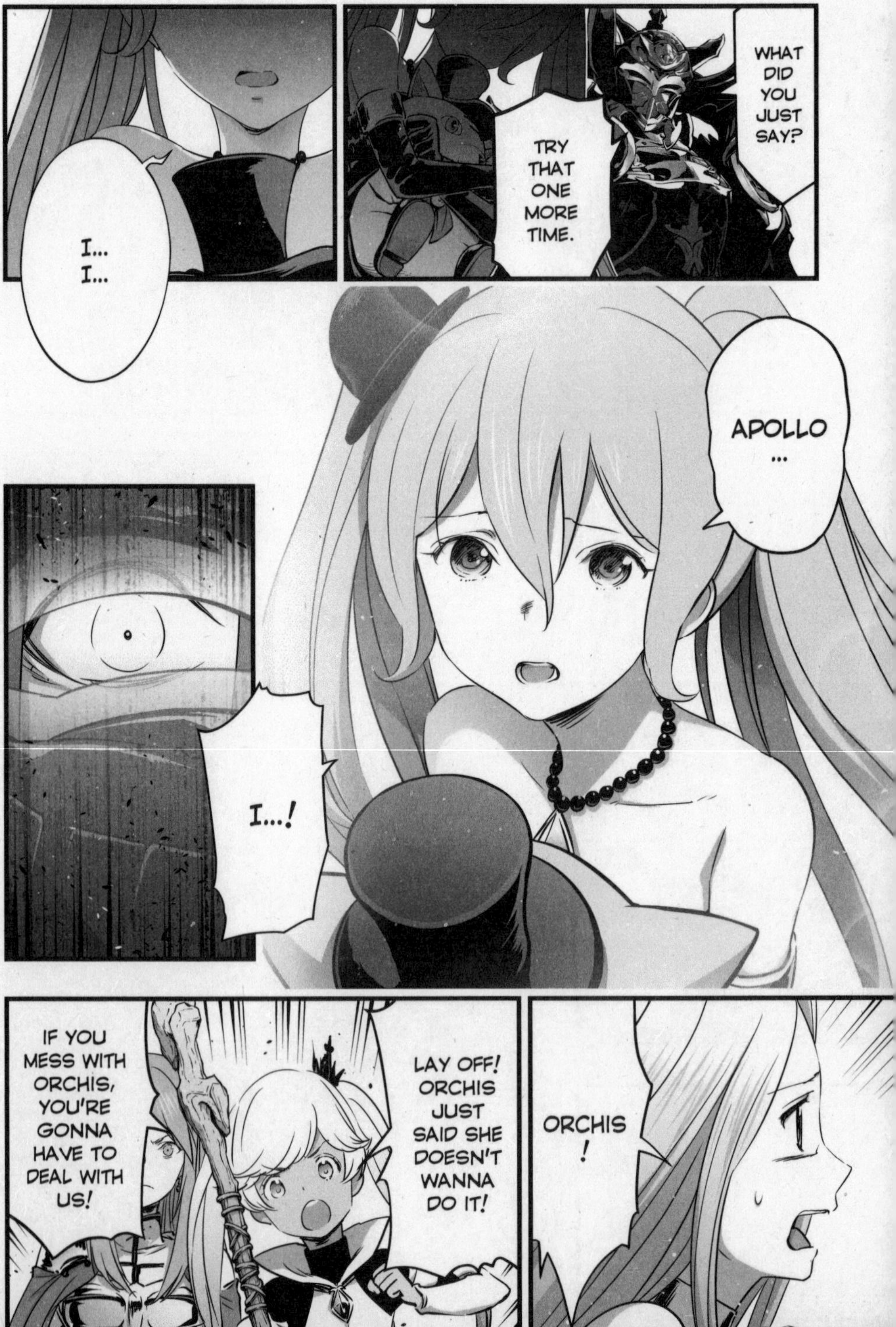
WHAT DID YOU JUST SAY?
TRY THAT ONE MORE TIME.
I... I...
APOLLO ...
I...!
ORCHIS!
LAY OFF! ORCHIS JUST SAID SHE DOESN'T WANNA DO IT!
IF YOU MESS WITH ORCHIS, YOU'RE GONNA HAVE TO DEAL WITH US!

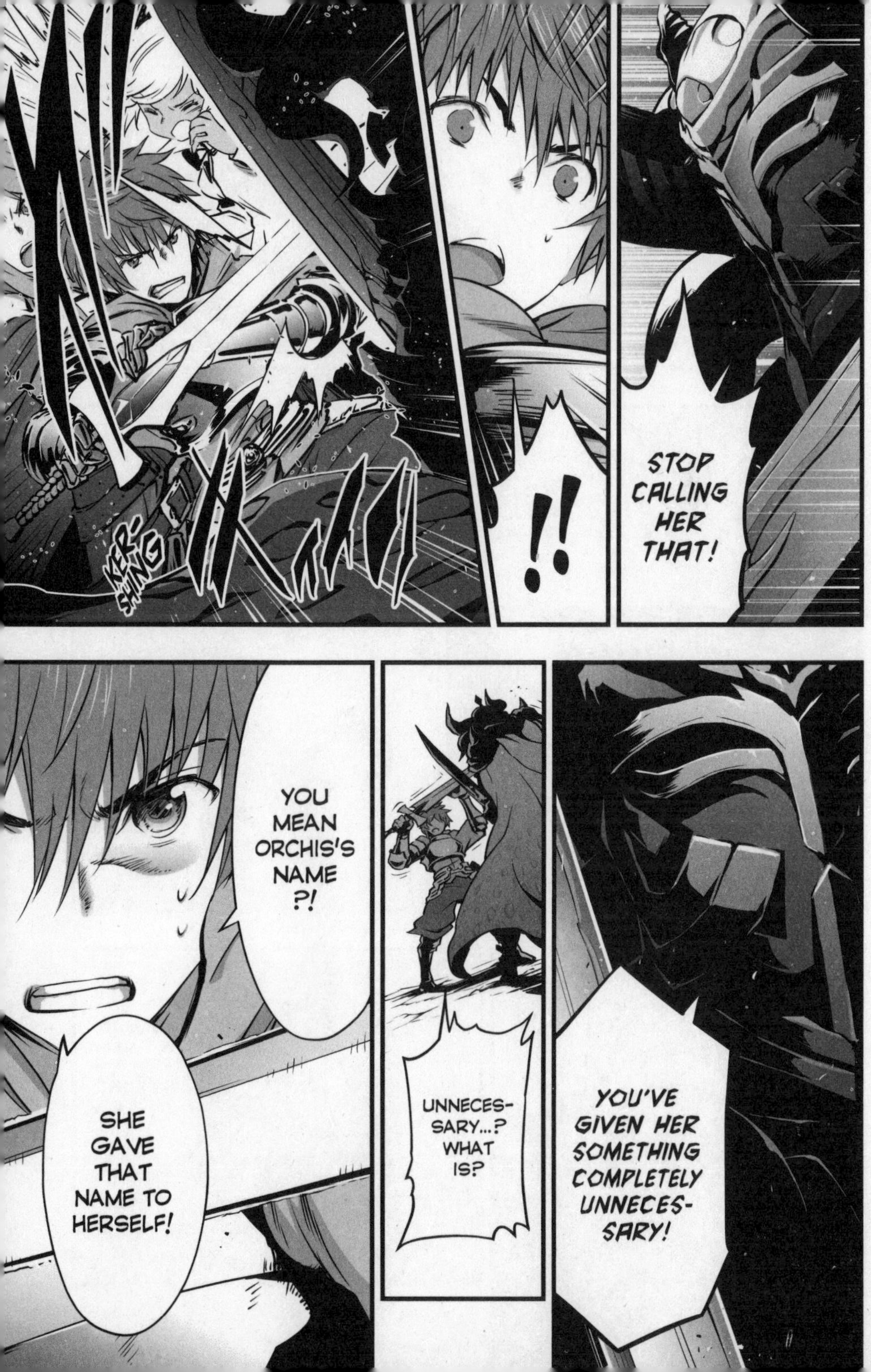
STOP CALLING HER THAT!
!!
KER-SHING
YOU'VE GIVEN HER SOMETHING COMPLETELY UNNECES-SARY!
UNNECES-SARY...? WHAT IS?
YOU MEAN ORCHIS'S NAME?!
SHE GAVE THAT NAME TO HERSELF!

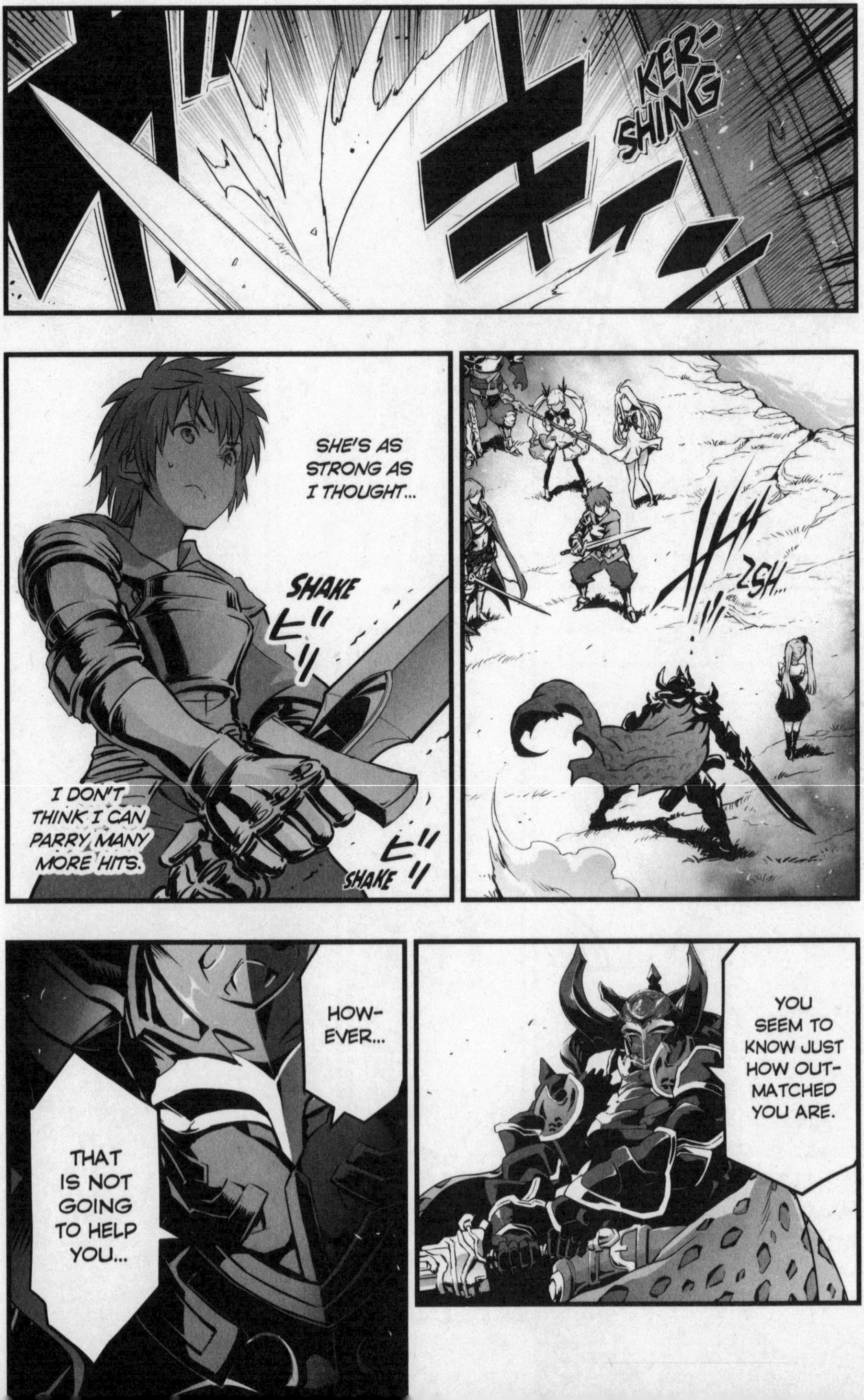
KER-SHING
Z-SH...
SHE'S AS STRONG AS I THOUGHT...
SHAKE
I DON'T THINK I CAN PARRY MANY MORE HITS.
SHAKE
YOU SEEM TO KNOW JUST HOW OUT-MATCHED YOU ARE.
HOW-EVER...
THAT IS NOT GOING TO HELP YOU...

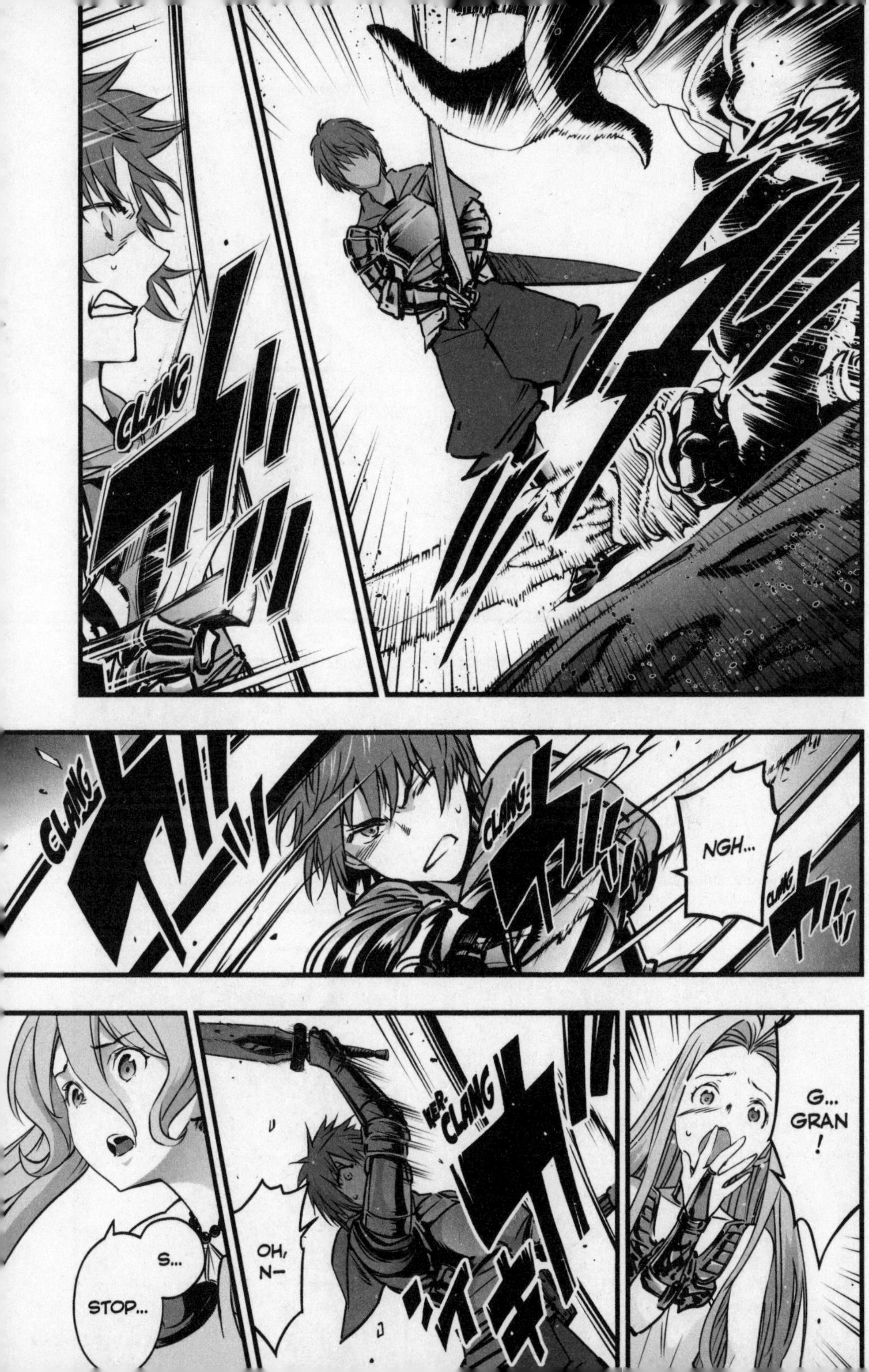
DASH
CLANG
NGH...
CLANG
CLANG
CLANG
G... GRAN!
KER-CLANG
OH, N—
S... STOP...

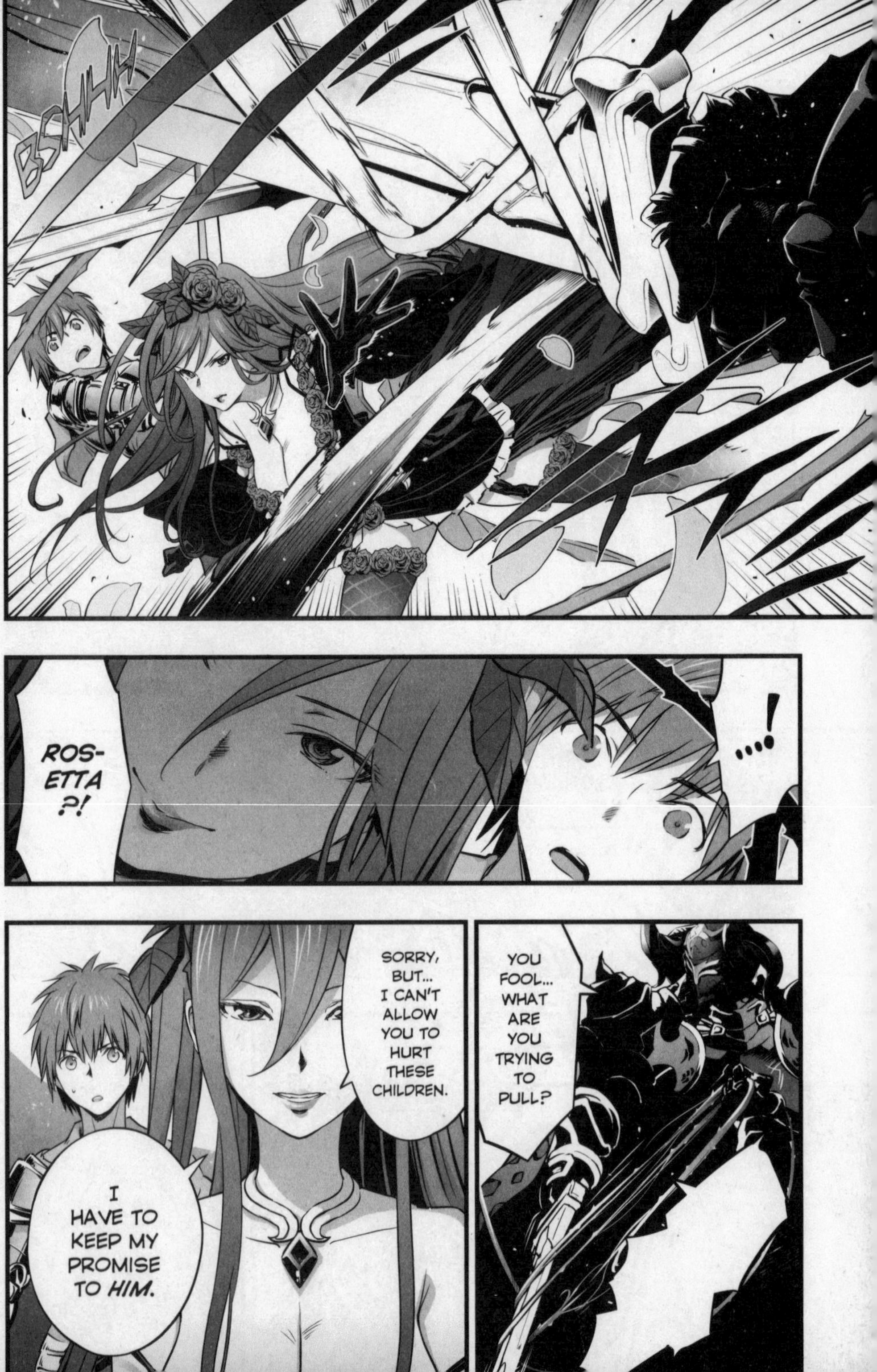
BSHHH
...!
ROS-ETTA?!
YOU FOOL... WHAT ARE YOU TRYING TO PULL?
SORRY, BUT... I CAN'T ALLOW YOU TO HURT THESE CHILDREN.
I HAVE TO KEEP MY PROMISE TO *HIM*.

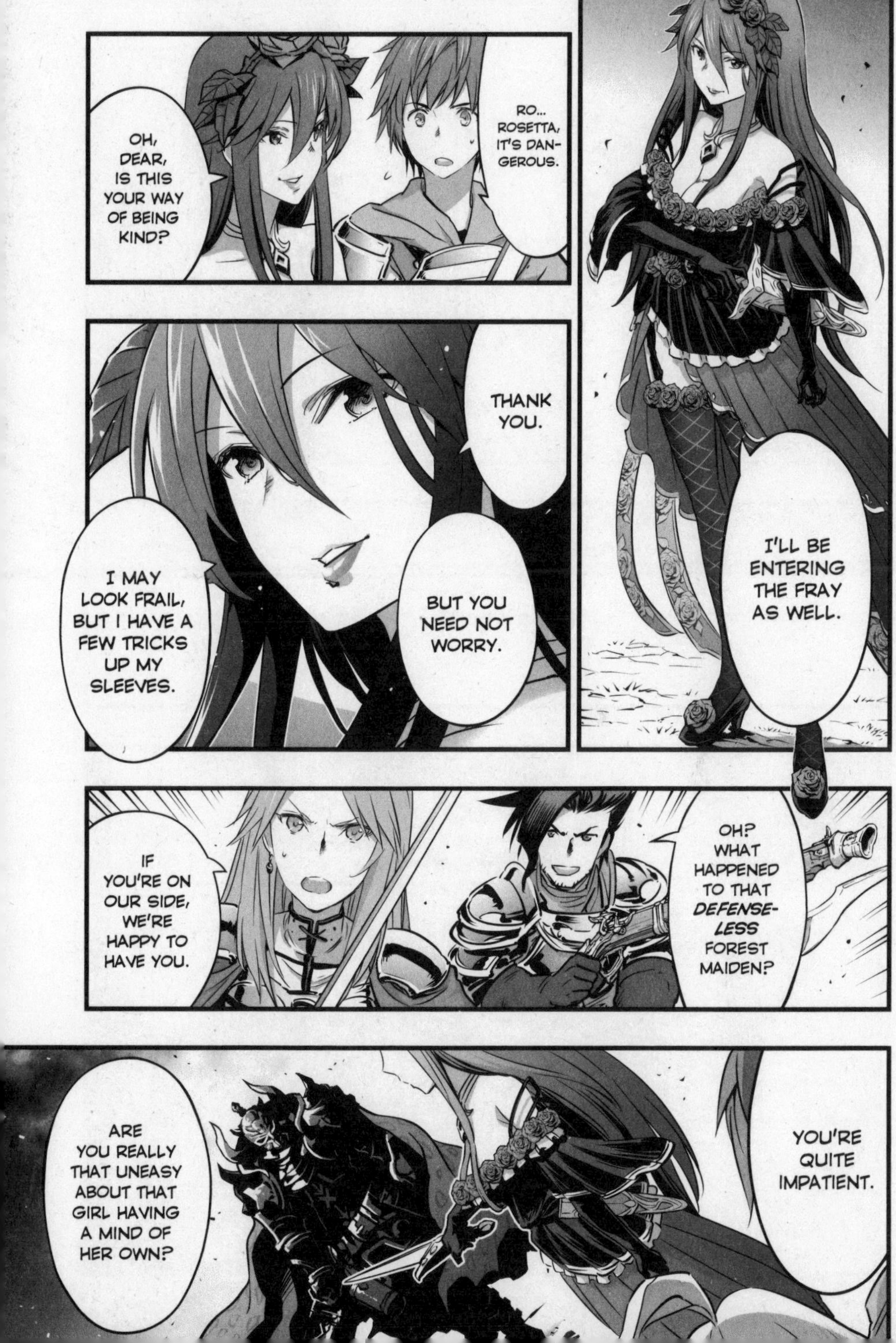
I'LL BE ENTERING THE FRAY AS WELL.
RO... ROSETTA, IT'S DAN-GEROUS.
OH, DEAR, IS THIS YOUR WAY OF BEING KIND?
THANK YOU.
BUT YOU NEED NOT WORRY.
I MAY LOOK FRAIL, BUT I HAVE A FEW TRICKS UP MY SLEEVES.
OH? WHAT HAPPENED TO THAT *DEFENSE-LESS* FOREST MAIDEN?
IF YOU'RE ON OUR SIDE, WE'RE HAPPY TO HAVE YOU.
YOU'RE QUITE IMPATIENT.
ARE YOU REALLY THAT UNEASY ABOUT THAT GIRL HAVING A MIND OF HER OWN?

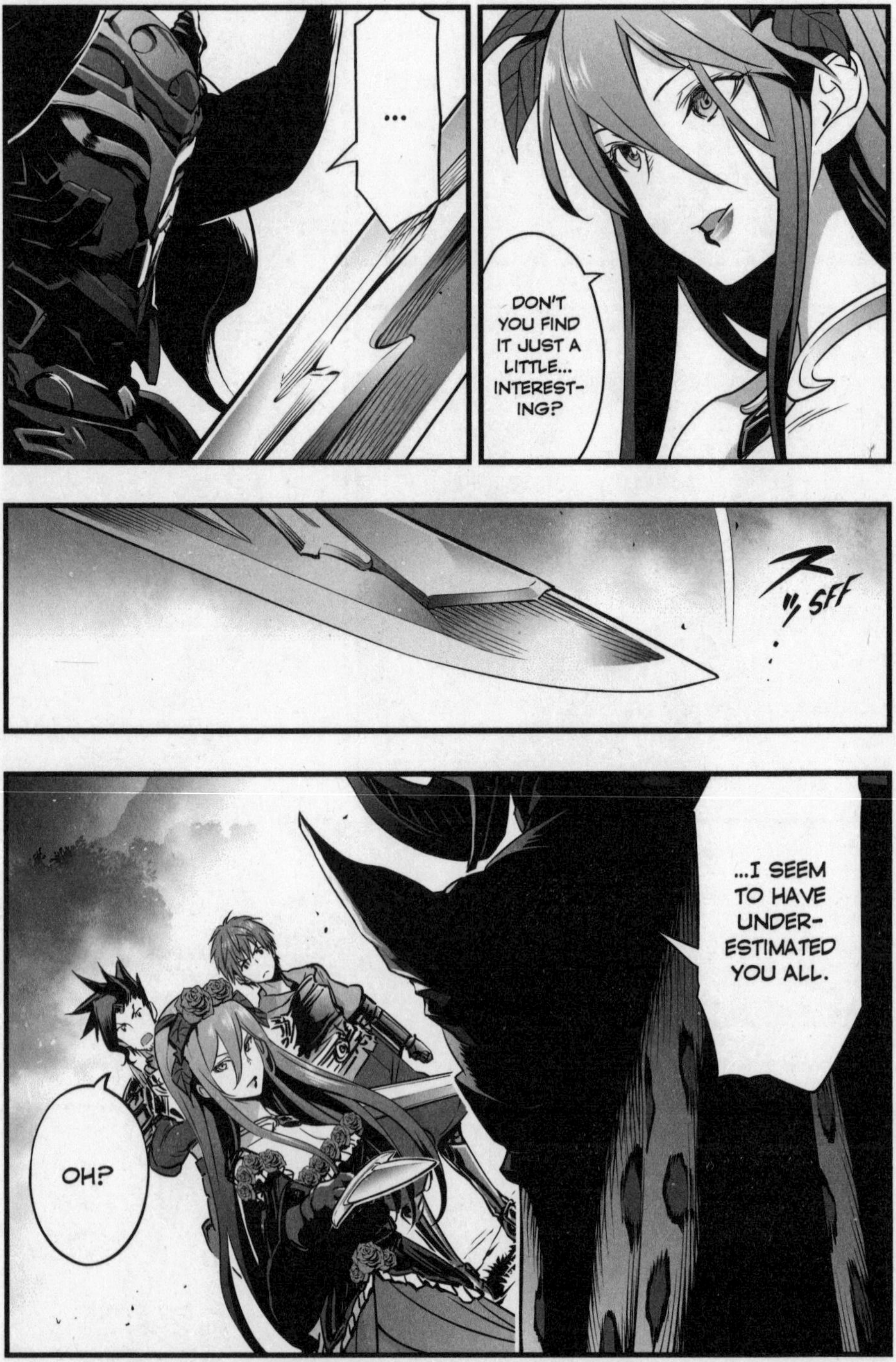
DON'T YOU FIND IT JUST A LITTLE... INTEREST-ING?
...
スッ SFF
...I SEEM TO HAVE UNDER-ESTIMATED YOU ALL.
OH?

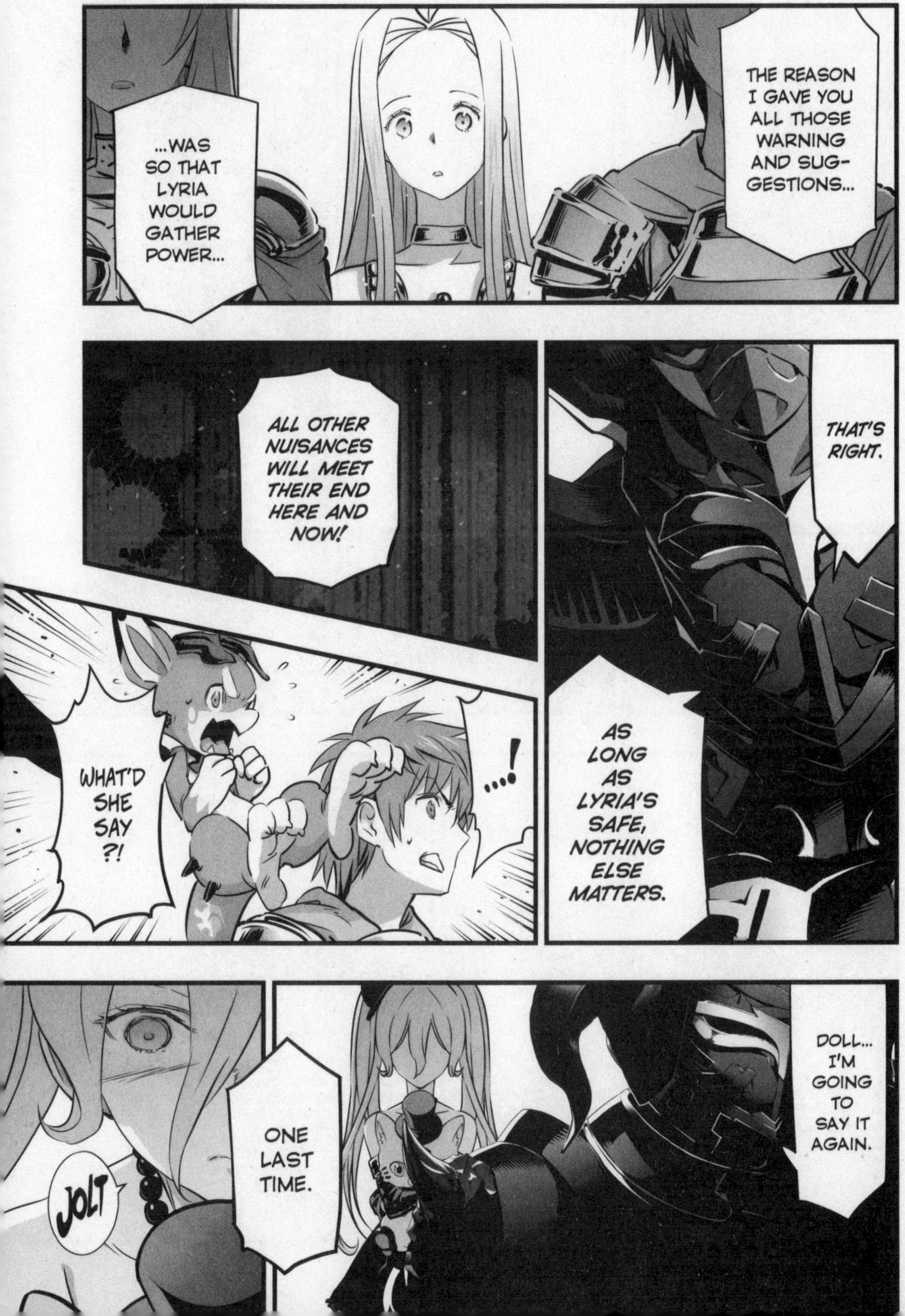
THE REASON I GAVE YOU ALL THOSE WARNING AND SUG-GESTIONS...
...WAS SO THAT LYRIA WOULD GATHER POWER...
THAT'S RIGHT.
AS LONG AS LYRIA'S SAFE, NOTHING ELSE MATTERS.
ALL OTHER NUISANCES WILL MEET THEIR END HERE AND NOW!
WHAT'D SHE SAY ?!
...!
DOLL... I'M GOING TO SAY IT AGAIN.
ONE LAST TIME.
JOLT

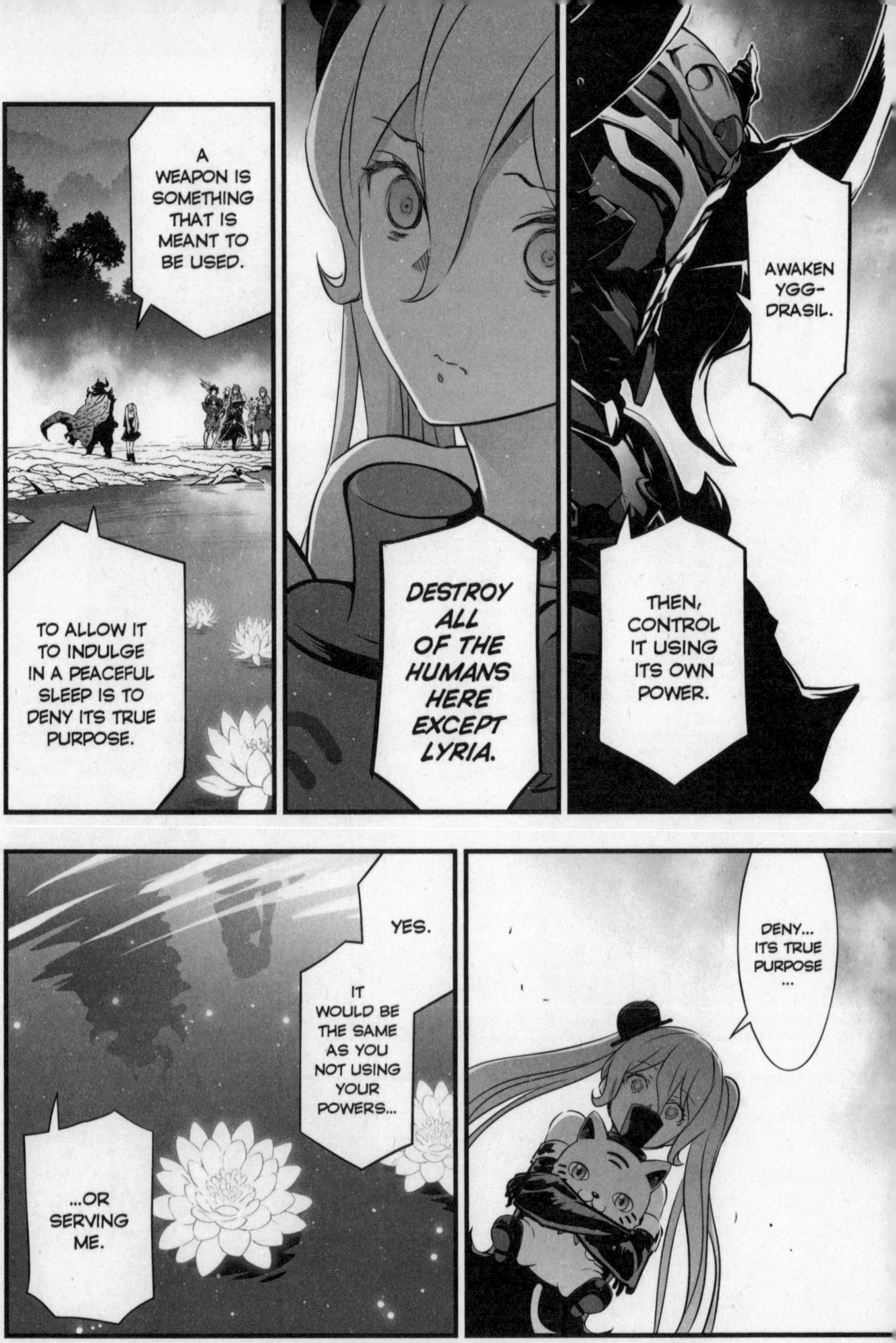
AWAKEN YGG-DRASIL.
THEN, CONTROL IT USING ITS OWN POWER.
DESTROY ALL OF THE HUMANS HERE EXCEPT LYRIA.
A WEAPON IS SOMETHING THAT IS MEANT TO BE USED.
TO ALLOW IT TO INDULGE IN A PEACEFUL SLEEP IS TO DENY ITS TRUE PURPOSE.
DENY... ITS TRUE PURPOSE ...
YES.
IT WOULD BE THE SAME AS YOU NOT USING YOUR POWERS...
...OR SERVING ME.

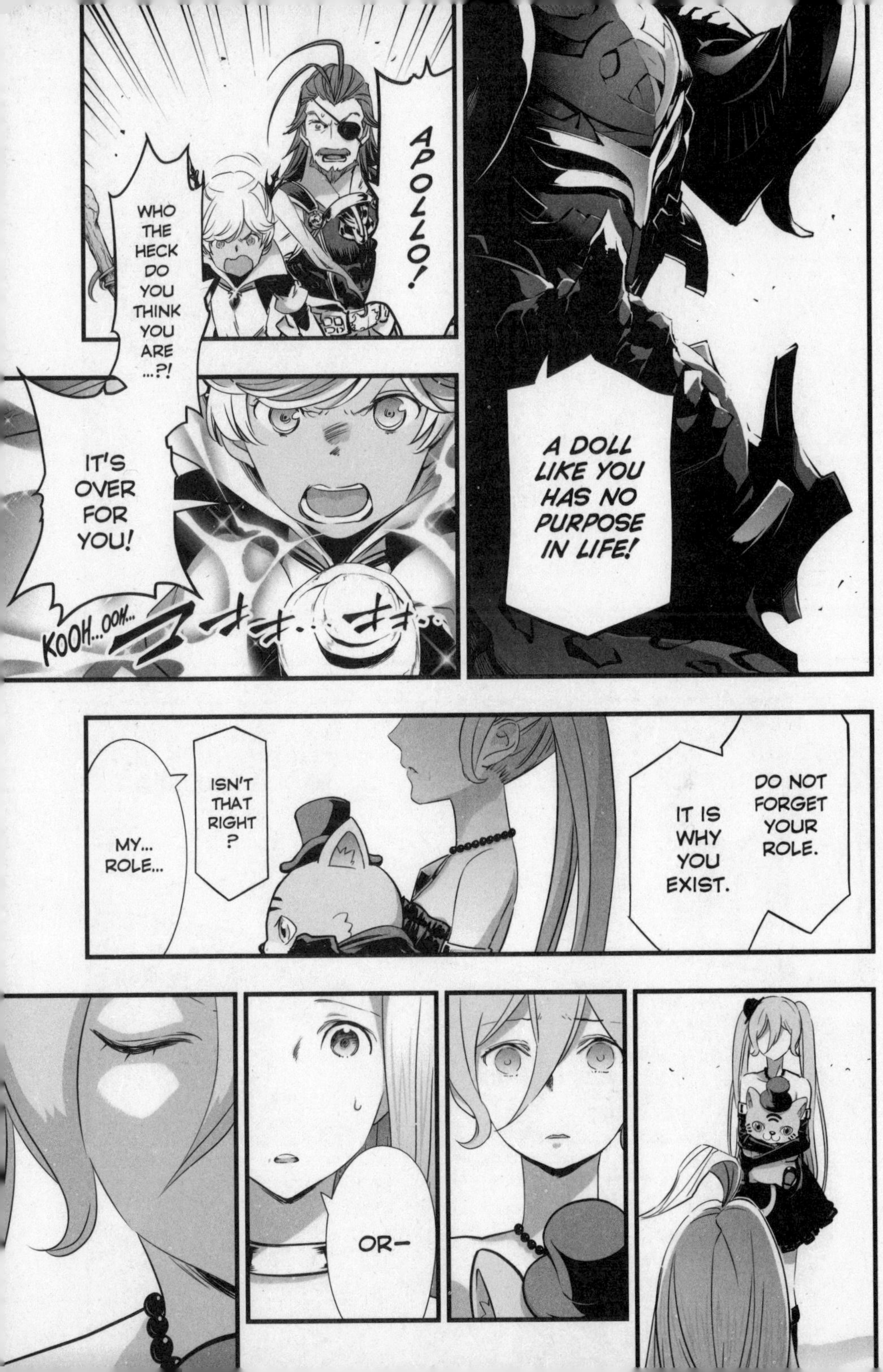
A DOLL LIKE YOU HAS NO PURPOSE IN LIFE!
APOLLO!
WHO THE HECK DO YOU THINK YOU ARE ...?!
IT'S OVER FOR YOU!
KOOH...OOH...
DO NOT FORGET YOUR ROLE.
IT IS WHY YOU EXIST.
ISN'T THAT RIGHT?
MY... ROLE...
OR-

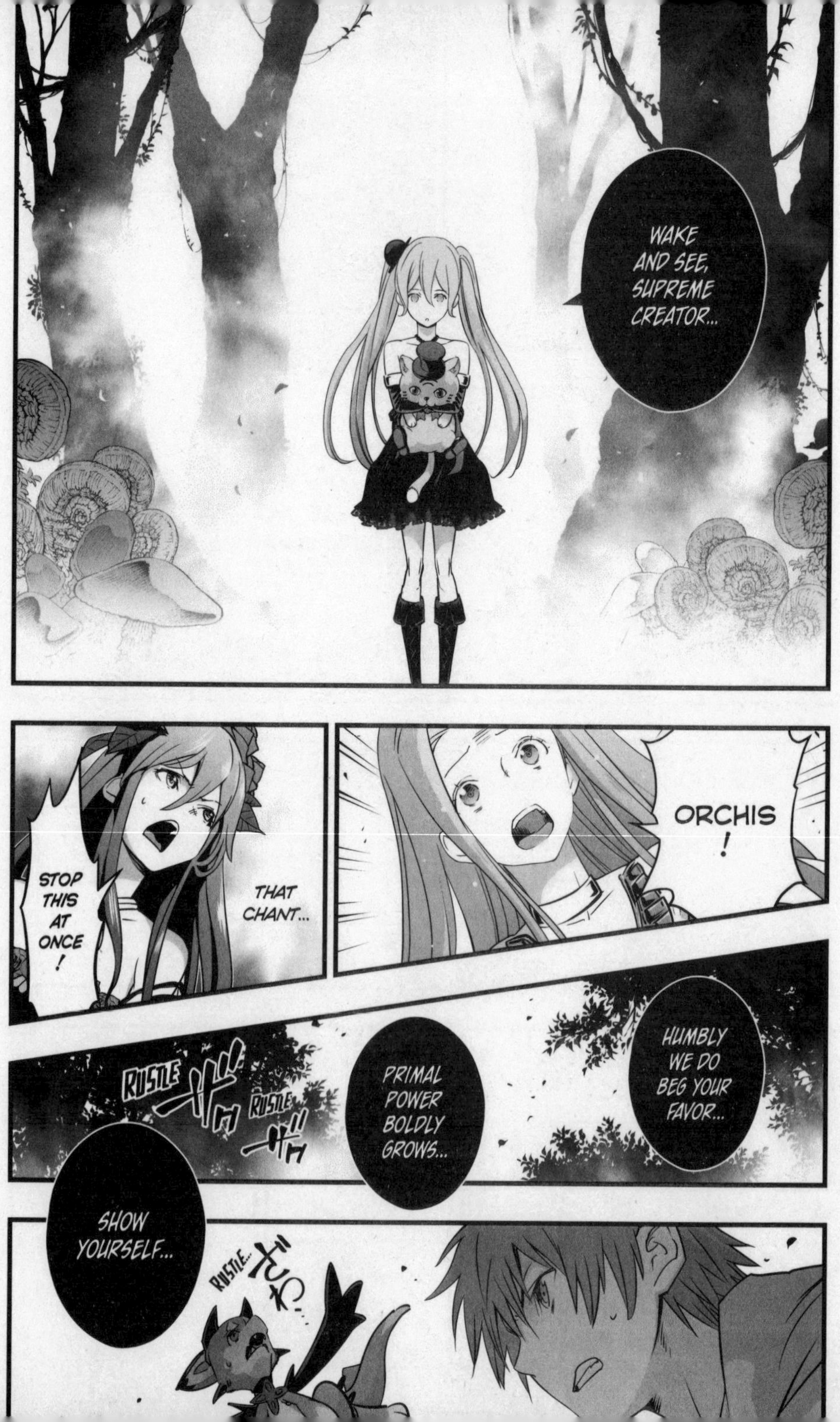
WAKE AND SEE, SUPREME CREATOR...
ORCHIS!
THAT CHANT...
STOP THIS AT ONCE!
HUMBLY WE DO BEG YOUR FAVOR...
PRIMAL POWER BOLDLY GROWS...
RUSTLE RUSTLE
SHOW YOURSELF...
RUSTLE...

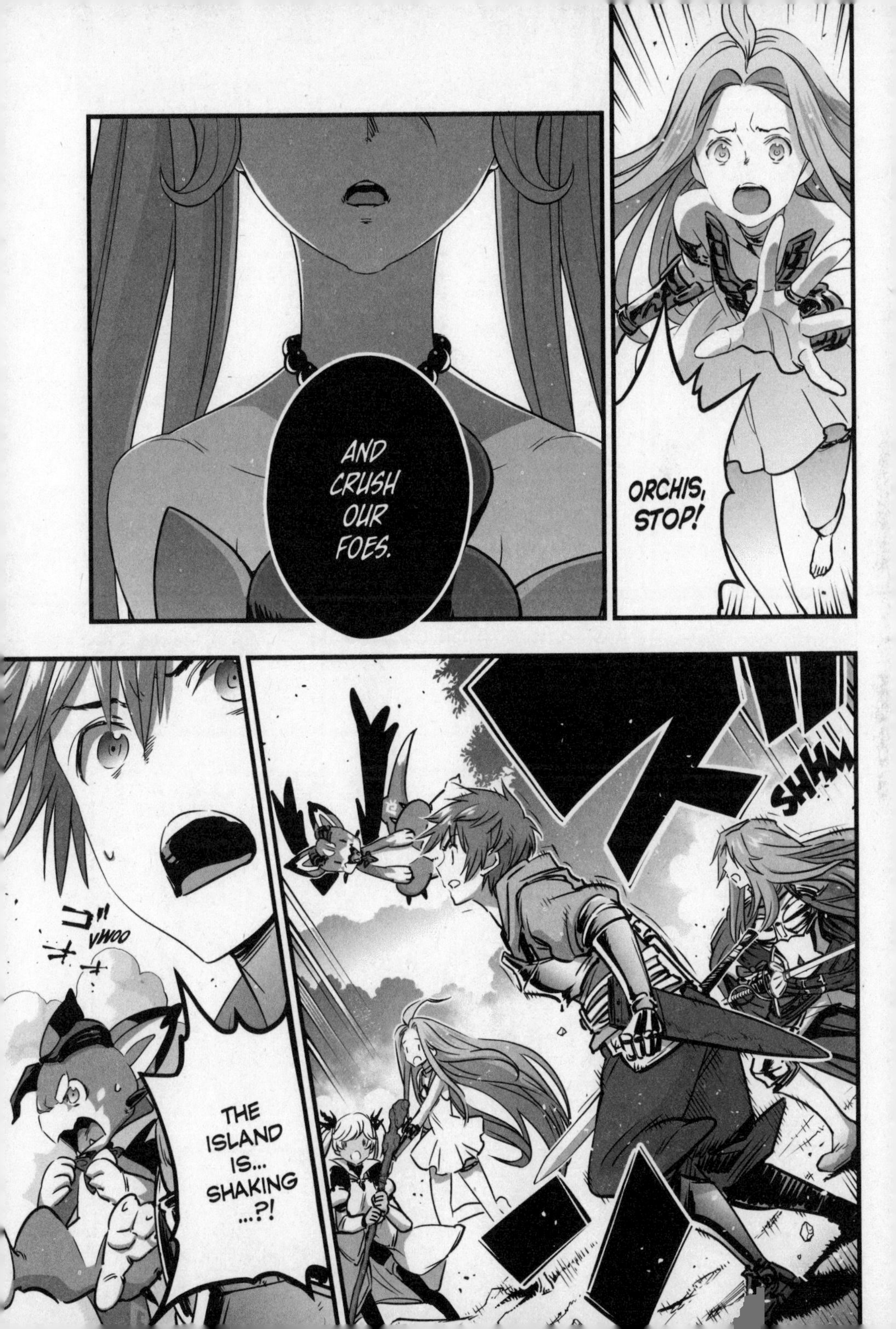
ORCHIS, STOP!
AND CRUSH OUR FOES.
SHHM
VWOO
THE ISLAND IS... SHAKING ...?!

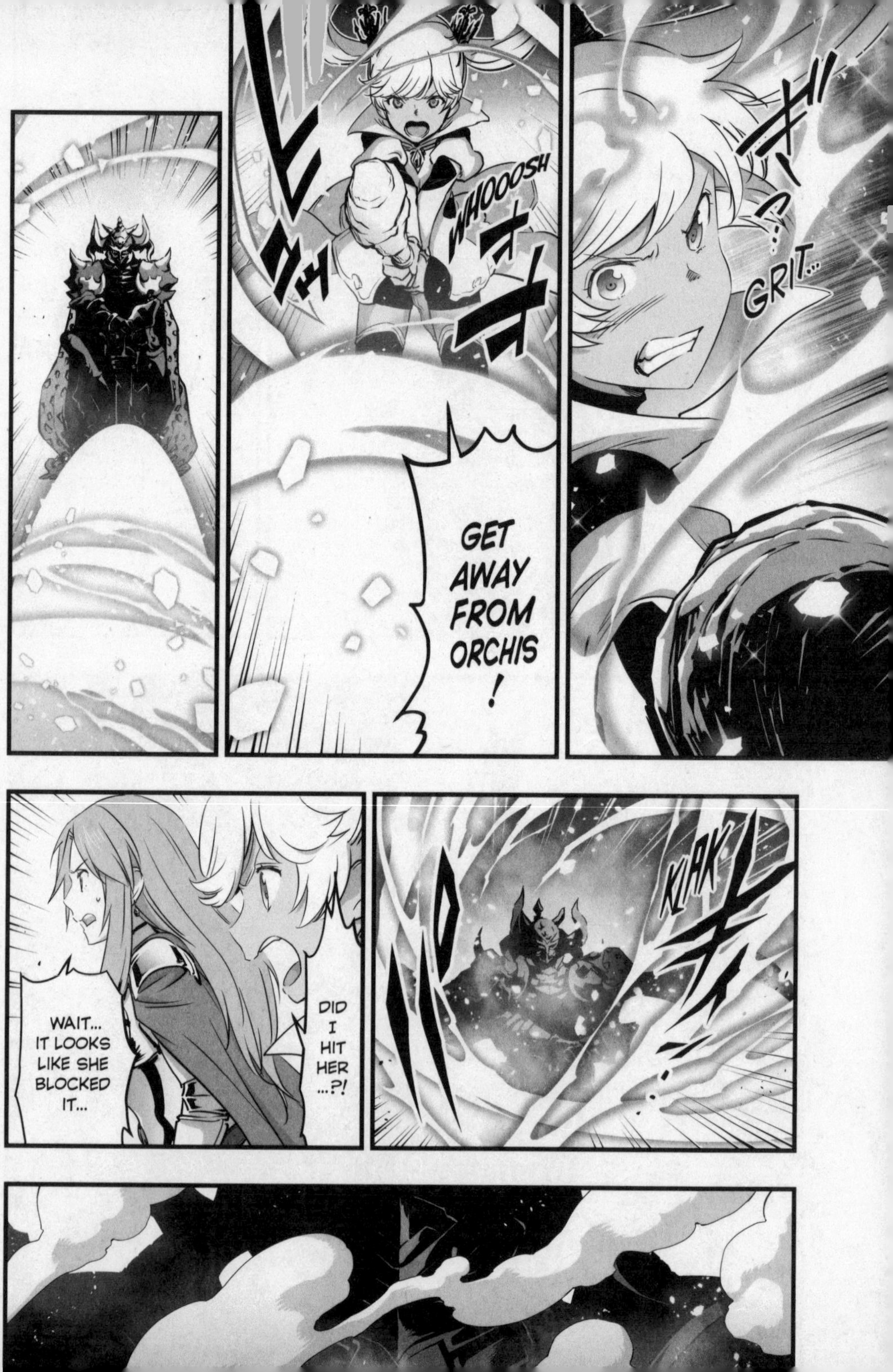
GRIT...
WHOOOSH
GET AWAY FROM ORCHIS!
KLAK
DID I HIT HER...?!
WAIT... IT LOOKS LIKE SHE BLOCKED IT...

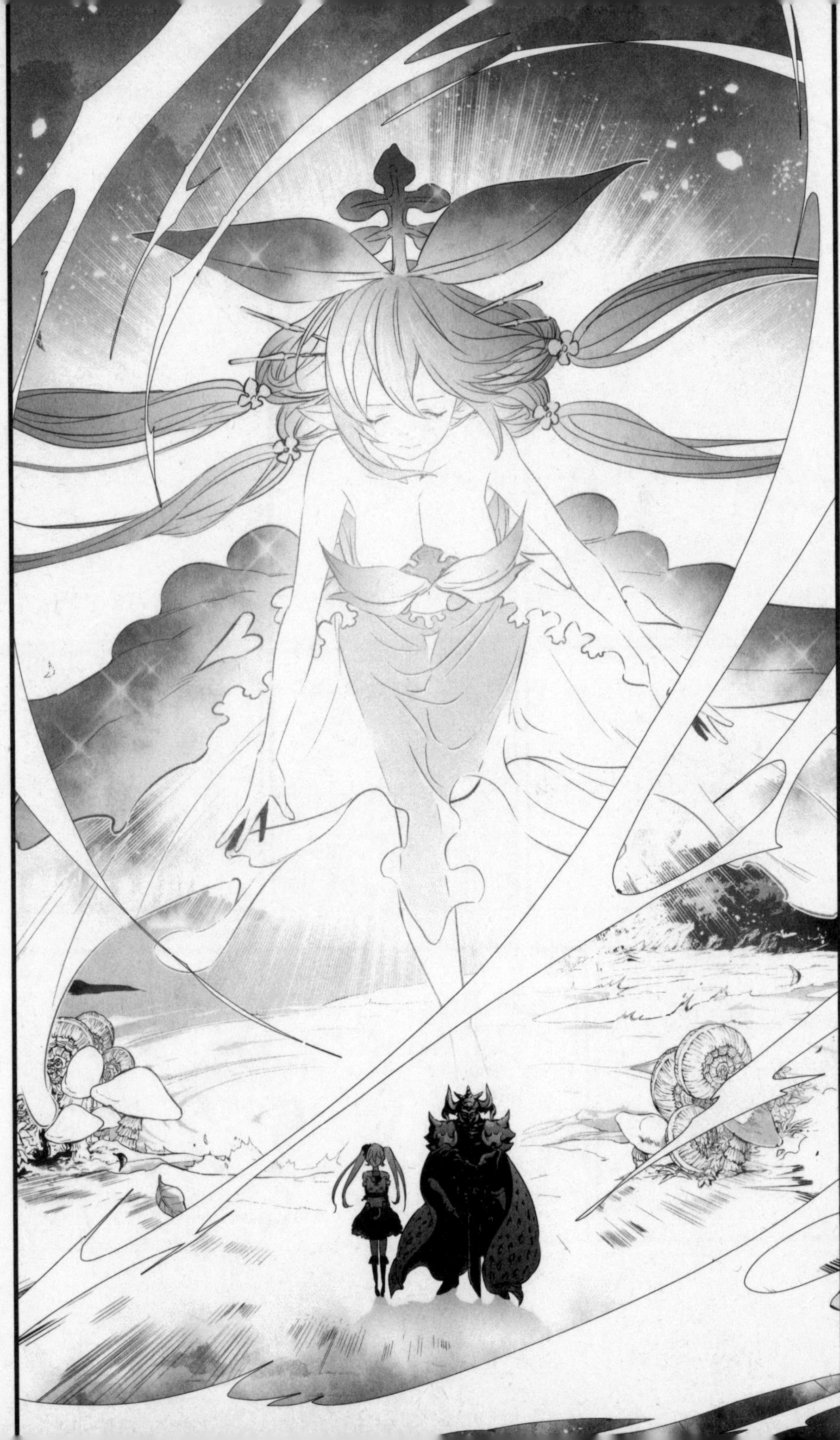

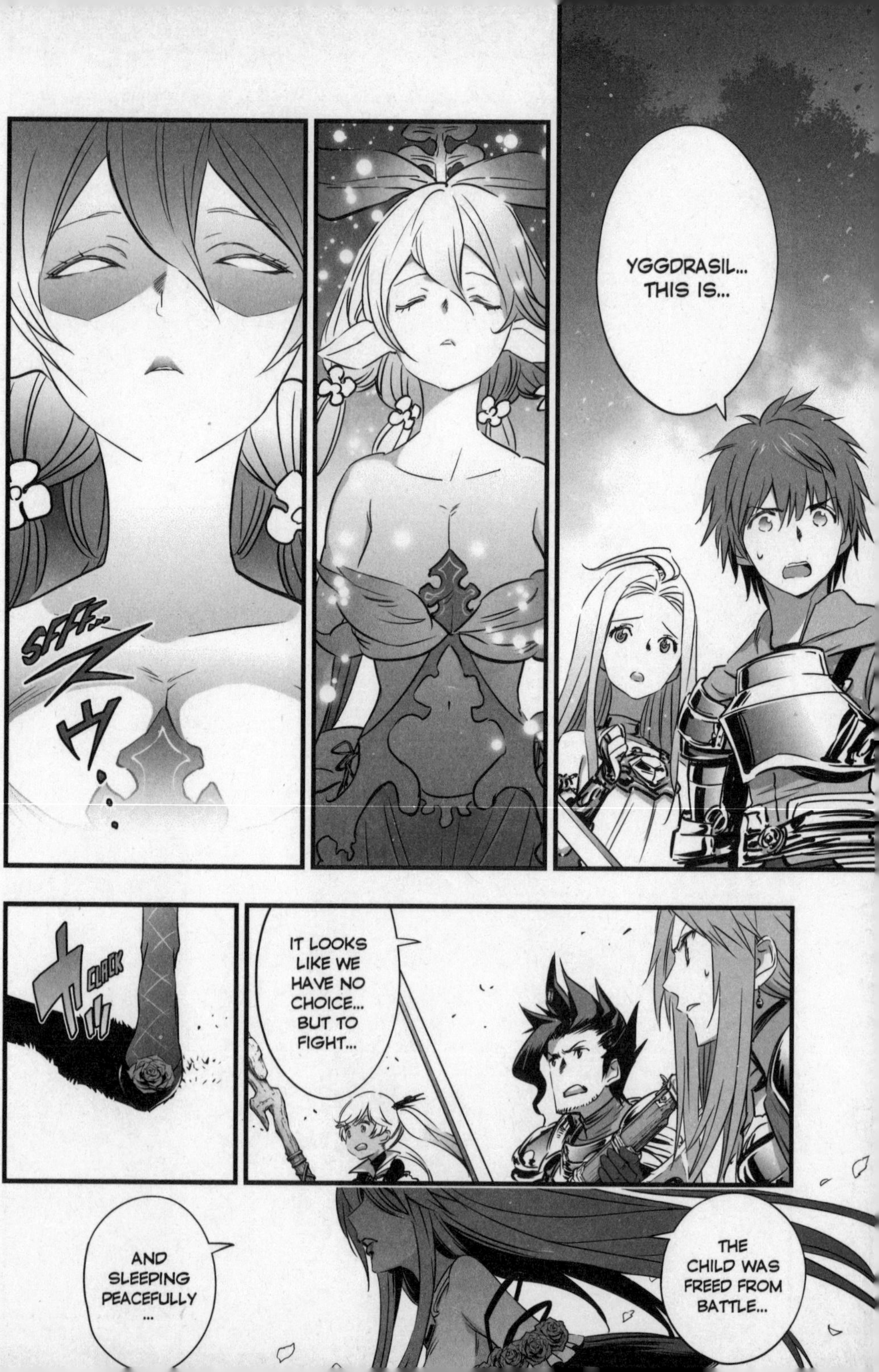
YGGDRASIL... THIS IS...
SFFF...
ヴ…
IT LOOKS LIKE WE HAVE NO CHOICE... BUT TO FIGHT...
CLACK
カッ
THE CHILD WAS FREED FROM BATTLE...
AND SLEEPING PEACEFULLY ...

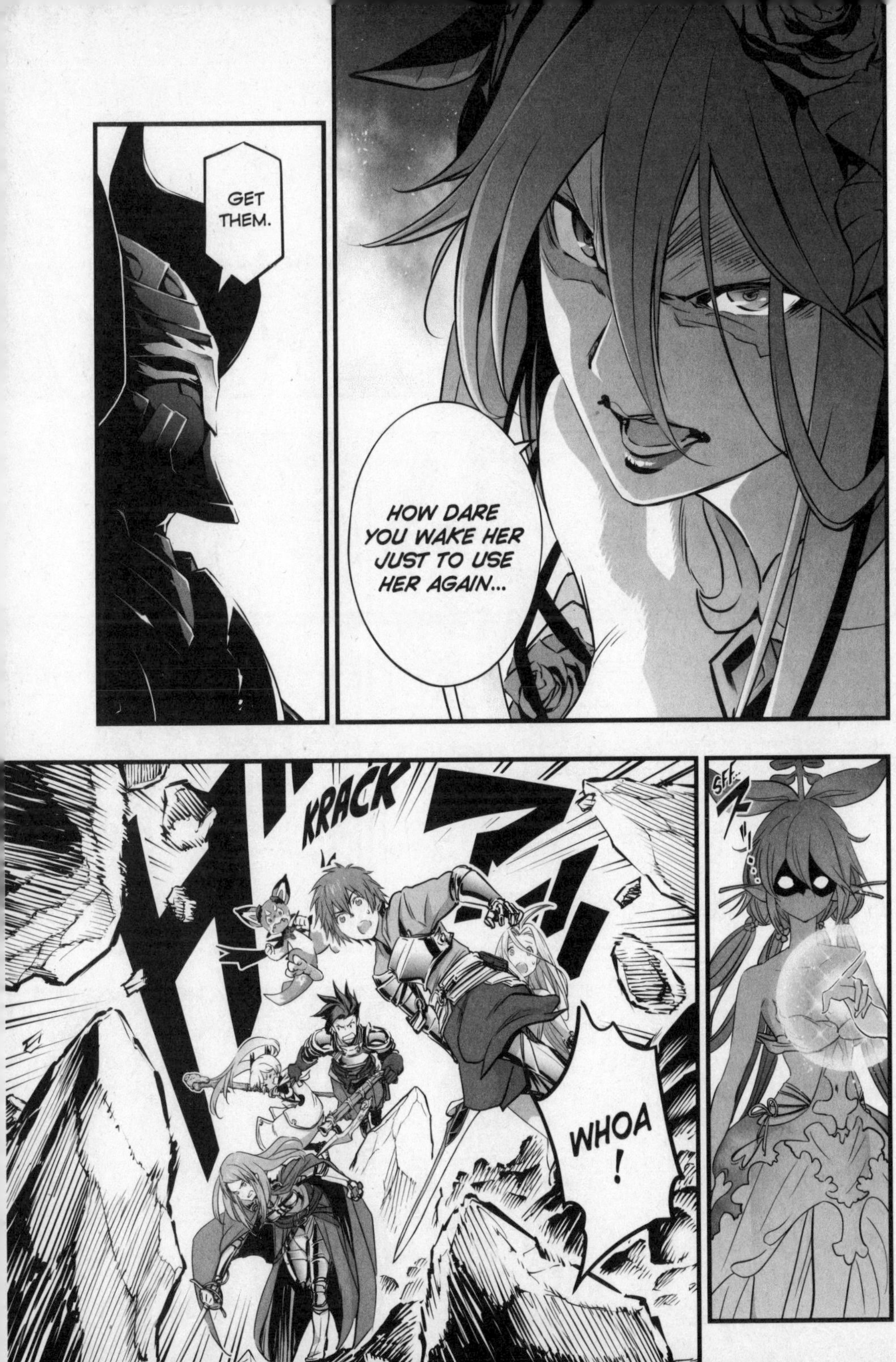
HOW DARE YOU WAKE HER JUST TO USE HER AGAIN...
GET THEM.
SFF...
KRACK
WHOA!

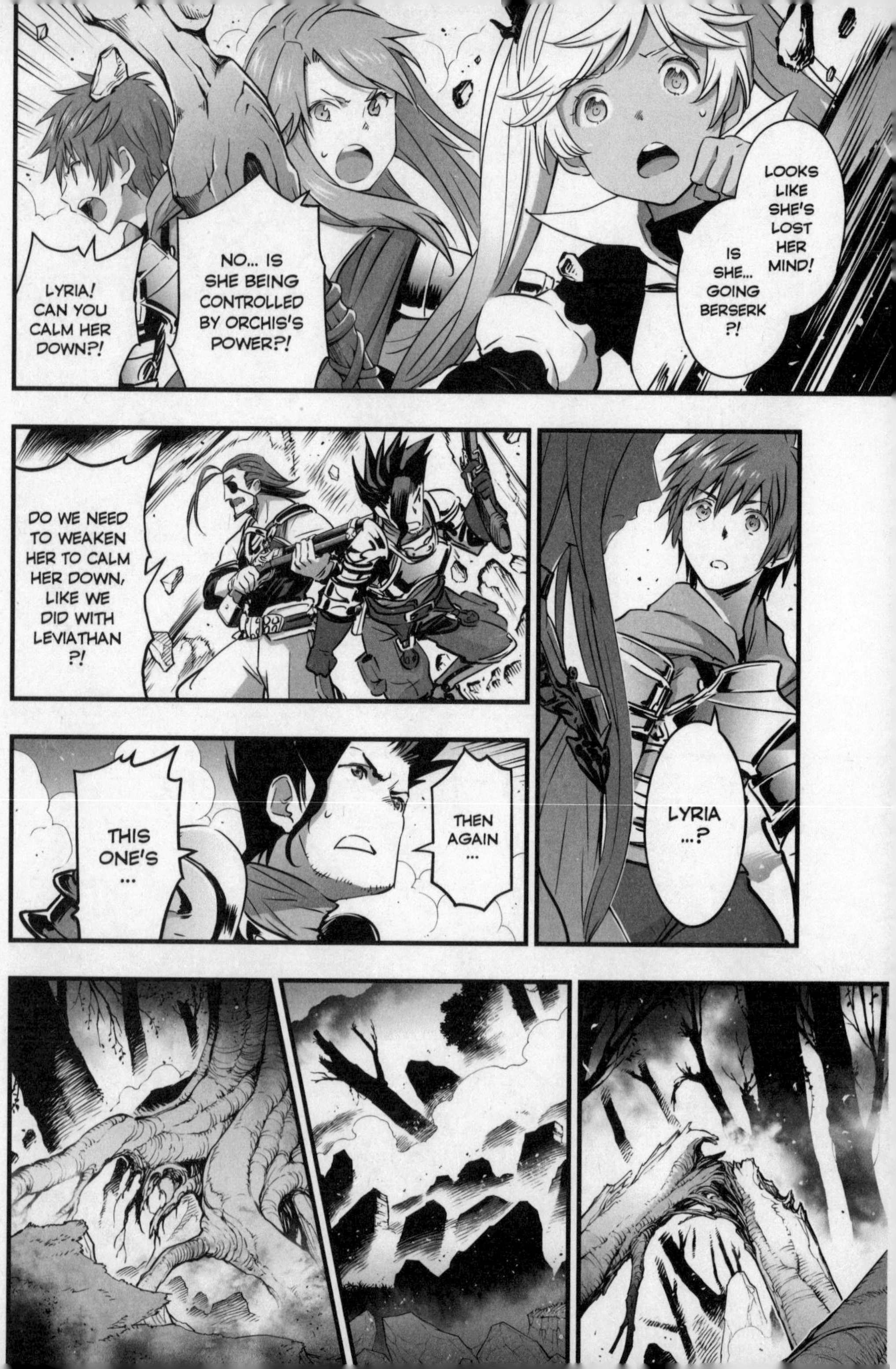
LOOKS LIKE SHE'S LOST HER MIND!
IS SHE... GOING BERSERK?!
NO... IS SHE BEING CONTROLLED BY ORCHIS'S POWER?!
LYRIA! CAN YOU CALM HER DOWN?!
LYRIA ...?
DO WE NEED TO WEAKEN HER TO CALM HER DOWN, LIKE WE DID WITH LEVIATHAN?!
THEN AGAIN ...
THIS ONE'S ...

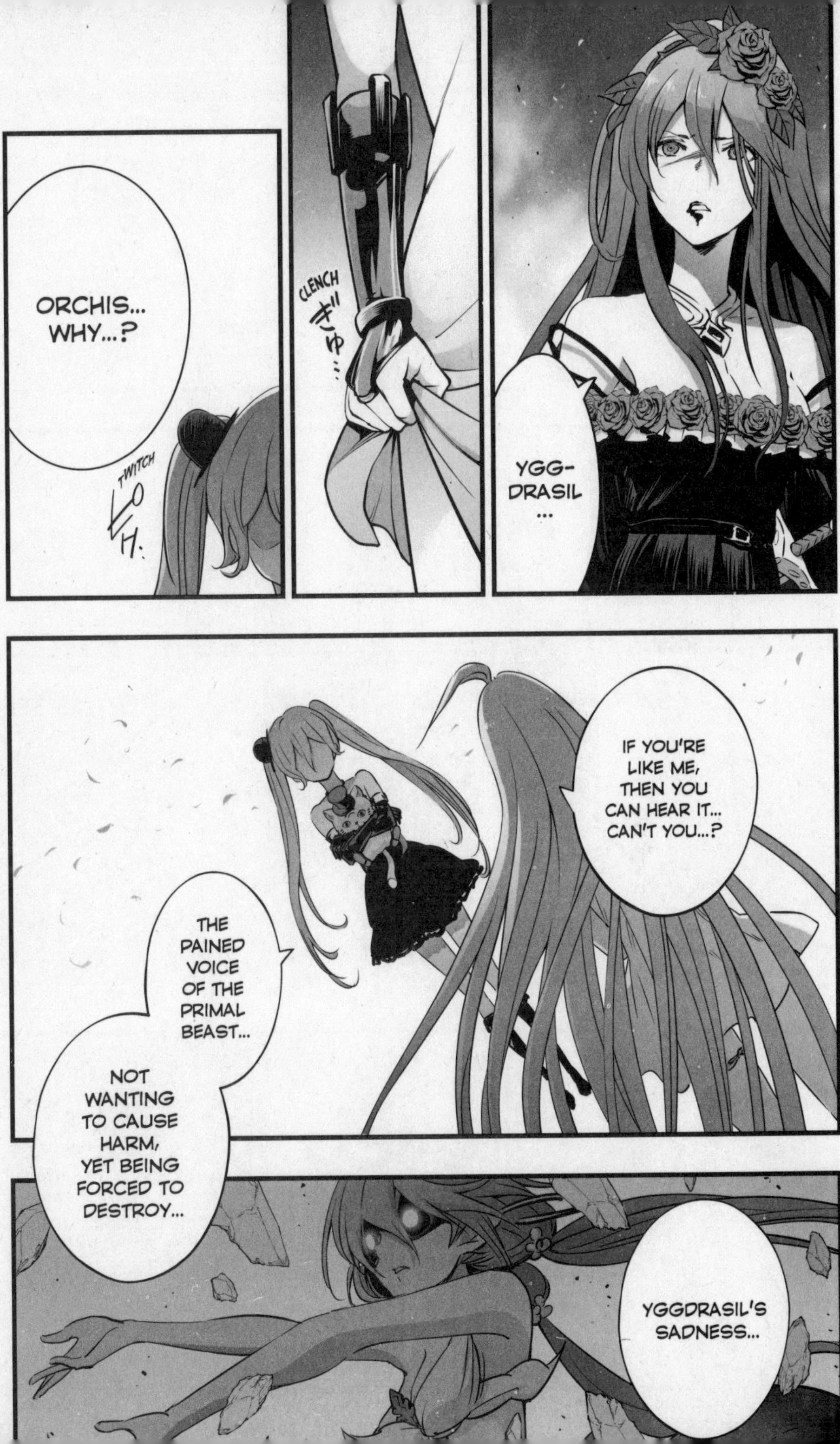
YGG-DRASIL...
CLENCH
ぎゅ
ORCHIS... WHY...?
TWITCH
IF YOU'RE LIKE ME, THEN YOU CAN HEAR IT... CAN'T YOU...?
THE PAINED VOICE OF THE PRIMAL BEAST...
NOT WANTING TO CAUSE HARM, YET BEING FORCED TO DESTROY...
YGGDRASIL'S SADNESS...

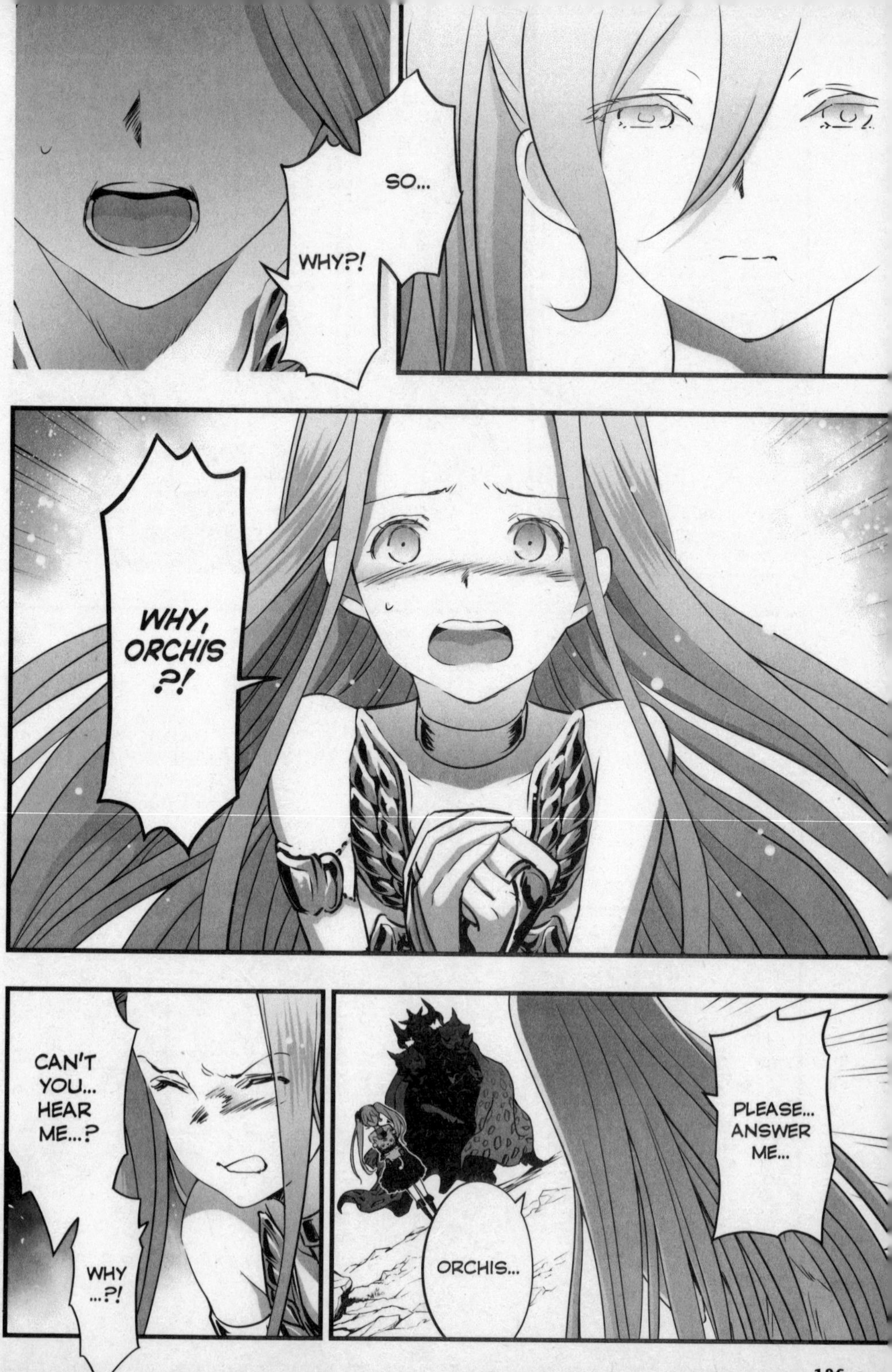
SO... WHY?!
WHY, ORCHIS ?!
PLEASE... ANSWER ME...
ORCHIS...
CAN'T YOU... HEAR ME...?
WHY ...?!

WHY...?

I'M SORRY.

HUH?

...HEY.

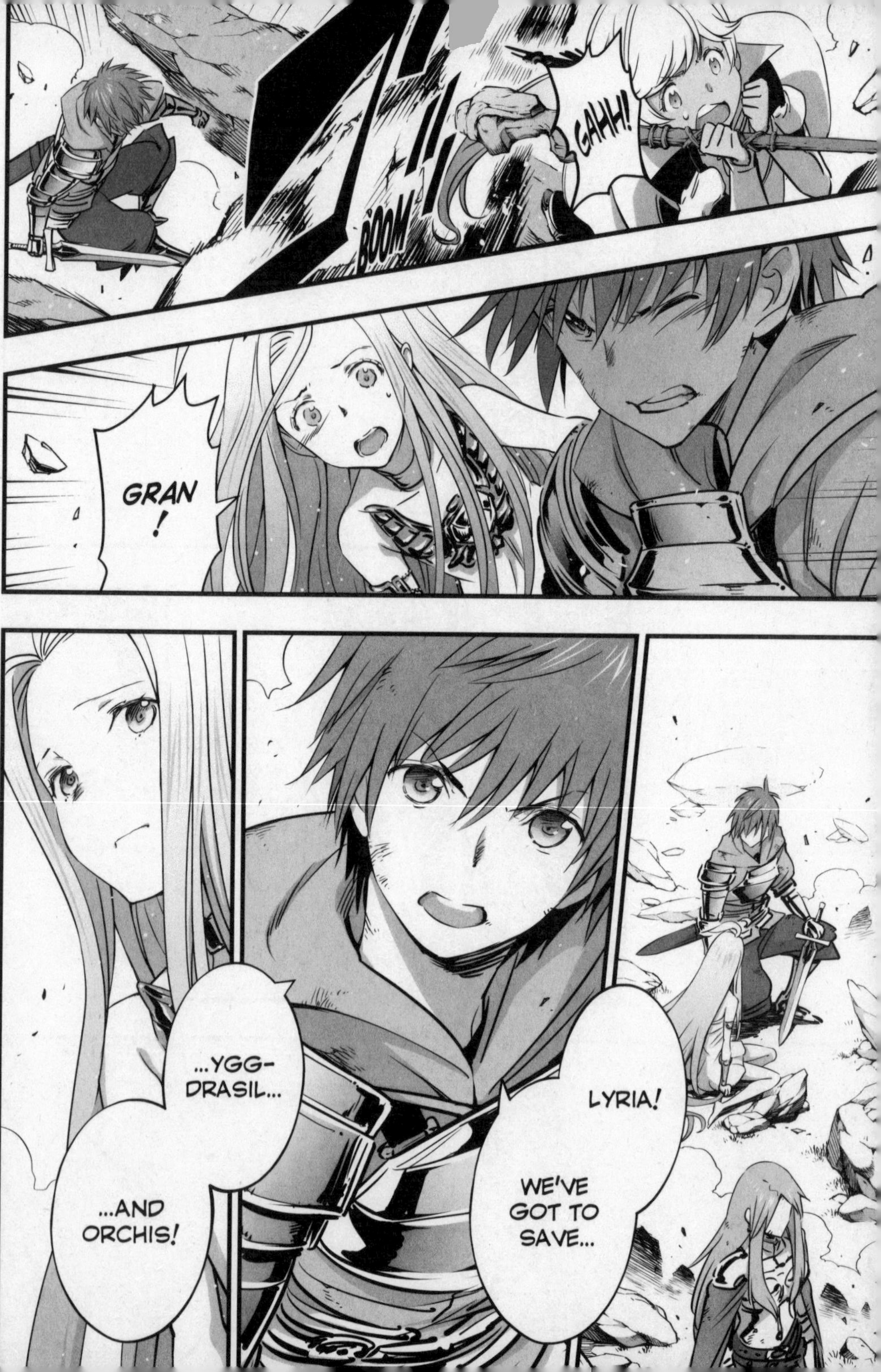
GAHH!
BOOM
GRAN!
LYRIA!
WE'VE GOT TO SAVE...
...YGG-DRASIL...
...AND ORCHIS!

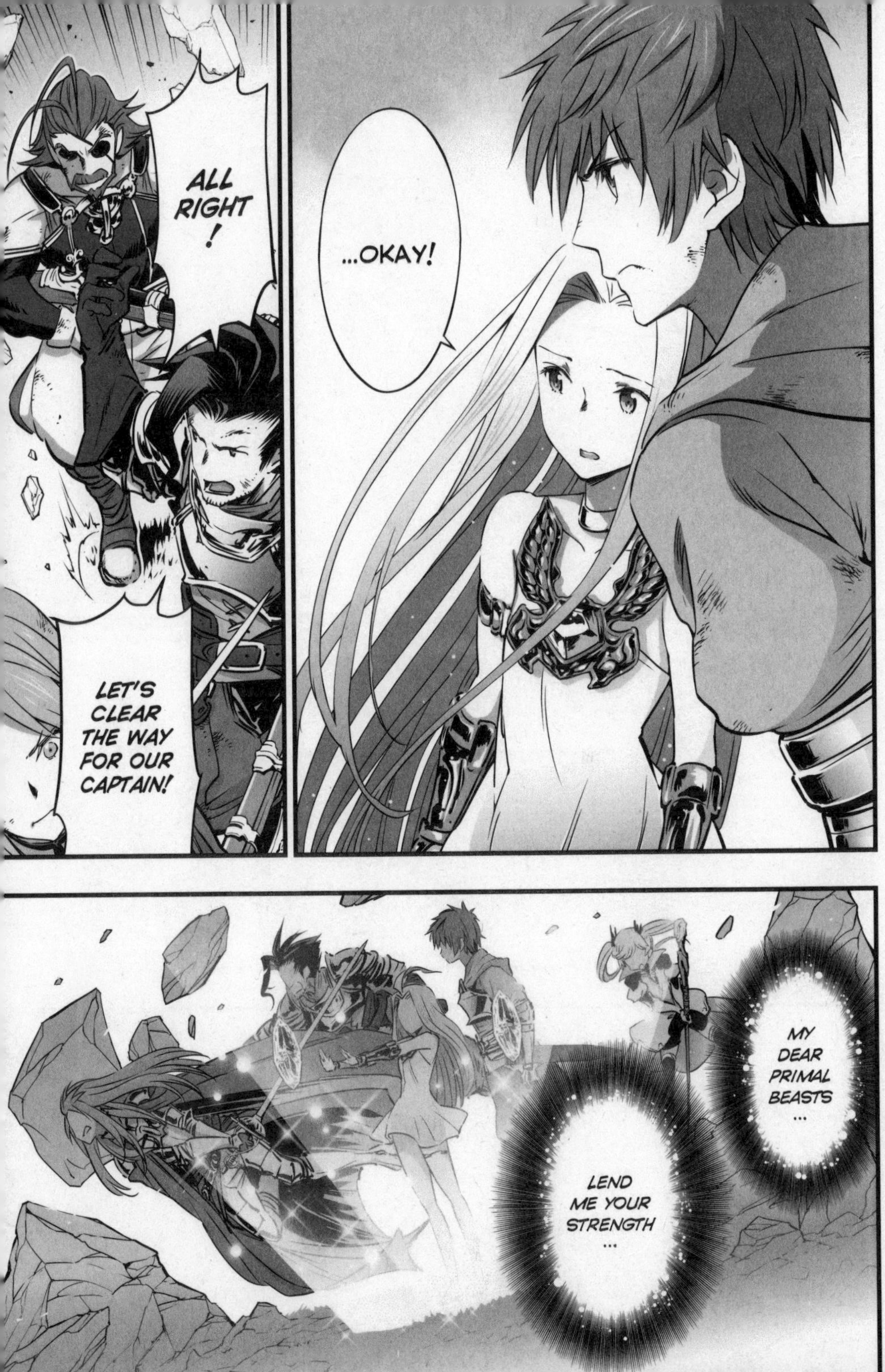
...OKAY!
ALL RIGHT!
LET'S CLEAR THE WAY FOR OUR CAPTAIN!
MY DEAR PRIMAL BEASTS...
LEND ME YOUR STRENGTH...

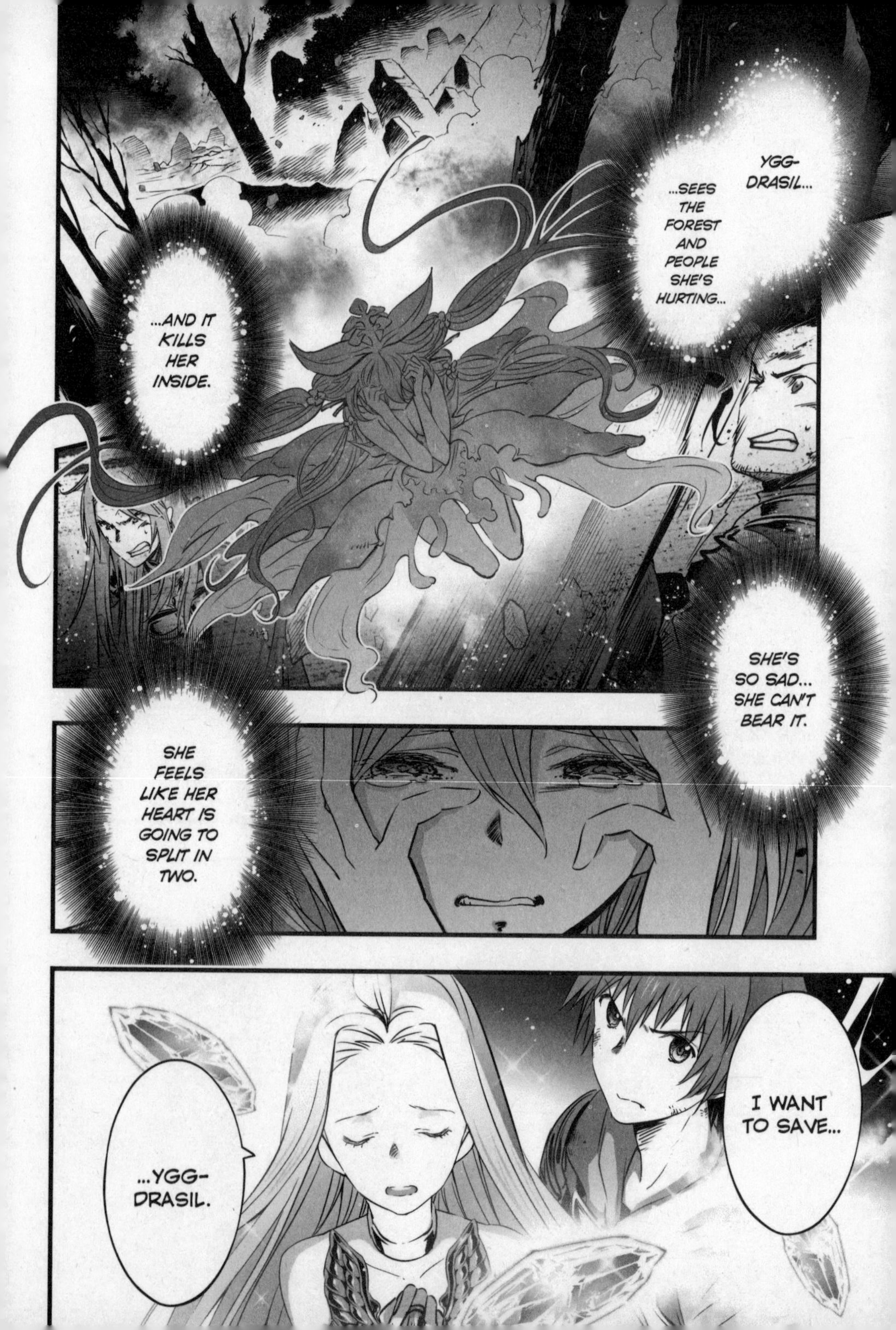
YGG-DRASIL...
...SEES THE FOREST AND PEOPLE SHE'S HURTING...
...AND IT KILLS HER INSIDE.
SHE'S SO SAD... SHE CAN'T BEAR IT.
SHE FEELS LIKE HER HEART IS GOING TO SPLIT IN TWO.
I WANT TO SAVE...
...YGG-DRASIL.

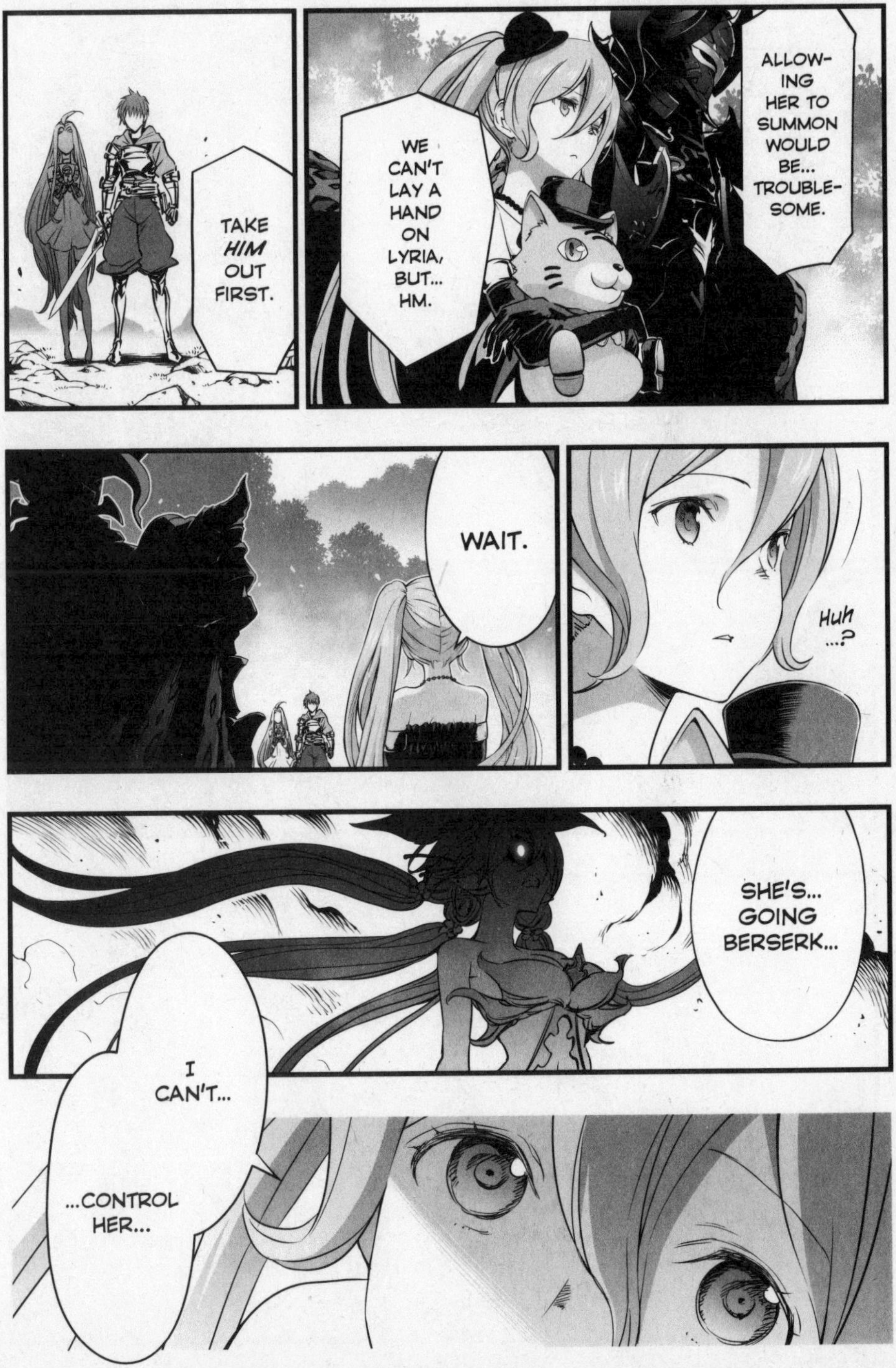
WE CAN'T LAY A HAND ON LYRIA, BUT... HM.
ALLOWING HER TO SUMMON WOULD BE... TROUBLESOME.
TAKE *HIM* OUT FIRST.
WAIT.
Huh ...?
SHE'S... GOING BERSERK...
I CAN'T...
...CONTROL HER...

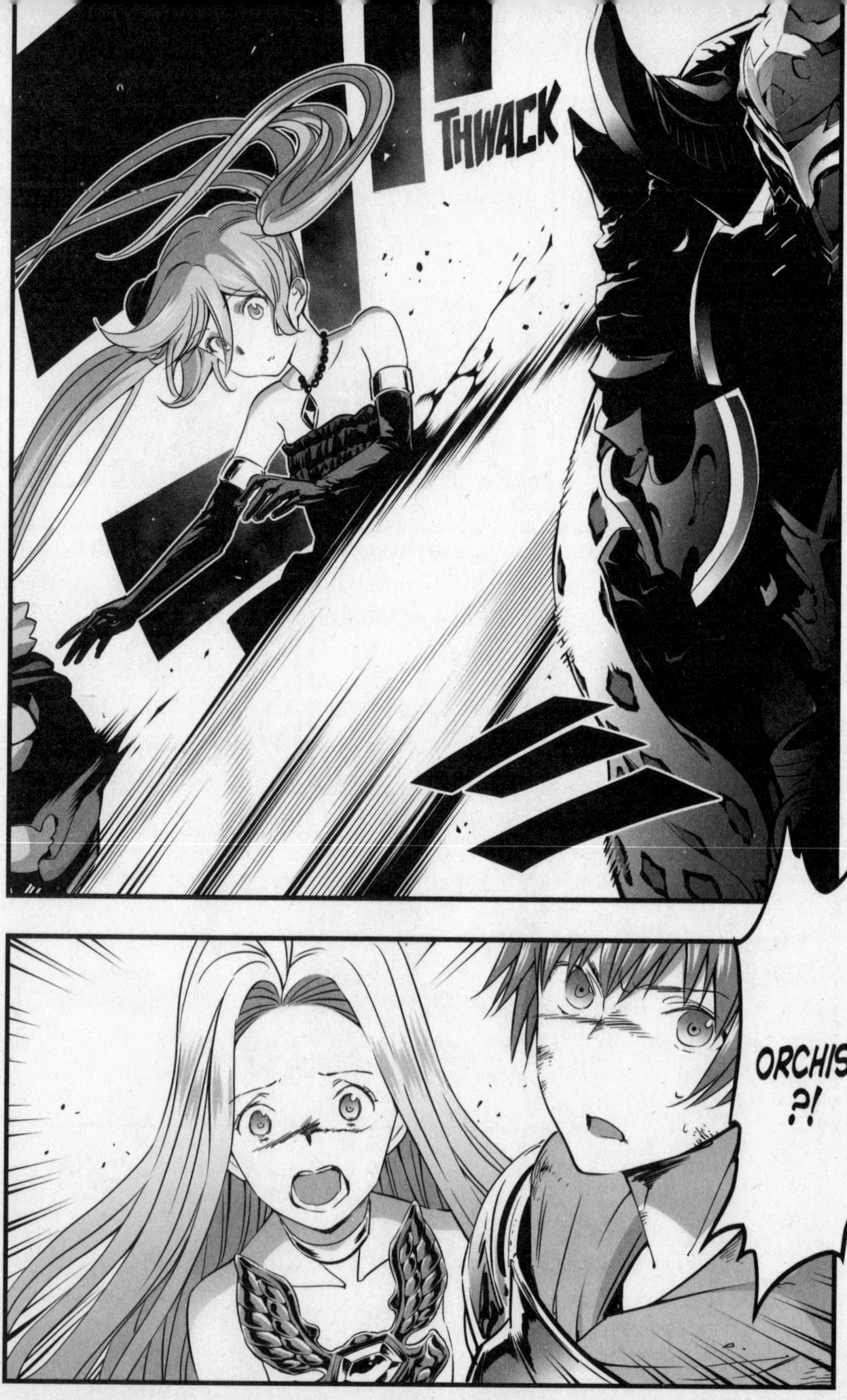
THWACK
ORCHIS ?!

NEXT

NEXT VOLUME PREVIEW

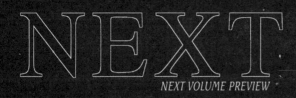

"Heh heh heh...
My dearest Katalina,
you and I will never
leave this place again.
We will be together
forever and ever..."

VOLUME.

06

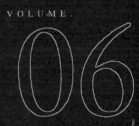

The curtain will open on
Albion Citadel!!

volume.

06

Volume Six
COMING SOON!

GRANBLUE FANTASY
グランブルーファンタジー

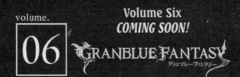

Magus of the Library

Mitsu Izumi

MITSU IZUMI'S STUNNING ARTWORK BRINGS A FANTASTICAL LITERARY ADVENTURE TO LUSH, THRILLING LIFE!

Young Theo adores books, but the prejudice and hatred of his village keeps them ever out of his reach. Then one day, he chances to meet Sedona, a traveling librarian who works for the great library of Aftzaak, City of Books, and his life changes forever...

‹ KAMOME ›
SHIRAHAMA

Witch Hat Atelier

A magical manga
adventure for
fans of Disney
and Studio
Ghibli!

Witch Hat Atelier © Kamome Shirahama/Kodansha Ltd.

The magical adventure that took Japan by storm is finally here, from acclaimed DC and Marvel cover artist Kamome Shirahama!

In a world where everyone takes wonders like magic spells and dragons for granted, Coco is a girl with a simple dream: She wants to be a witch. But everybody knows magicians are born, not made, and Coco was not born with a gift for magic. Resigned to her un-magical life, Coco is about to give up on her dream to become a witch...until the day she meets Qifrey, a mysterious, traveling magician. After secretly seeing Qifrey perform magic in a way she's never seen before, Coco soon learns what everybody "knows" might not be the truth, and discovers that her magical dream may not be as far away as it may seem...

Young characters and steampunk setting, like *Howl's Moving Castle* and *Battle Angel Alita*

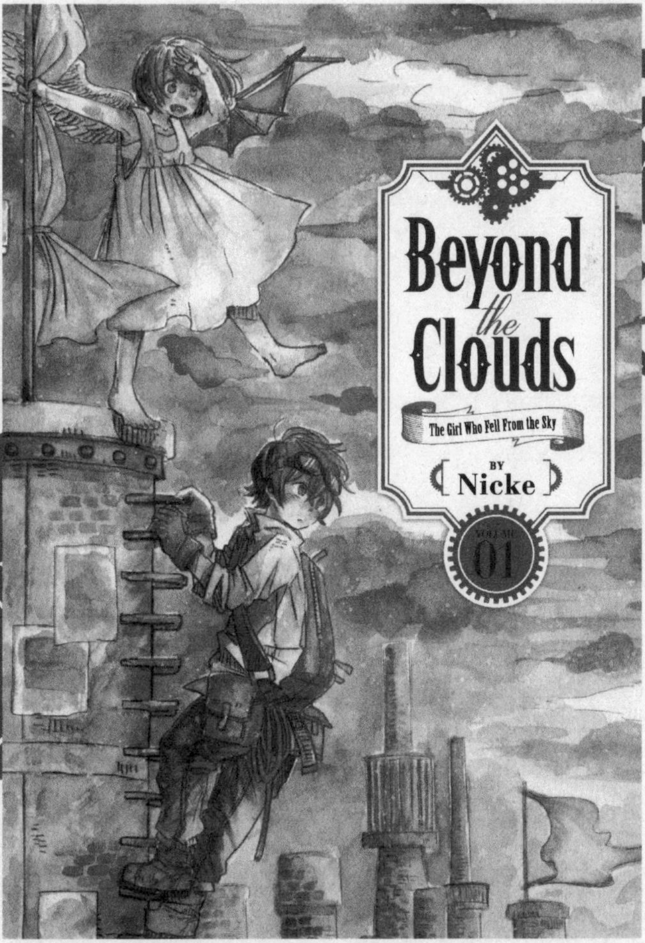
Beyond the Clouds
The Girl Who Fell From the Sky
BY Nicke
VOLUME 01
KC KODANSHA COMICS

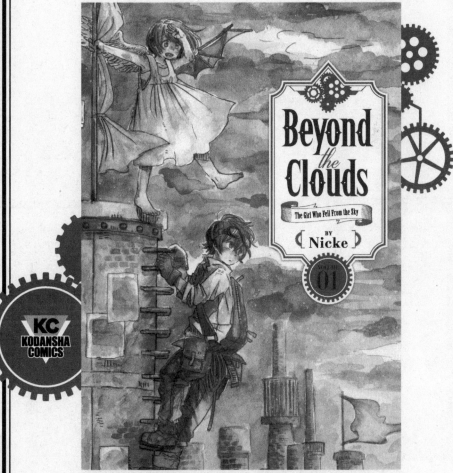

Beyond the Clouds © 2018 Nicke / Ki-oon

A boy with a talent for machines and a mysterious girl whose wings he's fixed will take you beyond the clouds! In the tradition of the high-flying, resonant adventure stories of Studio Ghibli comes a gorgeous tale about the longing of young hearts for adventure and friendship!

A SMART, NEW ROMANTIC COMEDY FOR FANS OF *SHORTCAKE CAKE* AND *TERRACE HOUSE!*

A romance manga starring high school girl Meeko, who learns to live on her own in a boarding house whose living room is home to the odd (but handsome) Matsunaga-san. She begins to adjust to her new life away from her parents, but Meeko soon learns that no matter how far away from home she is, she's still a young girl at heart — especially when she finds herself falling for Matsunaga-san.

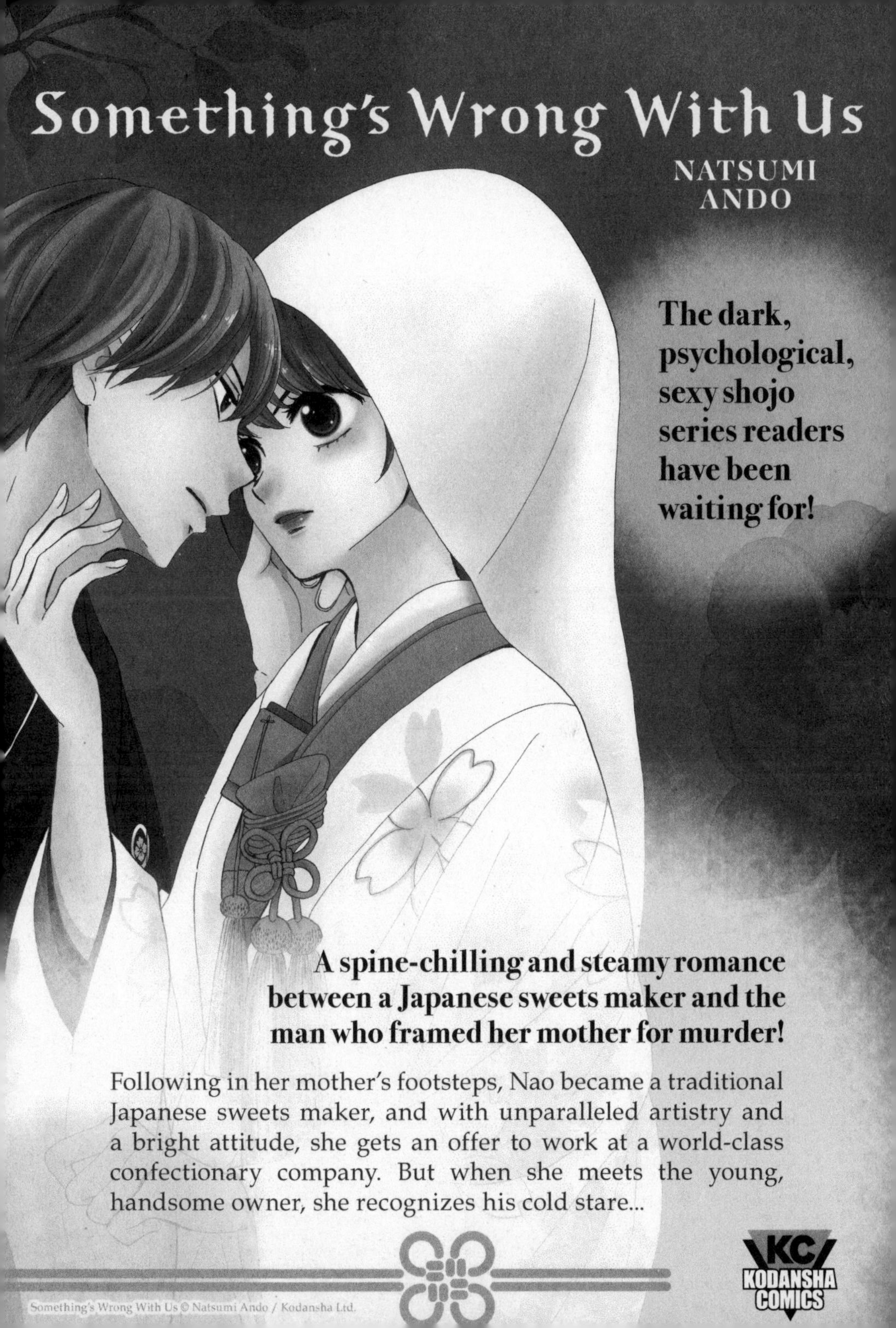
Something's Wrong With Us
NATSUMI ANDO
The dark, psychological, sexy shojo series readers have been waiting for!
A spine-chilling and steamy romance between a Japanese sweets maker and the man who framed her mother for murder!
Following in her mother's footsteps, Nao became a traditional Japanese sweets maker, and with unparalleled artistry and a bright attitude, she gets an offer to work at a world-class confectionary company. But when she meets the young, handsome owner, she recognizes his cold stare...
KC KODANSHA COMICS
Something's Wrong With Us © Natsumi Ando / Kodansha Ltd.

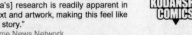

Knight of the Ice ©Yayoi Ogawa/Kodansha Ltd.

Yayoi Ogawa

SKATING THRILLS AND ICY CHILLS WITH THIS NEW TINGLY ROMANCE SERIES!

A rom-com on ice, perfect for fans of *Princess Jellyfish* and *Wotakoi*. Kokoro is the talk of the figure-skating world, winning trophies and hearts. But little do they know... he's actually a huge nerd! From the beloved creator of *You're My Pet (Tramps Like Us)*.

Chitose is a serious young woman, working for the health magazine *SASSO*. Or at least, she would be, if she wasn't constantly getting distracted by her childhood friend, international figure skating star Kokoro Kijinami! In the public eye and on the ice, Kokoro is a gallant, flawless knight, but behind his glittery costumes and breathtaking spins lies a secret: He's actually a hopelessly romantic otaku, who can only land his quad jumps when Chitose is on hand to recite a spell from his favorite magical girl anime!

EDENS ZERO
エデンズゼロ

HIRO MASHIMA IS BACK! JOIN THE CREATOR OF *FAIRY TAIL* AS HE TAKES TO THE STARS FOR ANOTHER THRILLING SAGA!

A high-flying space adventure! All the steadfast friendship and wild fighting you've been waiting for...IN SPACE!

At Granbell Kingdom, an abandoned amusement park, Shiki has lived his entire life among machines. But one day, Rebecca and her cat companion Happy appear at the park's front gates. Little do these newcomers know that this is the first human contact Granbell has had in a hundred years! As Shiki stumbles his way into making new friends, his former neighbors stir at an opportunity for a robo-rebellion... And when his old homeland becomes too dangerous, Shiki must join Rebecca and Happy on their spaceship and escape into the boundless cosmos.

The boys are back, in 400-page hardcovers that are as pretty and badass as they are!

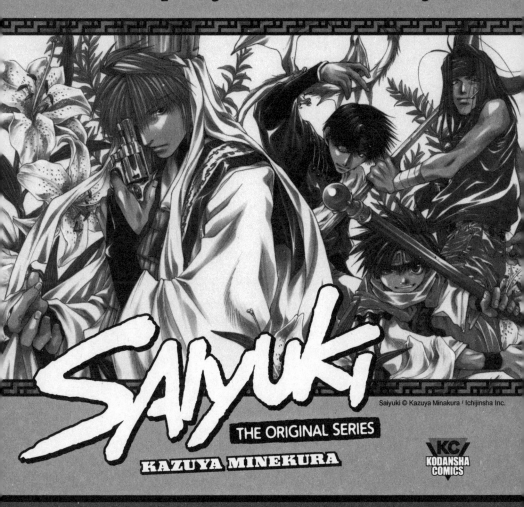

Saiyuki © Kazuya Minakura / Ichijinsha Inc.

SAIYUKI
THE ORIGINAL SERIES
KAZUYA MINEKURA

"AN EDGY COMIC LOOK AT AN ANCIENT CHINESE TALE." —YALSA

Genjo Sanzo is a Buddhist priest in the city of Togenkyo, which is being ravaged by yokai spirits that have fallen out of balance with the natural order. His superiors send him on a journey far to the west to discover why this is happening and how to stop it. His companions are three yokai with human souls. But this is no day trip — the four will encounter many discoveries and horrors on the way.

FEATURES NEW TRANSLATION, COLOR PAGES, AND BEAUTIFUL WRAPAROUND COVER ART!

A dark and sexy body-horror action manga perfect for fans of *Prison School* and *High School of the Dead*!

Shuichi Kagaya is a smart kid, and most smart kids his age would be thinking about college. Shuichi is also a monster, and he's smart enough to know that monsters don't go to college. But after he uses his monstrous form to save his classmate Claire Aoki, it doesn't matter what his plans for the future were, because he's not the one making the decisions anymore. Now that the seductive, sadistic Claire knows Shuichi's secret, she's got her own ideas about what a monster is good for—because he's not the first monster she's met...

**KC
KODANSHA
COMICS**

GLEIPNIR

"You and me together...we would be unstoppable."

THE SWEET SCENT OF LOVE IS IN THE AIR! FOR FANS OF OFFBEAT ROMANCES LIKE *WOTAKOI*

Sweat and Soap © Kintetsu Yamada / Kodansha Ltd.

In an office romance, there's a fine line between sexy and awkward... and that line is where Asako — a woman who sweats copiously — meets Koutarou — a perfume developer who can't get enough of Asako's, er, scent. Don't miss a romcom manga like no other!

KC
KODANSHA
COMICS

The adorable new odd-couple cat comedy manga from the creator of the beloved *Chi's Sweet Home*, in full color!

Sue & Tai-chan

Konami Kanata

Sue is an aging housecat who's looking forward to living out her life in peace... but her plans change when the mischievous black tomcat Tai-chan enters the picture! Hey! Sue never signed up to be a catsitter! *Sue & Tai-chan* is the latest from the reigning meow-narch of cute kitty comics, Konami Kanata.

KC
KODANSHA
COMICS

A Kodansha Comics Trade Paperback Original
Granblue Fantasy 5 copyright
© Cygames
© 2018 cocho
© 2018 Makoto Fugetsu

English translation copyright
© Cygames
© 2020 cocho
© 2020 Makoto Fugetsu

Published in the United States by Kodansha Comics, an imprint of Kodansha USA Publishing, LLC, New York.

Publication rights for this English edition arranged through Kodansha Ltd., Tokyo.

First published in Japan in 2018 by Kodansha Ltd., Tokyo as *Granblue Fantasy*, volume 5.

ISBN 978-1-63236-955-0

Original cover design by Yusuke Kurachi (Astrorb)

Printed in the United States of America.

www.kodanshacomics.com

9 8 7 6 5 4 3 2 1
Translation: Kristi Fernandez
Lettering: Evan Hayden
Editing: Vanessa Tenazas
Kodansha Comics edition cover design by Phil Balsman

Publisher: Kiichiro Sugawara
Vice president of marketing & publicity: Naho Yamada

Director of publishing services: Ben Applegate
Associate director of operations: Stephen Pakula
Publishing services managing editor: Noelle Webster
Assistant production manager: Emi Lotto, Angela Zurlo